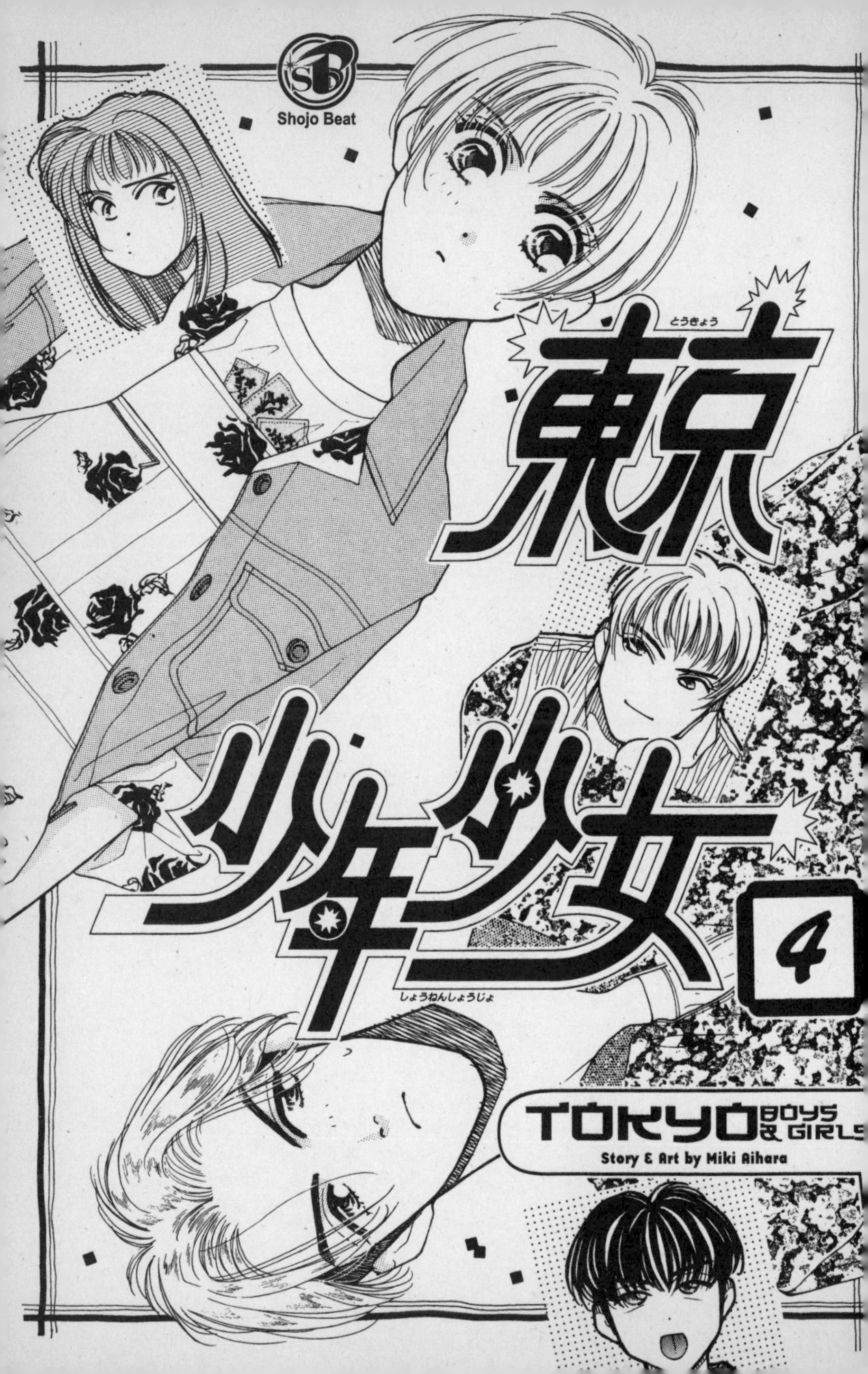
Shojo Beat
とうきょう
東京
少年少女
しょうねんしょうじょ
4
TOKYO BOYS & GIRLS
Story & Art by Miki Aihara

TOKYO BOYS & GIRLS

4

MAIN CHARACTERS

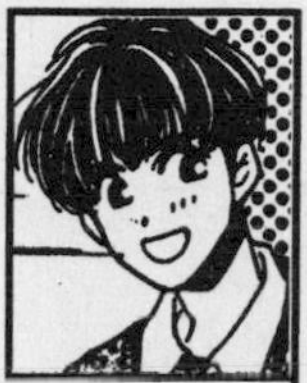

Ran Shingyoji

Member of Class 1-A, Boys' Division. A hot-blooded type and Kuniyasu's closest friend. Has a crush on Nana, but she doesn't have much interest in him.

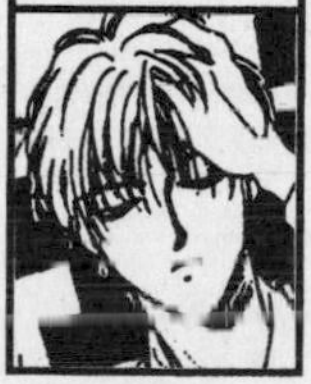

Member of Class 1-A, Boys' Division. He's got looks and brains. Usually cool, but acts weird around Mimori.

Kazukita Kuniyasu

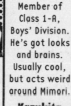

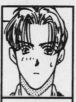

Atsushi Haruta

Member of Class 1-A, Boys' Division. A childhood friend of Mimori's, he was ruthlessly bullied as a kid.

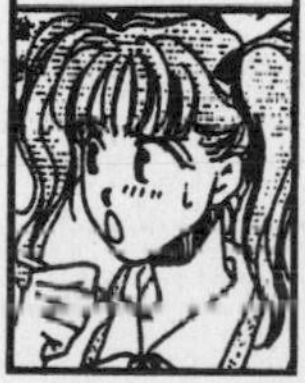

Mimori's classmate. She's the idol of the Boys' Division. She's in love with Kuniyasu, but he brushes her off.

Nana Takaichi

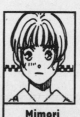

Mimori Kosaka

Member of Class 1-A, Girls' Division at Meidai Attached High School. She's dating Haruta, but trouble keeps cropping up between them.

The Story Thus Far

When Kuniyasu is arrested at a party, Mimori goes to the police station to help him. There, Ran tells her about Kuniyasu's unhappy home life. Mimori discovers that she can't stop thinking about Kuniyasu. This concerns Haruta, who's jealously protective of Mimori, and Nana, who has an unrequited crush on Kuniyasu.

When Kuniyasu doesn't show up for school the next day, Mimori becomes worried. She visits him at his apartment, where he lives alone. Nana tells Haruta, who goes to Kuniyasu's apartment to confront her. Meanwhile, in desperation, Nana gets physical with Ran, whom she doesn't even like! What will happen to these five as their relationships become even more confused?

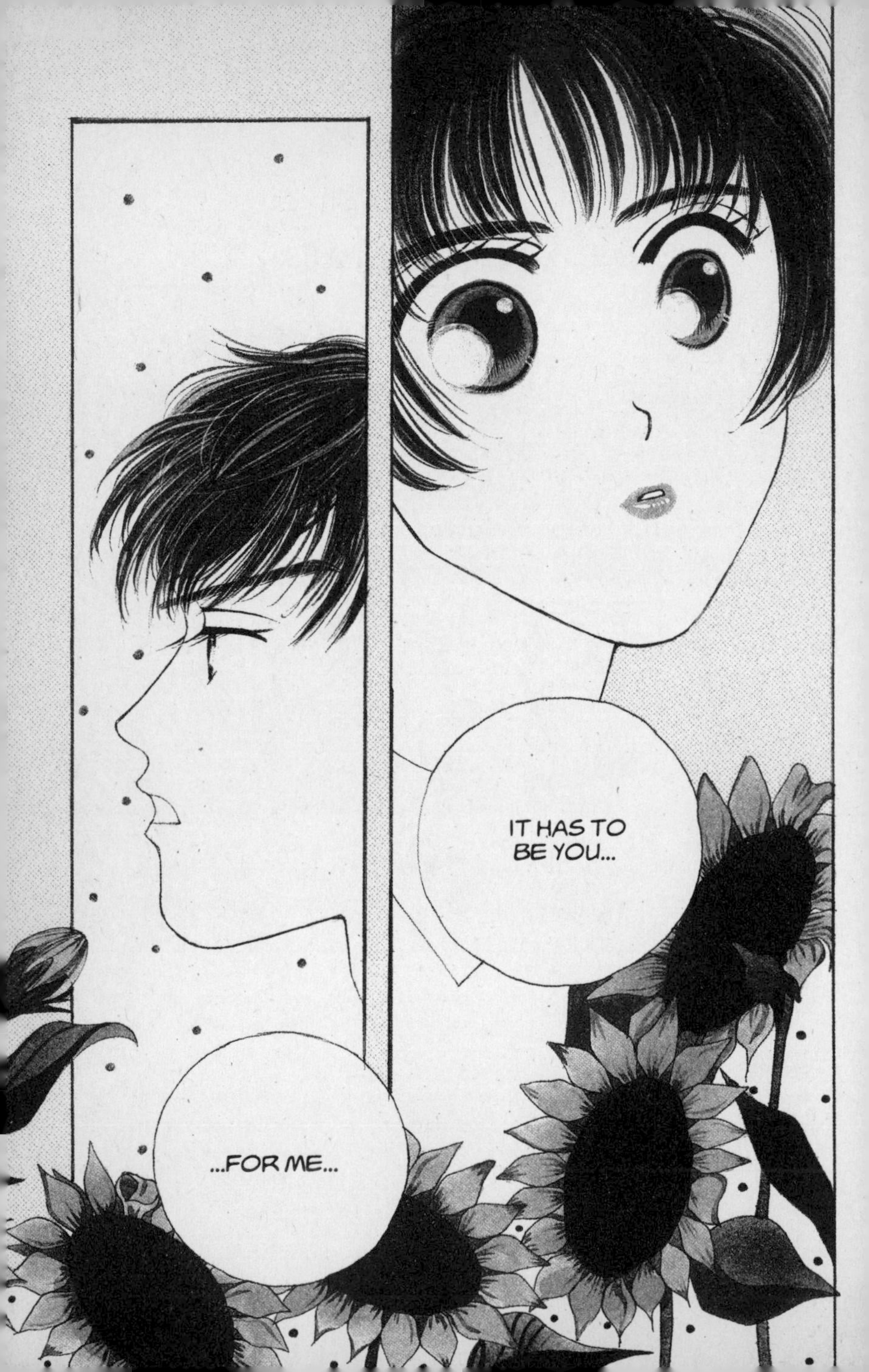
IT HAS TO BE YOU...
...FOR ME...

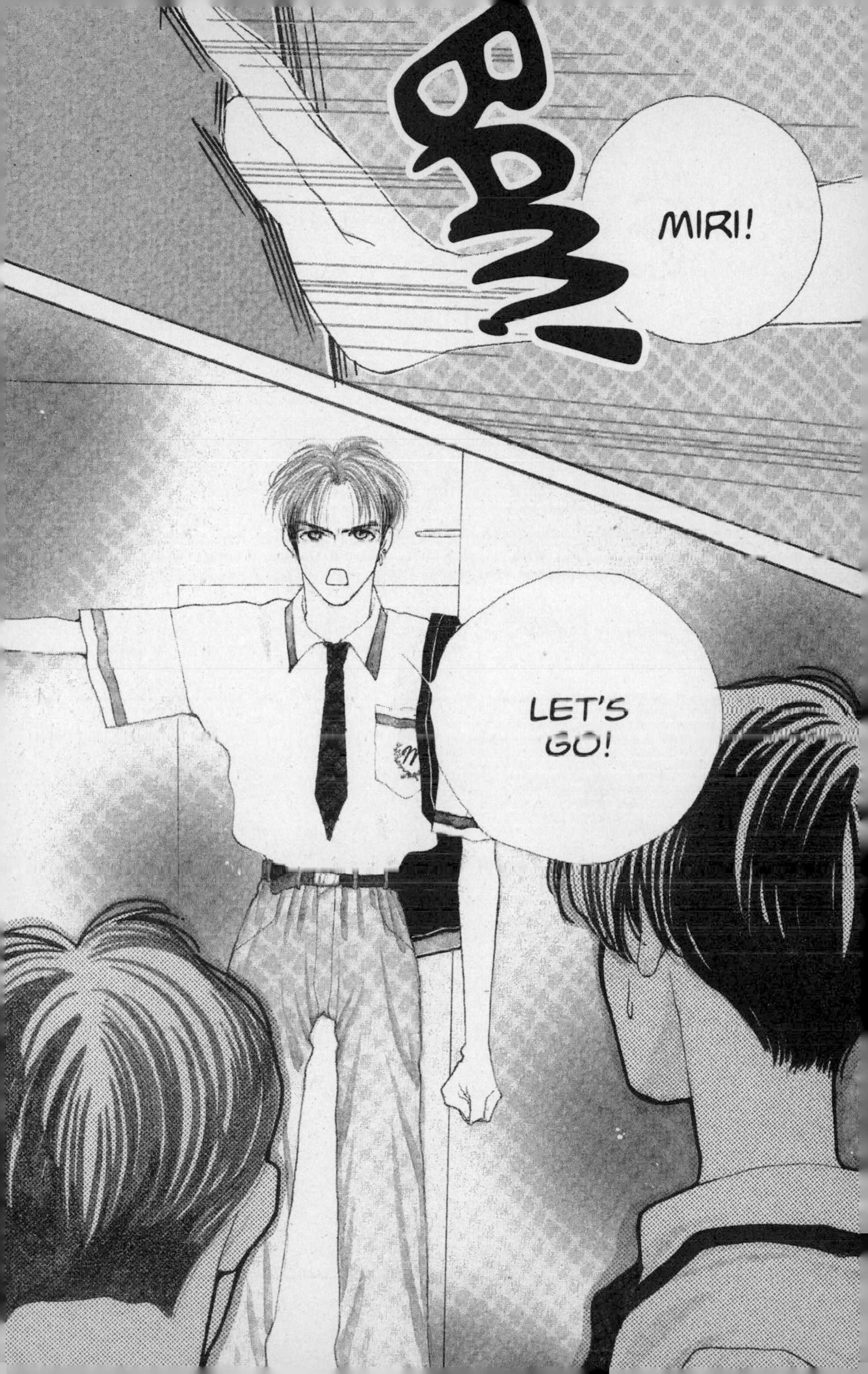
MIRI!
BAM!
LET'S GO!

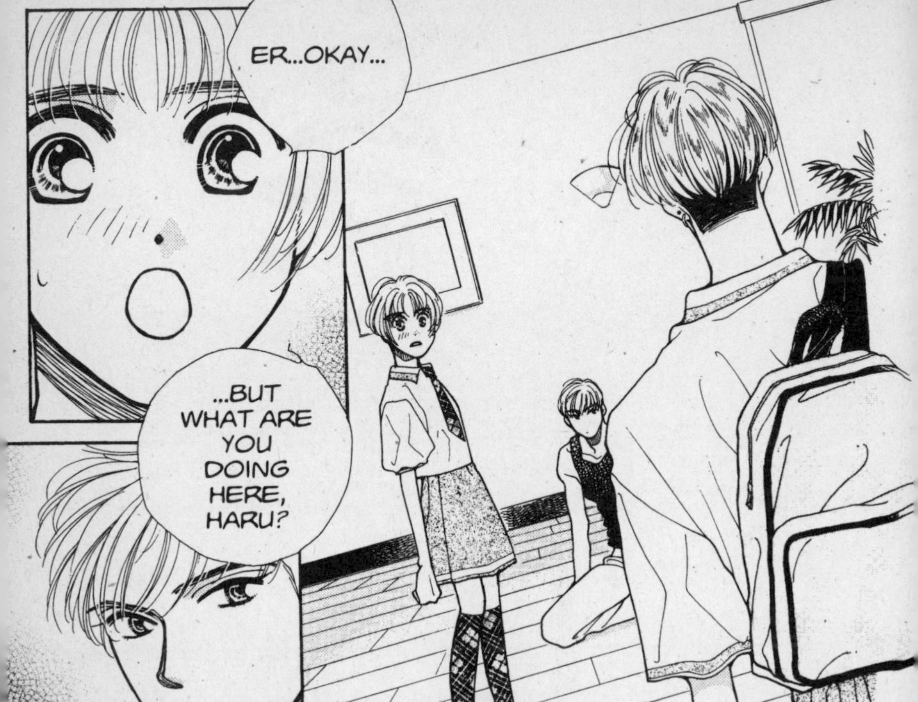
ER...OKAY...
...BUT WHAT ARE YOU DOING HERE, HARU?

Question Corner

*By Atsushi Haruta

No. 1

Question: "What's with the relationship between Terabayashi and Haruta?"

Answer: Ah, yes. Let's see. They went to the same junior high, where they both hung out in a bike gang. Terabayashi (smile) was thoroughly delinquent and hit puberty before anyone else, so he looked really scary. During that time, however, he saved Haruta from danger, and they became fast friends.

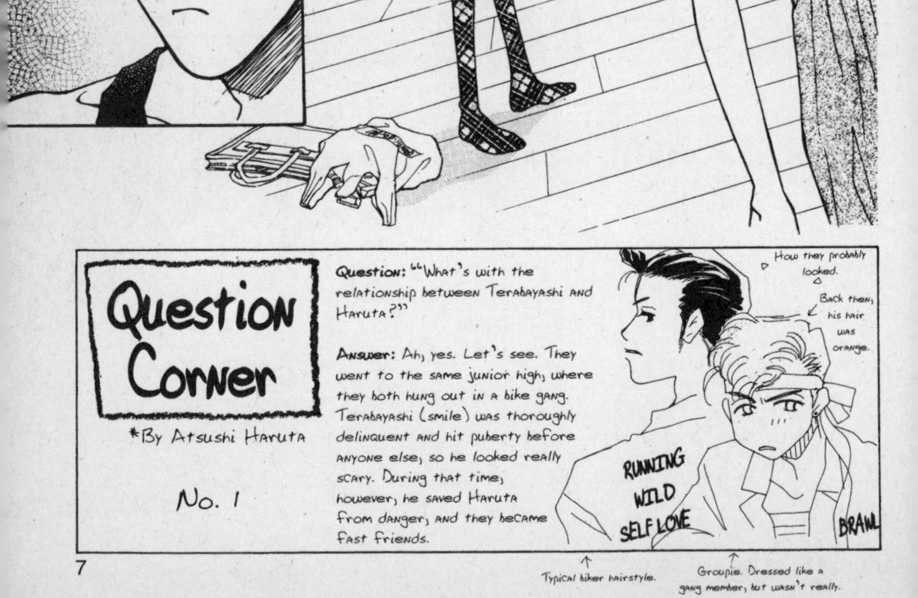
How they probably looked.
Back then, his hair was orange.
RUNNING WILD SELF LOVE
BRAWL
Typical biker hairstyle.
Groupie. Dressed like a gang member, but wasn't really.

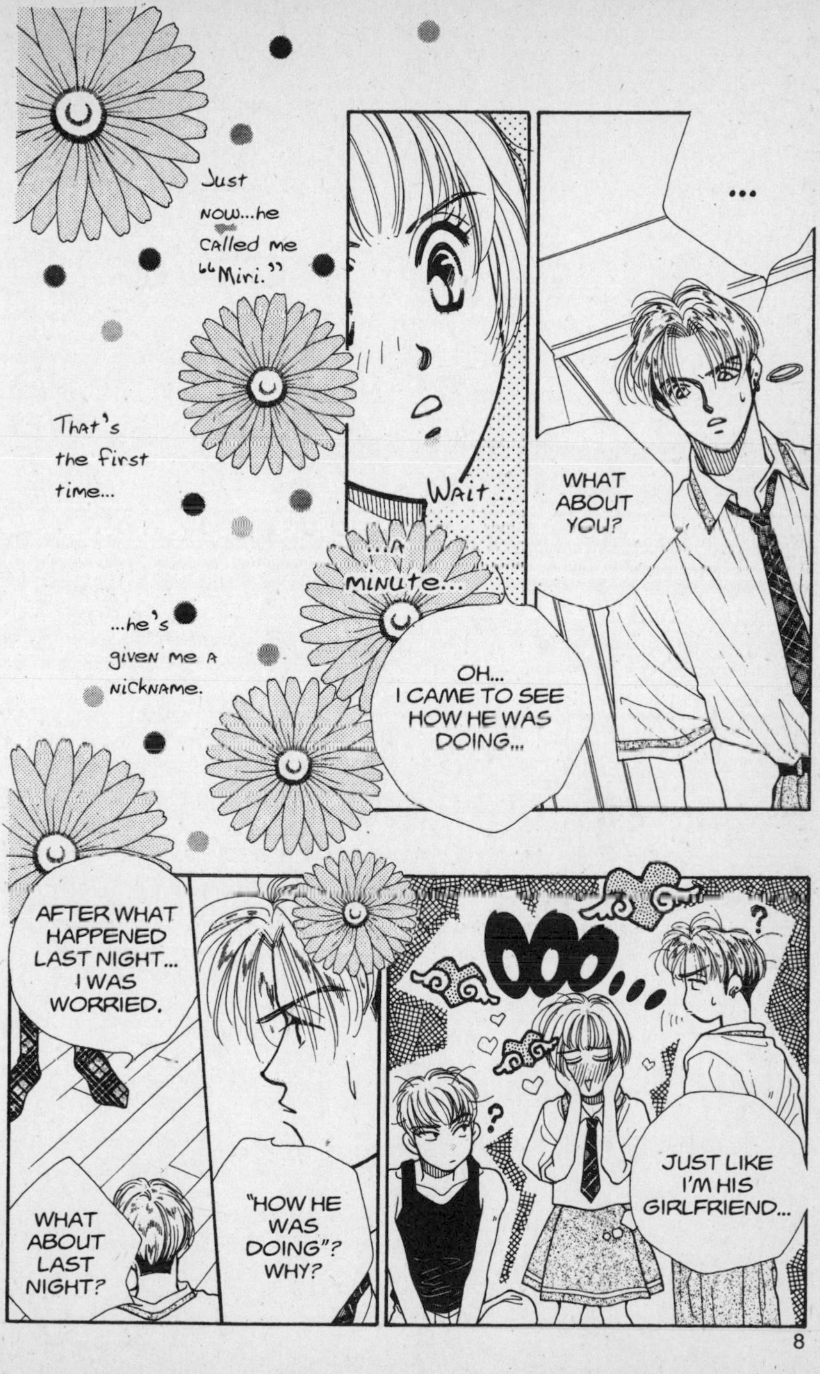
...
WHAT ABOUT YOU?
Wait...
...a minute...
OH... I CAME TO SEE HOW HE WAS DOING...
Just now...he called me "Miri."
That's the first time...
...he's given me a nickname.
OOO...
JUST LIKE I'M HIS GIRLFRIEND...
"HOW HE WAS DOING"? WHY?
AFTER WHAT HAPPENED LAST NIGHT... I WAS WORRIED.
WHAT ABOUT LAST NIGHT?

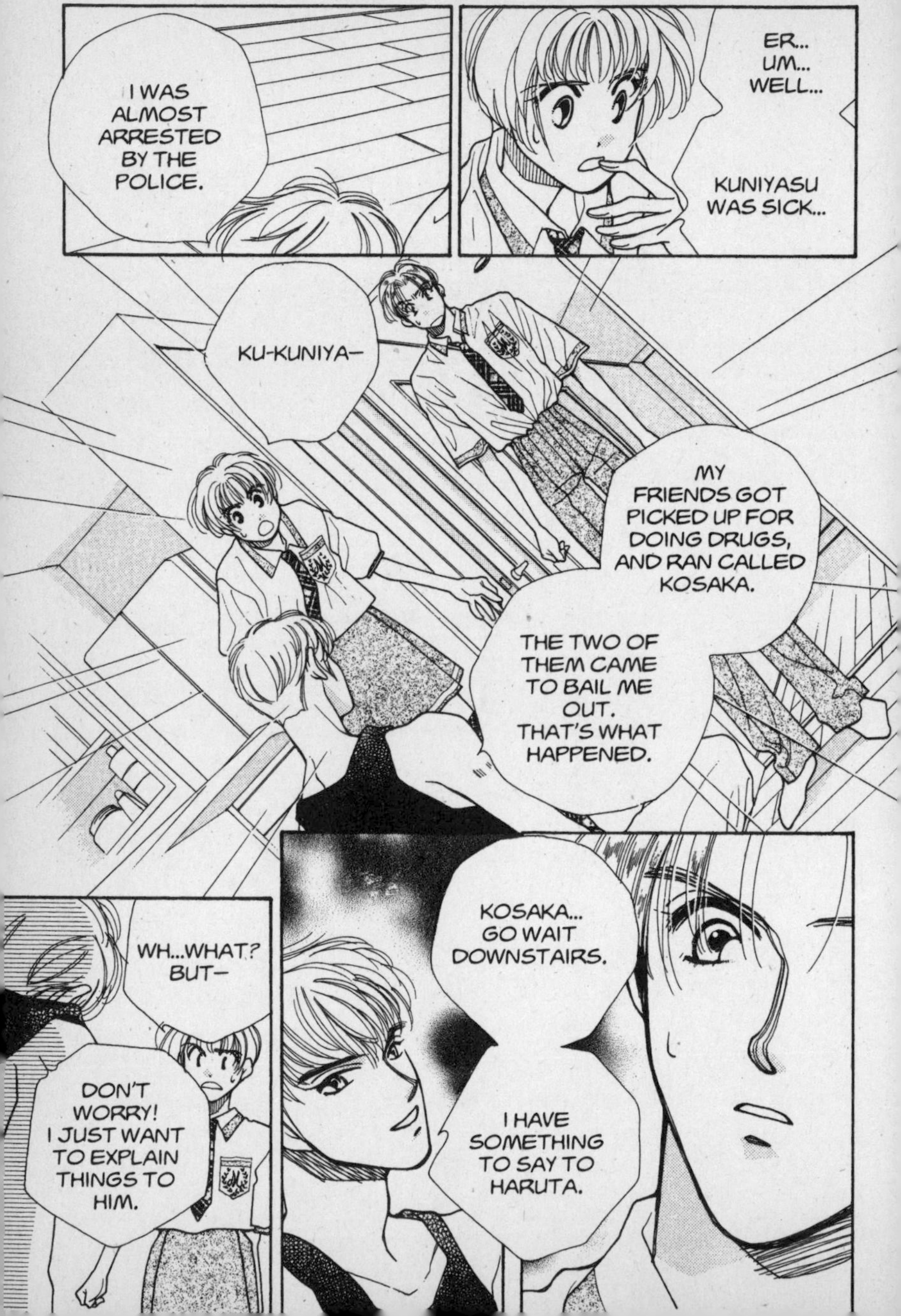
ER... UM... WELL...
KUNIYASU WAS SICK...
I WAS ALMOST ARRESTED BY THE POLICE.
KU-KUNIYA—
MY FRIENDS GOT PICKED UP FOR DOING DRUGS, AND RAN CALLED KOSAKA.
THE TWO OF THEM CAME TO BAIL ME OUT. THAT'S WHAT HAPPENED.
KOSAKA... GO WAIT DOWNSTAIRS.
I HAVE SOMETHING TO SAY TO HARUTA.
WH...WHAT? BUT—
DON'T WORRY! I JUST WANT TO EXPLAIN THINGS TO HIM.

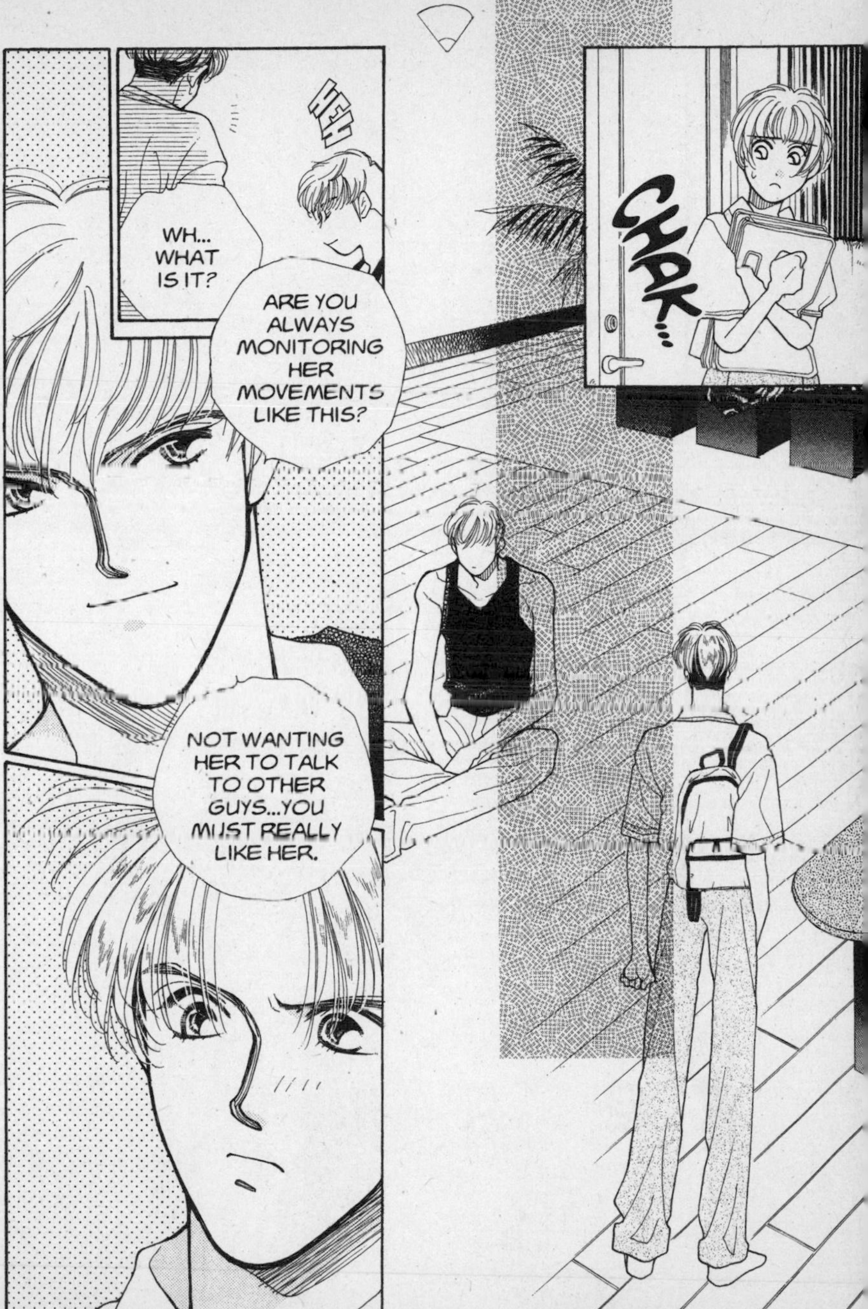
CHAK...
HEH
WH... WHAT IS IT?
ARE YOU ALWAYS MONITORING HER MOVEMENTS LIKE THIS?
NOT WANTING HER TO TALK TO OTHER GUYS...YOU MUST REALLY LIKE HER.

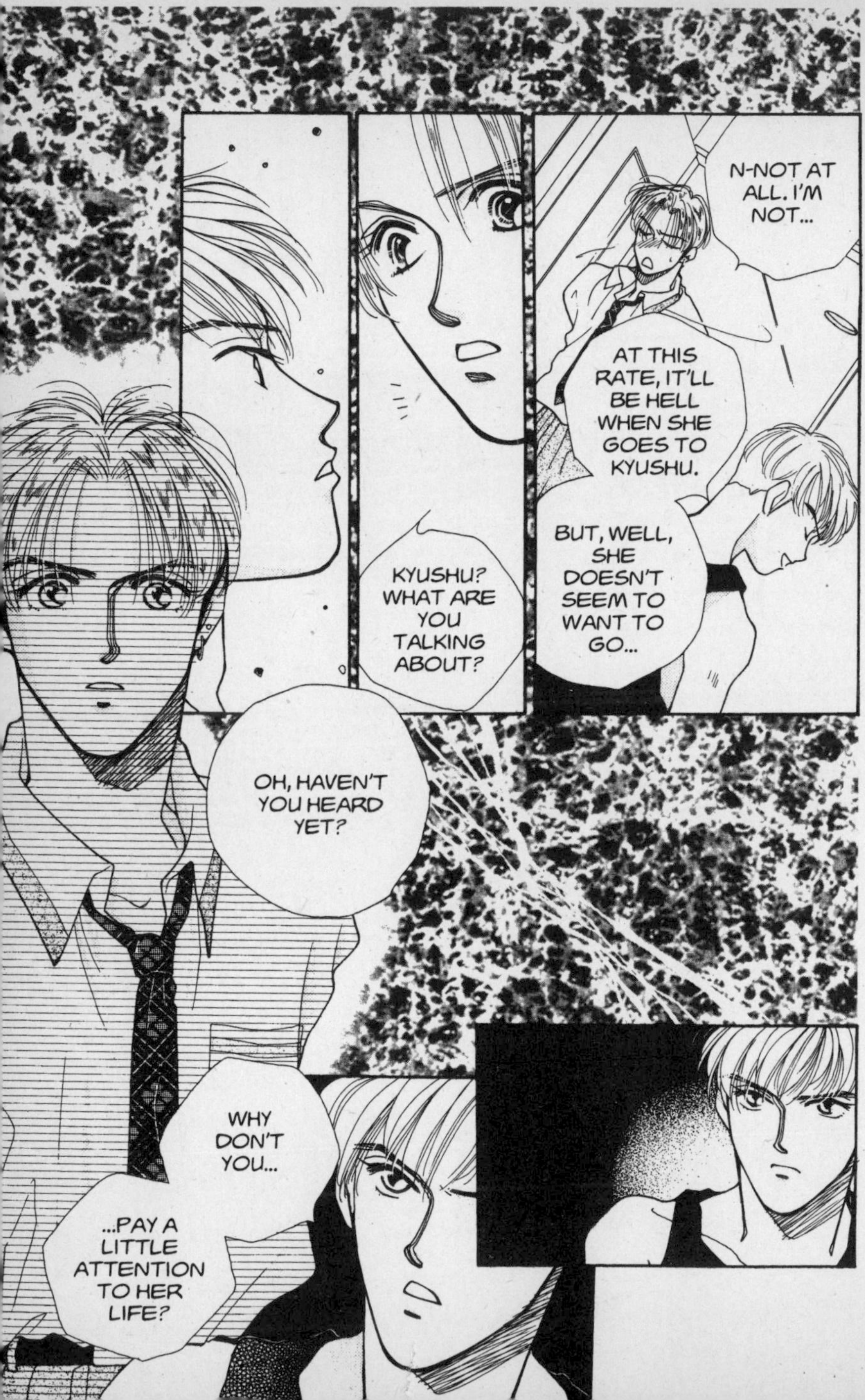
N-NOT AT ALL. I'M NOT...
AT THIS RATE, IT'LL BE HELL WHEN SHE GOES TO KYUSHU.
BUT, WELL, SHE DOESN'T SEEM TO WANT TO GO...
KYUSHU? WHAT ARE YOU TALKING ABOUT?
OH, HAVEN'T YOU HEARD YET?
WHY DON'T YOU...
...PAY A LITTLE ATTENTION TO HER LIFE?

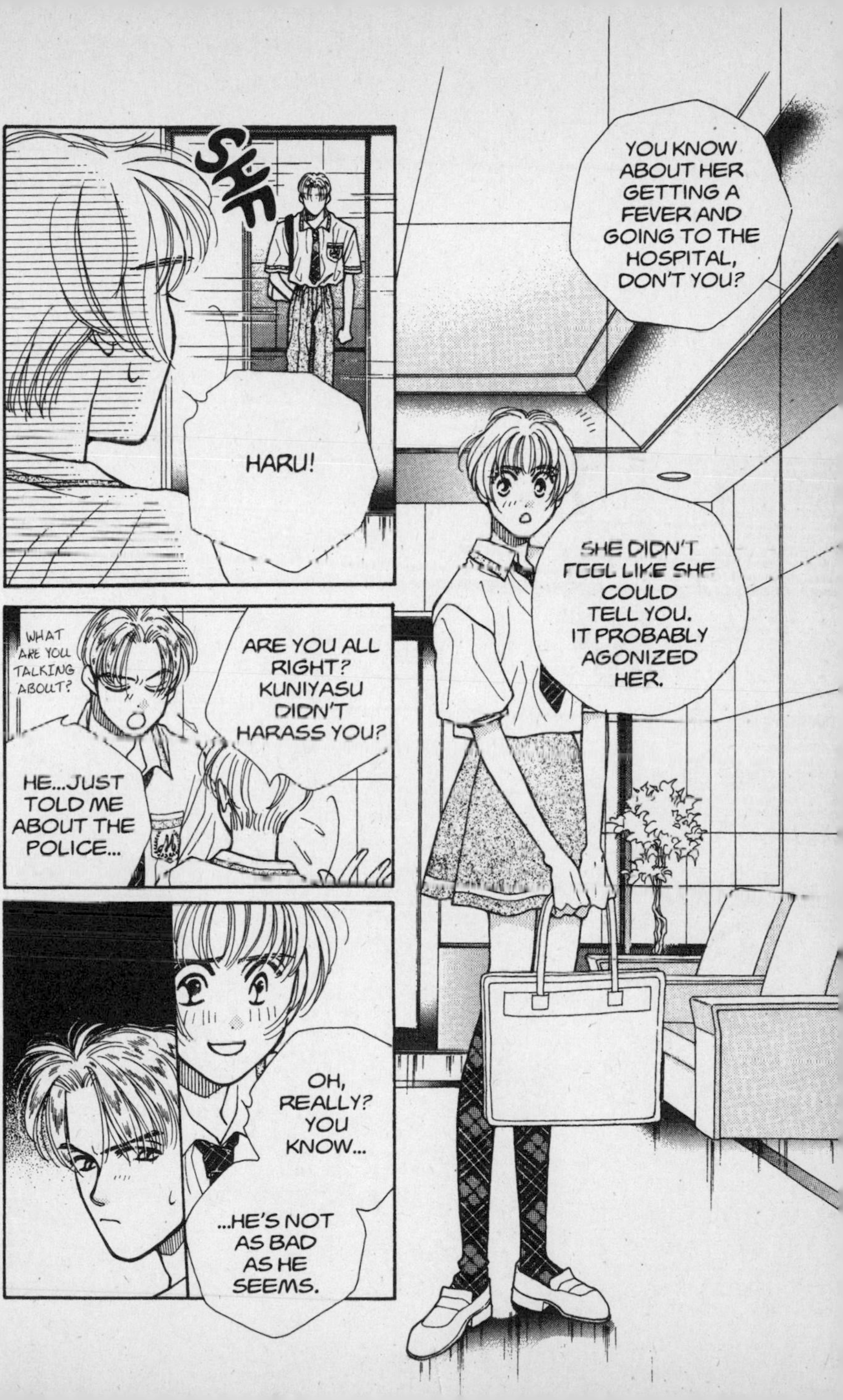
YOU KNOW ABOUT HER GETTING A FEVER AND GOING TO THE HOSPITAL, DON'T YOU?
SHE DIDN'T FEEL LIKE SHE COULD TELL YOU. IT PROBABLY AGONIZED HER.
SHF
HARU!
ARE YOU ALL RIGHT? KUNIYASU DIDN'T HARASS YOU?
WHAT ARE YOU TALKING ABOUT?
HE...JUST TOLD ME ABOUT THE POLICE...
OH, REALLY? YOU KNOW...
...HE'S NOT AS BAD AS HE SEEMS.

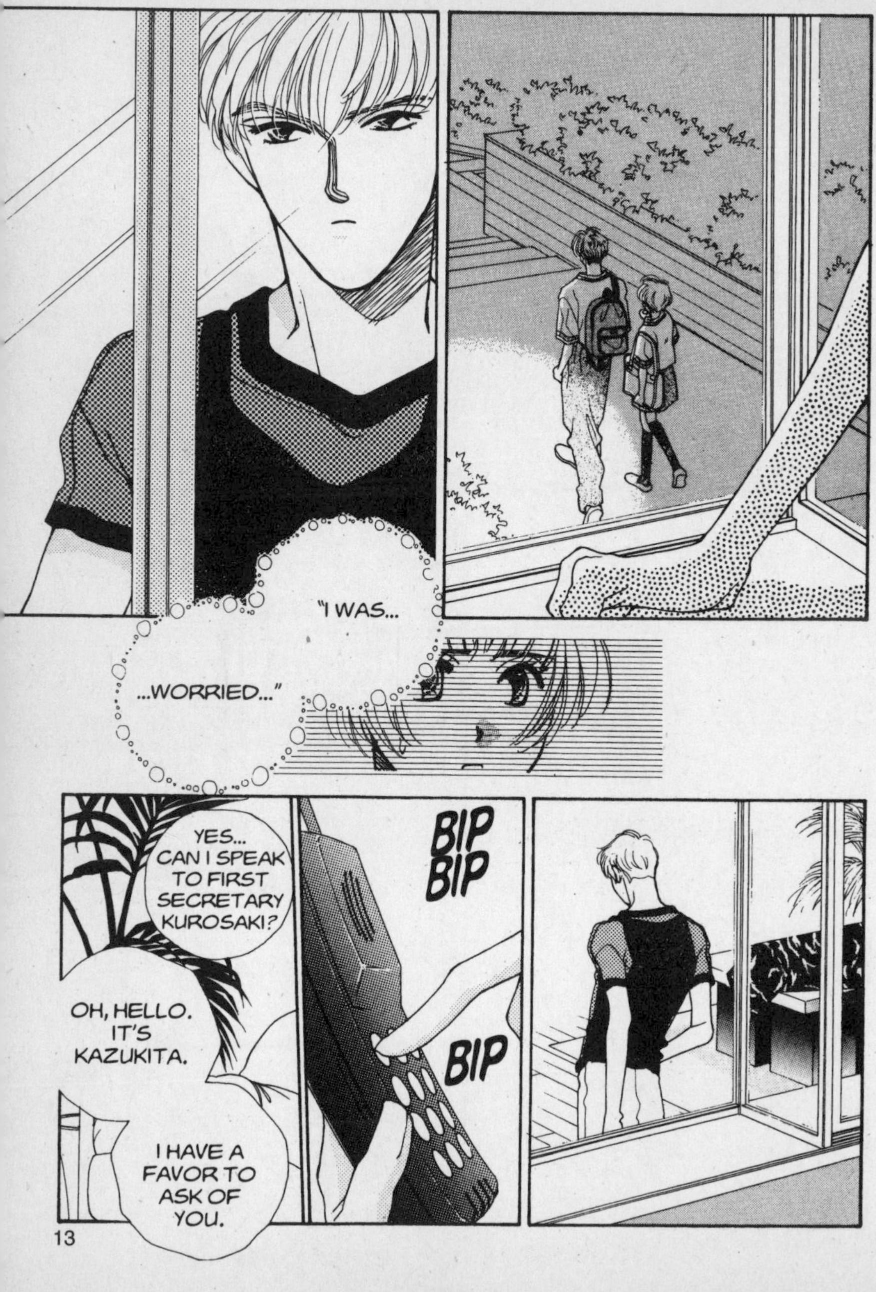
"I WAS...
...WORRIED..."
BIP BIP
BIP
YES... CAN I SPEAK TO FIRST SECRETARY KUROSAKI?
OH, HELLO. IT'S KAZUKITA.
I HAVE A FAVOR TO ASK OF YOU.

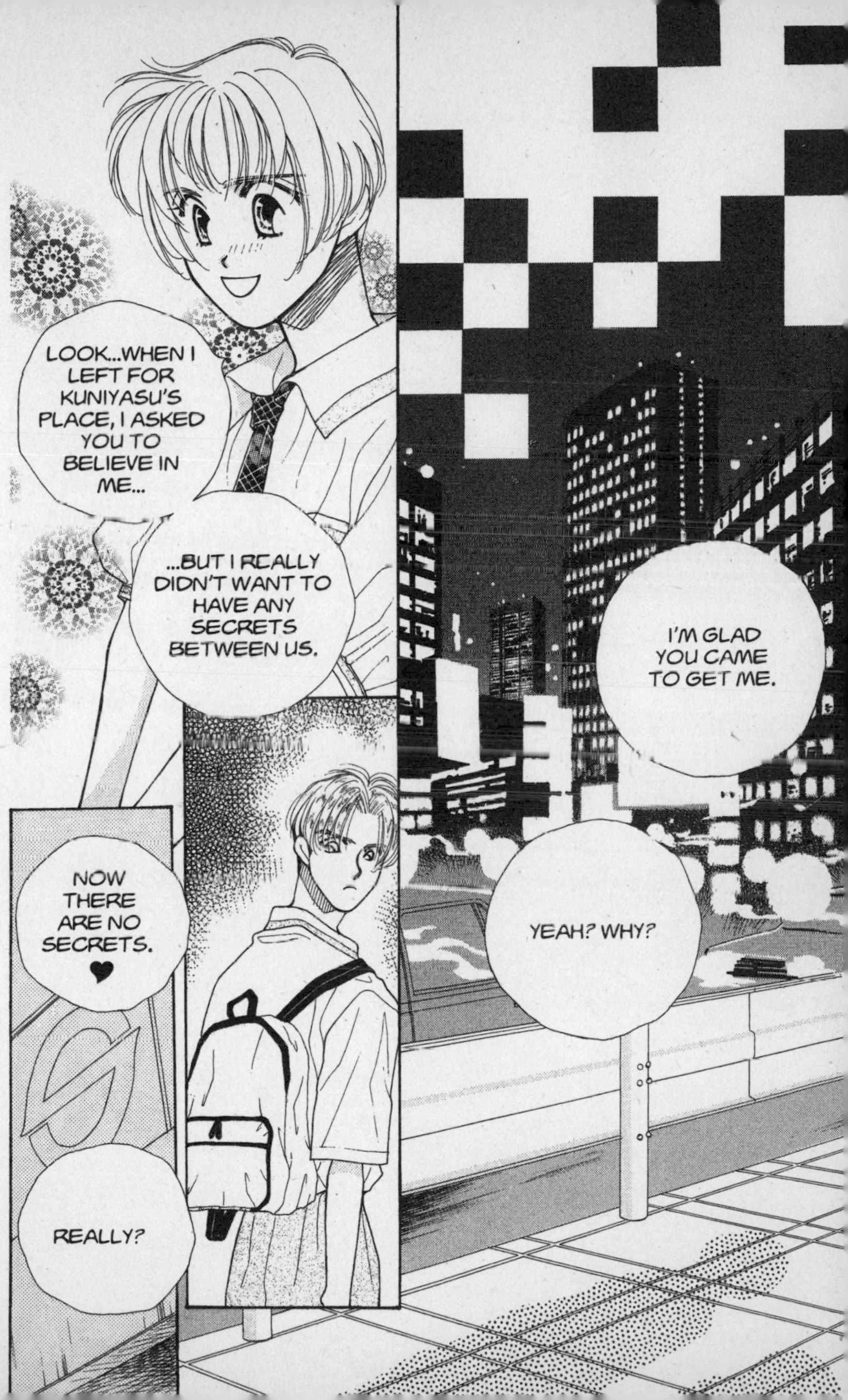
I'M GLAD YOU CAME TO GET ME.
YEAH? WHY?
LOOK...WHEN I LEFT FOR KUNIYASU'S PLACE, I ASKED YOU TO BELIEVE IN ME...
...BUT I REALLY DIDN'T WANT TO HAVE ANY SECRETS BETWEEN US.
NOW THERE ARE NO SECRETS. ♥
REALLY?

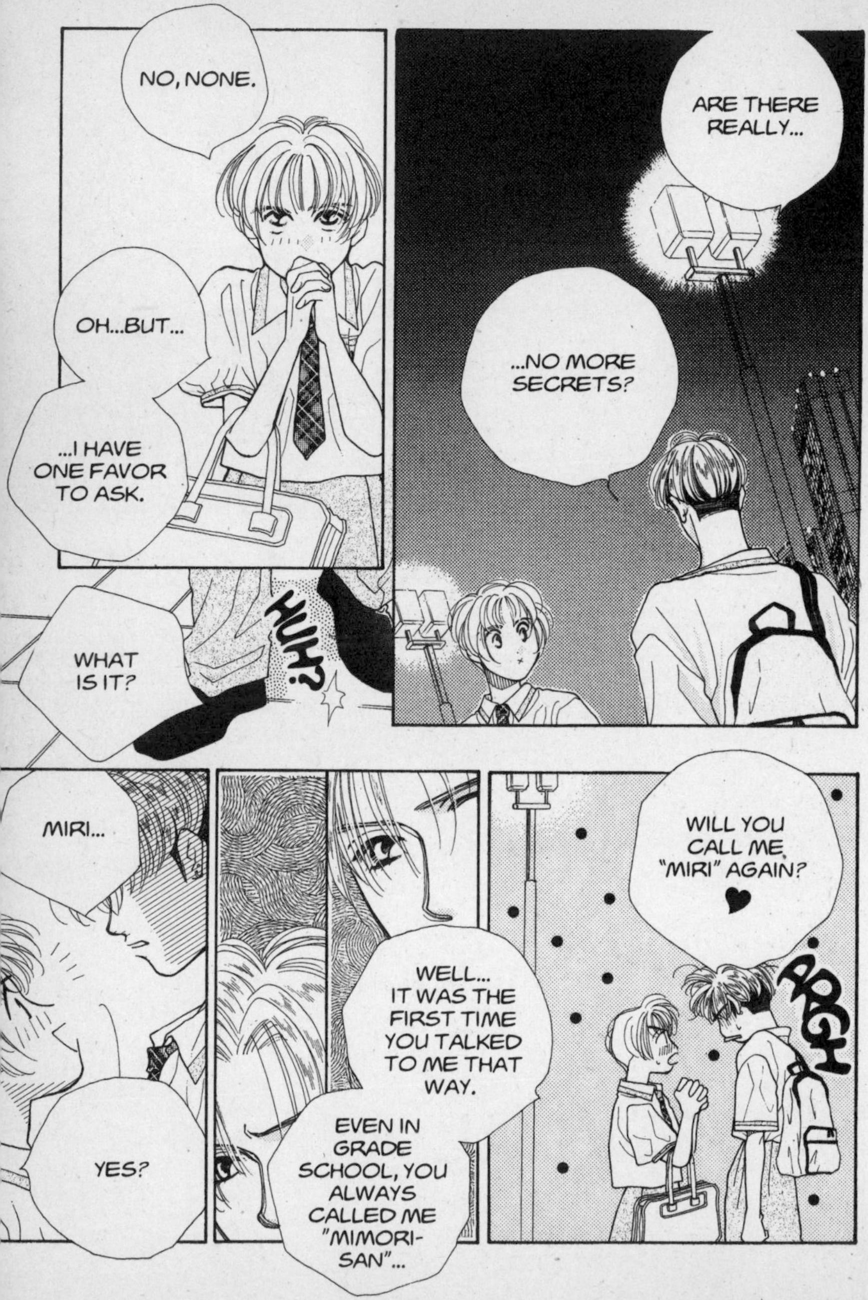
ARE THERE REALLY...
...NO MORE SECRETS?
NO, NONE.
OH...BUT...
...I HAVE ONE FAVOR TO ASK.
HUH?
WHAT IS IT?
WILL YOU CALL ME "MIRI" AGAIN? ♥
ARGH
WELL... IT WAS THE FIRST TIME YOU TALKED TO ME THAT WAY.
EVEN IN GRADE SCHOOL, YOU ALWAYS CALLED ME "MIMORI-SAN"...
MIRI...
YES?

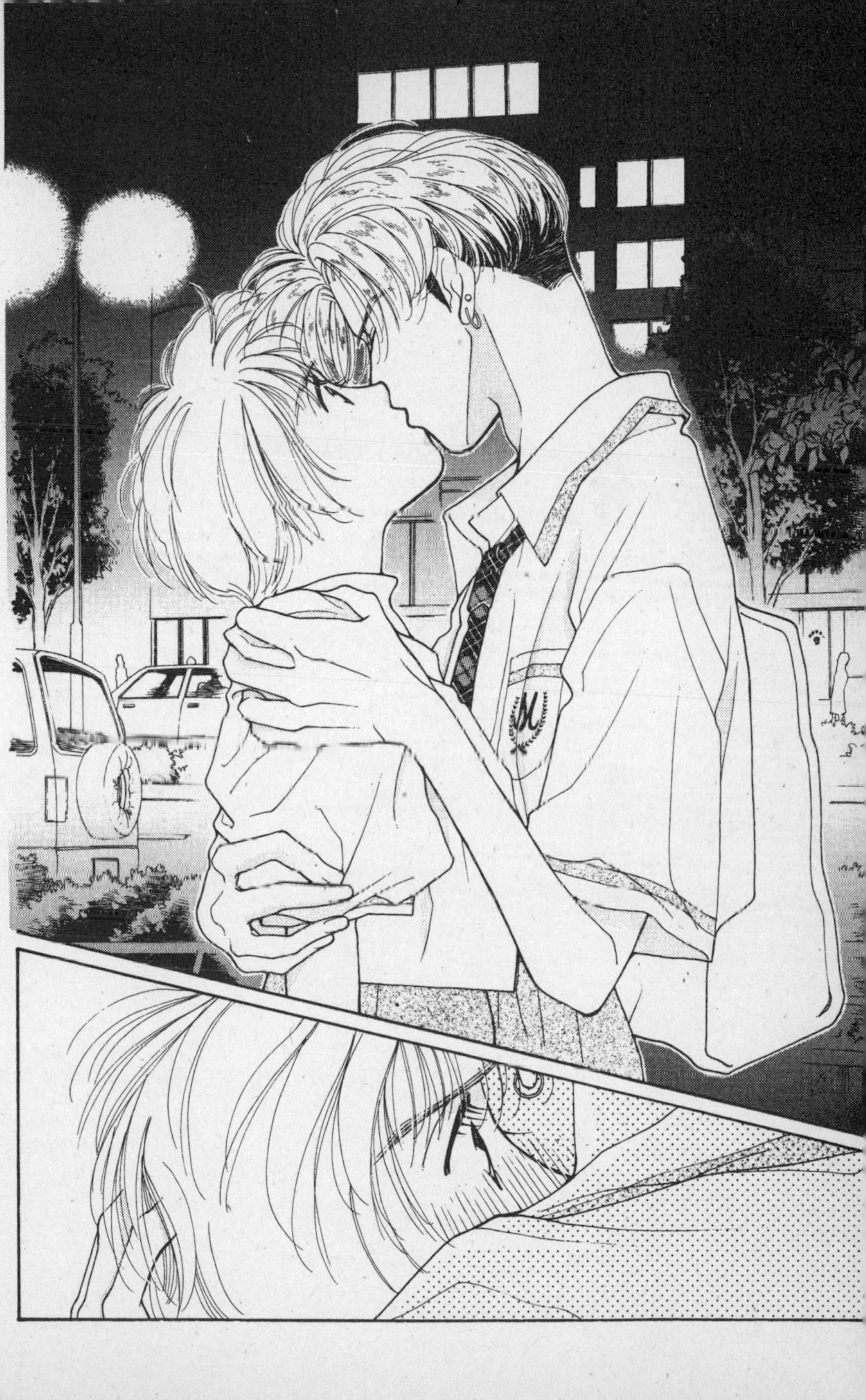

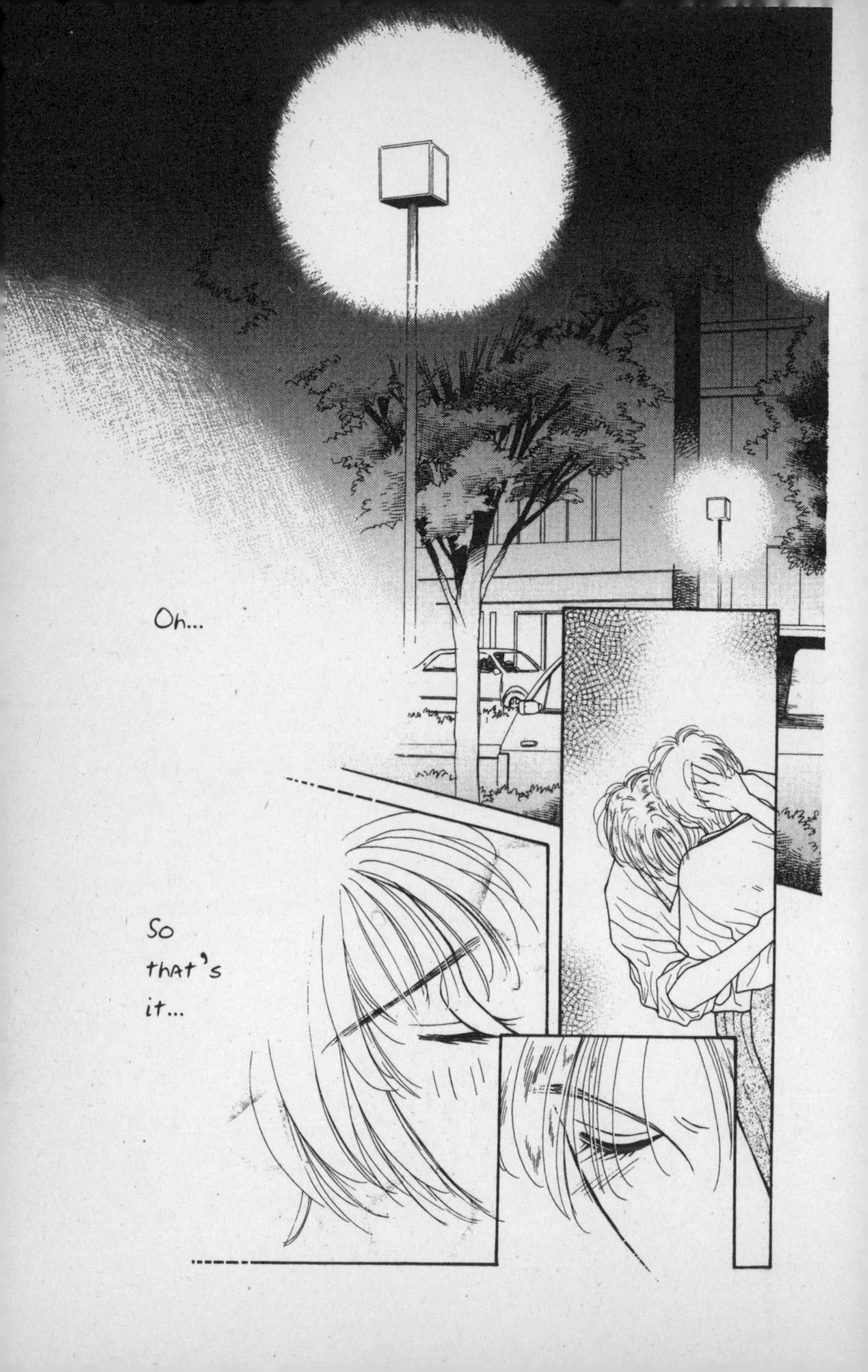
Oh...
So that's it...

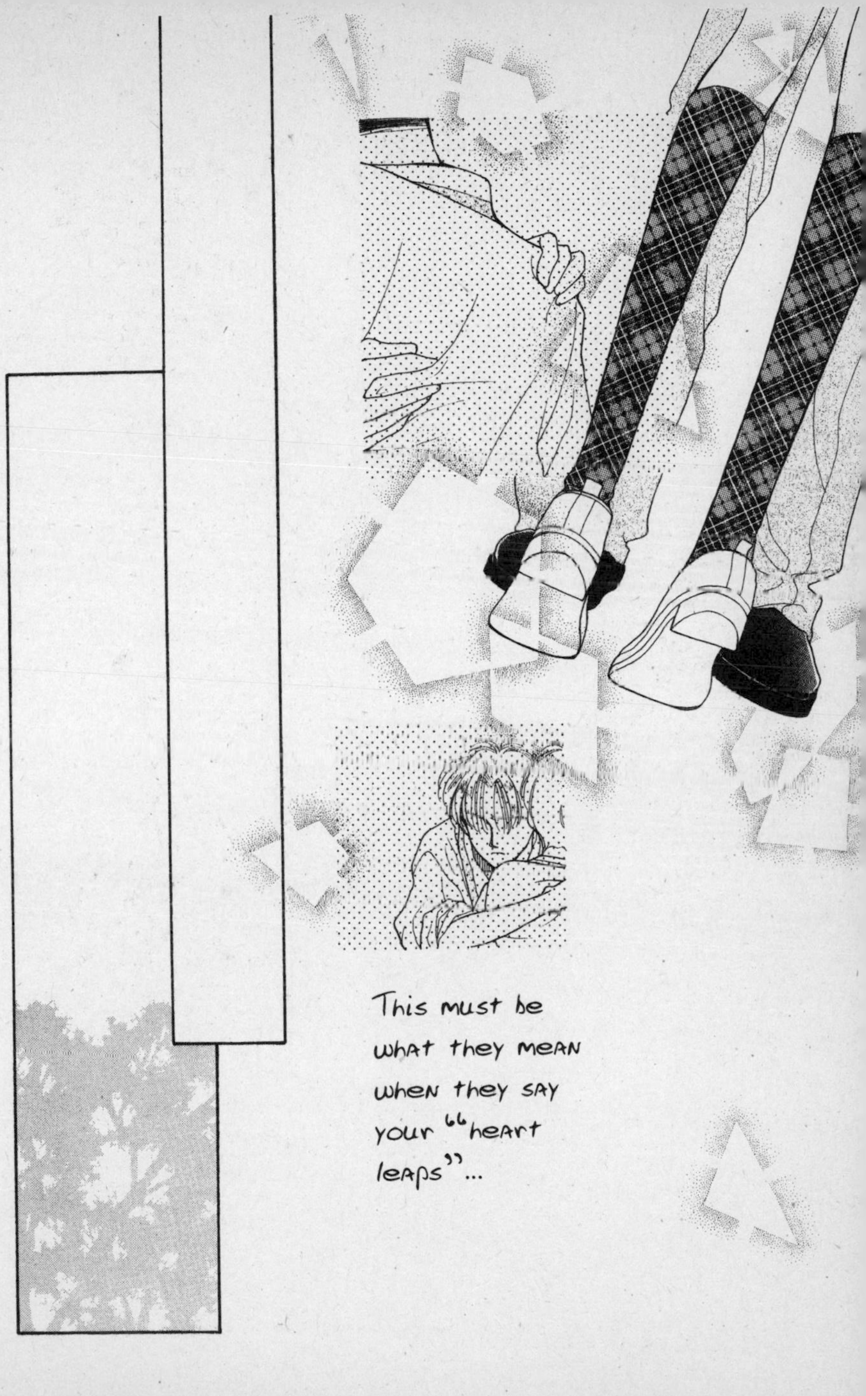
This must be what they mean when they say your "heart leaps"...

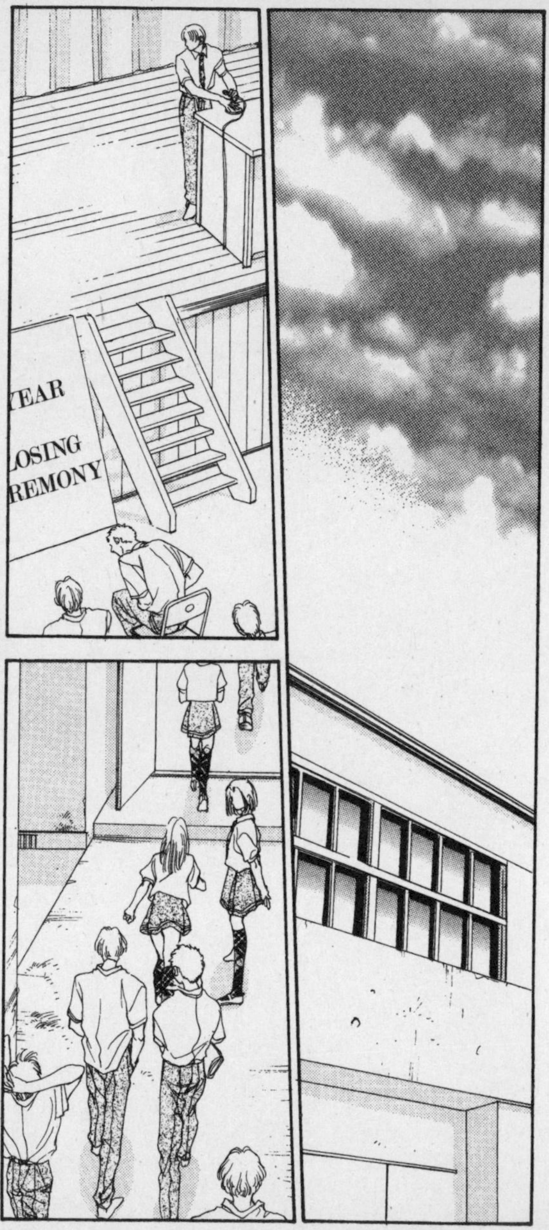
YEAR
LOSING
REMONY

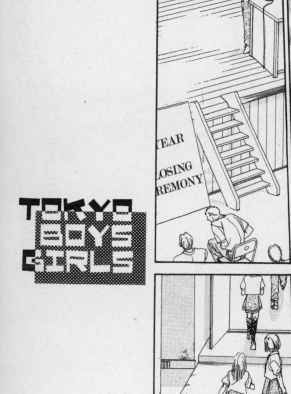

TOKYO BOYS GIRLS

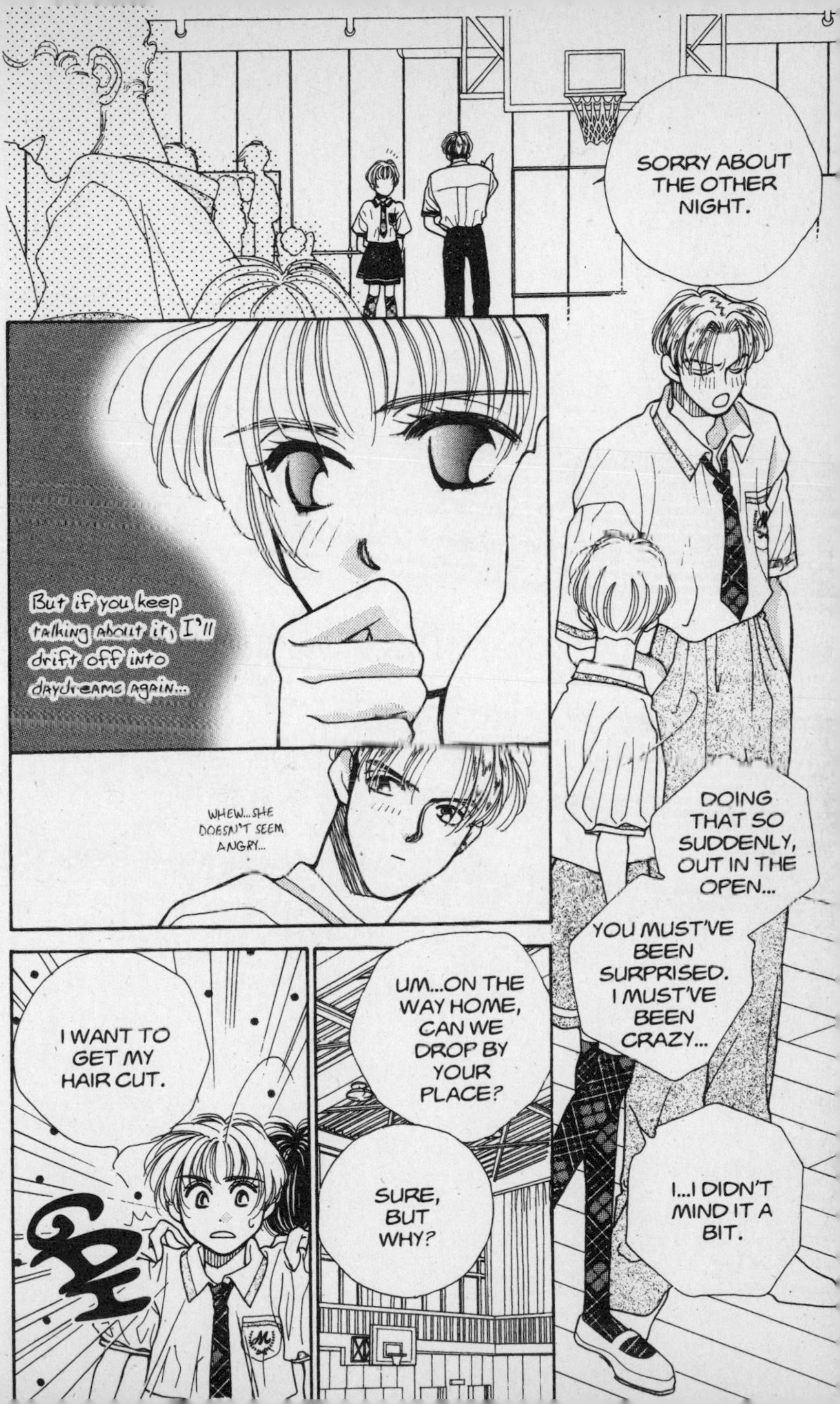
SORRY ABOUT THE OTHER NIGHT.
DOING THAT SO SUDDENLY, OUT IN THE OPEN...
YOU MUST'VE BEEN SURPRISED. I MUST'VE BEEN CRAZY...
I...I DIDN'T MIND IT A BIT.
But if you keep talking about it, I'll drift off into daydreams again...
WHEW...SHE DOESN'T SEEM ANGRY...
UM...ON THE WAY HOME, CAN WE DROP BY YOUR PLACE?
SURE, BUT WHY?
I WANT TO GET MY HAIR CUT.

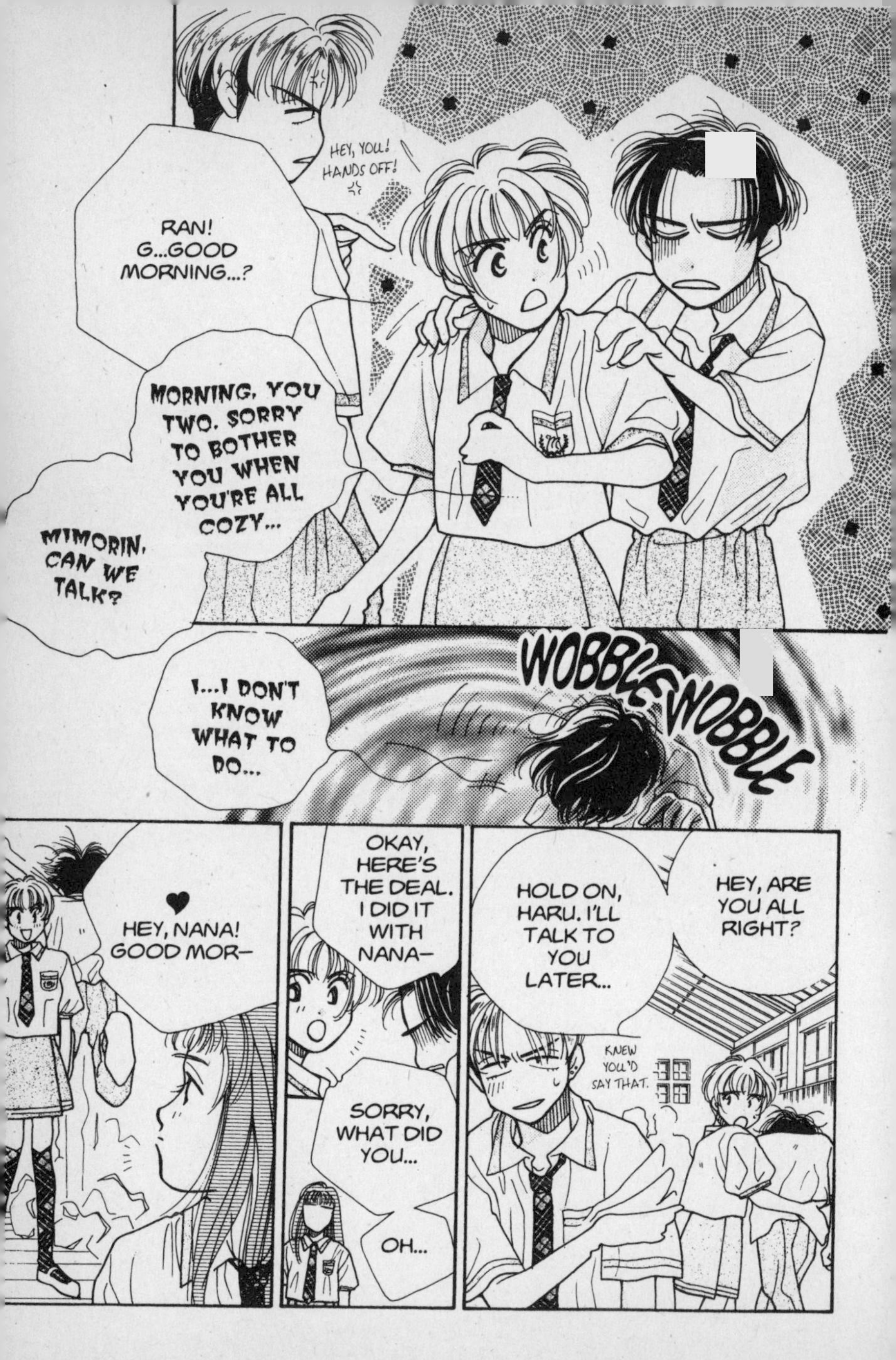
HEY, YOU! HANDS OFF!
RAN! G...GOOD MORNING...?
MORNING, YOU TWO. SORRY TO BOTHER YOU WHEN YOU'RE ALL COZY...
MIMORIN, CAN WE TALK?
WOBBLE WOBBLE
I...I DON'T KNOW WHAT TO DO...
HEY, ARE YOU ALL RIGHT?
HOLD ON, HARU. I'LL TALK TO YOU LATER...
KNEW YOU'D SAY THAT.
OKAY, HERE'S THE DEAL. I DID IT WITH NANA—
SORRY, WHAT DID YOU...
OH...
♥ HEY, NANA! GOOD MOR—

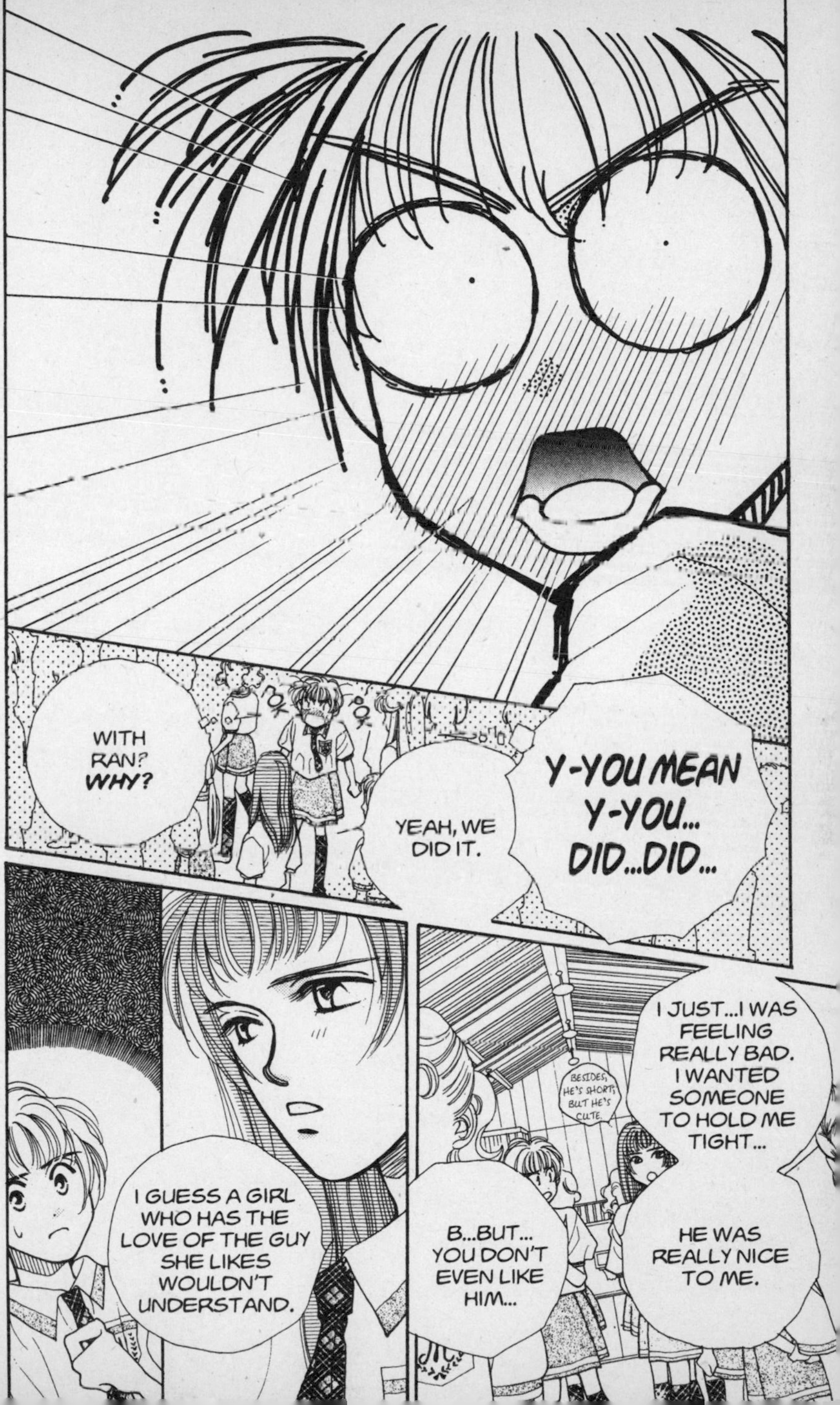
Y-YOU MEAN Y-YOU... DID...DID...
YEAH, WE DID IT.
WITH RAN? WHY?
I JUST...I WAS FEELING REALLY BAD. I WANTED SOMEONE TO HOLD ME TIGHT...
BESIDES, HE'S SHORT, BUT HE'S CUTE.
HE WAS REALLY NICE TO ME.
B...BUT... YOU DON'T EVEN LIKE HIM...
I GUESS A GIRL WHO HAS THE LOVE OF THE GUY SHE LIKES WOULDN'T UNDERSTAND.

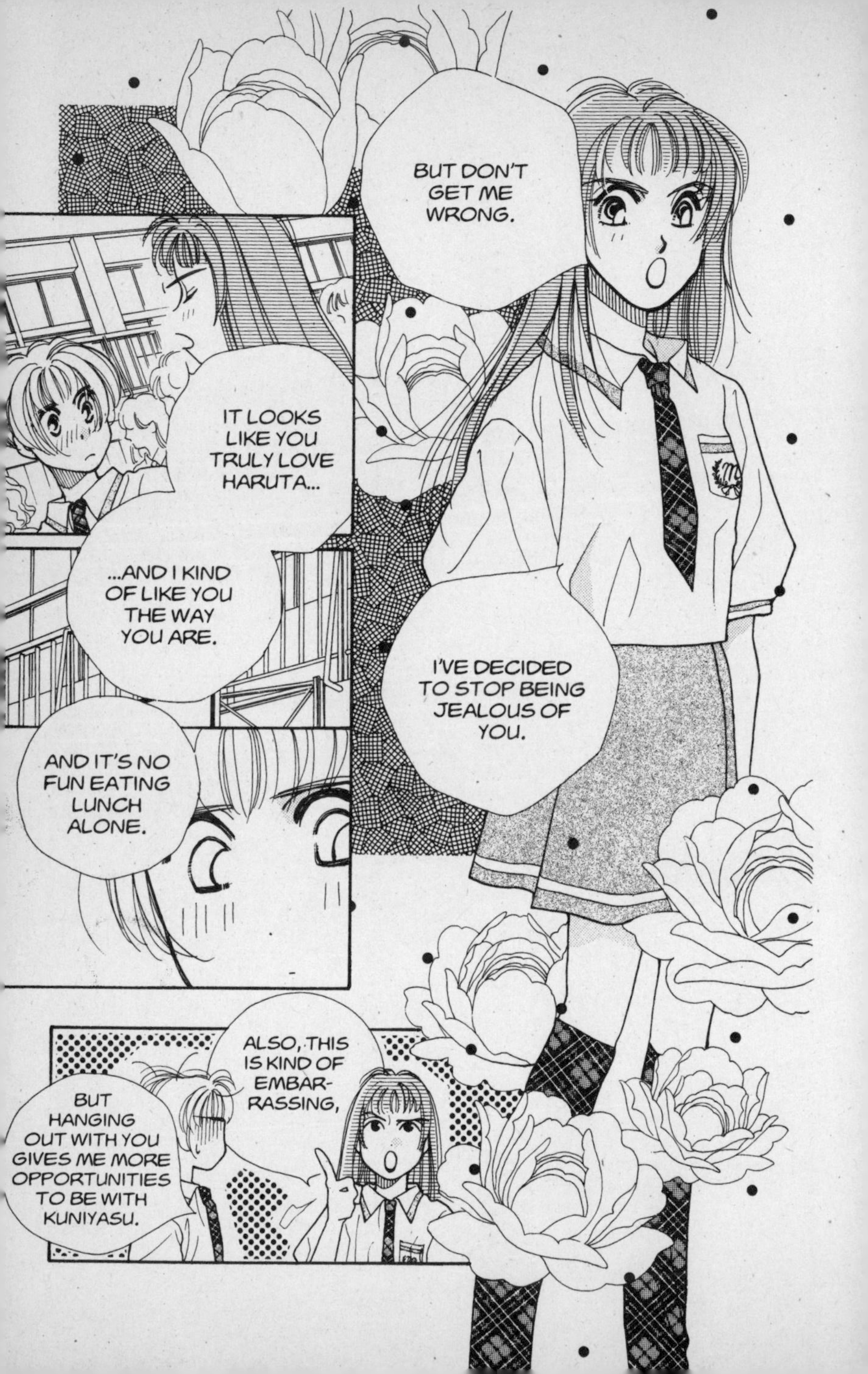
BUT DON'T GET ME WRONG.
I'VE DECIDED TO STOP BEING JEALOUS OF YOU.
IT LOOKS LIKE YOU TRULY LOVE HARUTA...
...AND I KIND OF LIKE YOU THE WAY YOU ARE.
AND IT'S NO FUN EATING LUNCH ALONE.
ALSO, THIS IS KIND OF EMBARRASSING,
BUT HANGING OUT WITH YOU GIVES ME MORE OPPORTUNITIES TO BE WITH KUNIYASU.

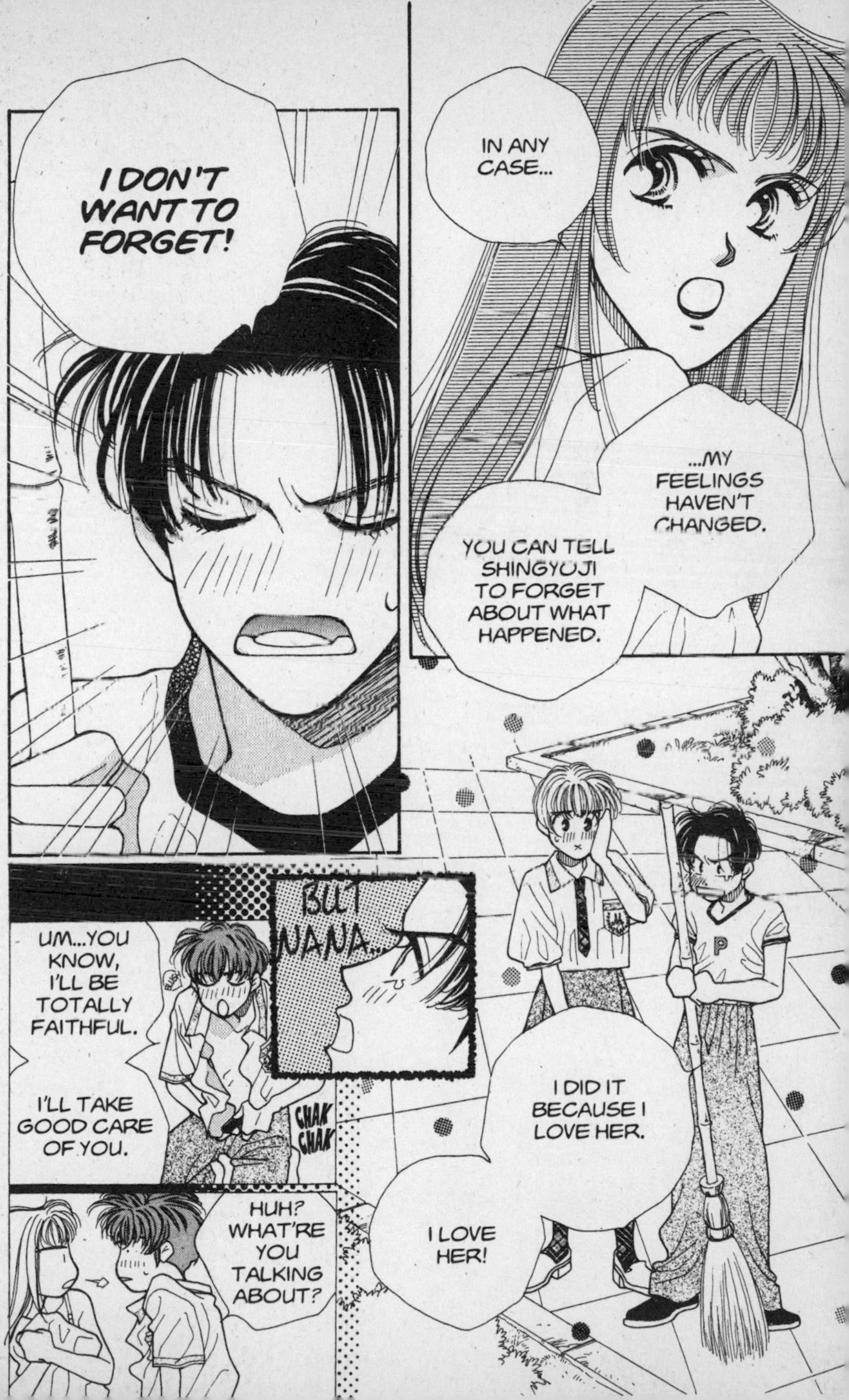
IN ANY CASE...
...MY FEELINGS HAVEN'T CHANGED.
YOU CAN TELL SHINGYOJI TO FORGET ABOUT WHAT HAPPENED.
I DON'T WANT TO FORGET!
I DID IT BECAUSE I LOVE HER.
I LOVE HER!
BUT NANA...
UM...YOU KNOW, I'LL BE TOTALLY FAITHFUL.
I'LL TAKE GOOD CARE OF YOU.
CHAK CHAK
HUH? WHAT'RE YOU TALKING ABOUT?

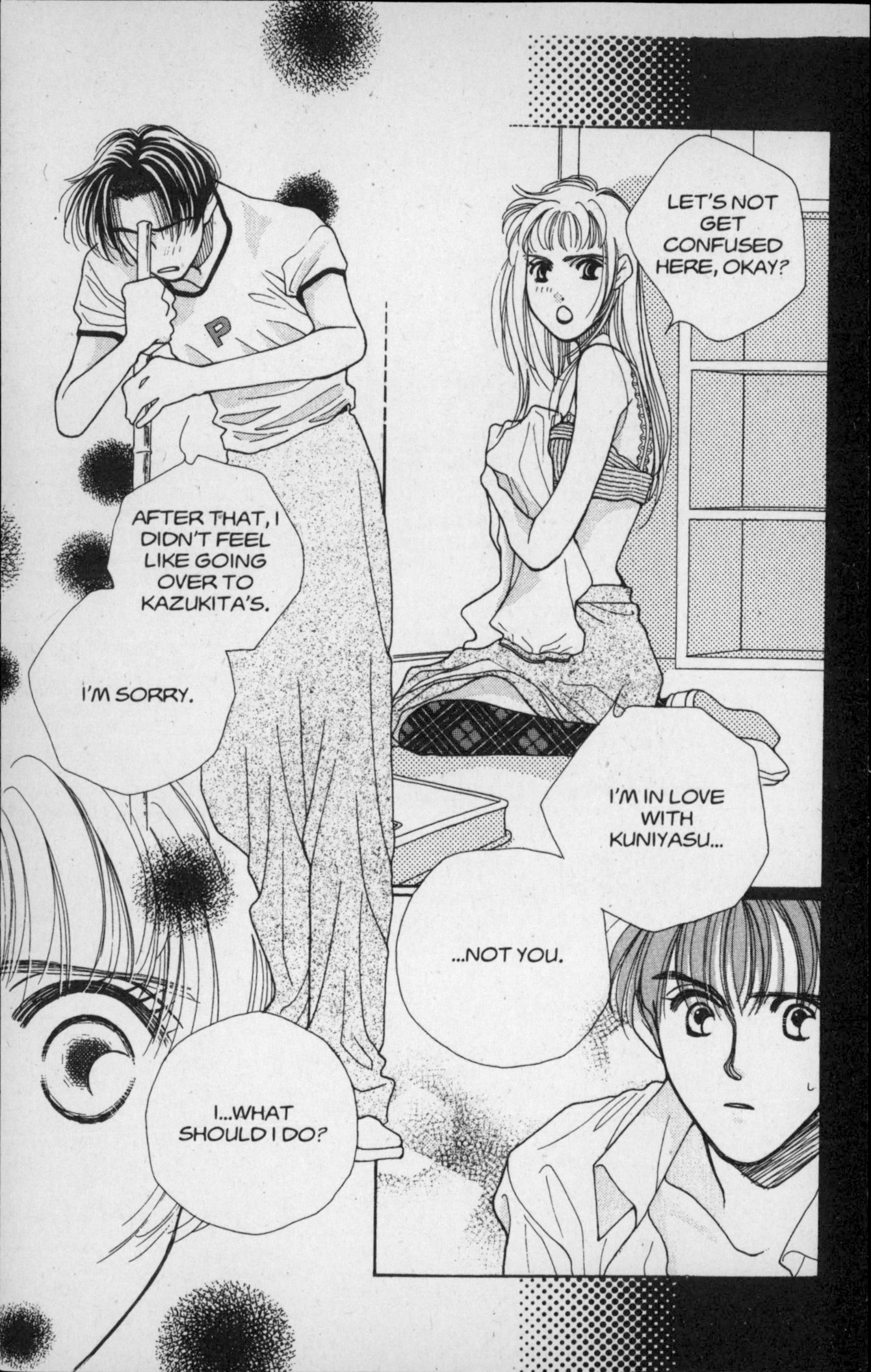
LET'S NOT GET CONFUSED HERE, OKAY?
I'M IN LOVE WITH KUNIYASU...
...NOT YOU.
AFTER THAT, I DIDN'T FEEL LIKE GOING OVER TO KAZUKITA'S.
I'M SORRY.
I...WHAT SHOULD I DO?

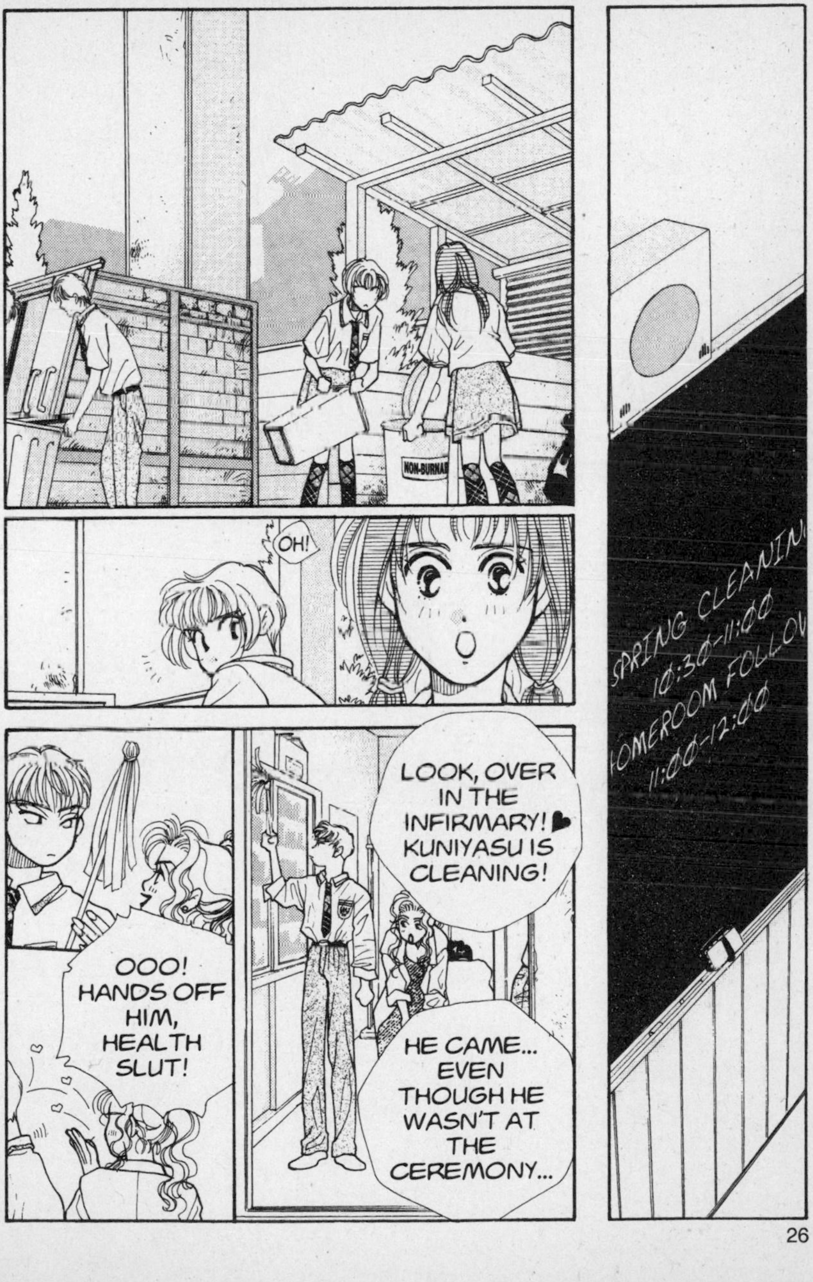
SPRING CLEANIN
10:30-11:00
HOMEROOM FOLLO
11:00-12:00
OH!
LOOK, OVER IN THE INFIRMARY! ♥ KUNIYASU IS CLEANING!
HE CAME... EVEN THOUGH HE WASN'T AT THE CEREMONY...
OOO! HANDS OFF HIM, HEALTH SLUT!

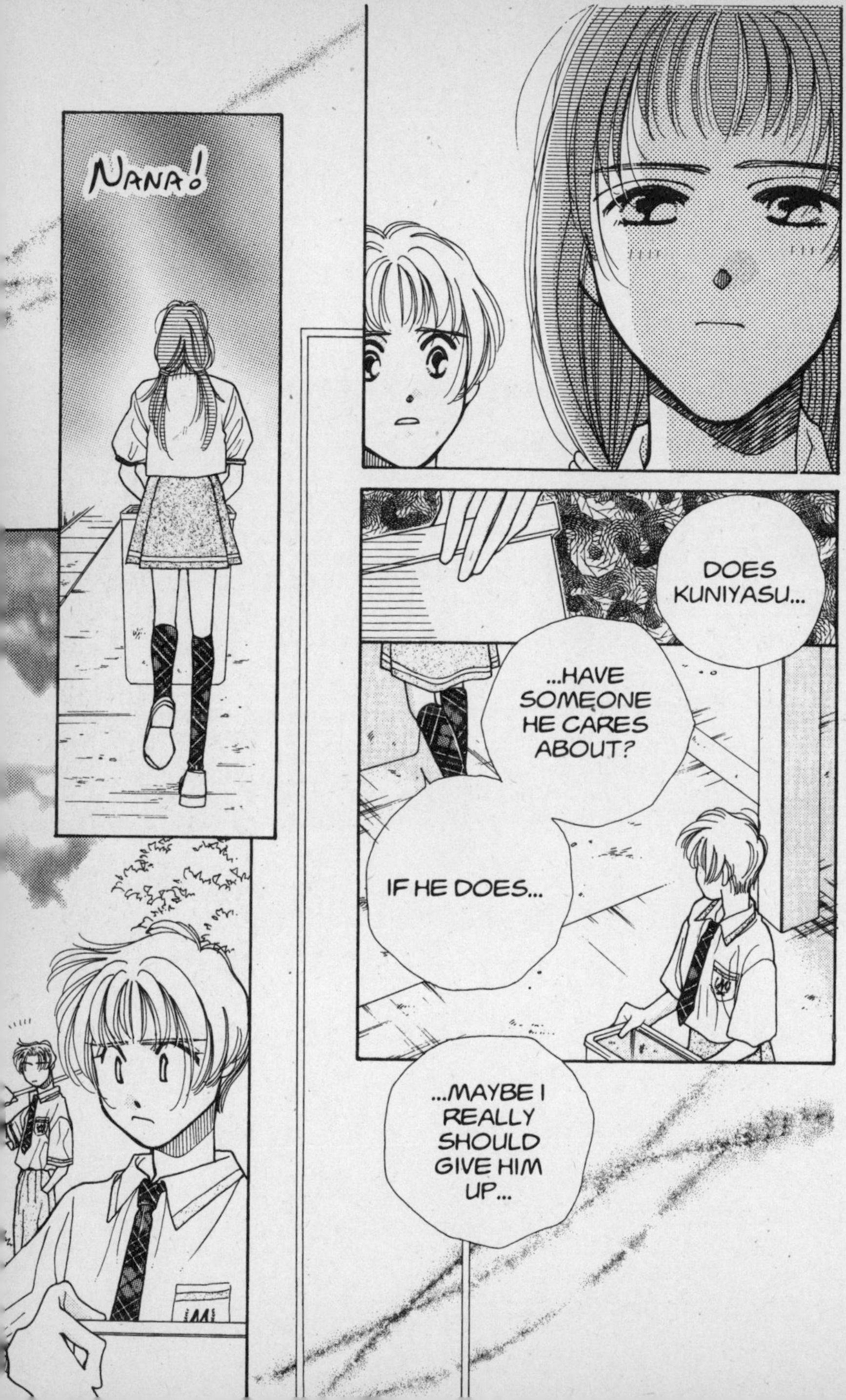
DOES KUNIYASU...
...HAVE SOMEONE HE CARES ABOUT?
IF HE DOES...
...MAYBE I REALLY SHOULD GIVE HIM UP...
NANA!

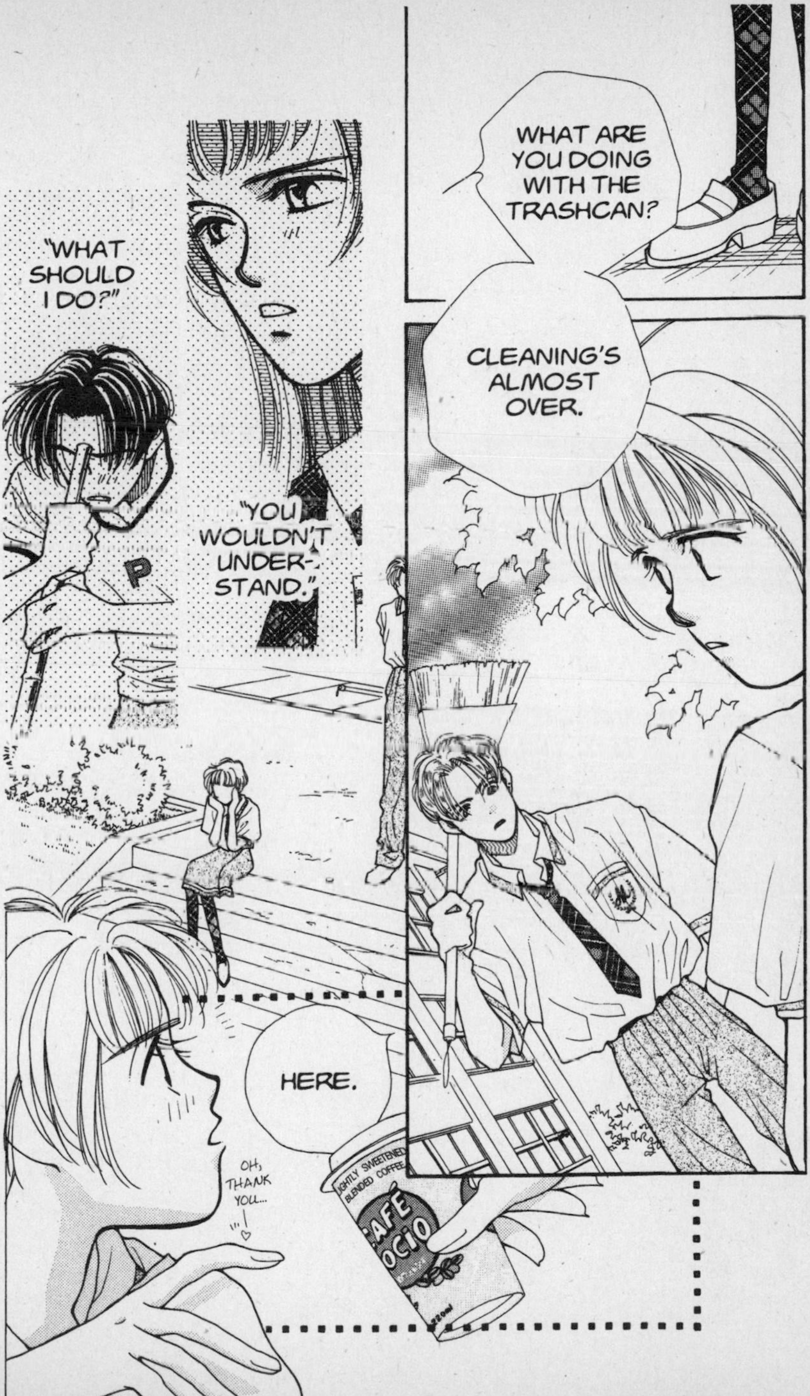
WHAT ARE YOU DOING WITH THE TRASHCAN?
CLEANING'S ALMOST OVER.
"YOU WOULDN'T UNDERSTAND."
"WHAT SHOULD I DO?"
HERE.
OH, THANK YOU...
BLENDED COFFEE

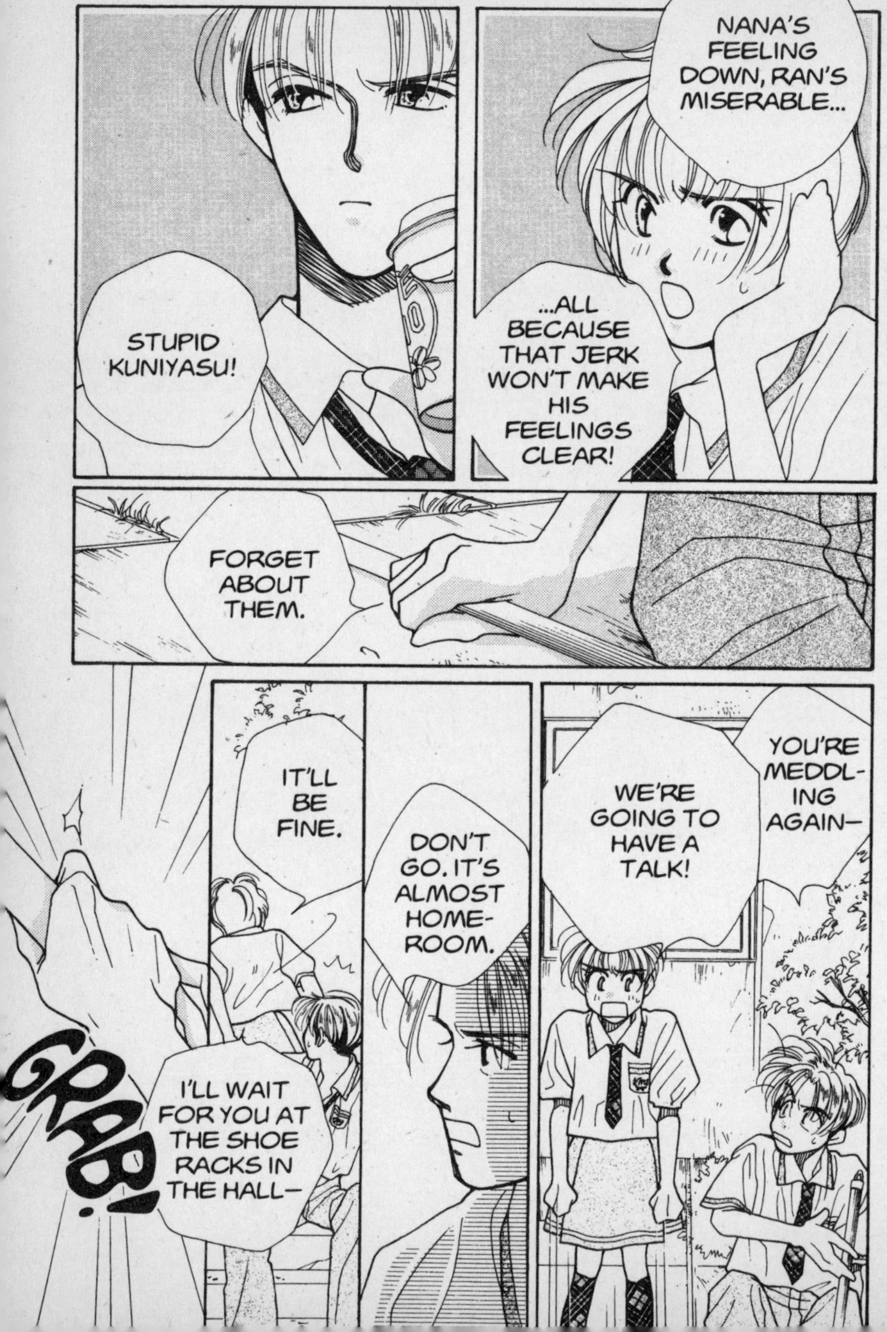
NANA'S FEELING DOWN, RAN'S MISERABLE...
...ALL BECAUSE THAT JERK WON'T MAKE HIS FEELINGS CLEAR!
STUPID KUNIYASU!
FORGET ABOUT THEM.
YOU'RE MEDDL-ING AGAIN—
WE'RE GOING TO HAVE A TALK!
DON'T GO. IT'S ALMOST HOME-ROOM.
IT'LL BE FINE.
I'LL WAIT FOR YOU AT THE SHOE RACKS IN THE HALL—
GRAB!

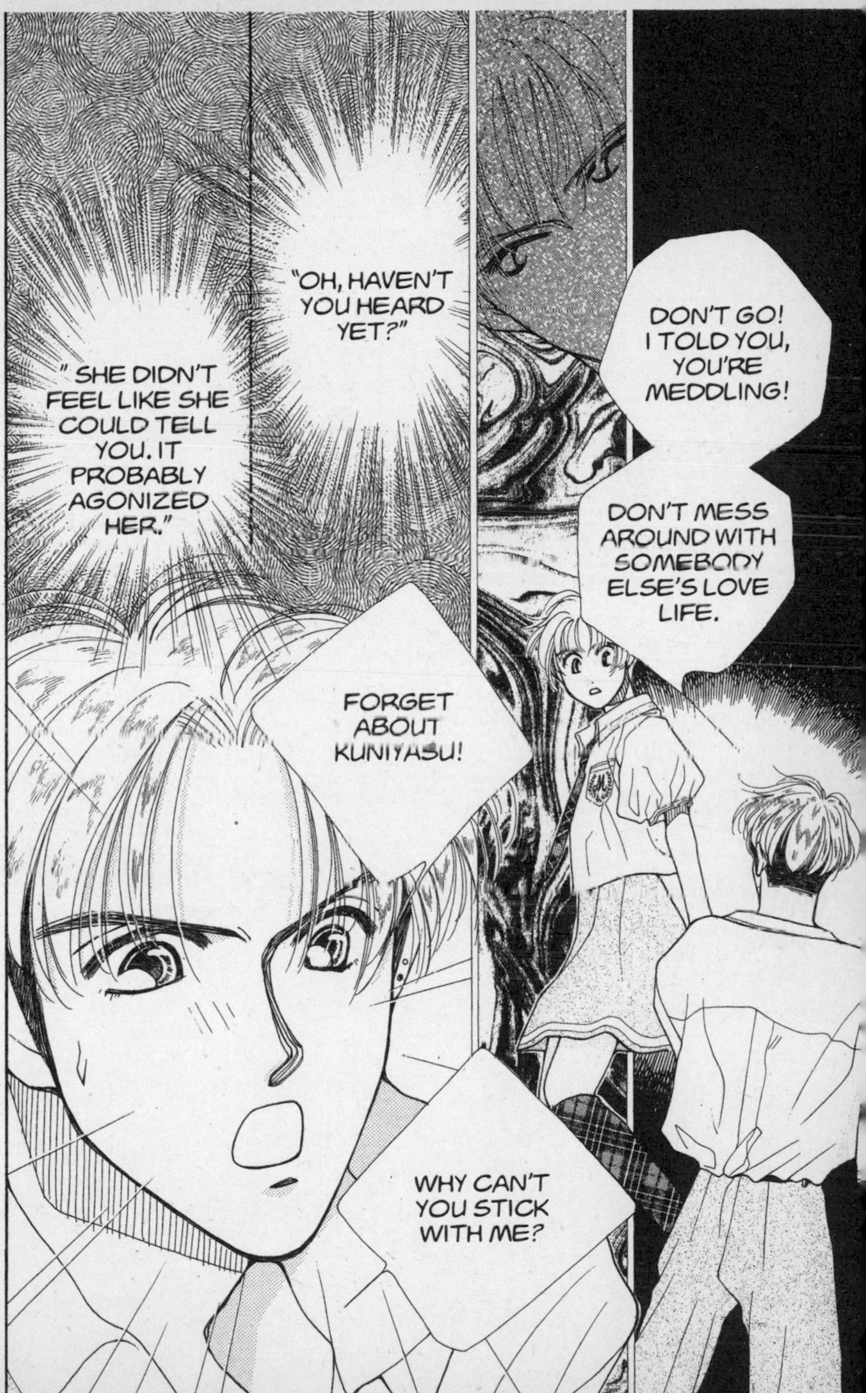
DON'T GO! I TOLD YOU, YOU'RE MEDDLING!
DON'T MESS AROUND WITH SOMEBODY ELSE'S LOVE LIFE.
"OH, HAVEN'T YOU HEARD YET?"
"SHE DIDN'T FEEL LIKE SHE COULD TELL YOU. IT PROBABLY AGONIZED HER."
FORGET ABOUT KUNIYASU!
WHY CAN'T YOU STICK WITH ME?

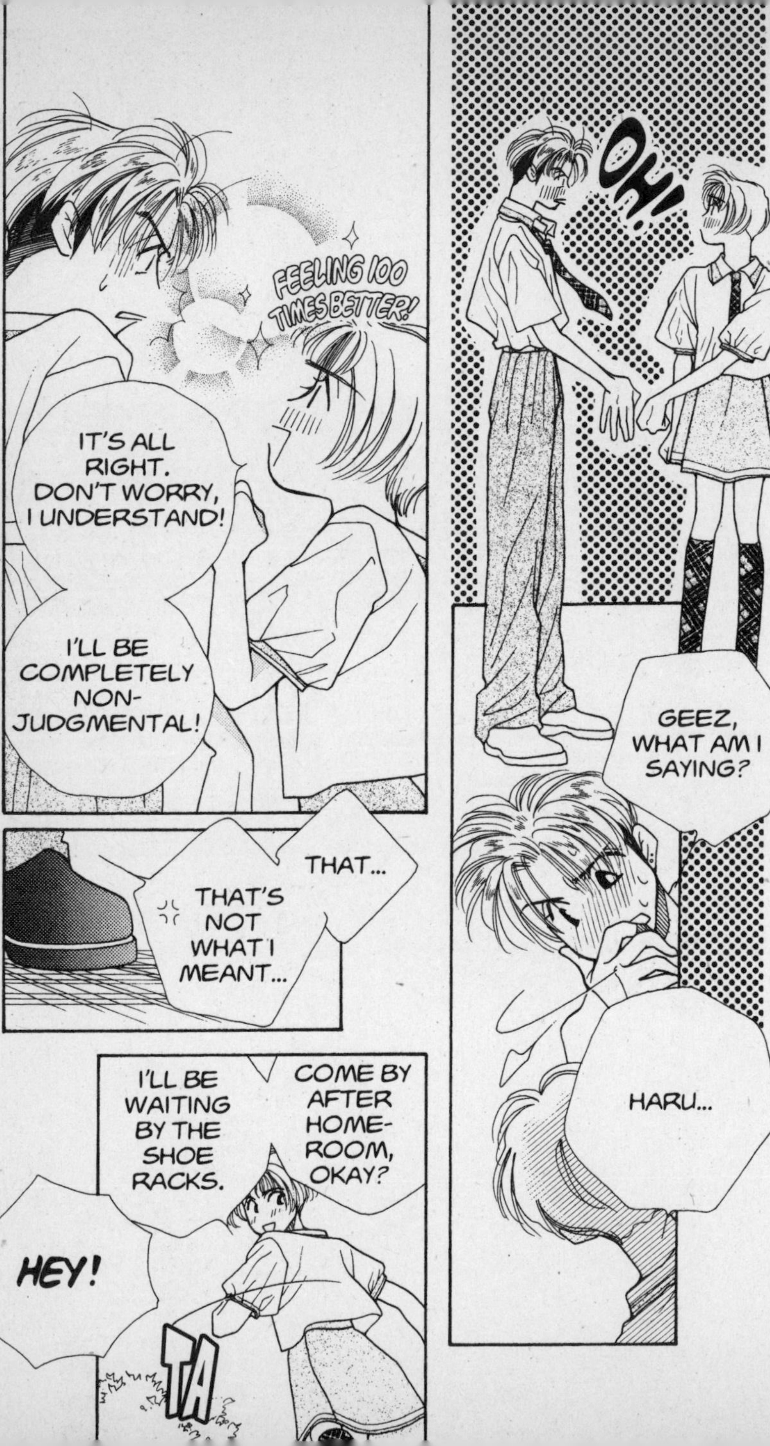
OH!
GEEZ, WHAT AM I SAYING?
HARU...
FEELING 100 TIMES BETTER!
IT'S ALL RIGHT. DON'T WORRY, I UNDERSTAND!
I'LL BE COMPLETELY NON-JUDGMENTAL!
THAT...
THAT'S NOT WHAT I MEANT...
COME BY AFTER HOME-ROOM, OKAY?
I'LL BE WAITING BY THE SHOE RACKS.
HEY!
TA

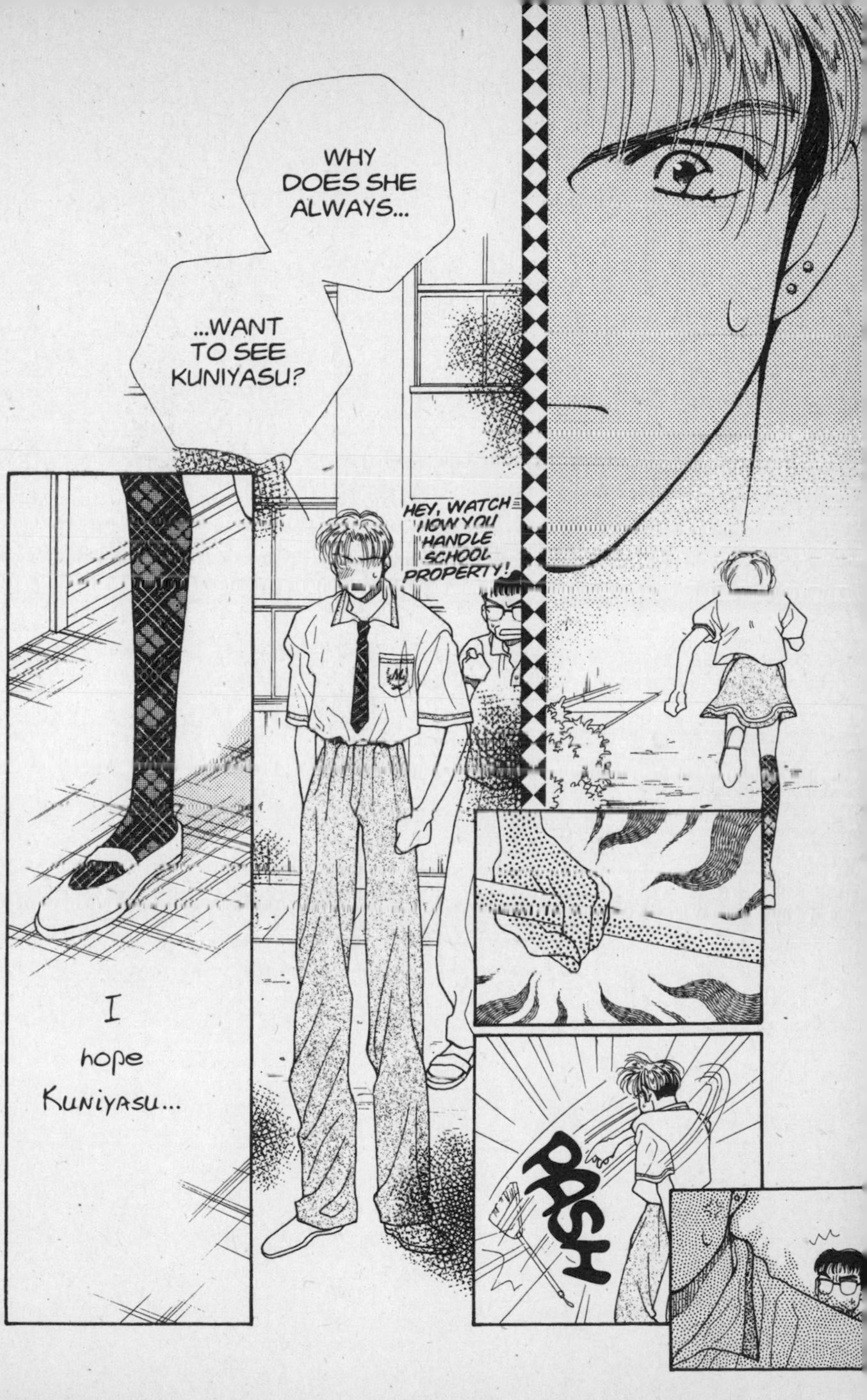
WHY DOES SHE ALWAYS...
...WANT TO SEE KUNIYASU?
PASH
HEY, WATCH HOW YOU HANDLE SCHOOL PROPERTY!
I hope Kuniyasu...

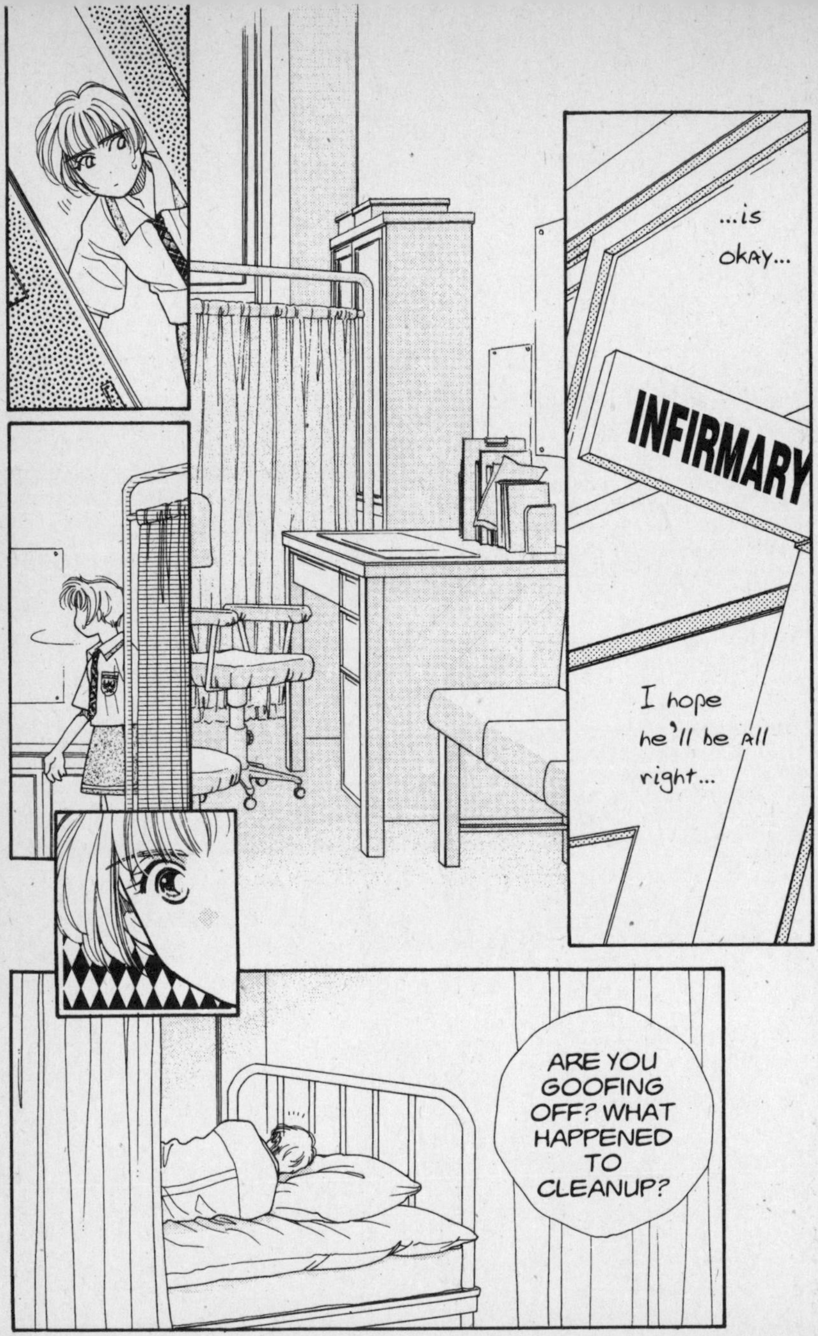
...is okay...
INFIRMARY
I hope he'll be all right...
ARE YOU GOOFING OFF? WHAT HAPPENED TO CLEANUP?

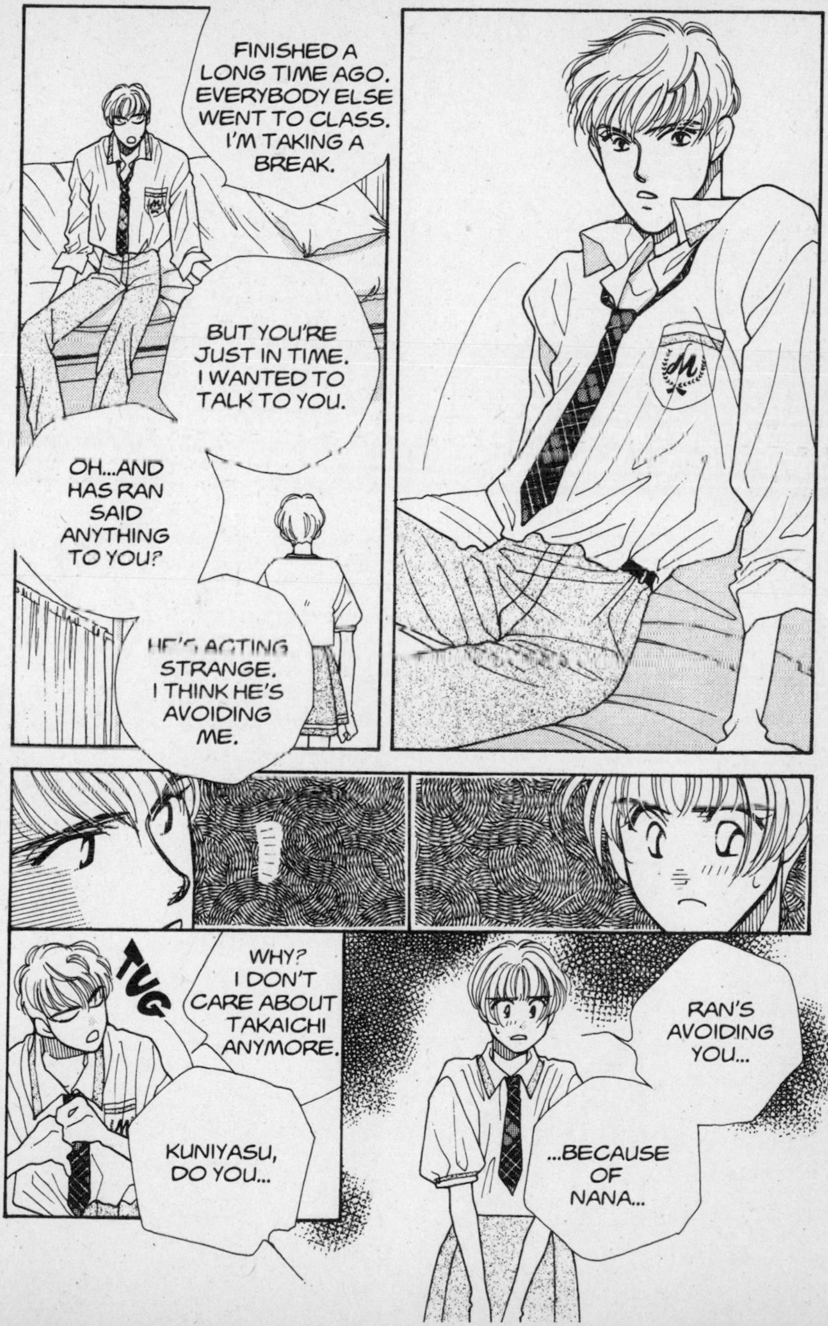
FINISHED A LONG TIME AGO. EVERYBODY ELSE WENT TO CLASS. I'M TAKING A BREAK.
BUT YOU'RE JUST IN TIME. I WANTED TO TALK TO YOU.
OH...AND HAS RAN SAID ANYTHING TO YOU?
HE'S ACTING STRANGE. I THINK HE'S AVOIDING ME.
RAN'S AVOIDING YOU...
...BECAUSE OF NANA...
WHY? I DON'T CARE ABOUT TAKAICHI ANYMORE.
TUG
KUNIYASU, DO YOU...

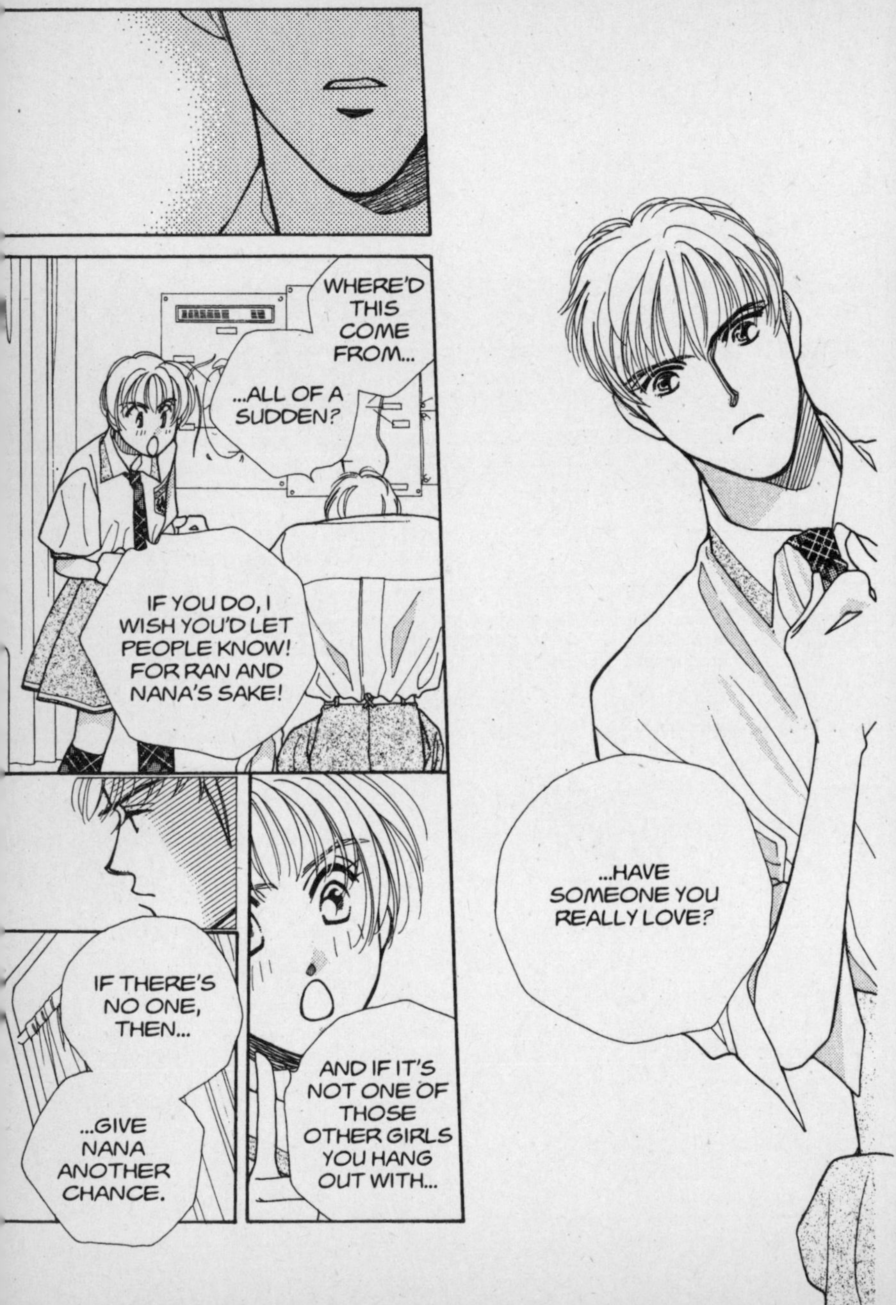
...HAVE SOMEONE YOU REALLY LOVE?
WHERE'D THIS COME FROM...
...ALL OF A SUDDEN?
IF YOU DO, I WISH YOU'D LET PEOPLE KNOW! FOR RAN AND NANA'S SAKE!
AND IF IT'S NOT ONE OF THOSE OTHER GIRLS YOU HANG OUT WITH...
IF THERE'S NO ONE, THEN...
...GIVE NANA ANOTHER CHANCE.

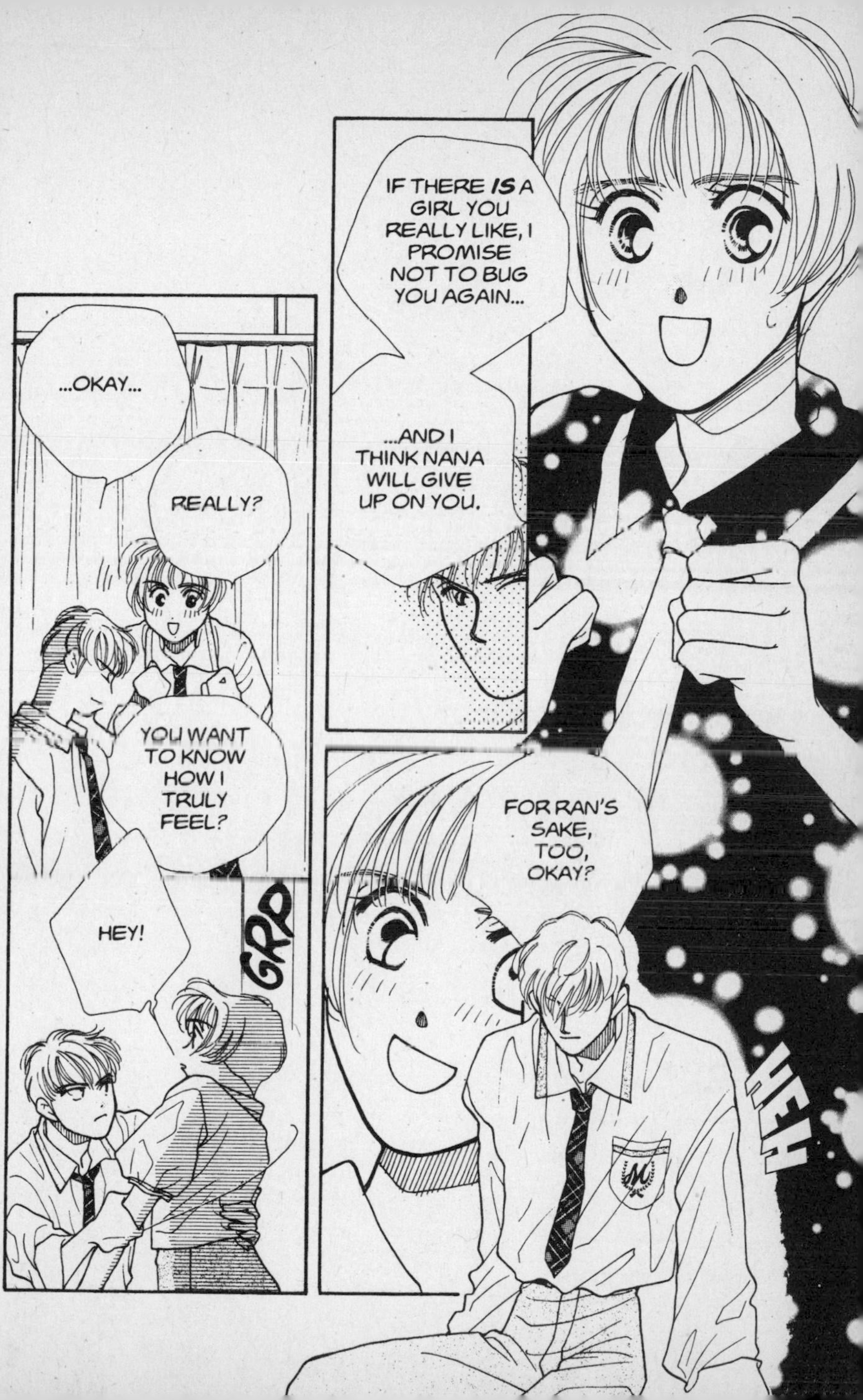
IF THERE *IS* A GIRL YOU REALLY LIKE, I PROMISE NOT TO BUG YOU AGAIN...
...AND I THINK NANA WILL GIVE UP ON YOU.
FOR RAN'S SAKE, TOO, OKAY?
HEH
...OKAY...
REALLY?
YOU WANT TO KNOW HOW I TRULY FEEL?
HEY!
GRP

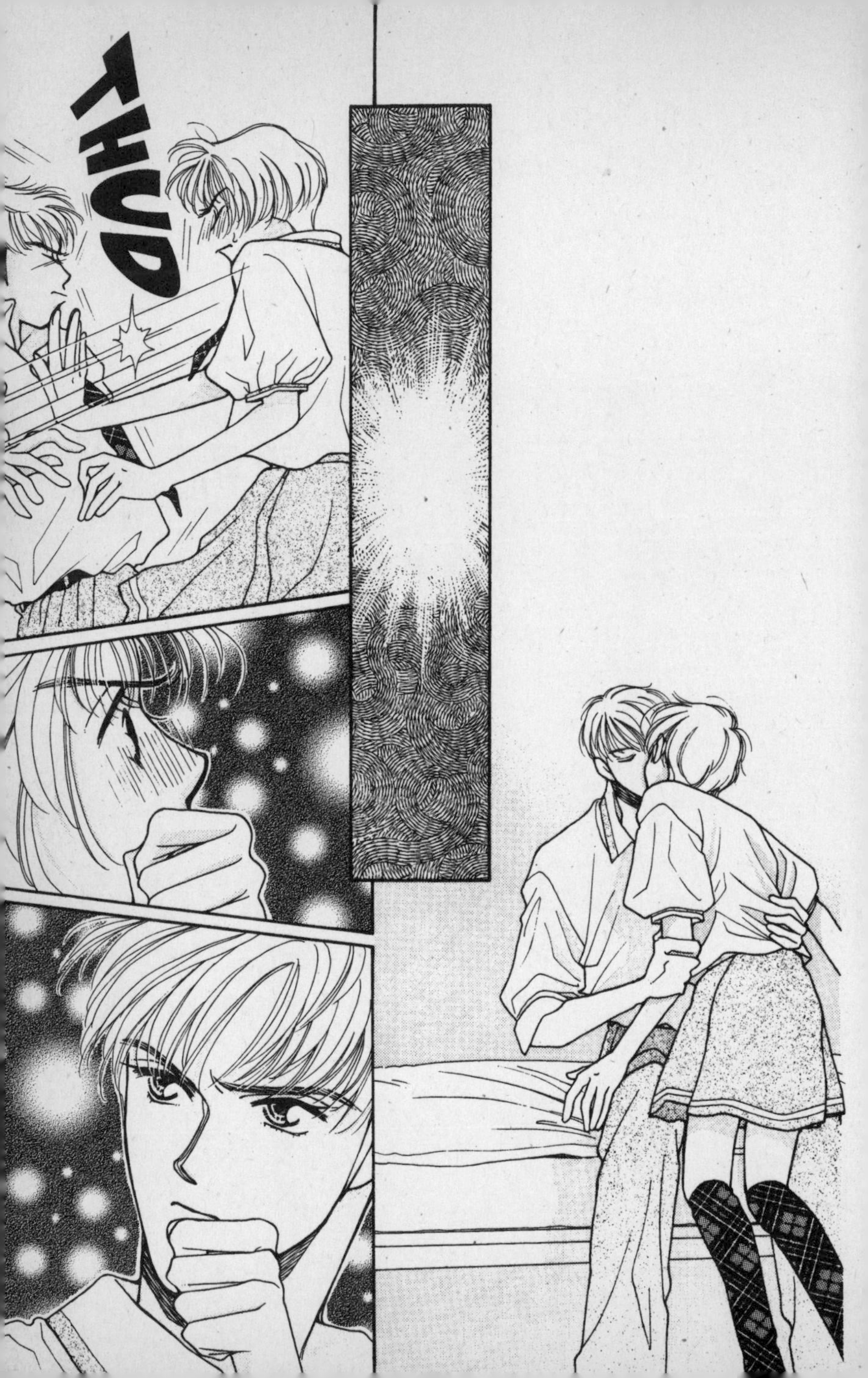
THUD

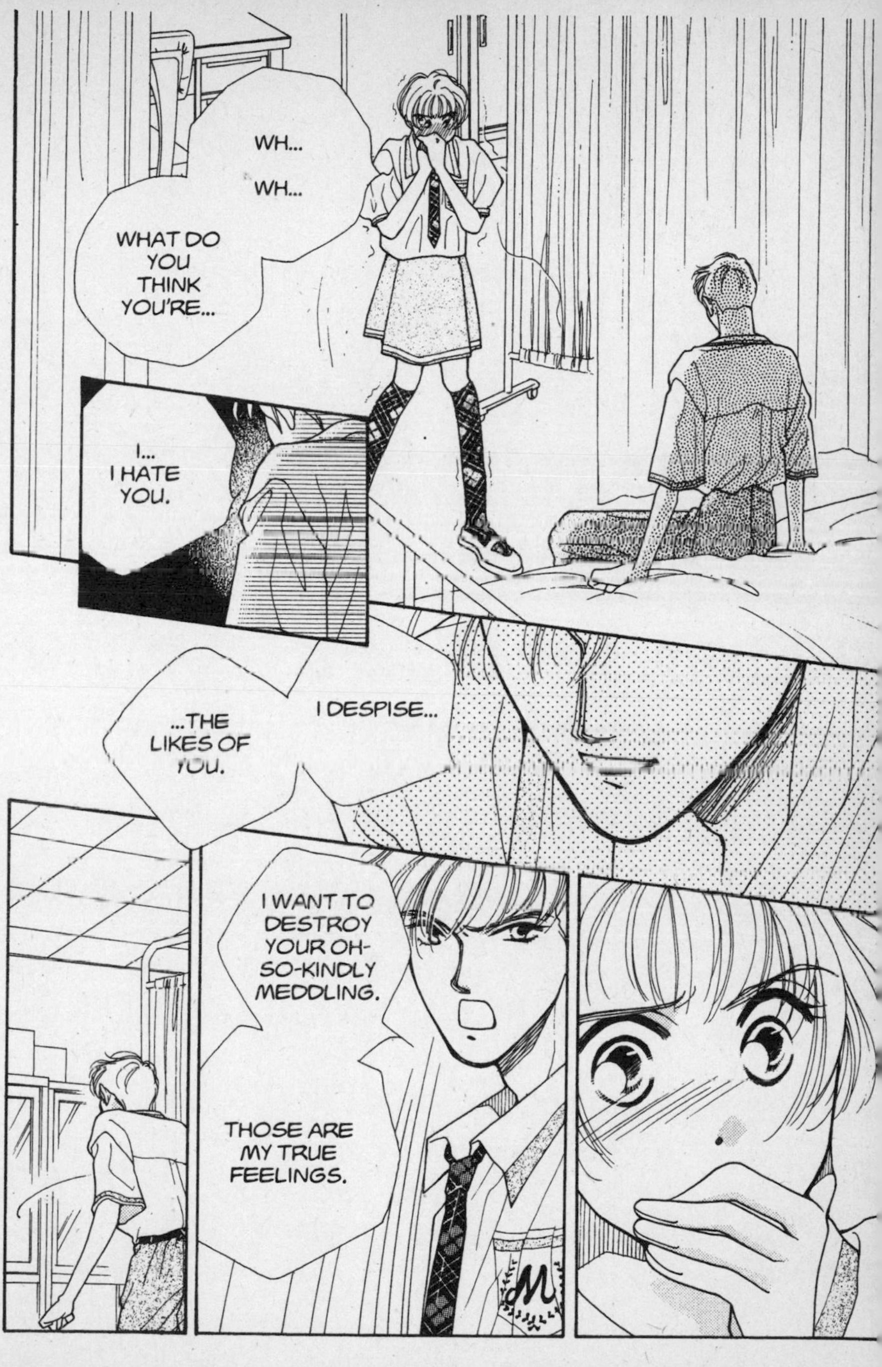
WH...
WH...
WHAT DO YOU THINK YOU'RE...
I... I HATE YOU.
I DESPISE...
...THE LIKES OF YOU.
I WANT TO DESTROY YOUR OH-SO-KINDLY MEDDLING.
THOSE ARE MY TRUE FEELINGS.

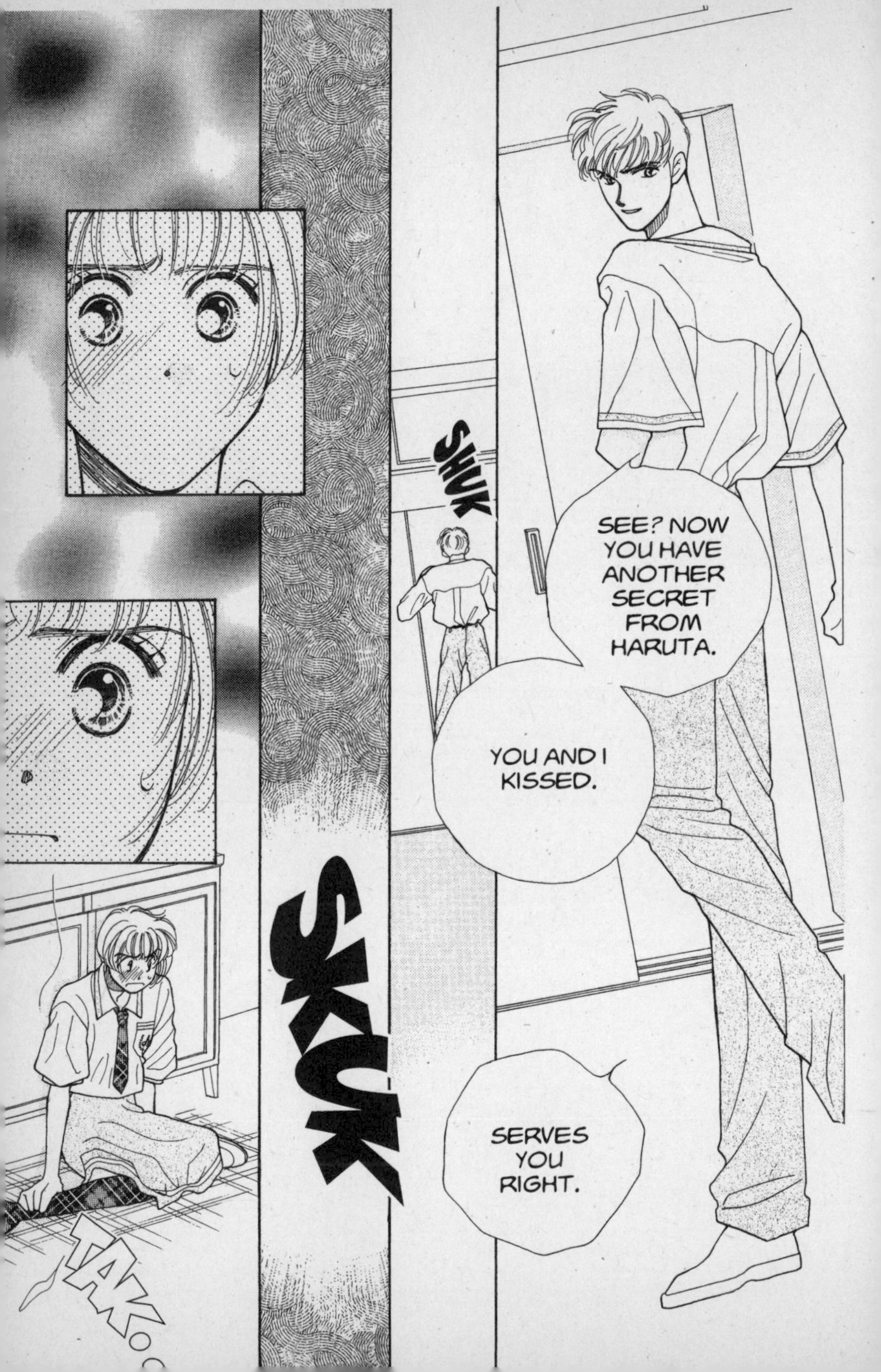
SEE? NOW YOU HAVE ANOTHER SECRET FROM HARUTA.
YOU AND I KISSED.
SHUK
SERVES YOU RIGHT.
SKUK
TAK

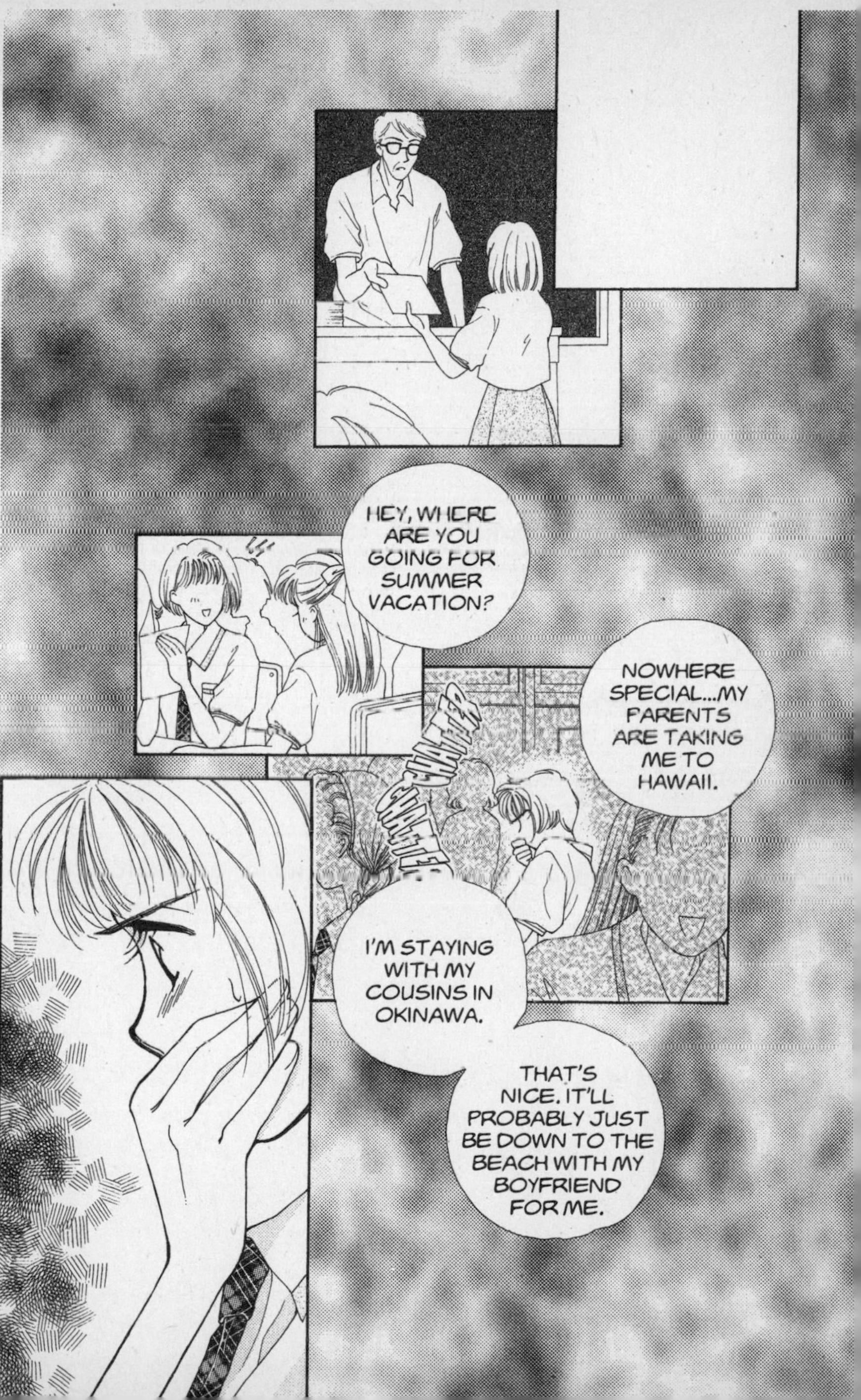
HEY, WHERE ARE YOU GOING FOR SUMMER VACATION?
NOWHERE SPECIAL...MY PARENTS ARE TAKING ME TO HAWAII.
CHATTER CHATTER
I'M STAYING WITH MY COUSINS IN OKINAWA.
THAT'S NICE. IT'LL PROBABLY JUST BE DOWN TO THE BEACH WITH MY BOYFRIEND FOR ME.

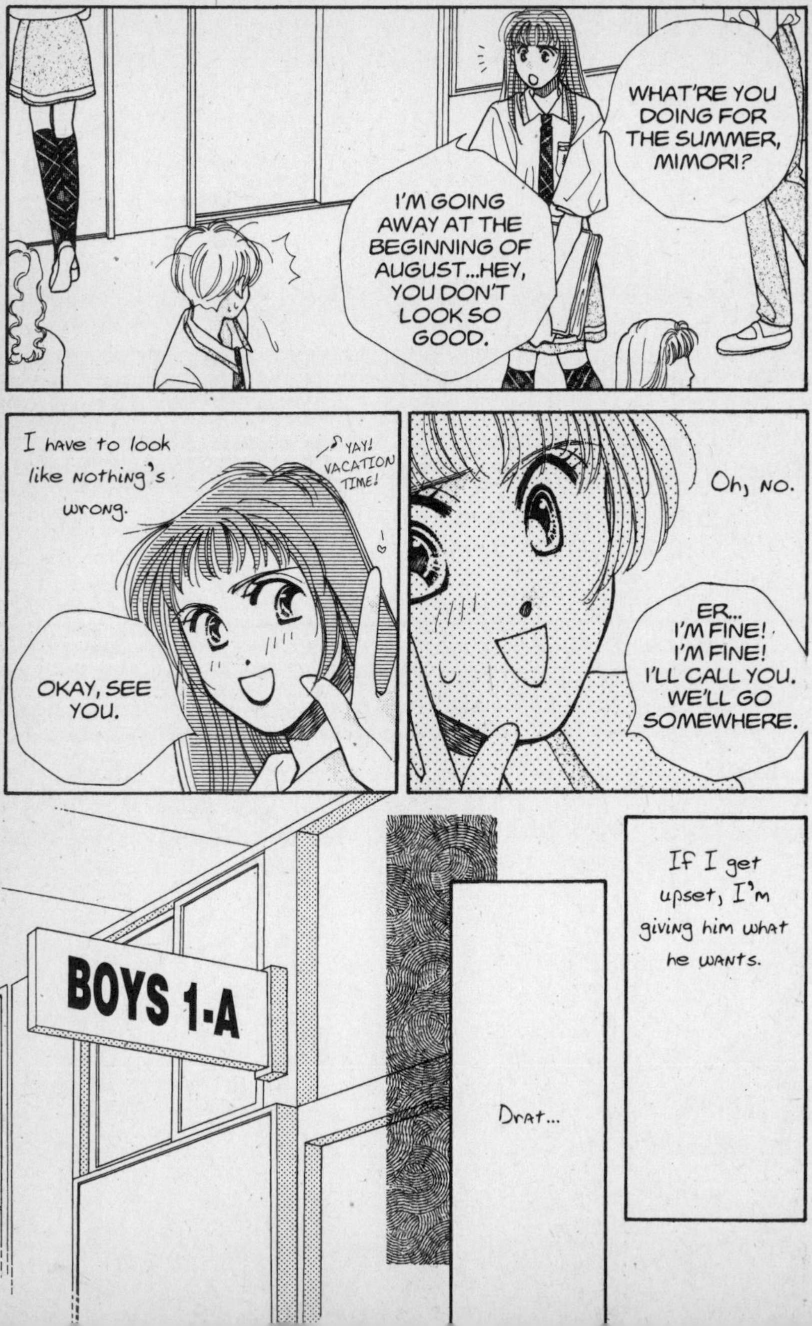
WHAT'RE YOU DOING FOR THE SUMMER, MIMORI?
I'M GOING AWAY AT THE BEGINNING OF AUGUST...HEY, YOU DON'T LOOK SO GOOD.
Oh, no.
ER... I'M FINE! I'M FINE! I'LL CALL YOU. WE'LL GO SOMEWHERE.
YAY! VACATION TIME!
I have to look like nothing's wrong.
OKAY, SEE YOU.
If I get upset, I'm giving him what he wants.
Drat...
BOYS 1-A

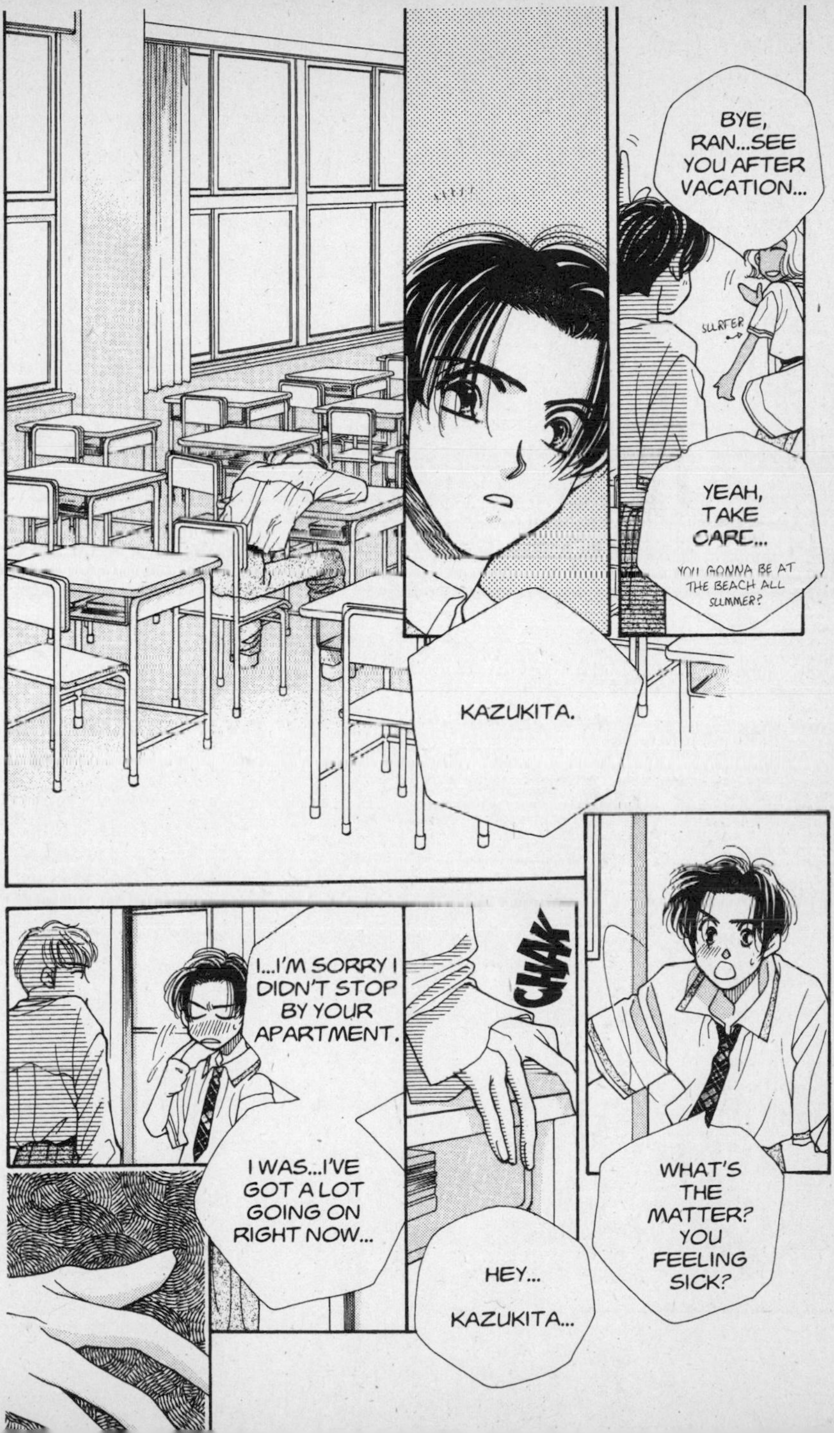
BYE, RAN...SEE YOU AFTER VACATION...
SURFER
YEAH, TAKE CARE...
YOU GONNA BE AT THE BEACH ALL SUMMER?
KAZUKITA.
WHAT'S THE MATTER? YOU FEELING SICK?
CHAK
HEY... KAZUKITA...
I...I'M SORRY I DIDN'T STOP BY YOUR APARTMENT.
I WAS...I'VE GOT A LOT GOING ON RIGHT NOW...

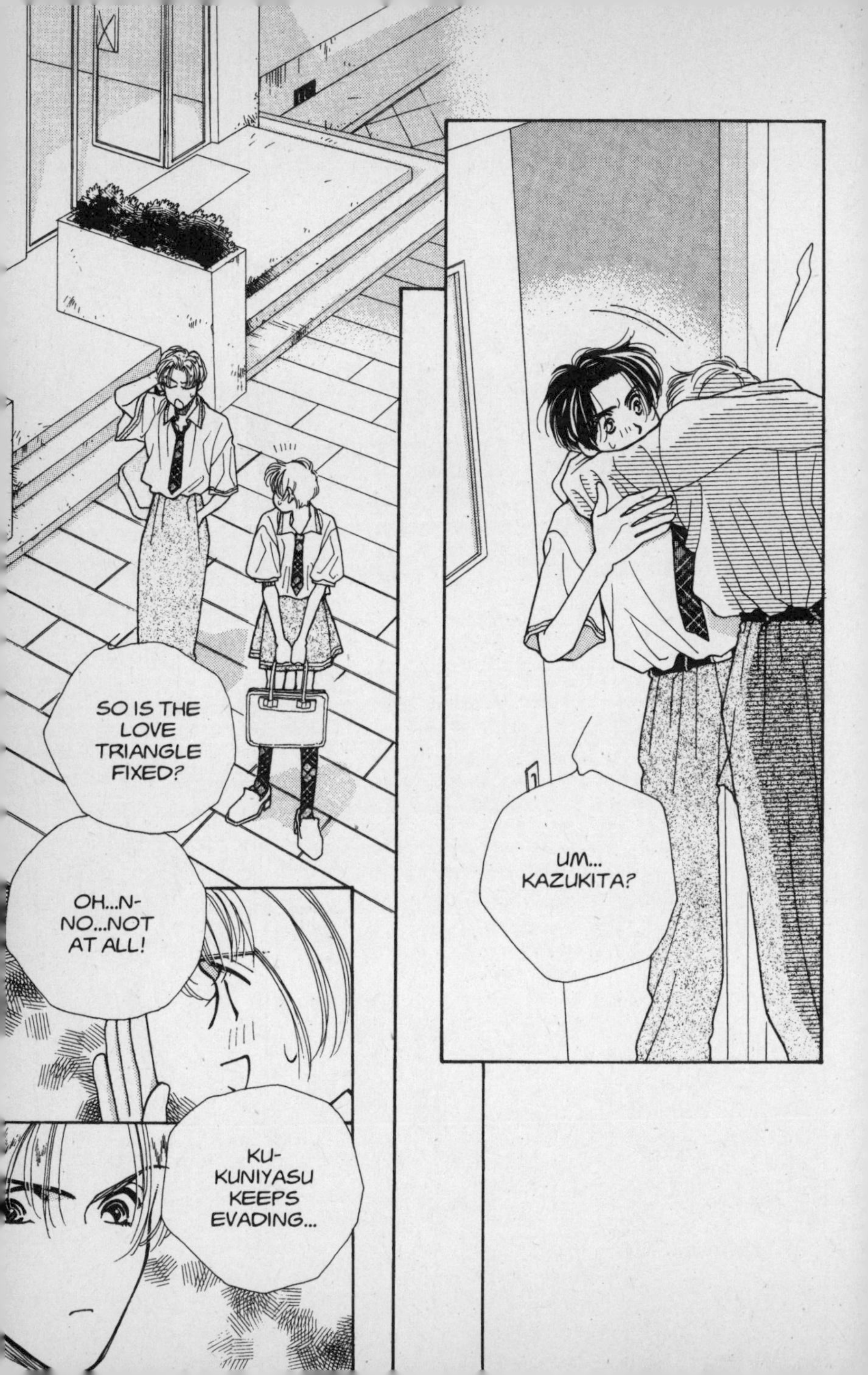
SO IS THE LOVE TRIANGLE FIXED?
OH...N-NO...NOT AT ALL!
KU-KUNIYASU KEEPS EVADING...
UM... KAZUKITA?

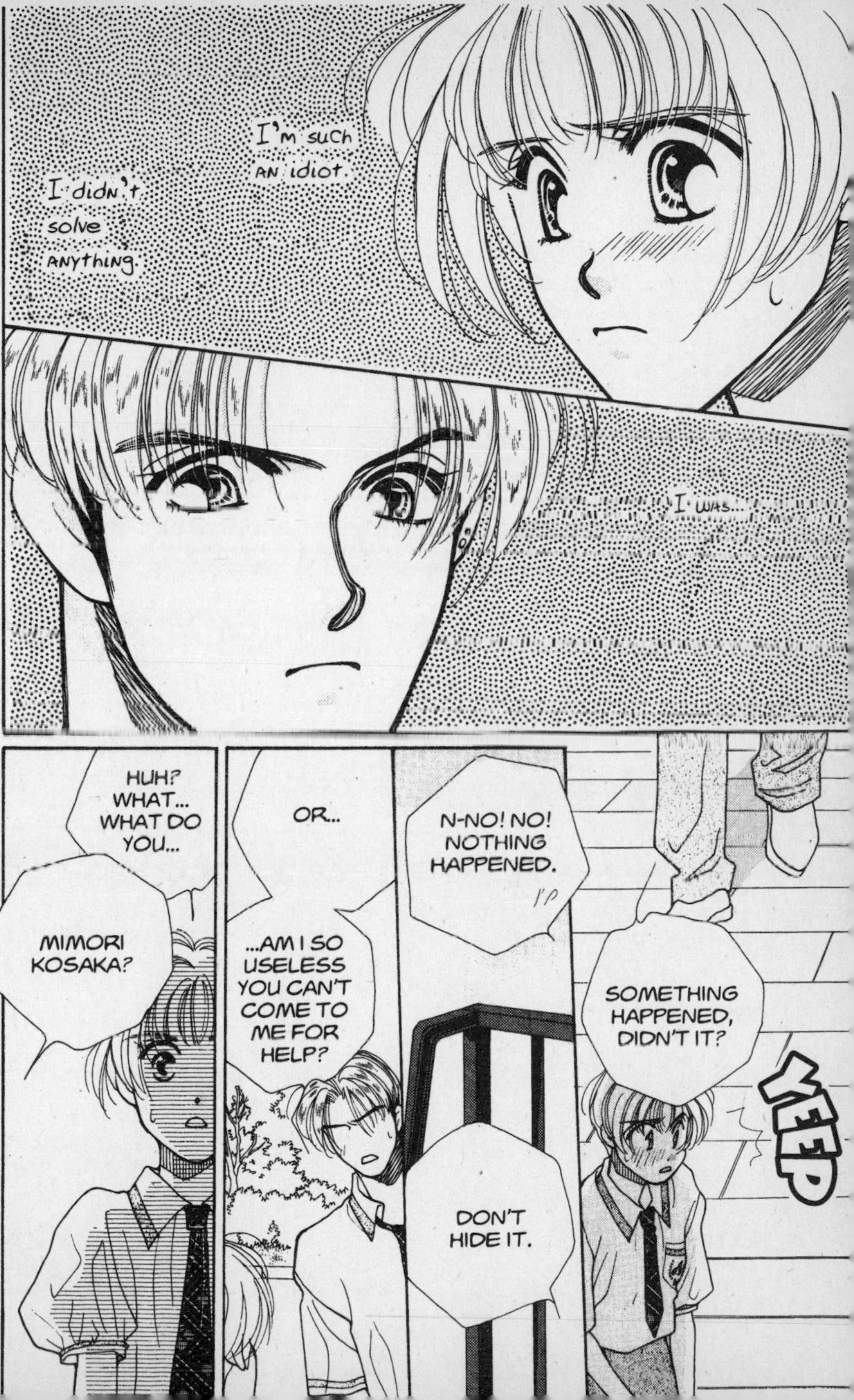
I'm such an idiot.
I didn't solve anything.
I was...
SOMETHING HAPPENED, DIDN'T IT?
YEEP
N-NO! NO! NOTHING HAPPENED.
DON'T HIDE IT.
OR...
...AM I SO USELESS YOU CAN'T COME TO ME FOR HELP?
HUH? WHAT... WHAT DO YOU...
MIMORI KOSAKA?

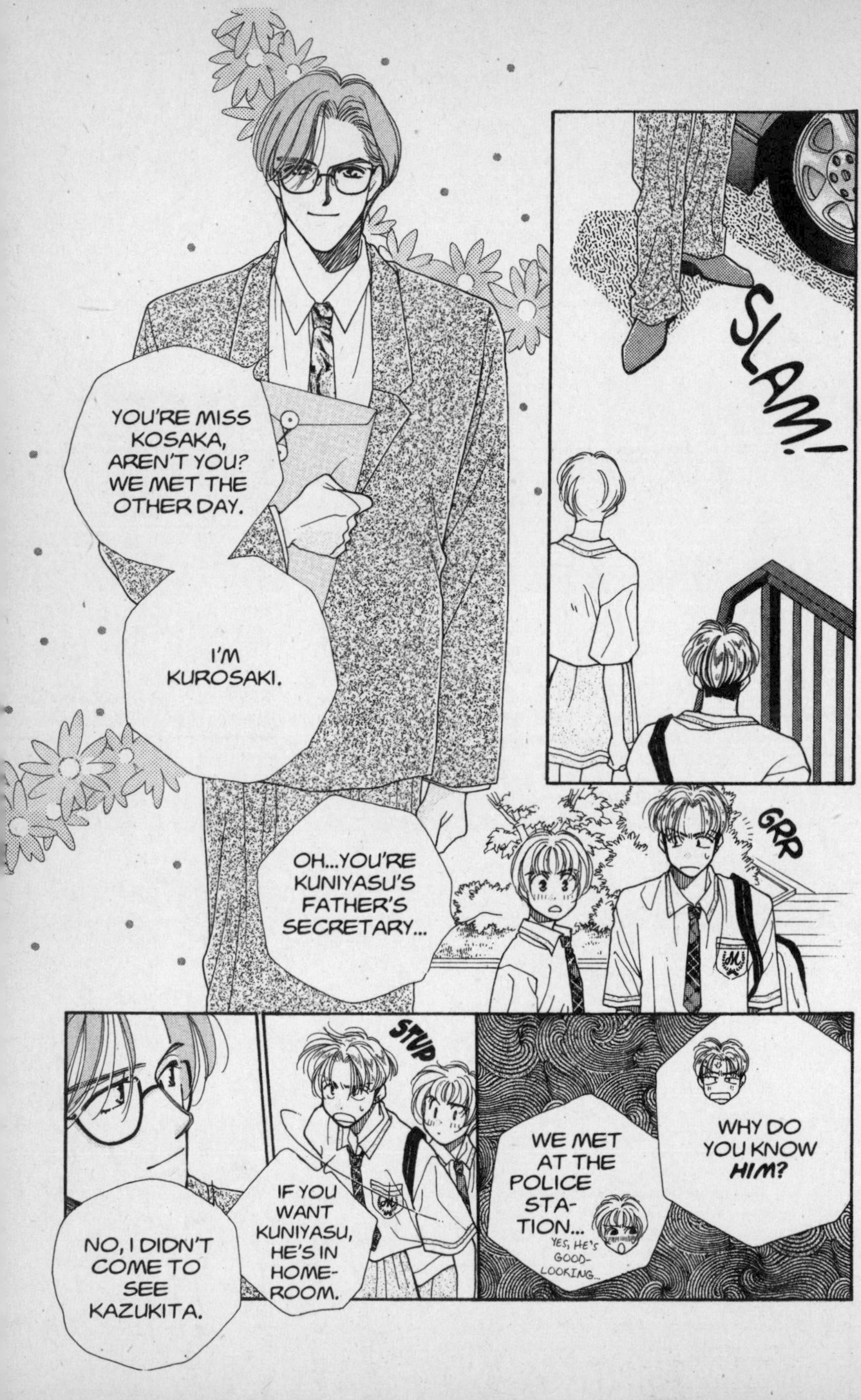
SLAM!
YOU'RE MISS KOSAKA, AREN'T YOU? WE MET THE OTHER DAY.
I'M KUROSAKI.
OH...YOU'RE KUNIYASU'S FATHER'S SECRETARY...
GRR
WHY DO YOU KNOW HIM?
WE MET AT THE POLICE STATION...
YES, HE'S GOOD-LOOKING...
STUP
IF YOU WANT KUNIYASU, HE'S IN HOMEROOM.
NO, I DIDN'T COME TO SEE KAZUKITA.

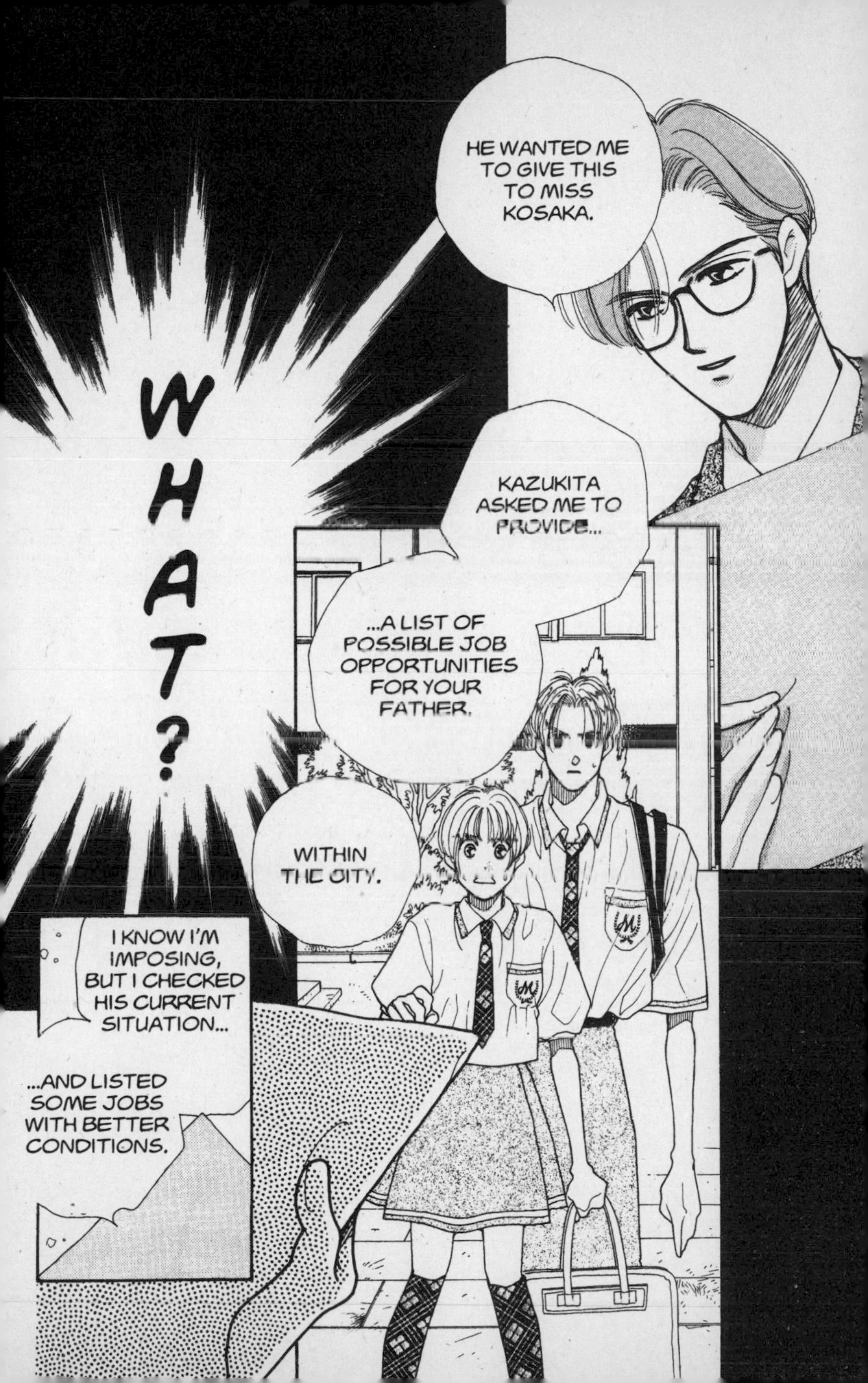
HE WANTED ME TO GIVE THIS TO MISS KOSAKA.
KAZUKITA ASKED ME TO PROVIDE...
...A LIST OF POSSIBLE JOB OPPORTUNITIES FOR YOUR FATHER.
WITHIN THE CITY.
WHAT?
I KNOW I'M IMPOSING, BUT I CHECKED HIS CURRENT SITUATION...
...AND LISTED SOME JOBS WITH BETTER CONDITIONS.

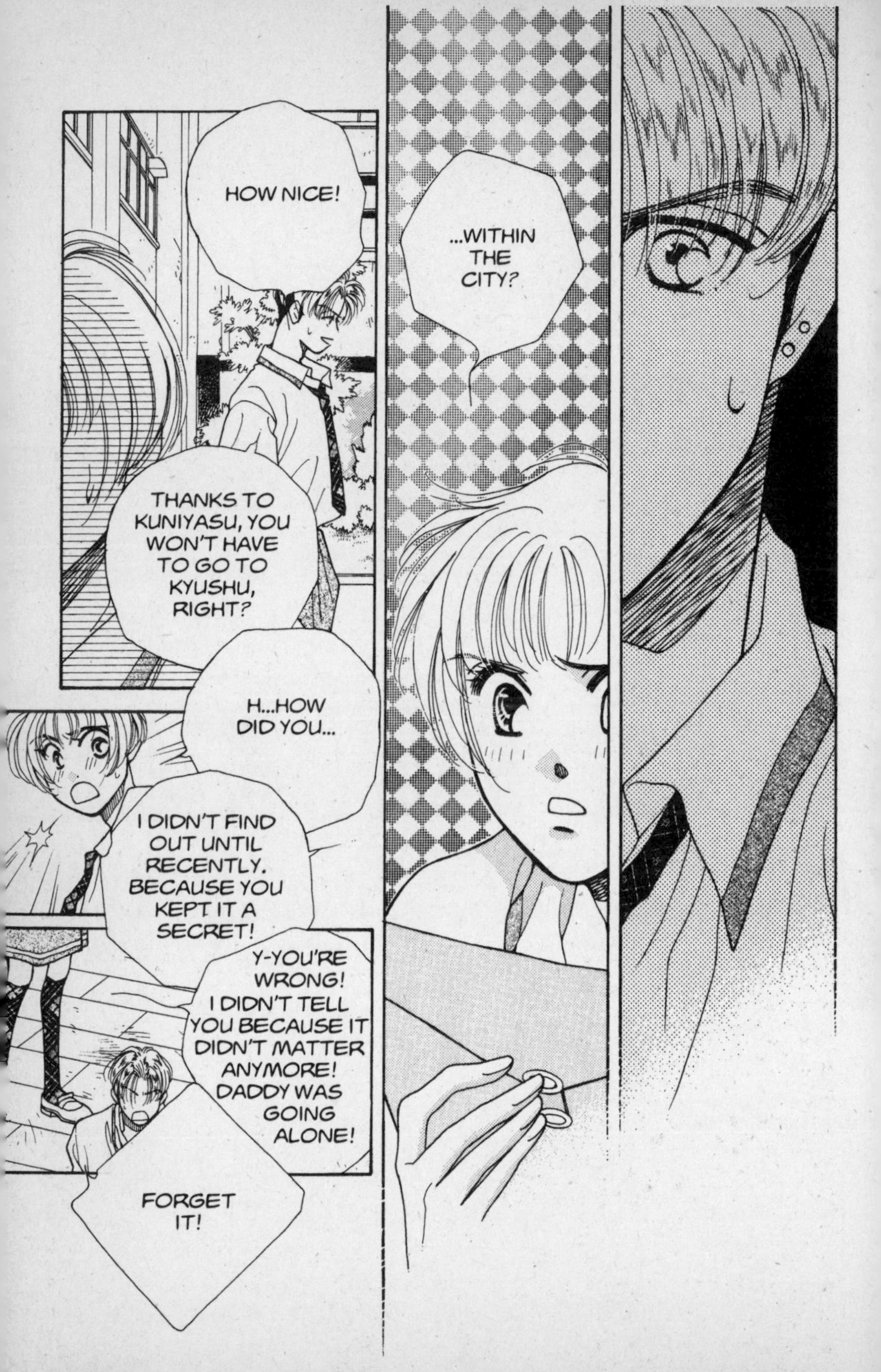
...WITHIN THE CITY?
HOW NICE!
THANKS TO KUNIYASU, YOU WON'T HAVE TO GO TO KYUSHU, RIGHT?
H...HOW DID YOU...
I DIDN'T FIND OUT UNTIL RECENTLY. BECAUSE YOU KEPT IT A SECRET!
Y-YOU'RE WRONG! I DIDN'T TELL YOU BECAUSE IT DIDN'T MATTER ANYMORE! DADDY WAS GOING ALONE!
FORGET IT!

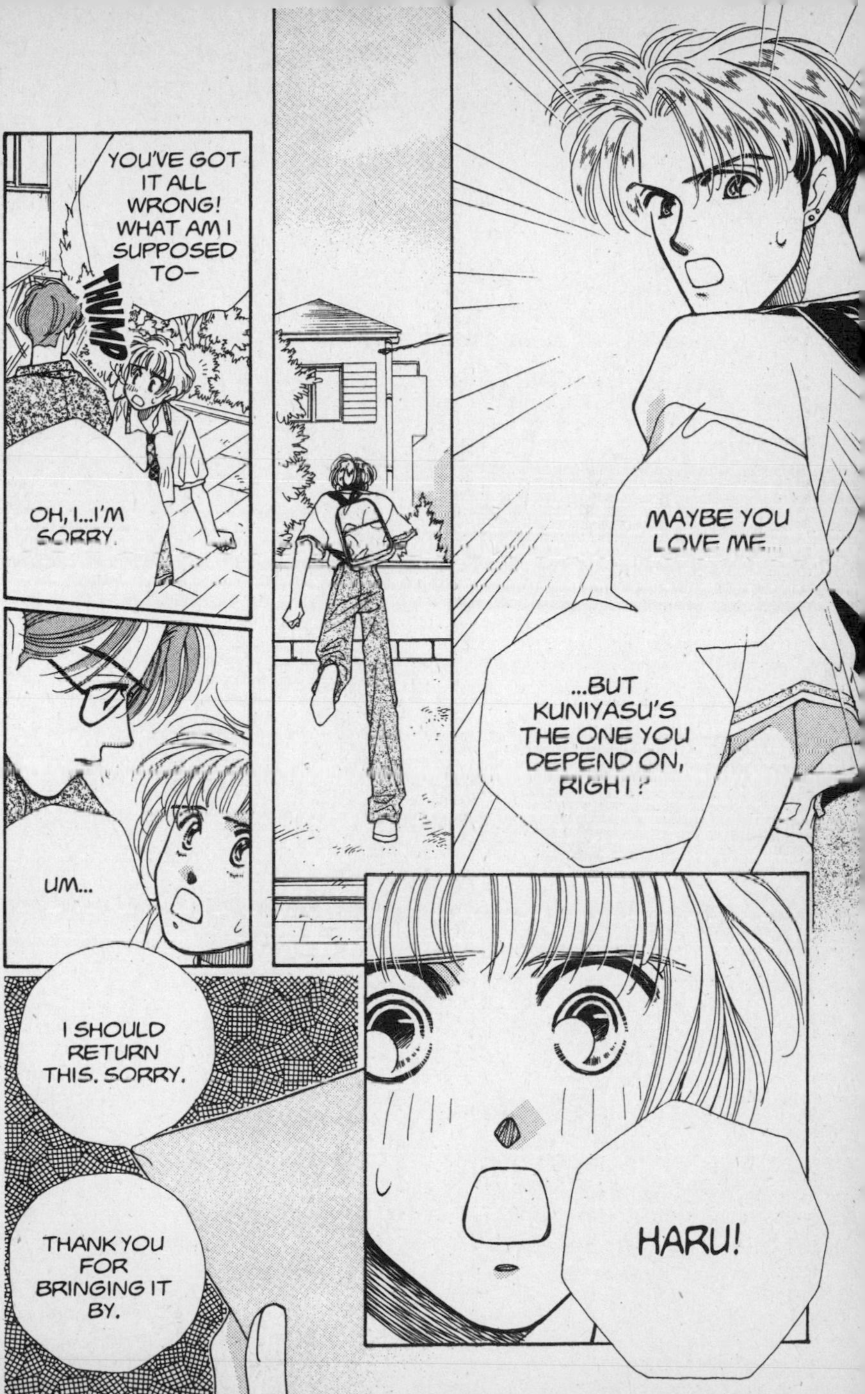
MAYBE YOU LOVE ME...
...BUT KUNIYASU'S THE ONE YOU DEPEND ON, RIGHT?
YOU'VE GOT IT ALL WRONG! WHAT AM I SUPPOSED TO—
THUMP
OH, I...I'M SORRY.
UM...
HARU!
I SHOULD RETURN THIS. SORRY.
THANK YOU FOR BRINGING IT BY.

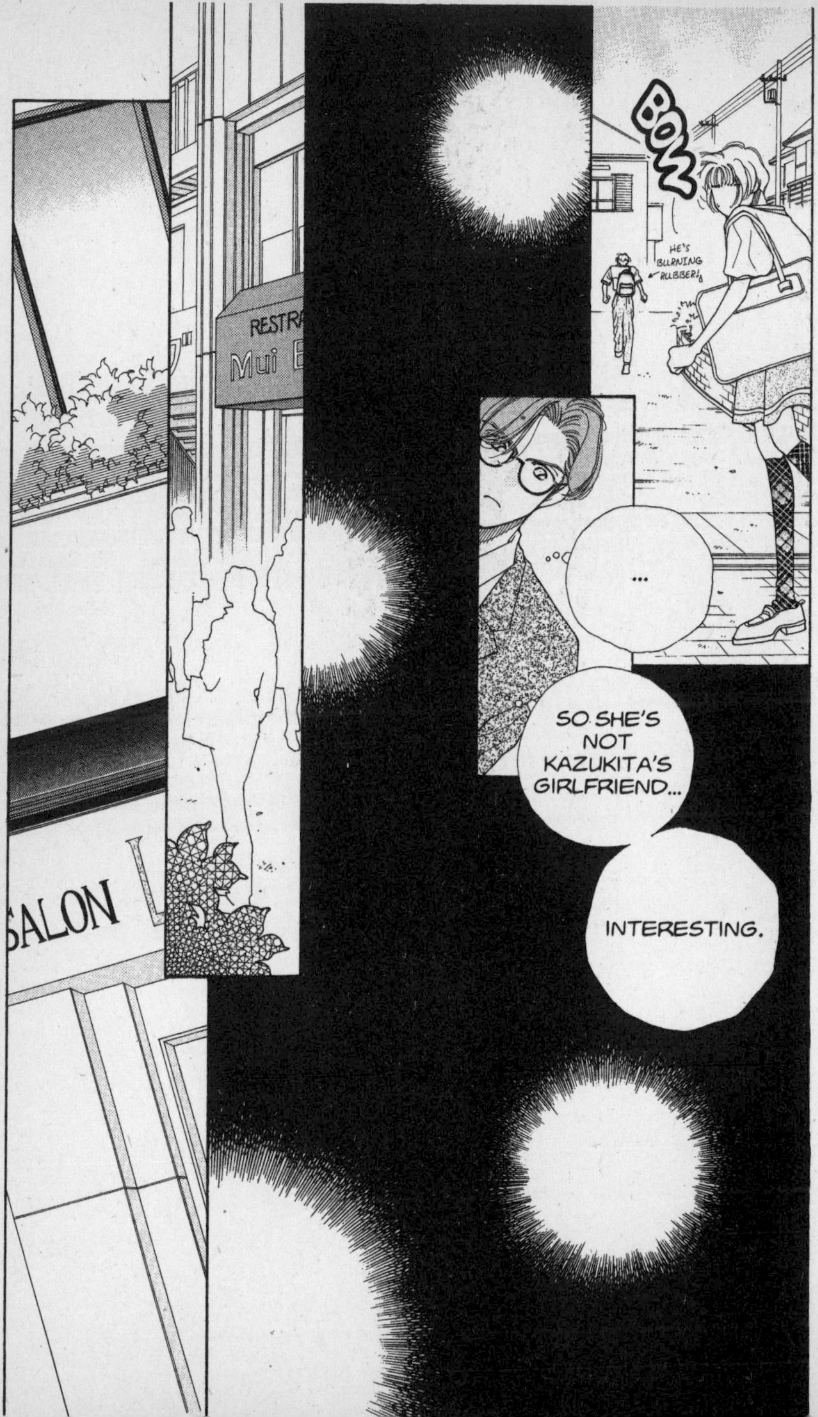
BOW
HE'S BURNING RUBBER!
...
SO SHE'S NOT KAZUKITA'S GIRLFRIEND...
INTERESTING.
RESTRA
Mui E
SALON

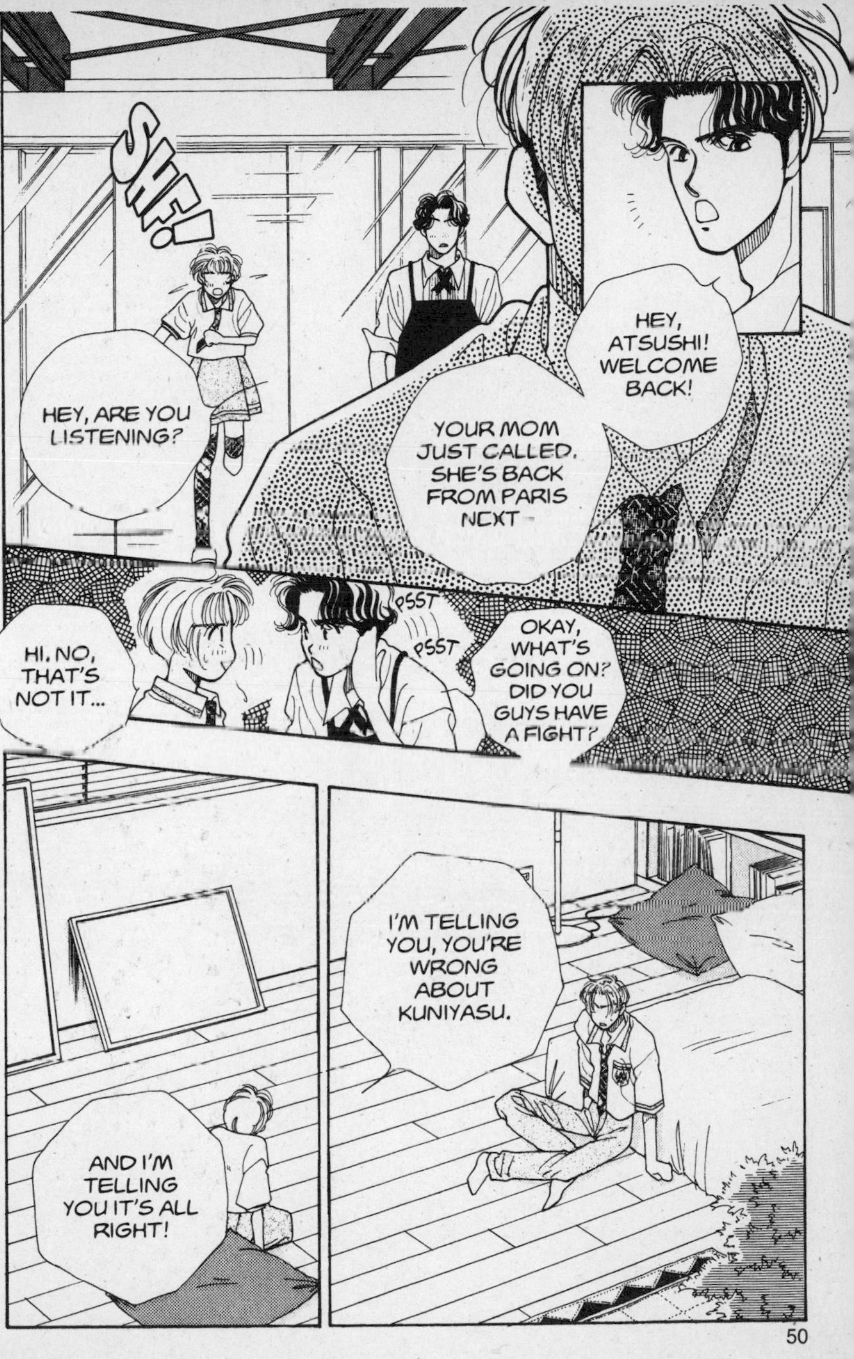
HEY, ATSUSHI! WELCOME BACK!
YOUR MOM JUST CALLED. SHE'S BACK FROM PARIS NEXT —
SHF!
HEY, ARE YOU LISTENING?
OKAY, WHAT'S GOING ON? DID YOU GUYS HAVE A FIGHT?
PSST
PSST
HI. NO, THAT'S NOT IT...
I'M TELLING YOU, YOU'RE WRONG ABOUT KUNIYASU.
AND I'M TELLING YOU IT'S ALL RIGHT!

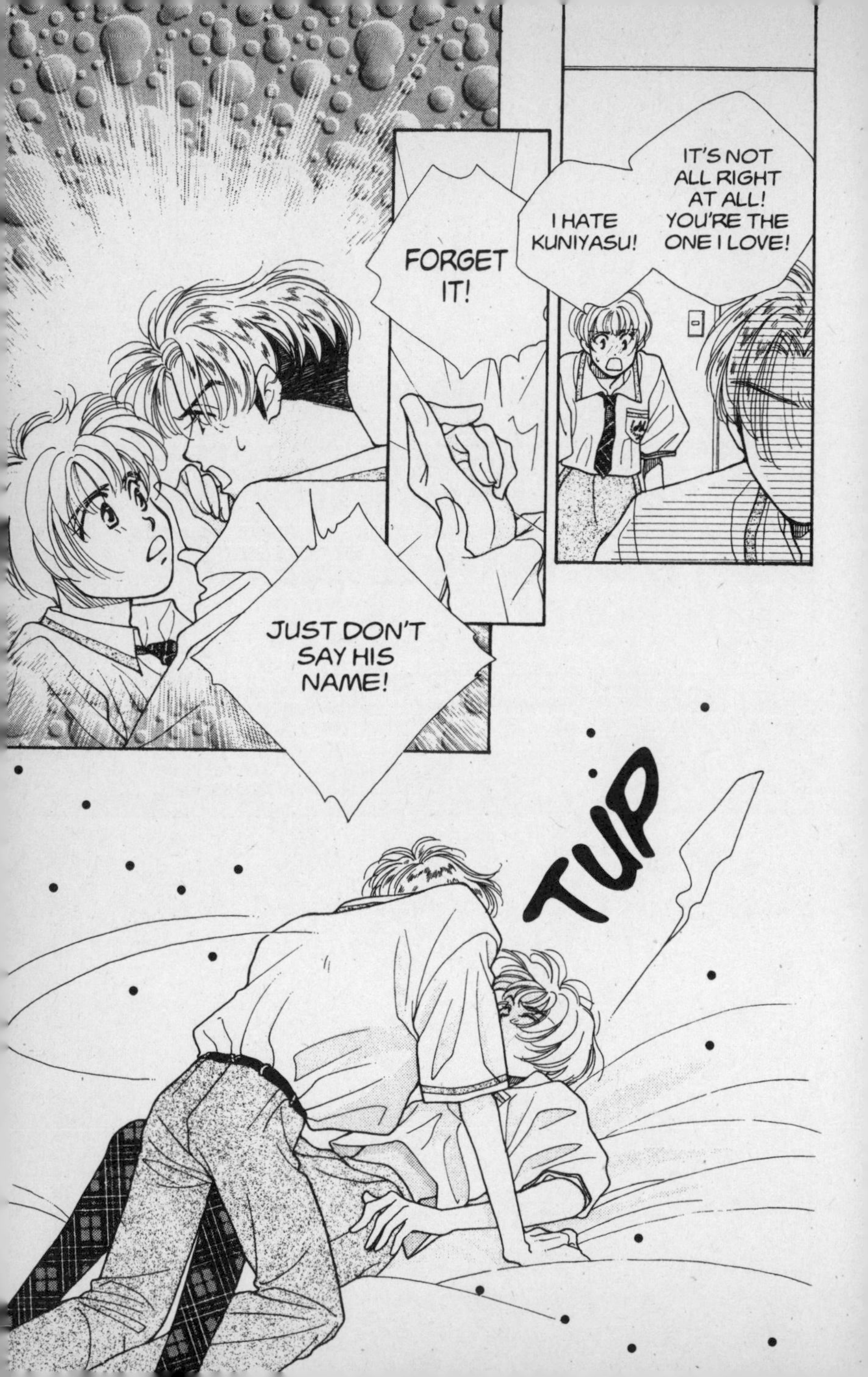
IT'S NOT ALL RIGHT AT ALL! YOU'RE THE ONE I LOVE!
I HATE KUNIYASU!
FORGET IT!
JUST DON'T SAY HIS NAME!
TUP

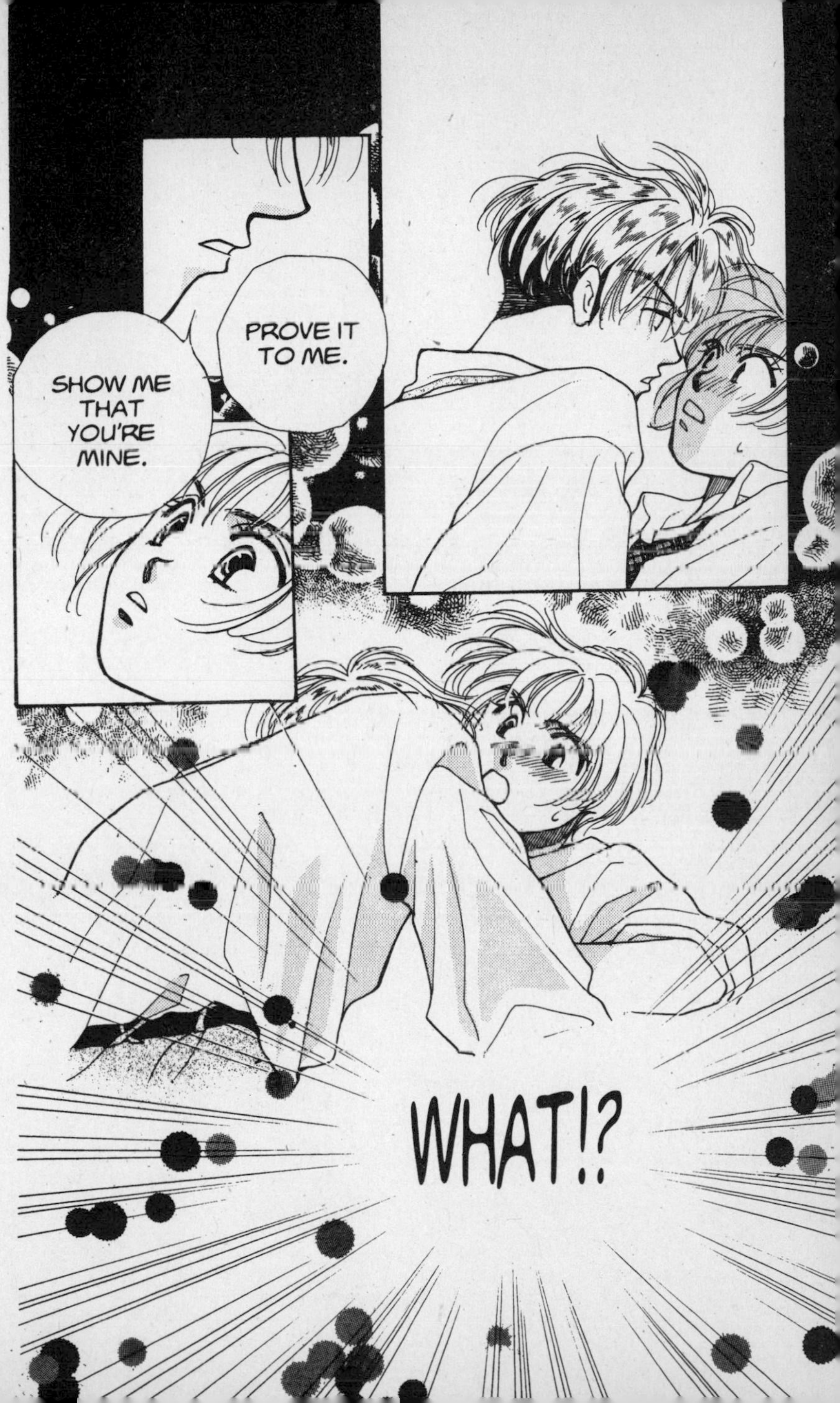
PROVE IT TO ME.
SHOW ME THAT YOU'RE MINE.
WHAT!?

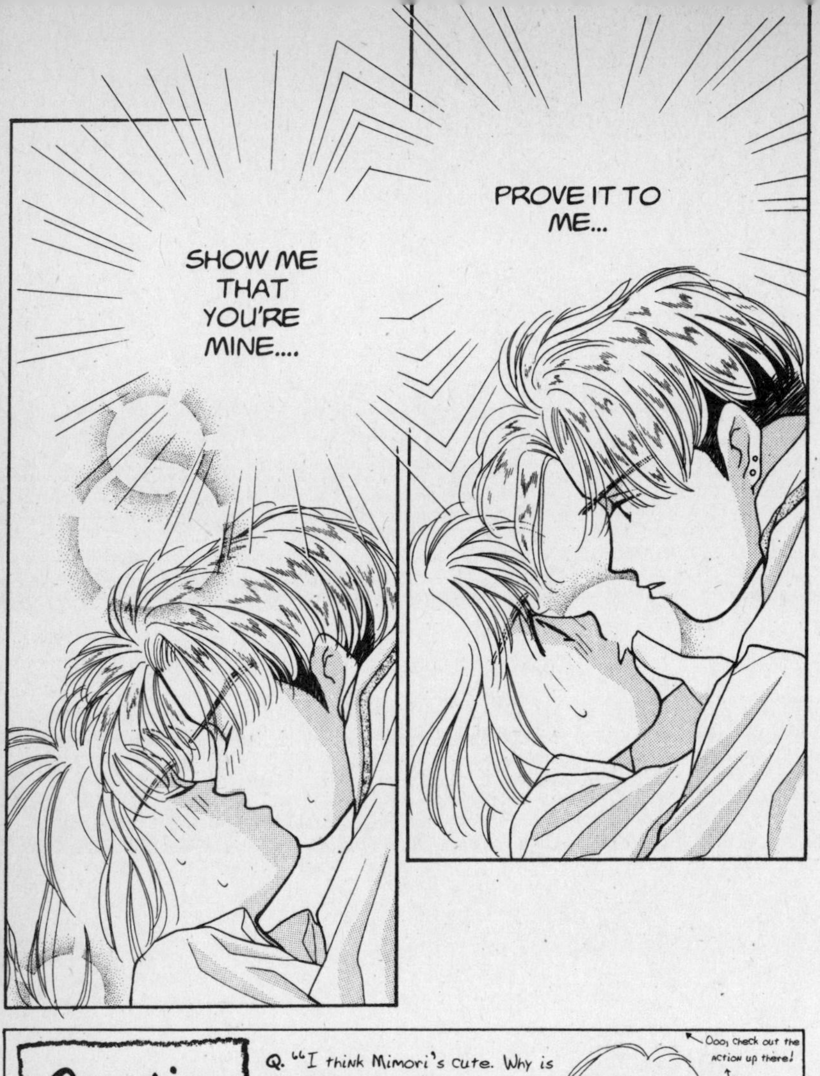
PROVE IT TO ME...
SHOW ME THAT YOU'RE MINE....

Question Corner

*The Heroine

Q. "I think Mimori's cute. Why is Nana the one who's always being told she's pretty?"

A. Readers who are older than junior high can tell, I think. There's a subtle difference between the girls who are cute to other girls and the ones all the boys think are hot. (smile) That's the reason.

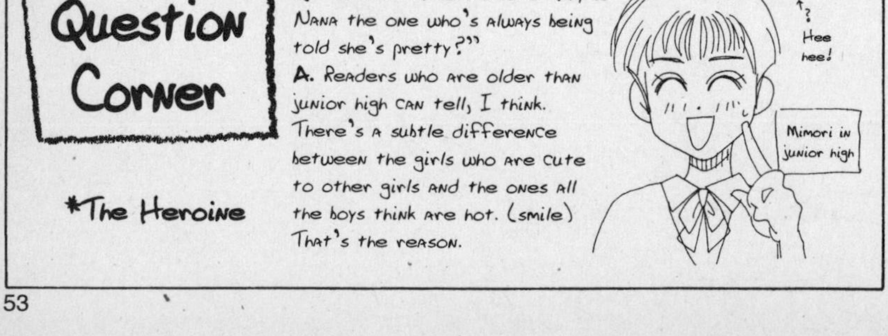
Ooo, check out the action up there!
?
Hee hee!
Mimori in junior high

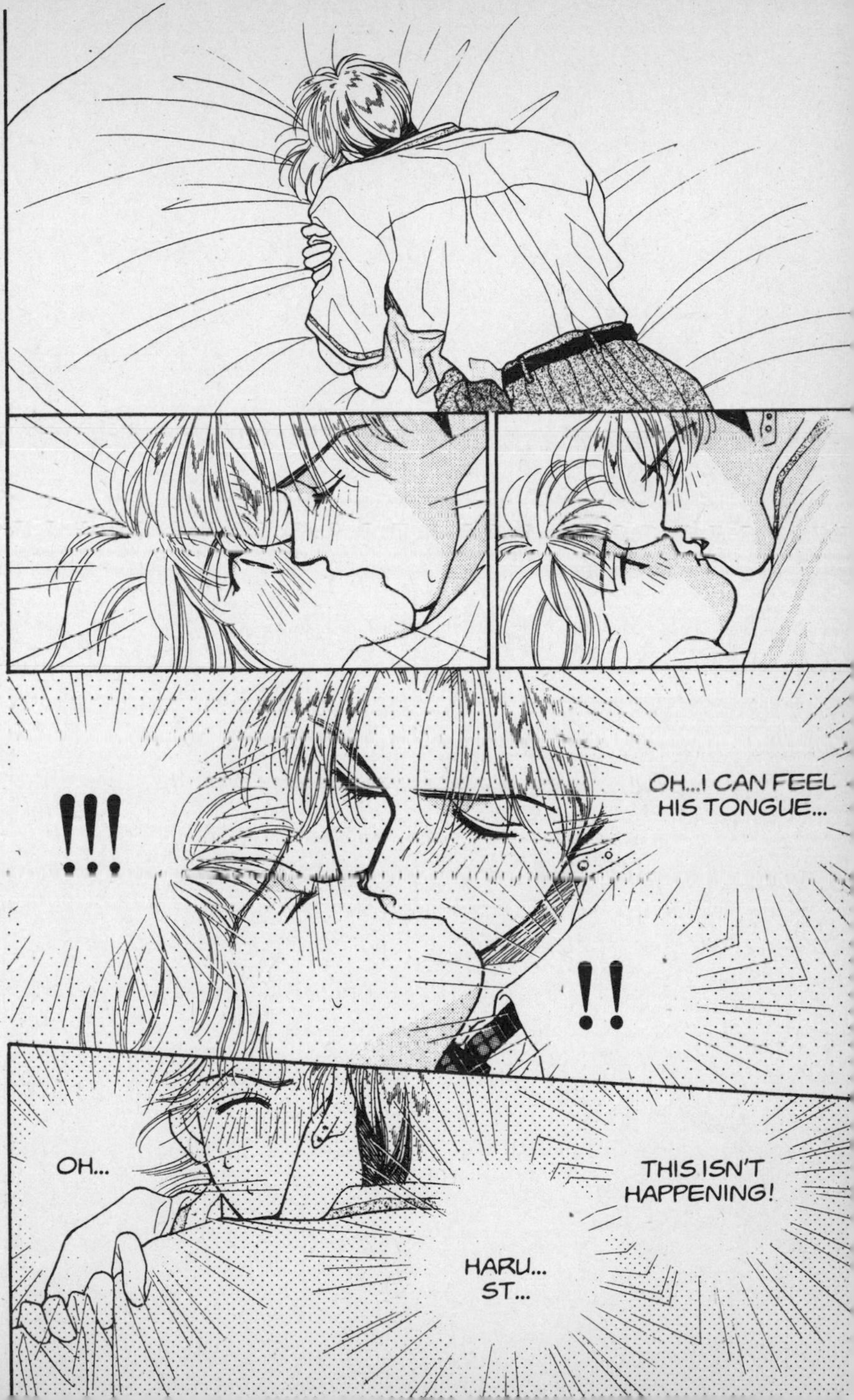
OH...I CAN FEEL HIS TONGUE...
!!!
!!
THIS ISN'T HAPPENING!
OH...
HARU... ST...

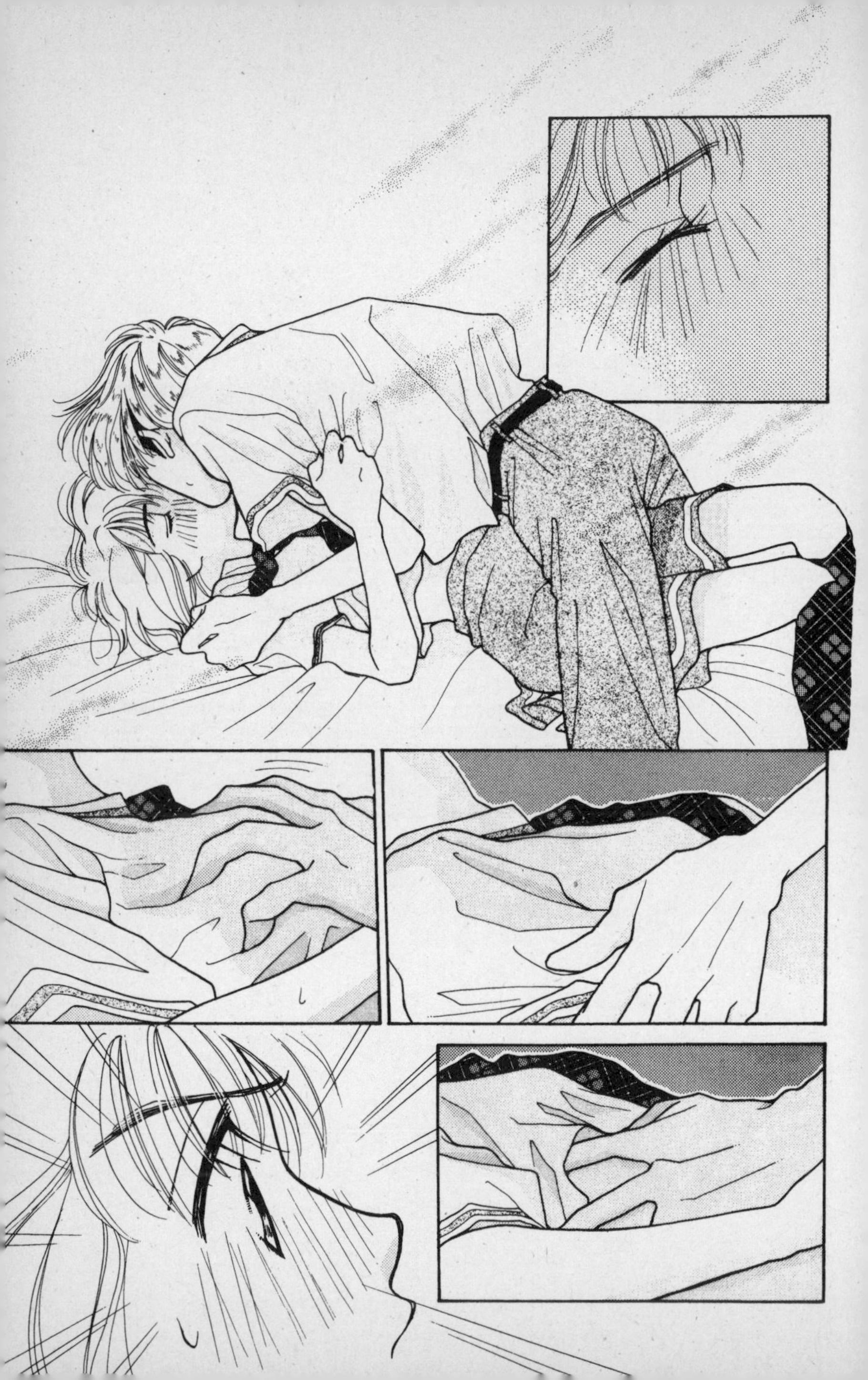

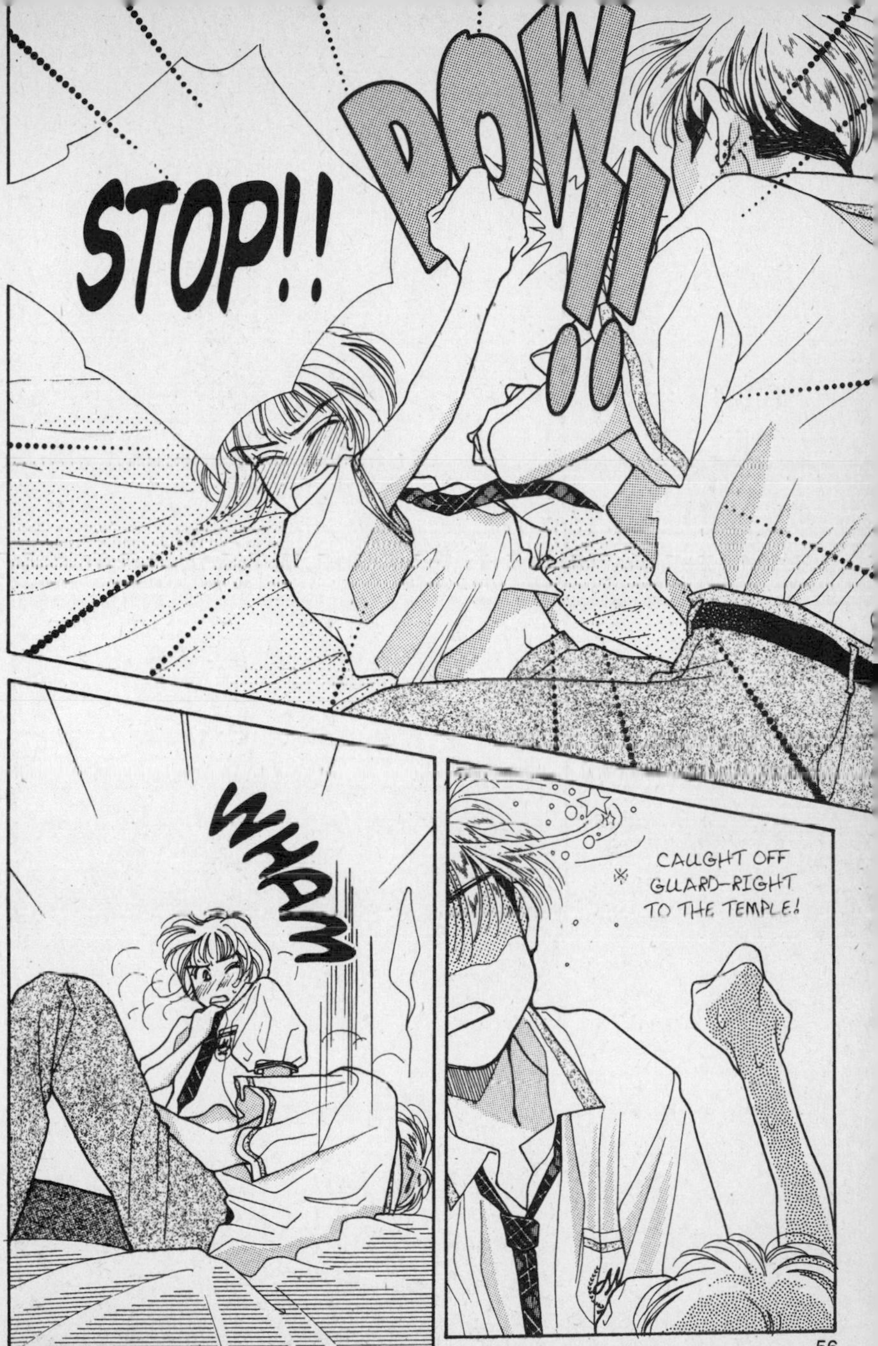
POW!!
STOP!!
CAUGHT OFF GUARD—RIGHT TO THE TEMPLE!
WHAM

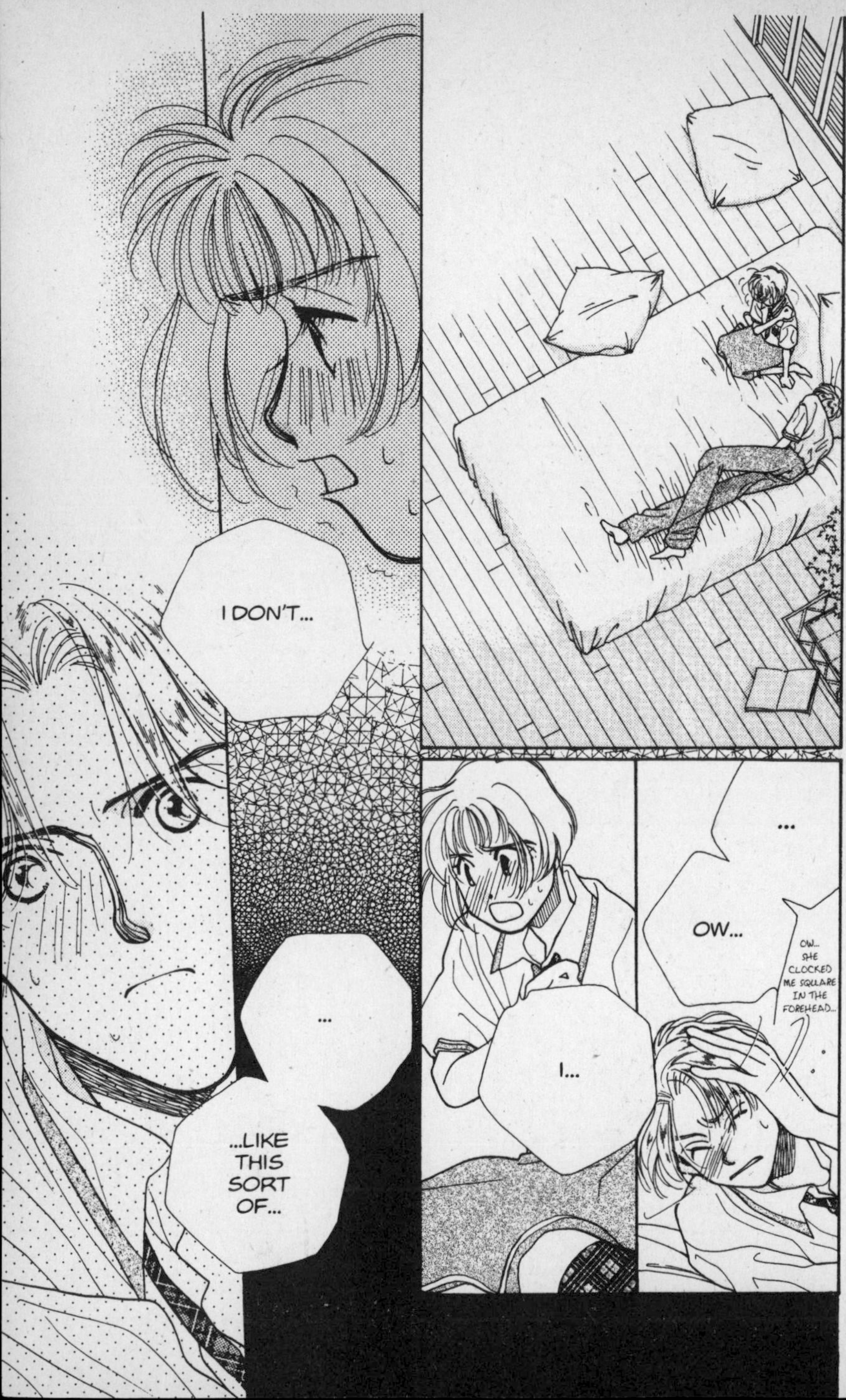
...
OW...
OW... SHE CLOCKED ME SQUARE IN THE FOREHEAD...
I...
I DON'T...
...
...LIKE THIS SORT OF...

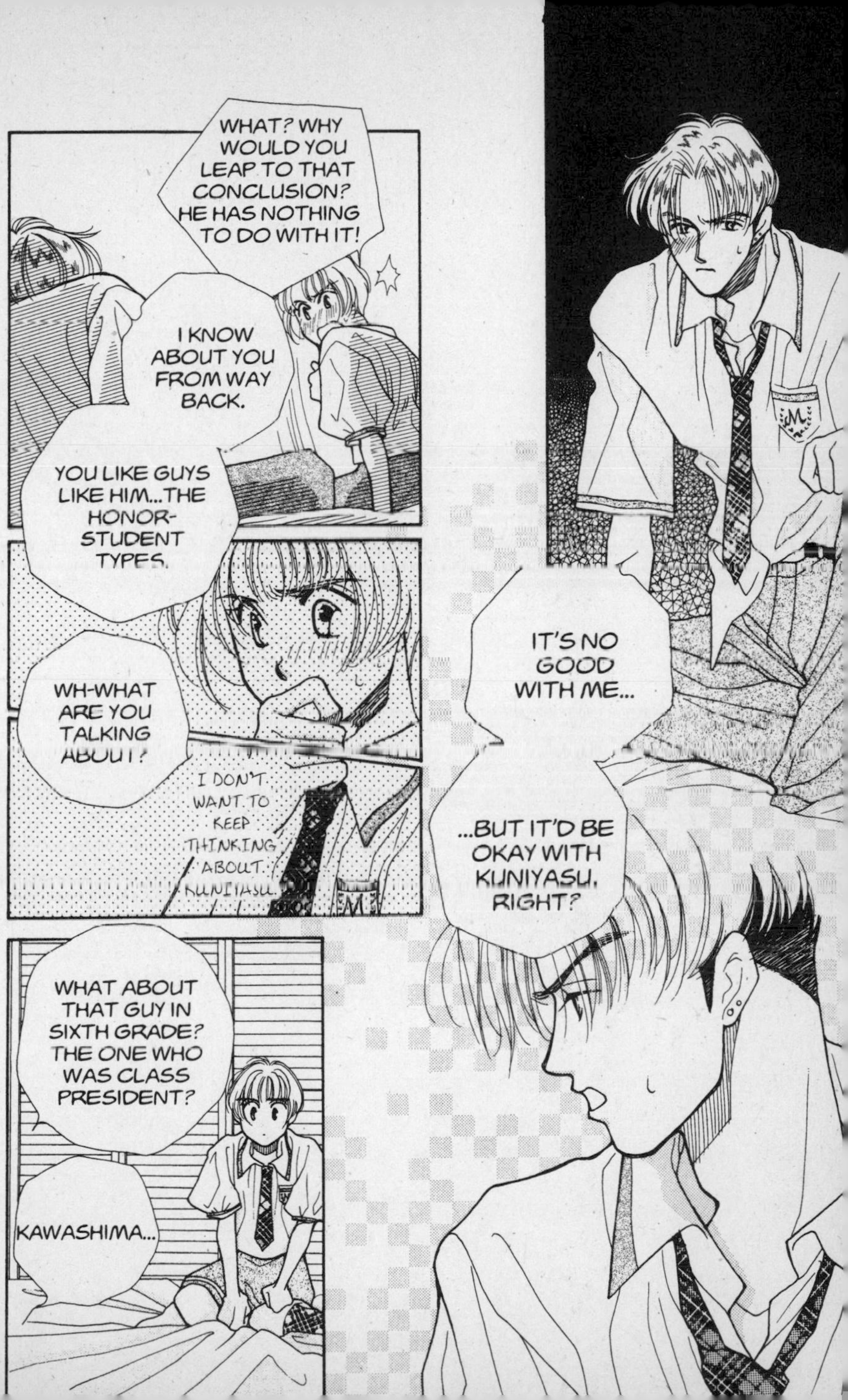
IT'S NO GOOD WITH ME...
...BUT IT'D BE OKAY WITH KUNIYASU, RIGHT?
WHAT? WHY WOULD YOU LEAP TO THAT CONCLUSION? HE HAS NOTHING TO DO WITH IT!
I KNOW ABOUT YOU FROM WAY BACK.
YOU LIKE GUYS LIKE HIM...THE HONOR-STUDENT TYPES.
WH-WHAT ARE YOU TALKING ABOUT?
I DON'T WANT TO KEEP THINKING ABOUT KUNIYASU.
WHAT ABOUT THAT GUY IN SIXTH GRADE? THE ONE WHO WAS CLASS PRESIDENT?
KAWASHIMA...

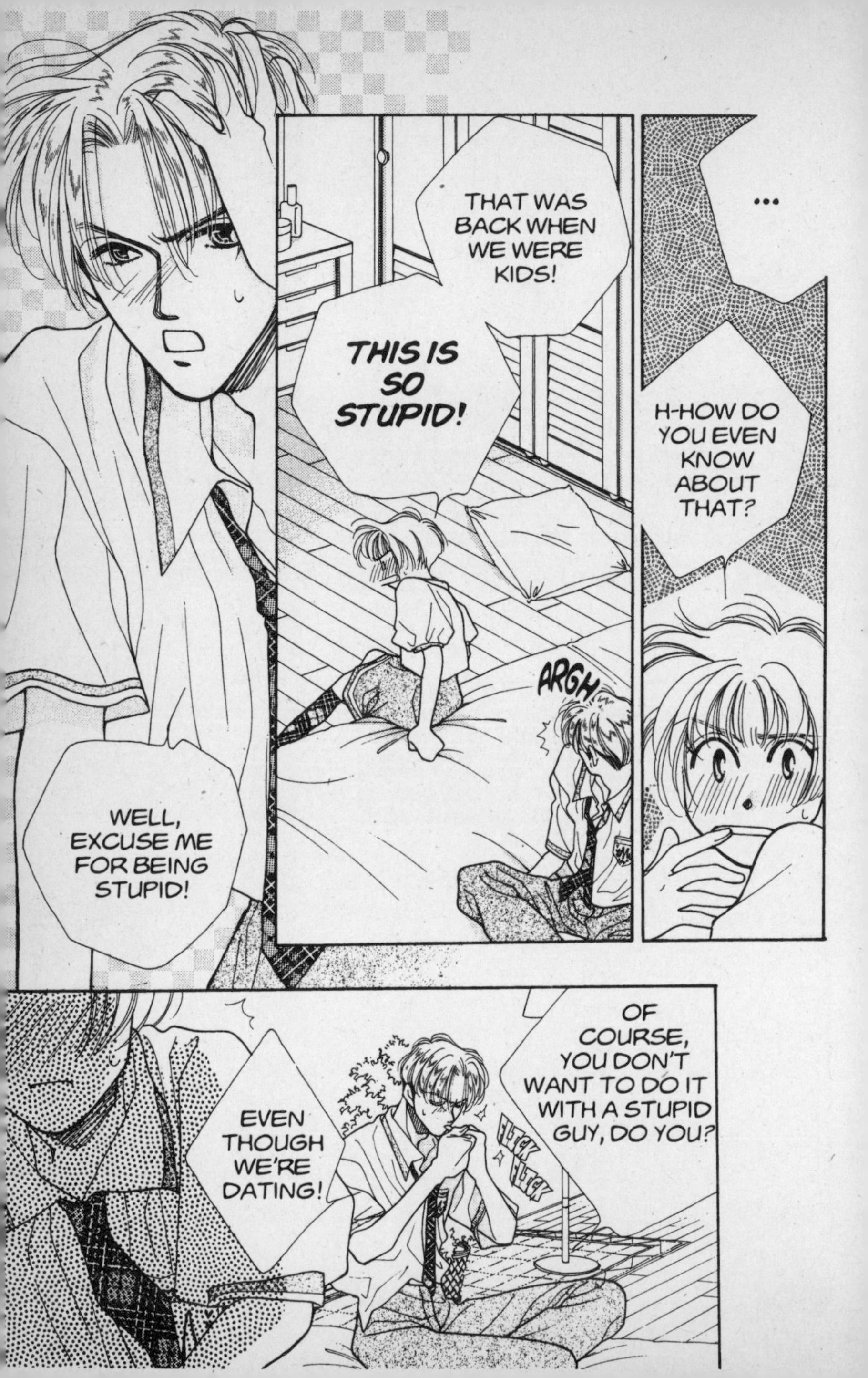
...
H-HOW DO YOU EVEN KNOW ABOUT THAT?
THAT WAS BACK WHEN WE WERE KIDS!
THIS IS SO STUPID!
ARGH
WELL, EXCUSE ME FOR BEING STUPID!
OF COURSE, YOU DON'T WANT TO DO IT WITH A STUPID GUY, DO YOU?
FLICK FLICK
EVEN THOUGH WE'RE DATING!

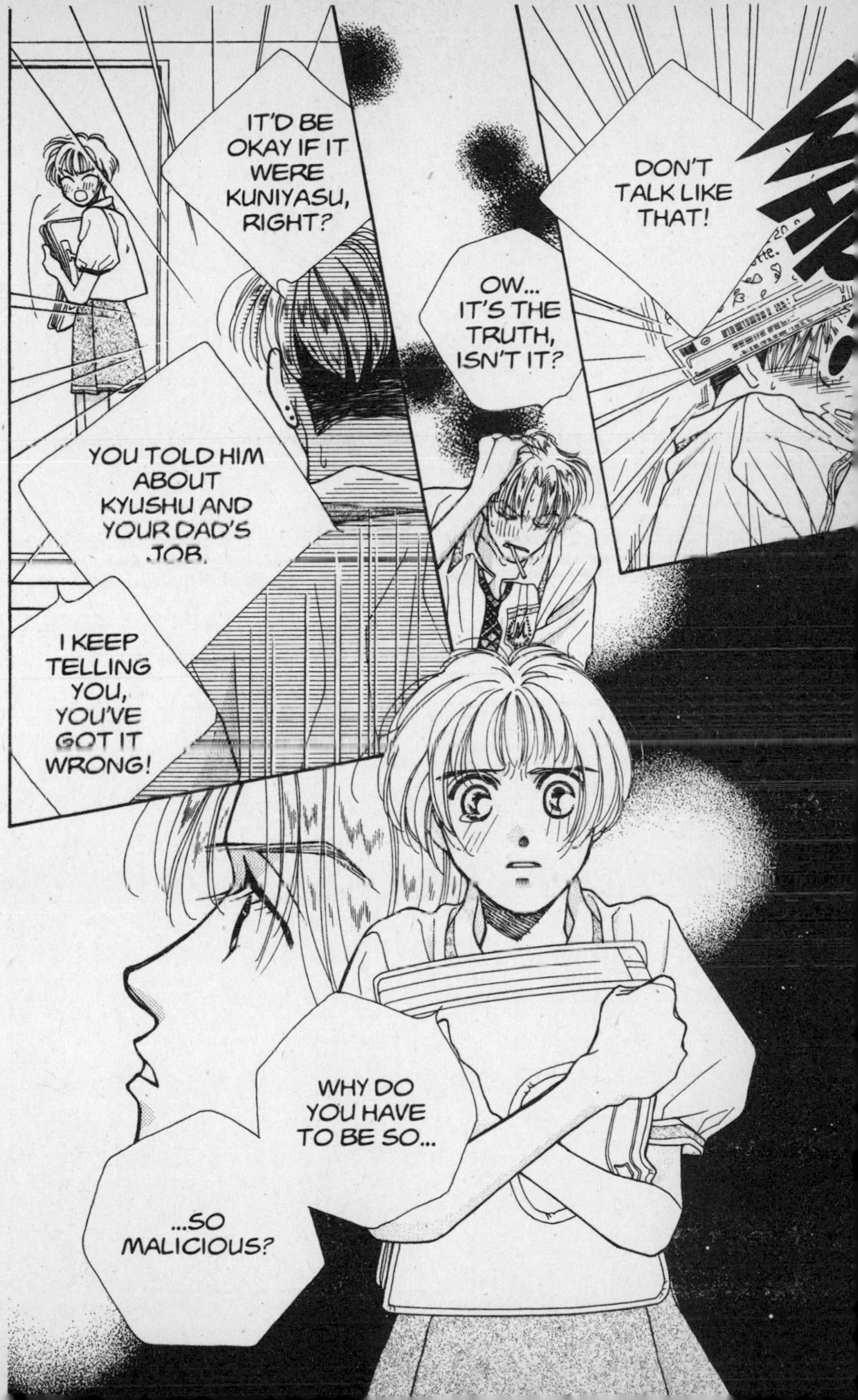
DON'T TALK LIKE THAT!
OW... IT'S THE TRUTH, ISN'T IT?
IT'D BE OKAY IF IT WERE KUNIYASU, RIGHT?
YOU TOLD HIM ABOUT KYUSHU AND YOUR DAD'S JOB.
I KEEP TELLING YOU, YOU'VE GOT IT WRONG!
WHY DO YOU HAVE TO BE SO...
...SO MALICIOUS?

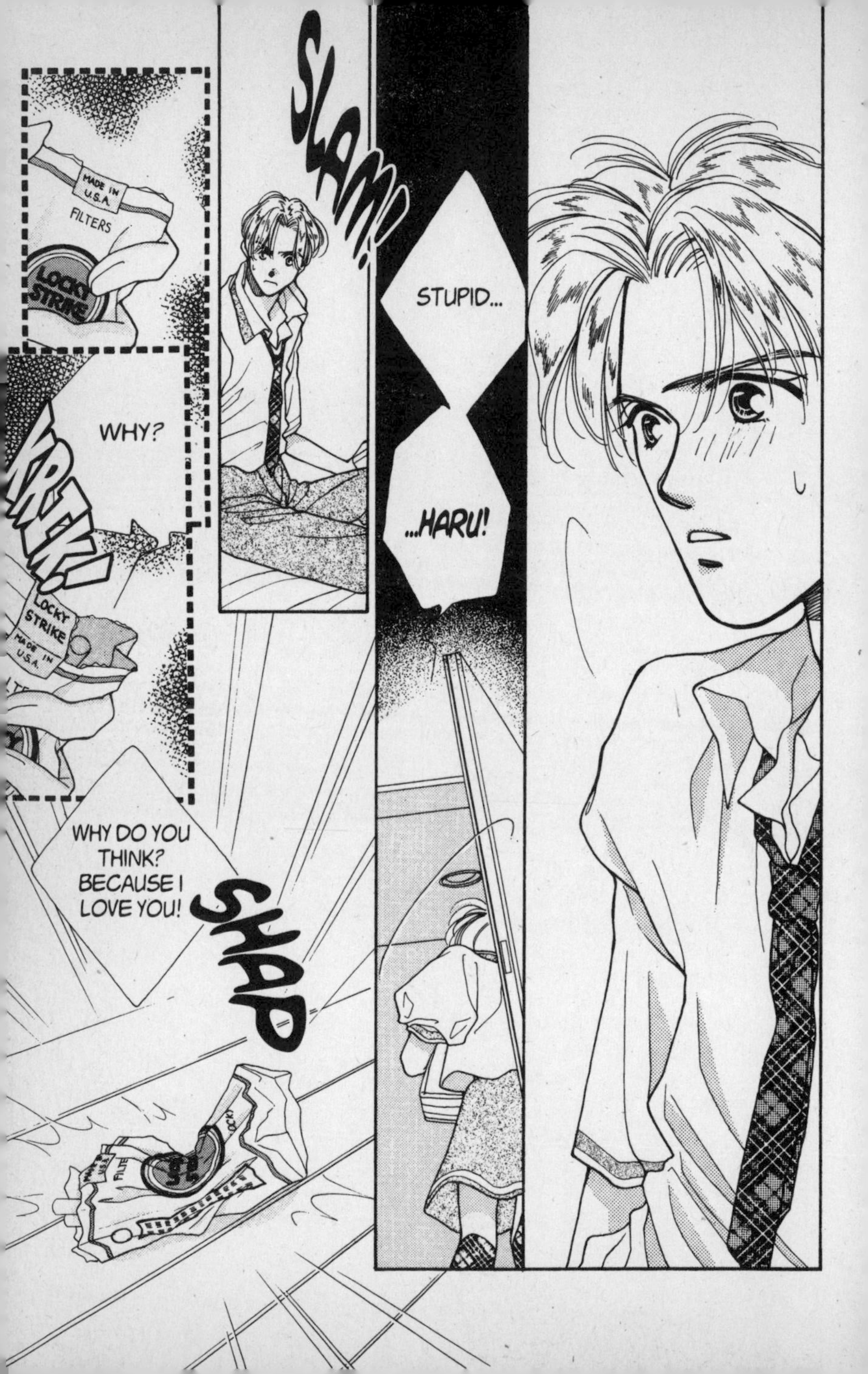
STUPID...
...HARU!
SLAM!
MADE IN U.S.A.
FILTERS
LOCKY STRIKE
WHY?
KRAK!
LOCKY STRIKE
MADE IN U.S.A.
WHY DO YOU THINK? BECAUSE I LOVE YOU!
SHAP

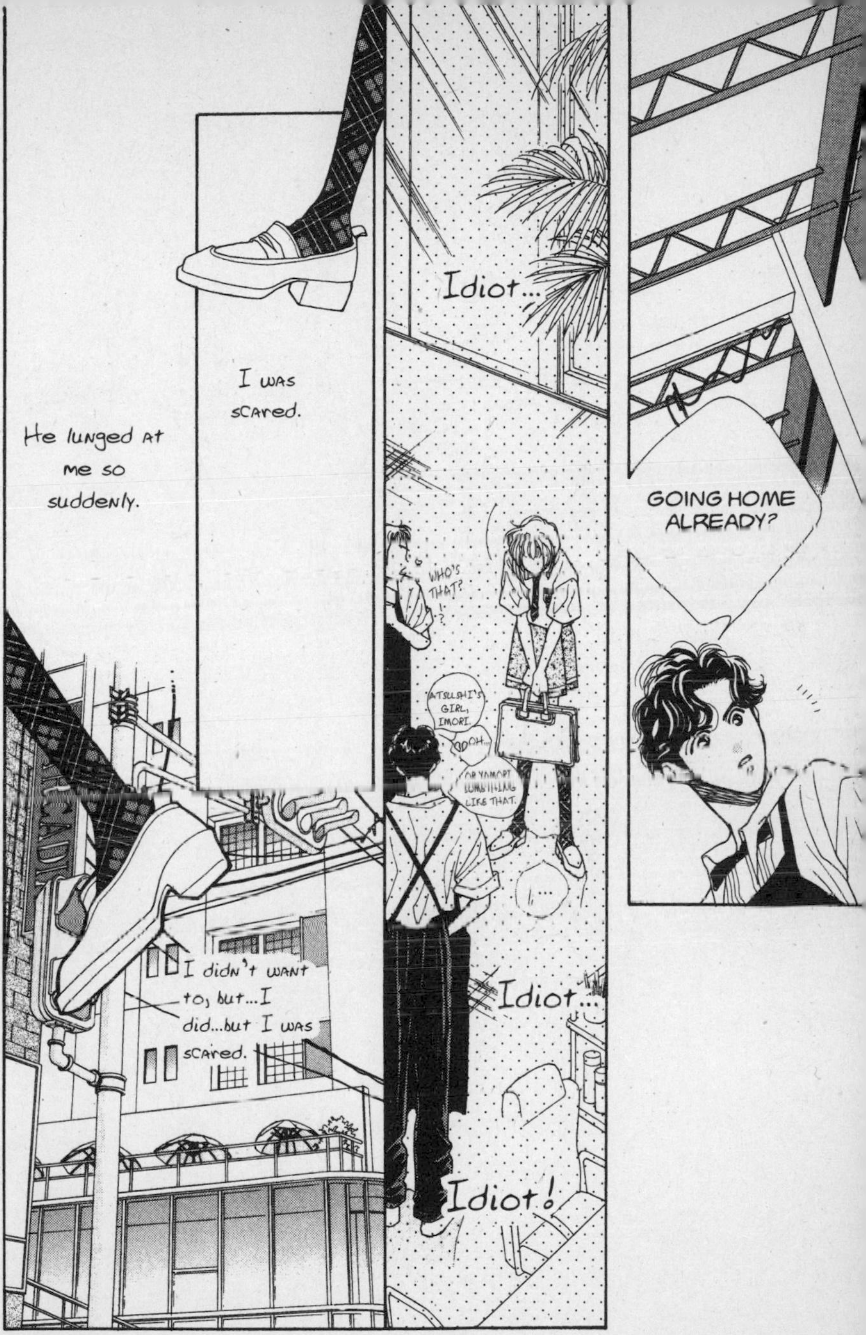
GOING HOME ALREADY?
Idiot...
WHO'S THAT?
!?
ATSUSHI'S GIRL, IMORI.
OOH...
OR YAMORI SOMETHING LIKE THAT.
...
Idiot...
Idiot!
I was scared.
He lunged at me so suddenly.
I didn't want to, but...I did...but I was scared.

TOKYO BOYS GIRLS

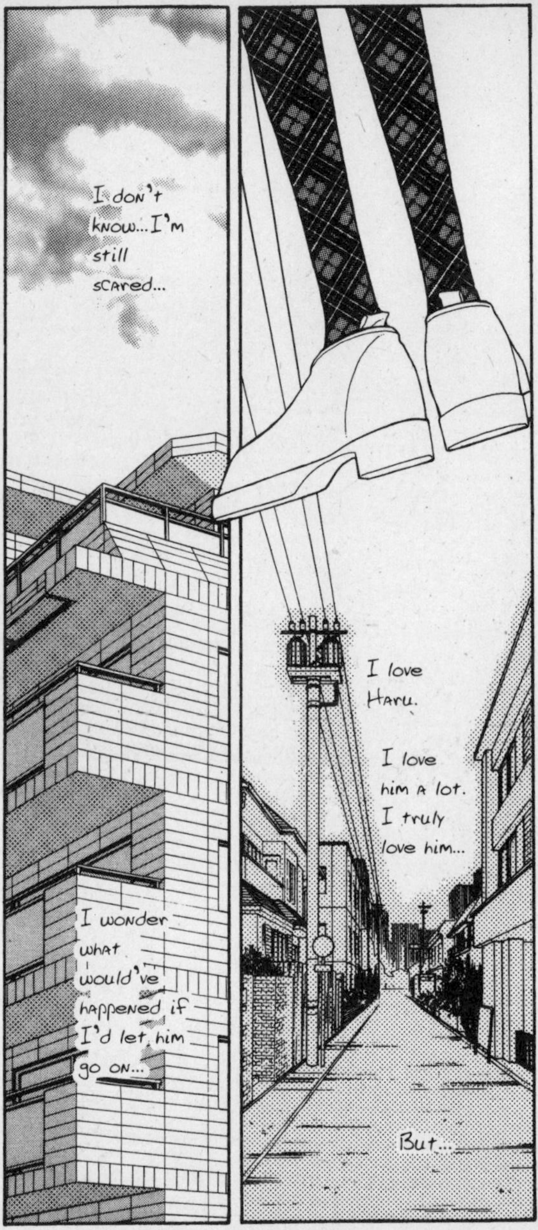
I love Haru.
I love him a lot. I truly love him...
But...
I don't know... I'm still scared...
I wonder what would've happened if I'd let him go on...

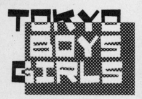

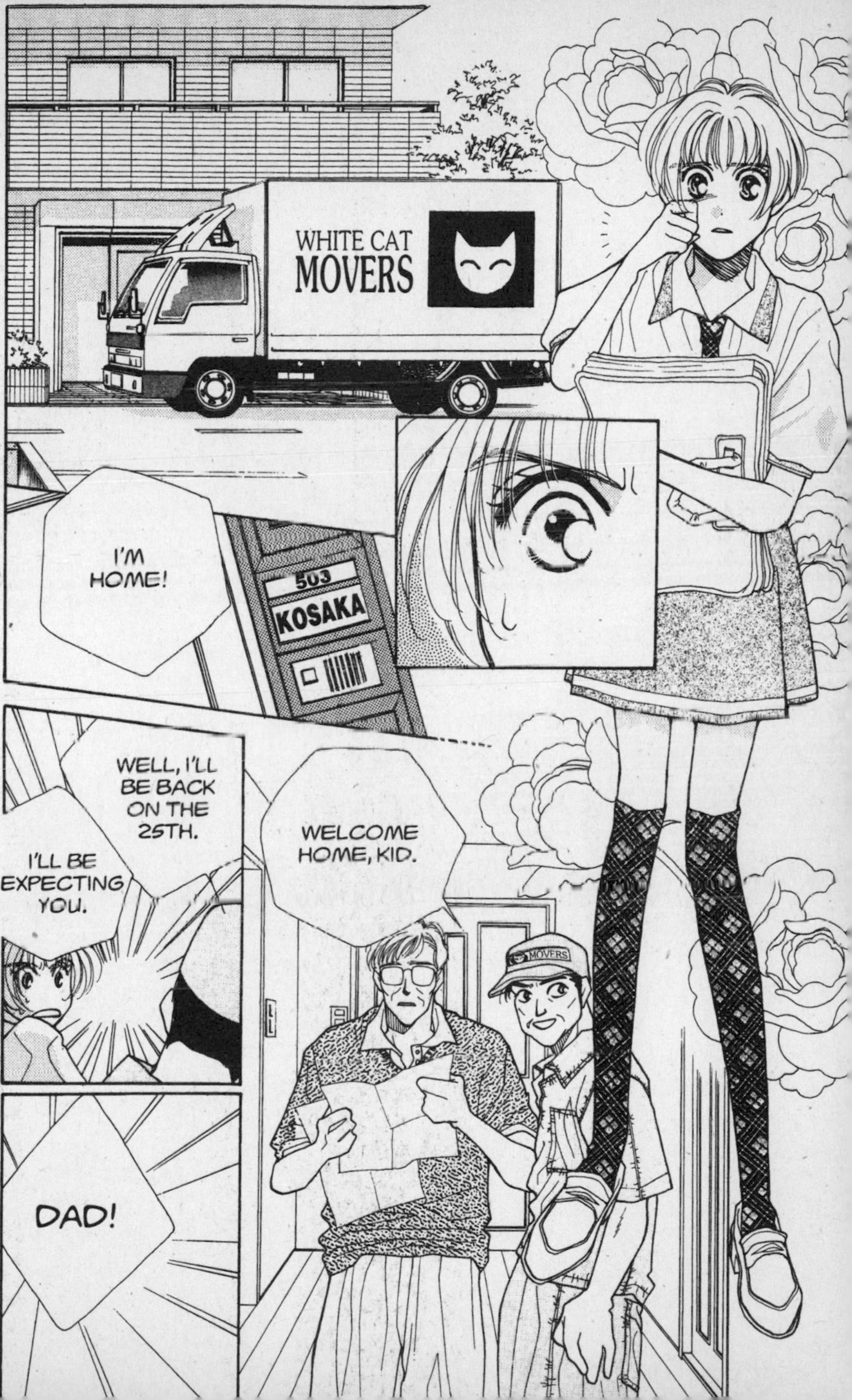
WHITE CAT MOVERS
503
KOSAKA
I'M HOME!
MOVERS
WELCOME HOME, KID.
WELL, I'LL BE BACK ON THE 25TH.
I'LL BE EXPECTING YOU.
DAD!

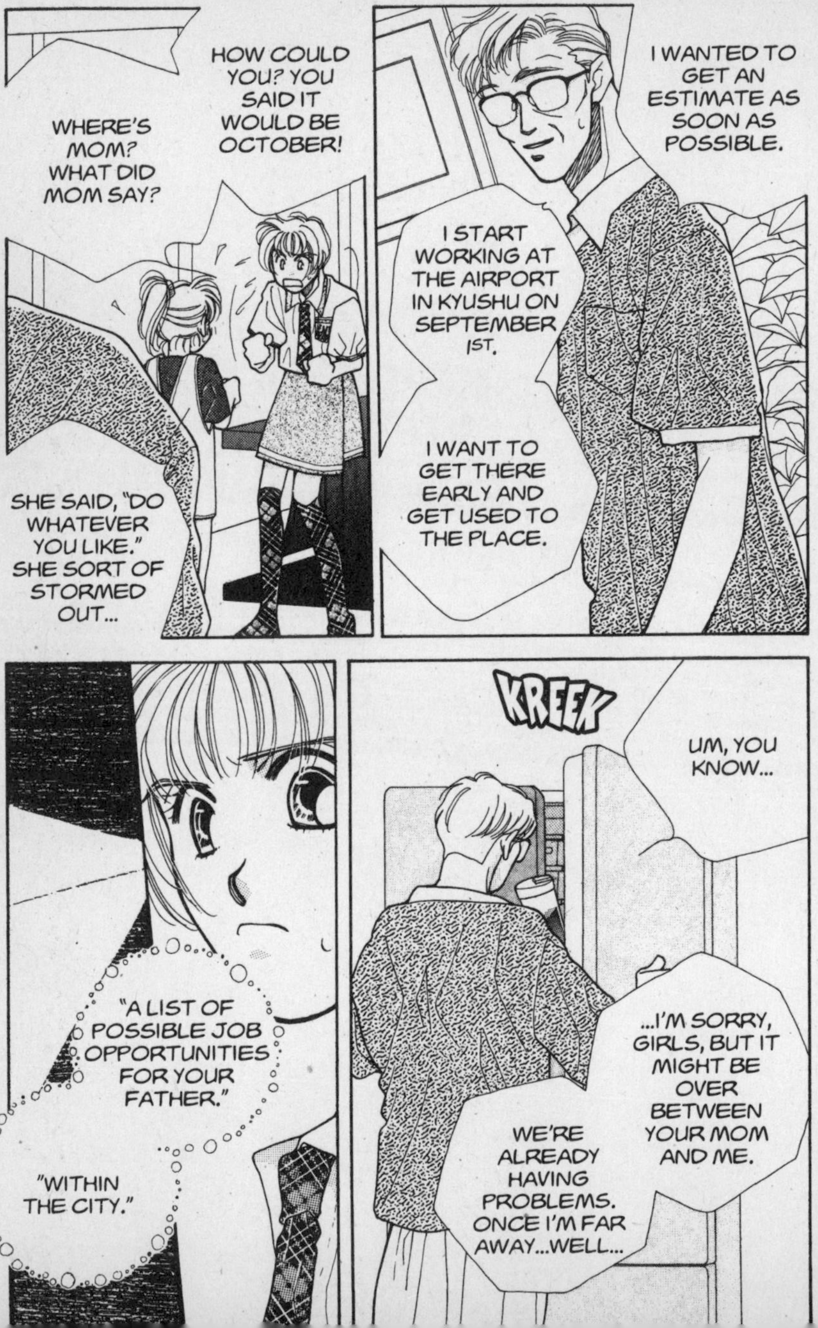
I WANTED TO GET AN ESTIMATE AS SOON AS POSSIBLE.
I START WORKING AT THE AIRPORT IN KYUSHU ON SEPTEMBER 1ST.
I WANT TO GET THERE EARLY AND GET USED TO THE PLACE.
HOW COULD YOU? YOU SAID IT WOULD BE OCTOBER!
WHERE'S MOM? WHAT DID MOM SAY?
SHE SAID, "DO WHATEVER YOU LIKE." SHE SORT OF STORMED OUT...
KREEK
UM, YOU KNOW...
...I'M SORRY, GIRLS, BUT IT MIGHT BE OVER BETWEEN YOUR MOM AND ME.
WE'RE ALREADY HAVING PROBLEMS. ONCE I'M FAR AWAY...WELL...
"A LIST OF POSSIBLE JOB OPPORTUNITIES FOR YOUR FATHER."
"WITHIN THE CITY."

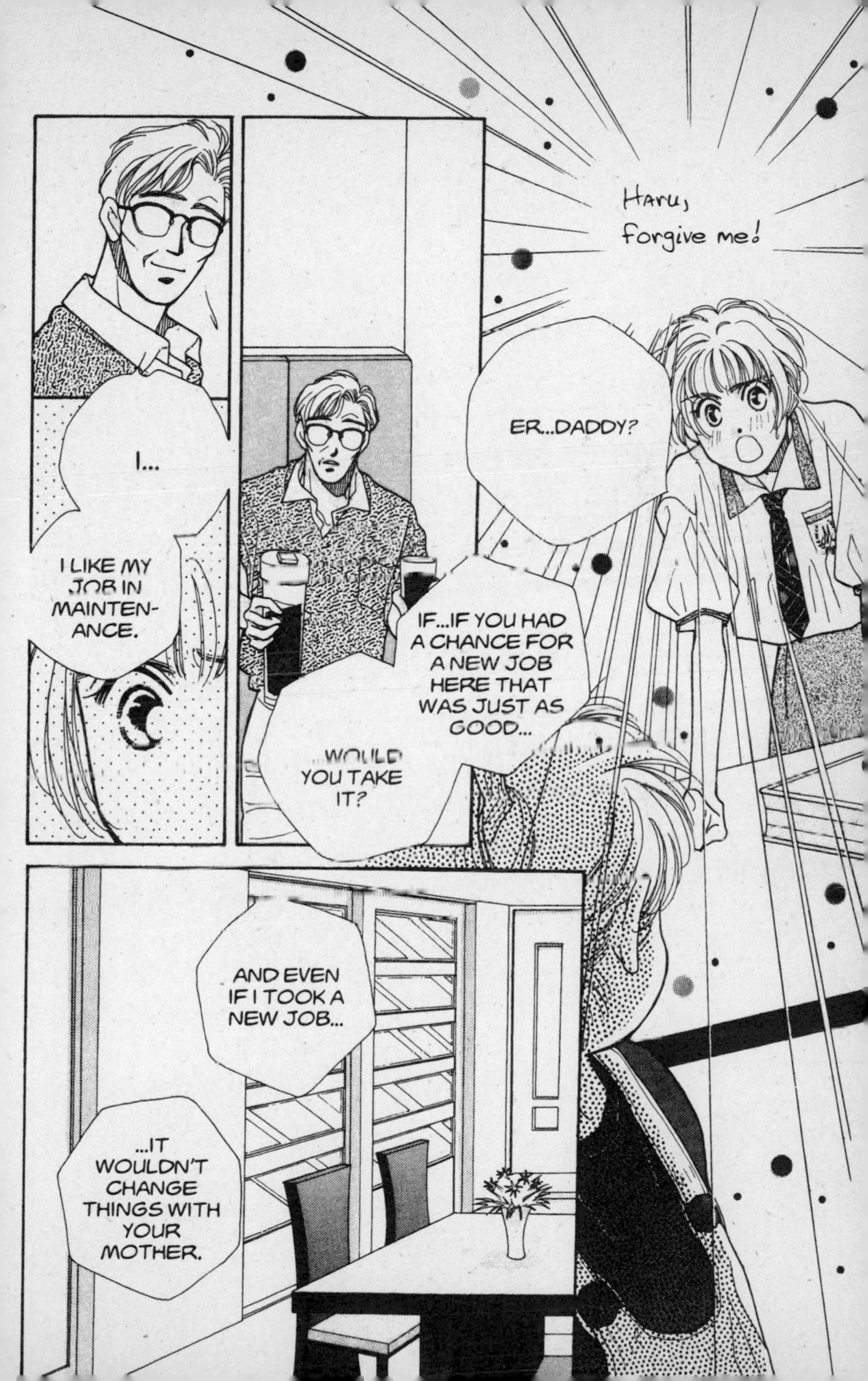
Haru, forgive me!
ER...DADDY?
IF...IF YOU HAD A CHANCE FOR A NEW JOB HERE THAT WAS JUST AS GOOD...
WOULD YOU TAKE IT?
I...
I LIKE MY JOB IN MAINTEN-ANCE.
AND EVEN IF I TOOK A NEW JOB...
...IT WOULDN'T CHANGE THINGS WITH YOUR MOTHER.

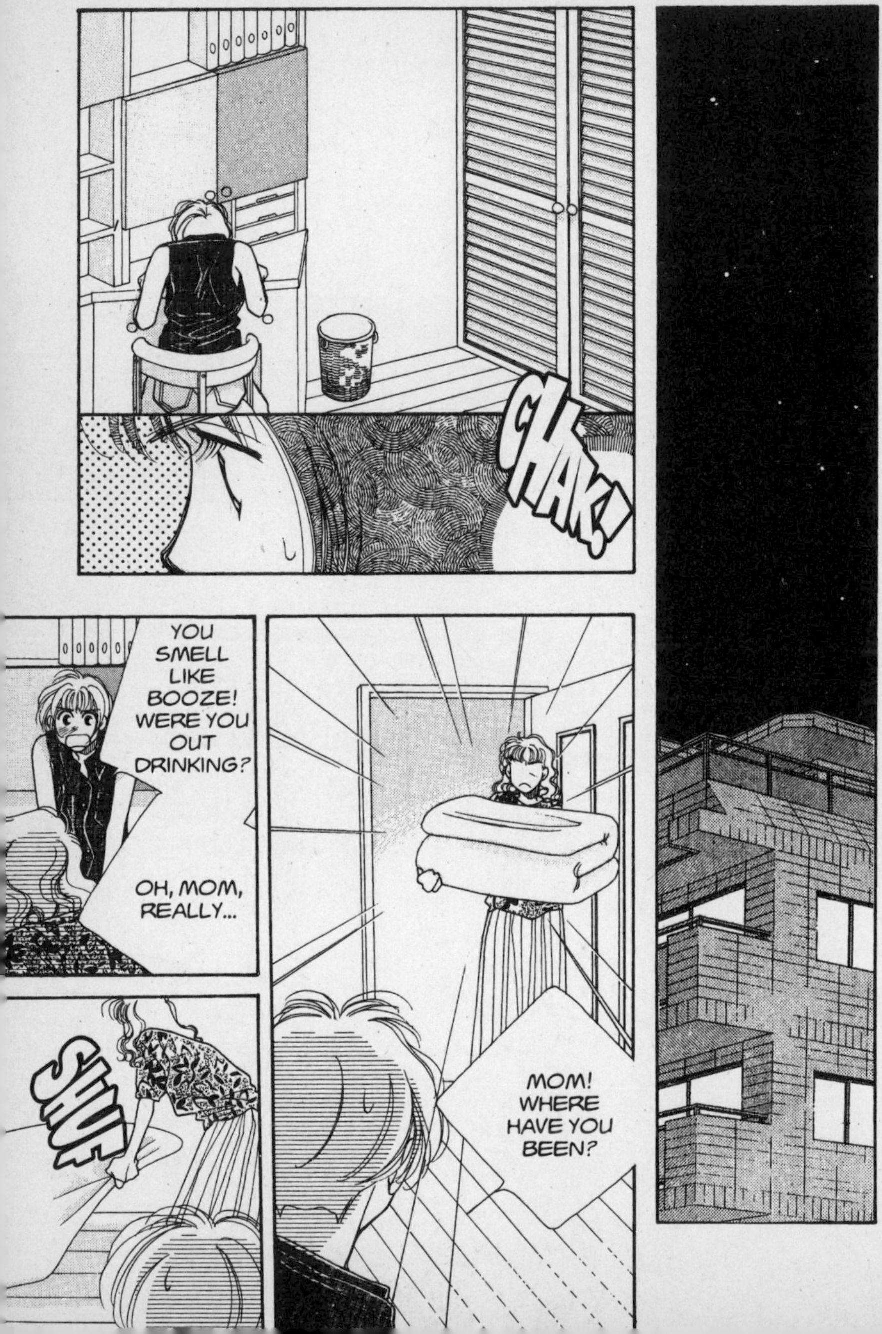
CHAK!
MOM! WHERE HAVE YOU BEEN?
YOU SMELL LIKE BOOZE! WERE YOU OUT DRINKING?
OH, MOM, REALLY...
SHUF

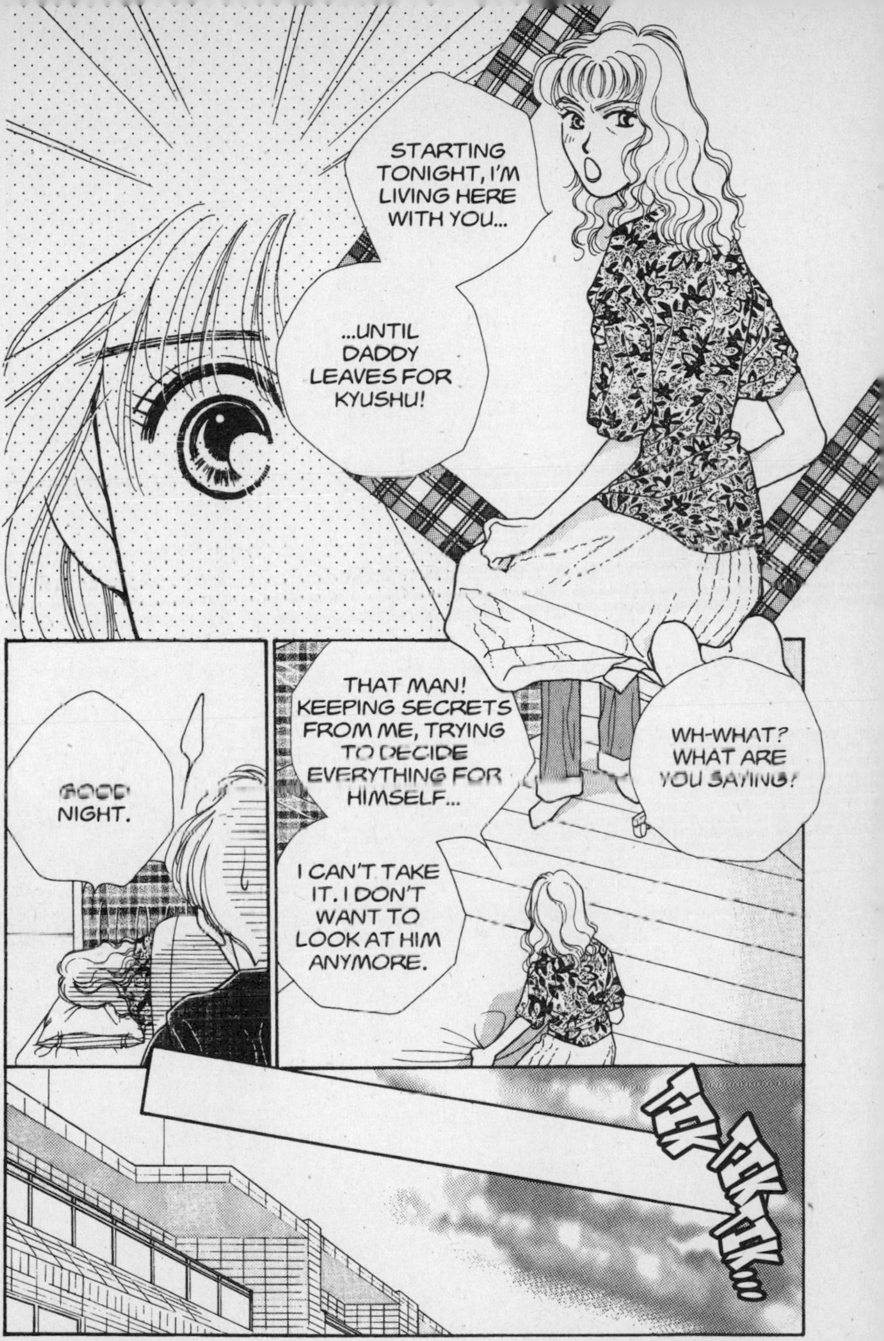
STARTING TONIGHT, I'M LIVING HERE WITH YOU...
...UNTIL DADDY LEAVES FOR KYUSHU!
WH-WHAT? WHAT ARE YOU SAYING?
THAT MAN! KEEPING SECRETS FROM ME, TRYING TO DECIDE EVERYTHING FOR HIMSELF...
I CAN'T TAKE IT. I DON'T WANT TO LOOK AT HIM ANYMORE.
GOOD NIGHT.
TPK TPK TPK...

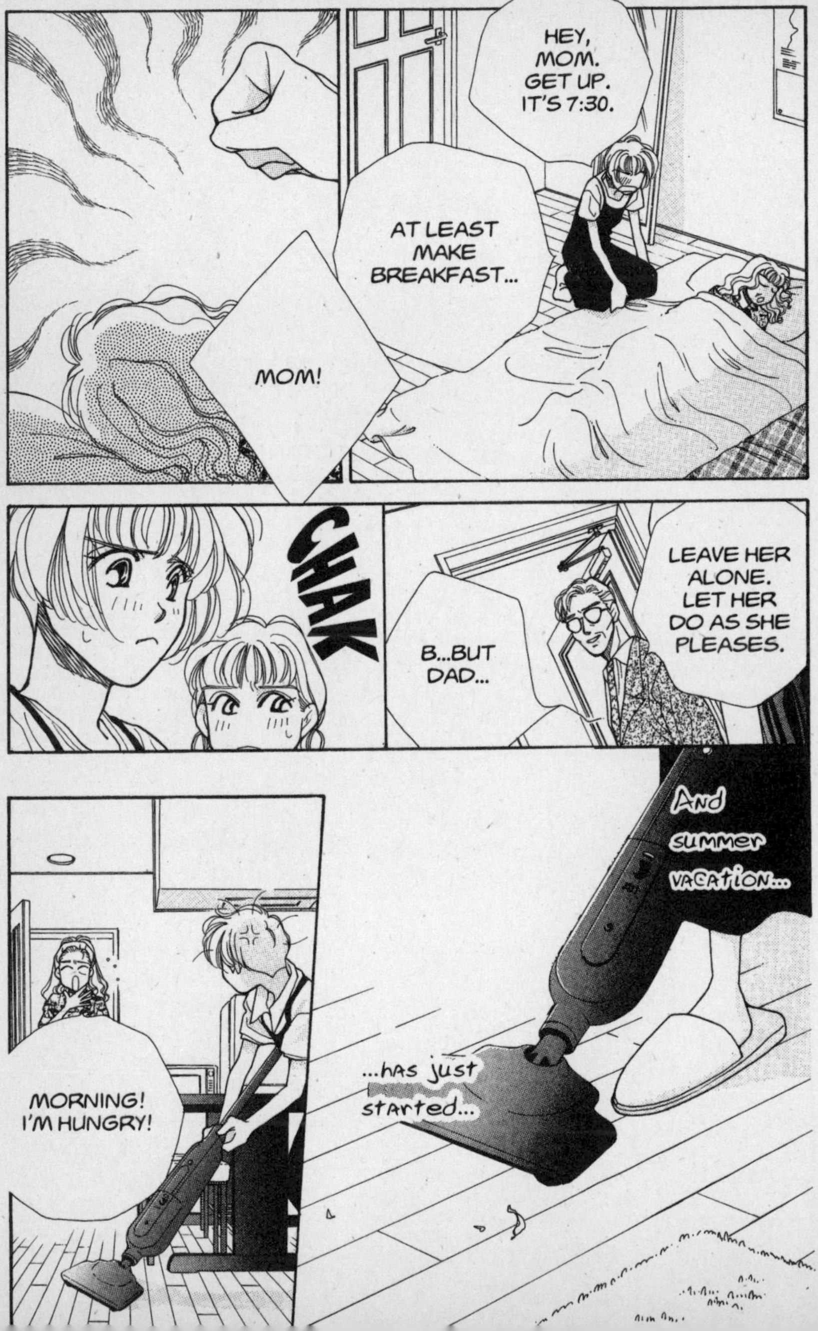
HEY, MOM. GET UP. IT'S 7:30.
AT LEAST MAKE BREAKFAST...
MOM!
LEAVE HER ALONE. LET HER DO AS SHE PLEASES.
B...BUT DAD...
CHAK
And summer vacation...
...has just started...
MORNING! I'M HUNGRY!

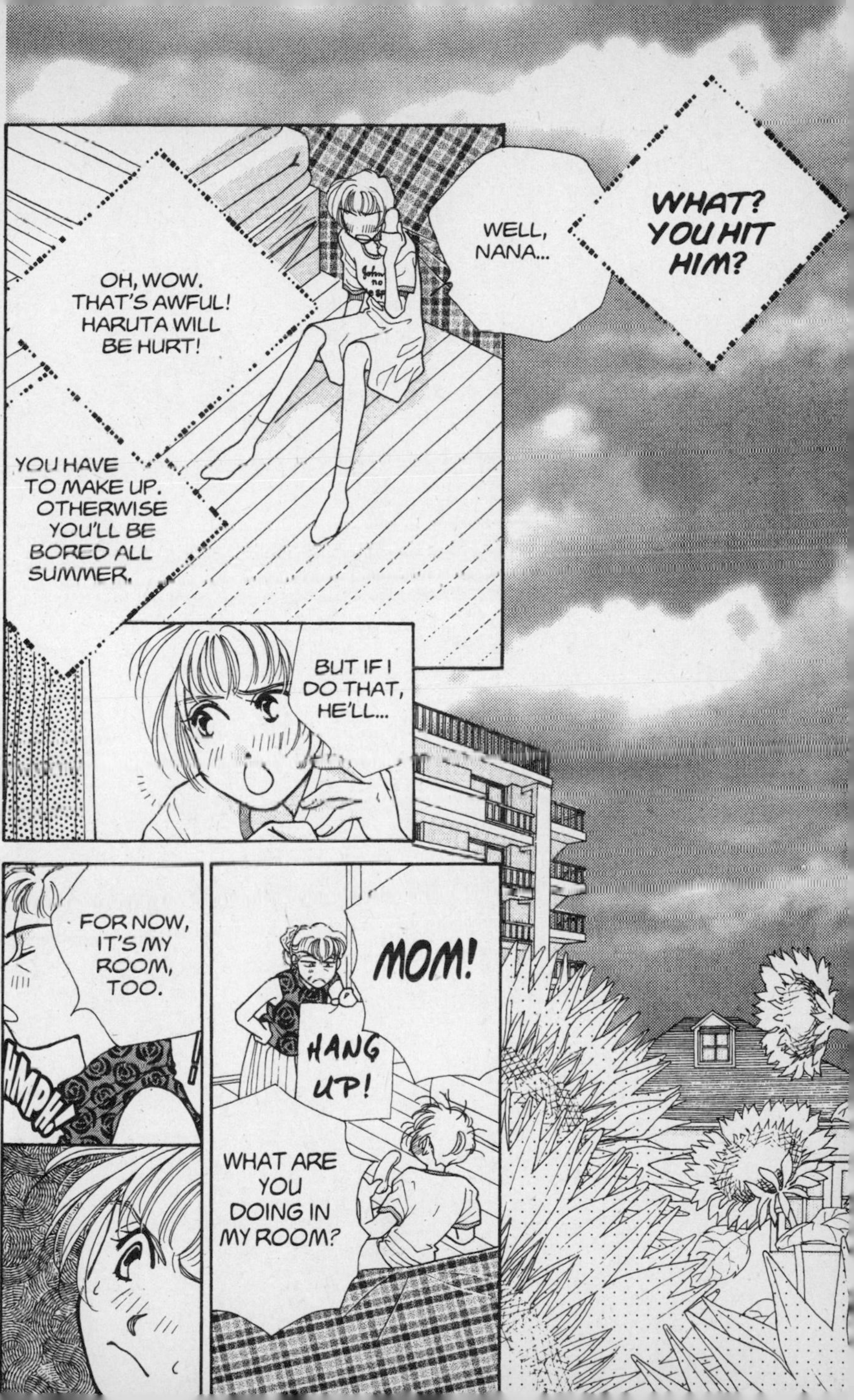
WHAT? YOU HIT HIM?
WELL, NANA...
OH, WOW. THAT'S AWFUL! HARUTA WILL BE HURT!
YOU HAVE TO MAKE UP. OTHERWISE YOU'LL BE BORED ALL SUMMER.
BUT IF I DO THAT, HE'LL...
MOM!
HANG UP!
WHAT ARE YOU DOING IN MY ROOM?
FOR NOW, IT'S MY ROOM, TOO.
HMPH!

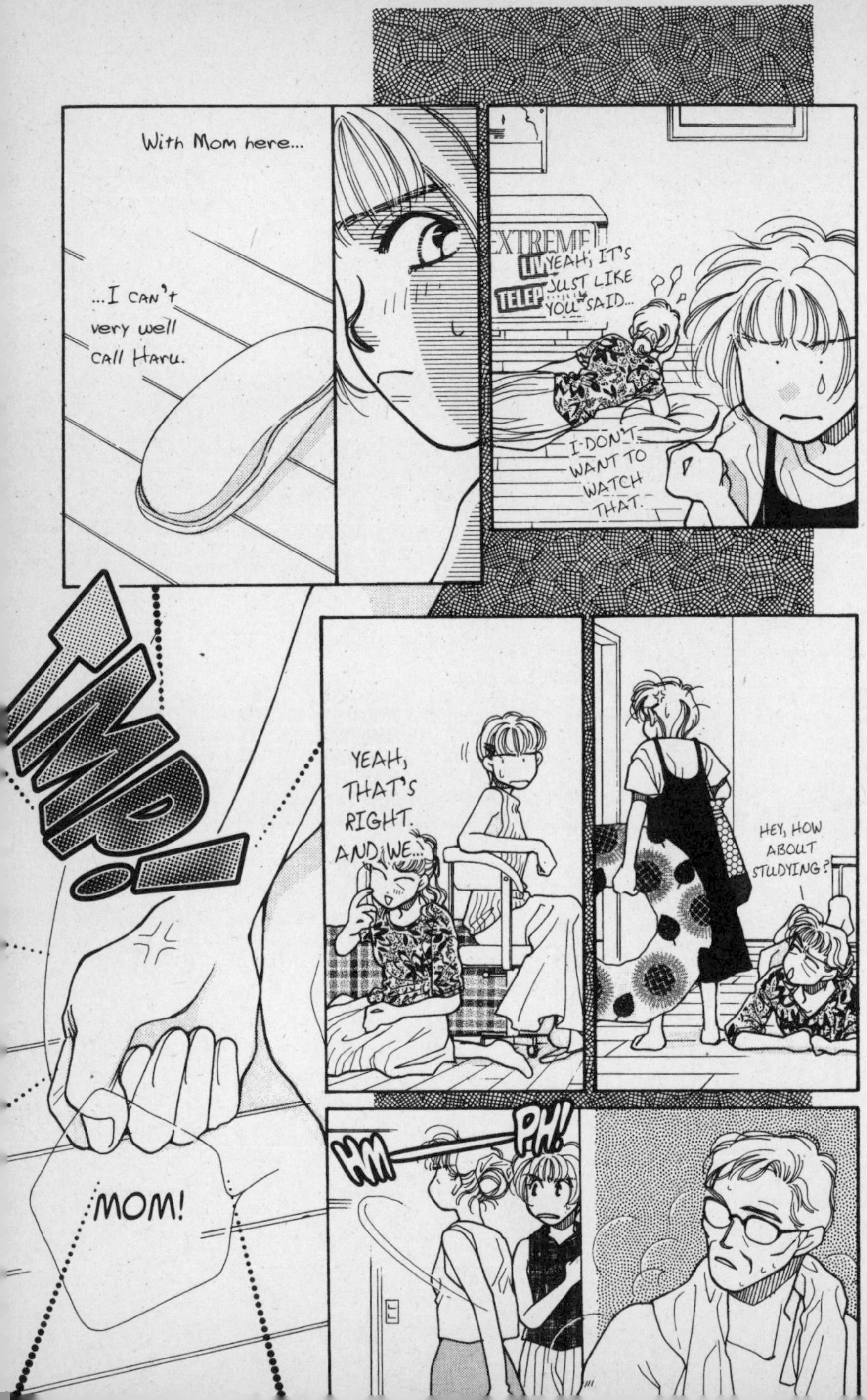
EXTREME
YEAH, IT'S JUST LIKE YOU SAID...
I DON'T WANT TO WATCH THAT.
With Mom here...
...I can't very well call Haru.
HEY, HOW ABOUT STUDYING?
YEAH, THAT'S RIGHT. AND WE...
HMPH!
TMP!
MOM!

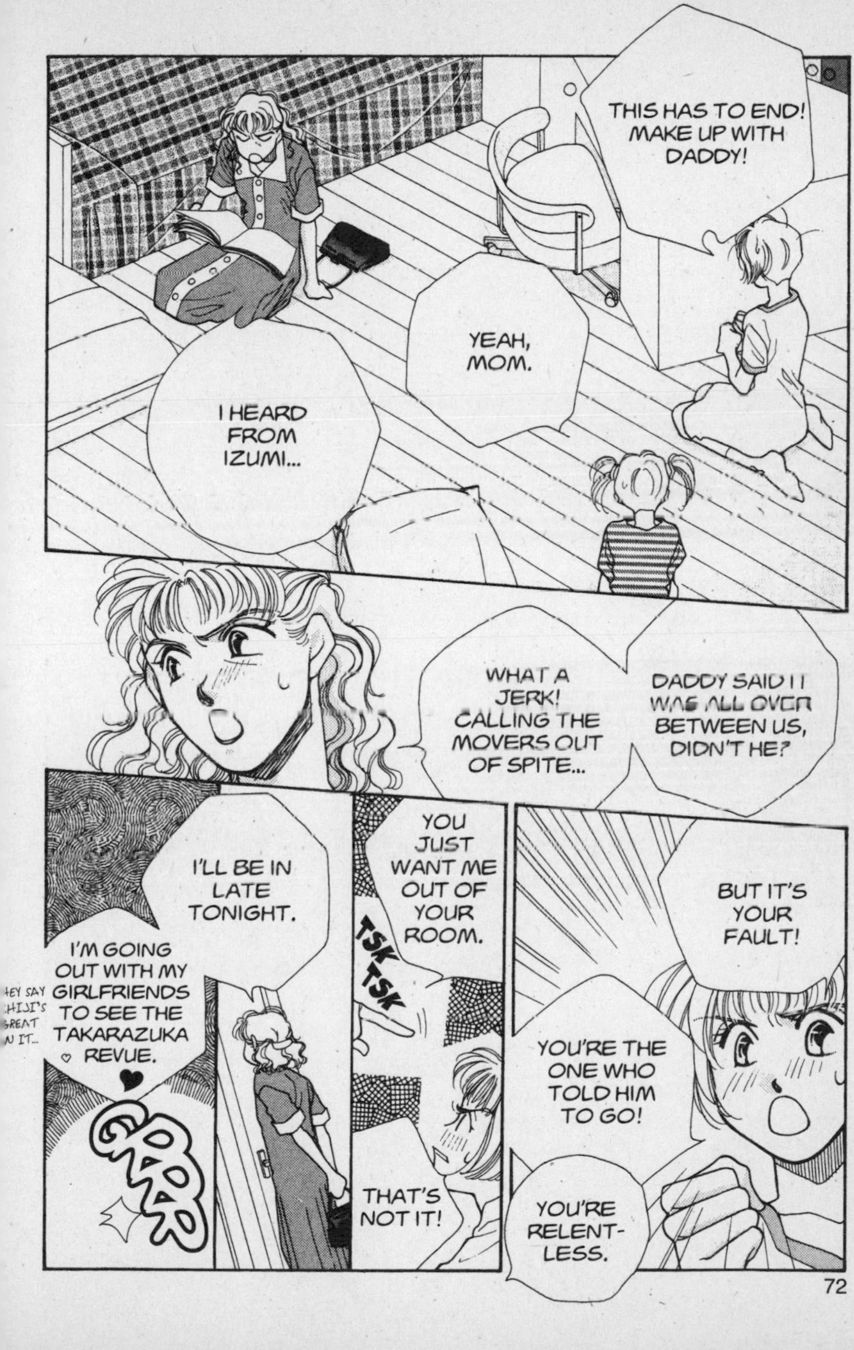
THIS HAS TO END! MAKE UP WITH DADDY!
YEAH, MOM.
I HEARD FROM IZUMI...
DADDY SAID IT WAS ALL OVER BETWEEN US, DIDN'T HE?
WHAT A JERK! CALLING THE MOVERS OUT OF SPITE...
BUT IT'S YOUR FAULT!
YOU'RE THE ONE WHO TOLD HIM TO GO!
YOU'RE RELENT-LESS.
YOU JUST WANT ME OUT OF YOUR ROOM.
TSK TSK
THAT'S NOT IT!
I'LL BE IN LATE TONIGHT.
I'M GOING OUT WITH MY GIRLFRIENDS TO SEE THE TAKARAZUKA REVUE.
GRAB

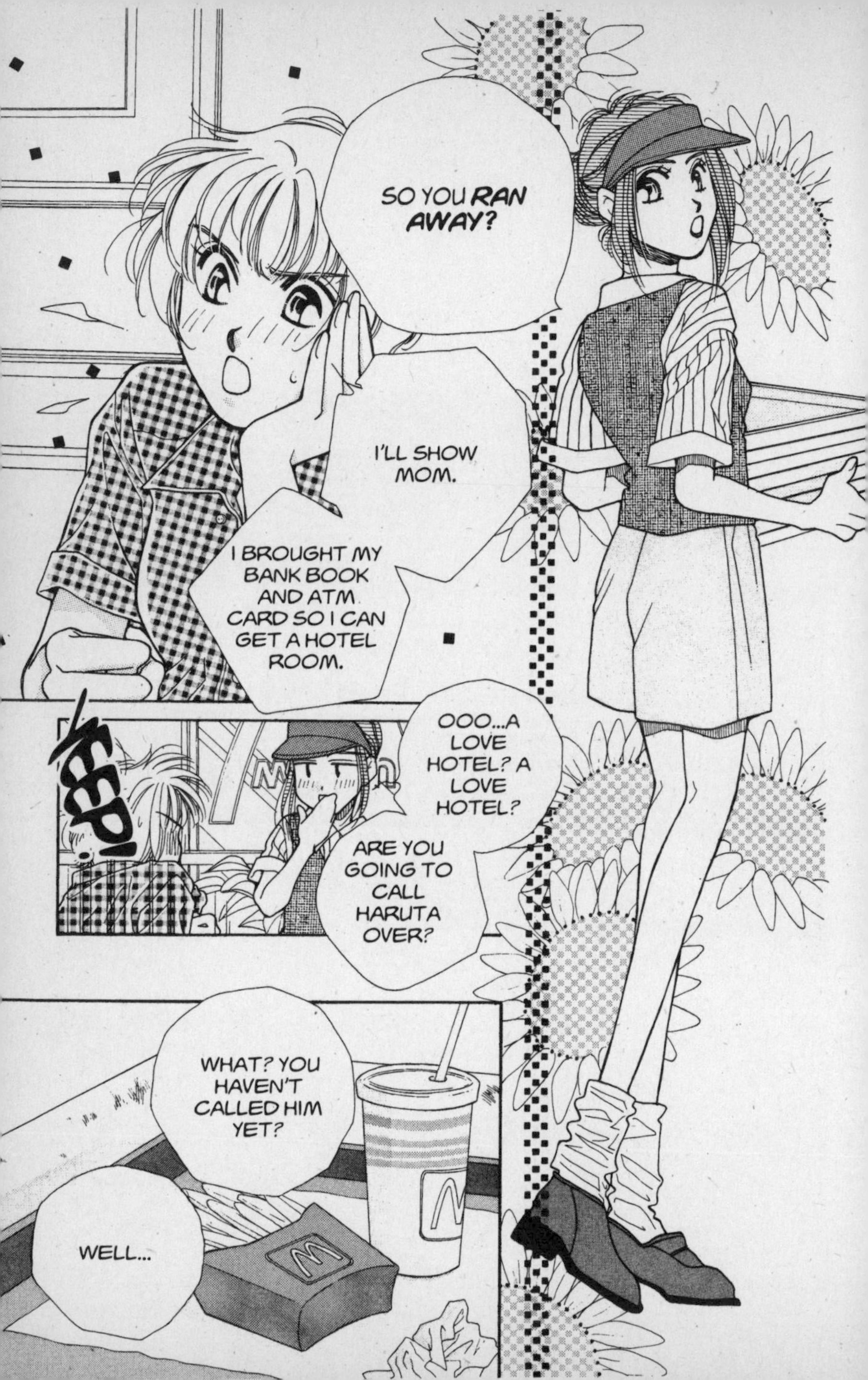
SO YOU RAN AWAY?
I'LL SHOW MOM.
I BROUGHT MY BANK BOOK AND ATM CARD SO I CAN GET A HOTEL ROOM.
OOO...A LOVE HOTEL? A LOVE HOTEL?
YEEP!
ARE YOU GOING TO CALL HARUTA OVER?
WHAT? YOU HAVEN'T CALLED HIM YET?
WELL...

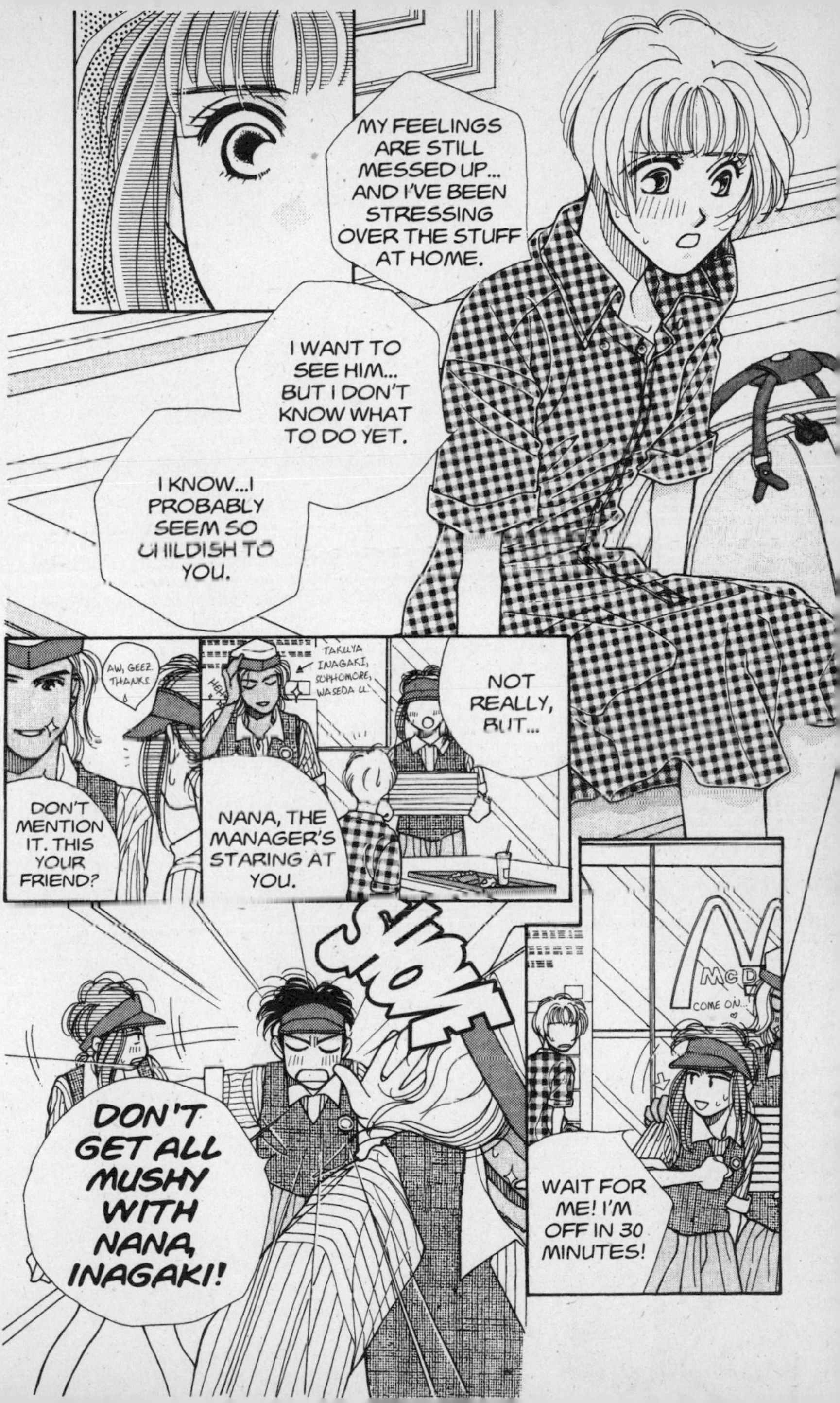
MY FEELINGS ARE STILL MESSED UP... AND I'VE BEEN STRESSING OVER THE STUFF AT HOME.
I WANT TO SEE HIM... BUT I DON'T KNOW WHAT TO DO YET.
I KNOW...I PROBABLY SEEM SO CHILDISH TO YOU.
NOT REALLY, BUT...
TAKUYA INAGAKI, SOPHOMORE, WASEDA U.
NANA, THE MANAGER'S STARING AT YOU.
AW, GEEZ. THANKS.
DON'T MENTION IT. THIS YOUR FRIEND?
McD
COME ON...
WAIT FOR ME! I'M OFF IN 30 MINUTES!
SHOVE
DON'T GET ALL MUSHY WITH NANA, INAGAKI!

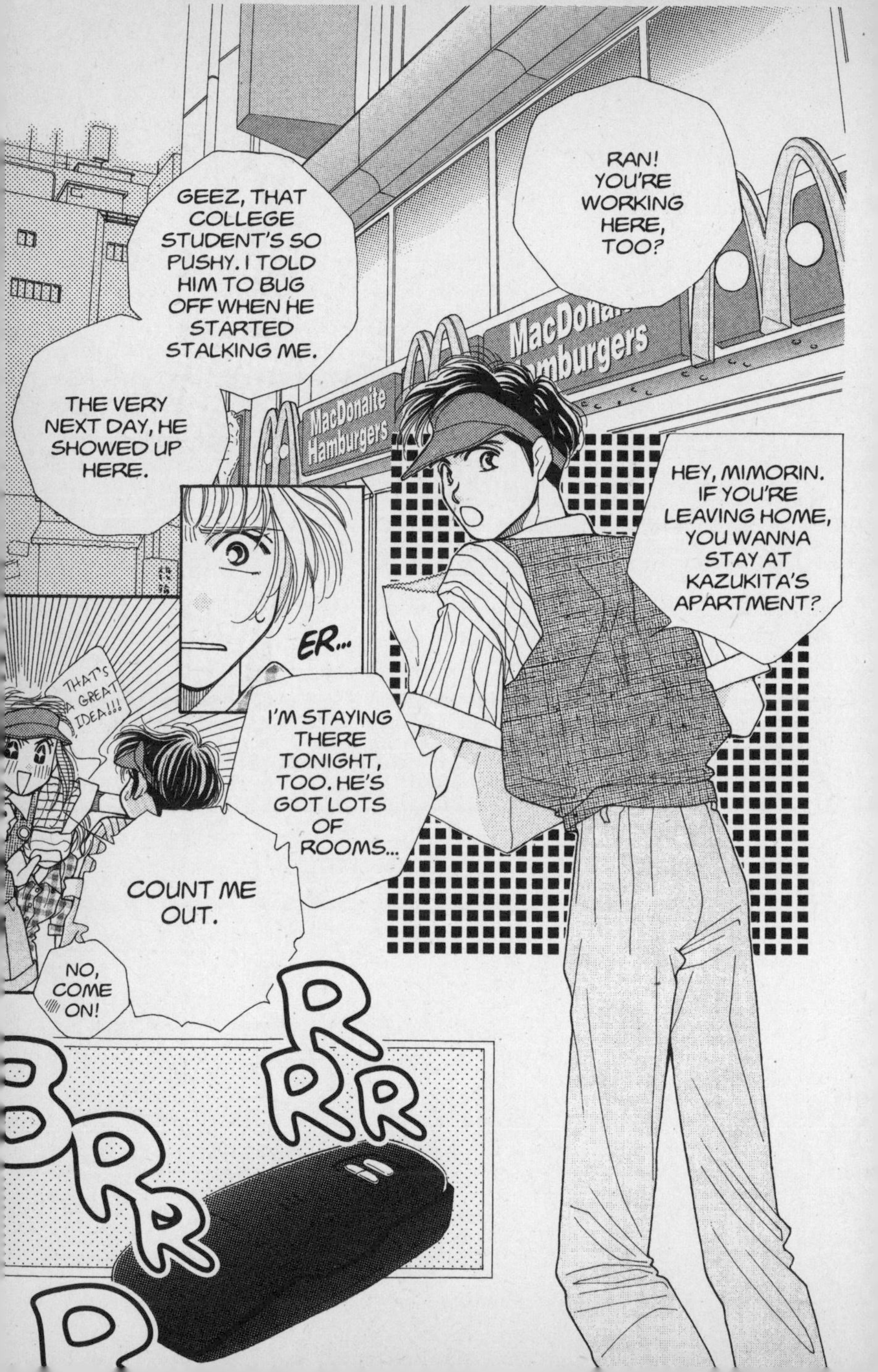
RAN! YOU'RE WORKING HERE, TOO?
GEEZ, THAT COLLEGE STUDENT'S SO PUSHY. I TOLD HIM TO BUG OFF WHEN HE STARTED STALKING ME.
THE VERY NEXT DAY, HE SHOWED UP HERE.
MacDonaite Hamburgers
HEY, MIMORIN. IF YOU'RE LEAVING HOME, YOU WANNA STAY AT KAZUKITA'S APARTMENT?
ER...
I'M STAYING THERE TONIGHT, TOO. HE'S GOT LOTS OF ROOMS...
THAT'S A GREAT IDEA!!!
COUNT ME OUT.
NO, COME ON!
RRR
BRR

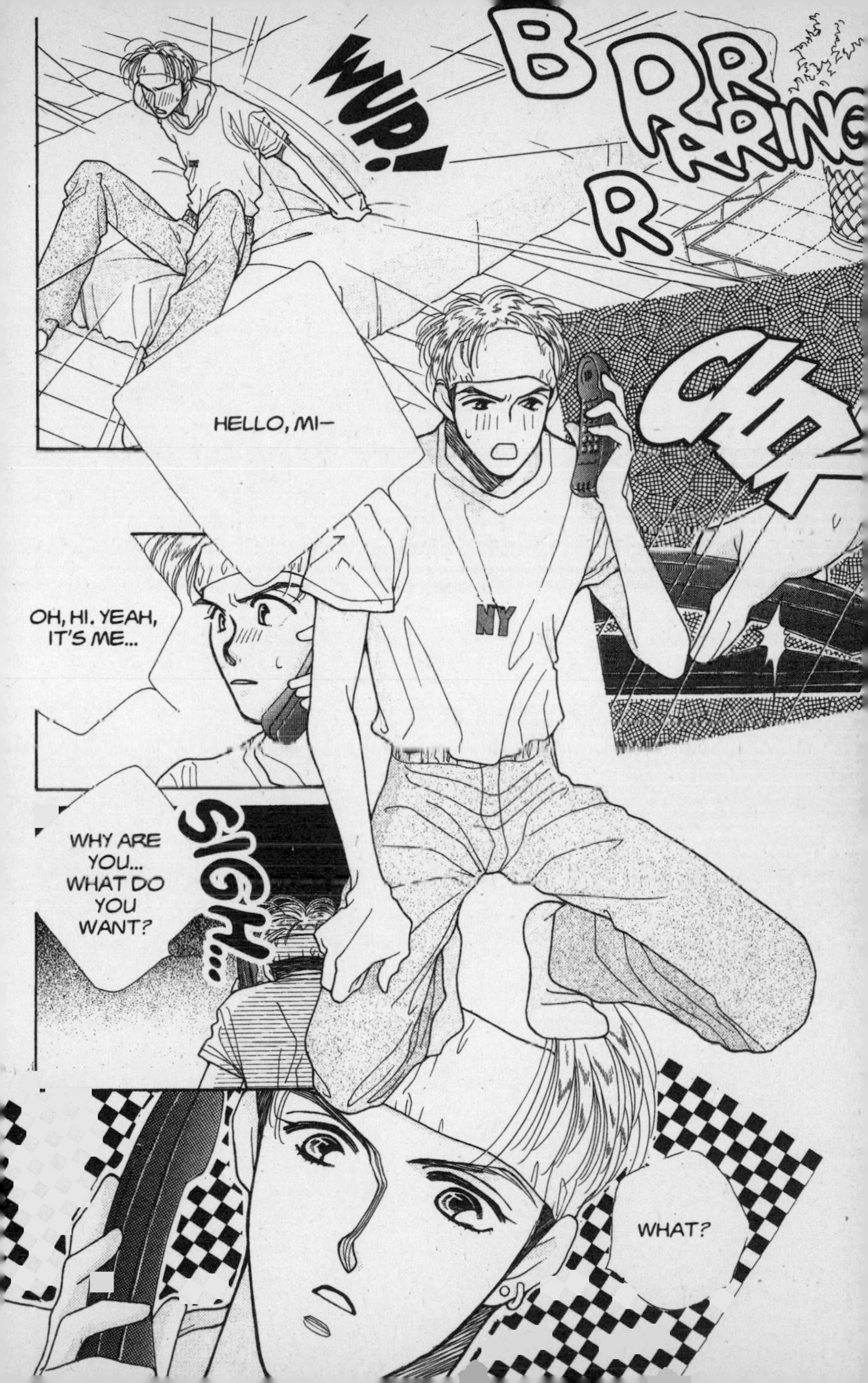
BRRR RRING
WUP!
CHK
HELLO, MI—
OH, HI. YEAH, IT'S ME...
SIGH...
WHY ARE YOU... WHAT DO YOU WANT?
WHAT?

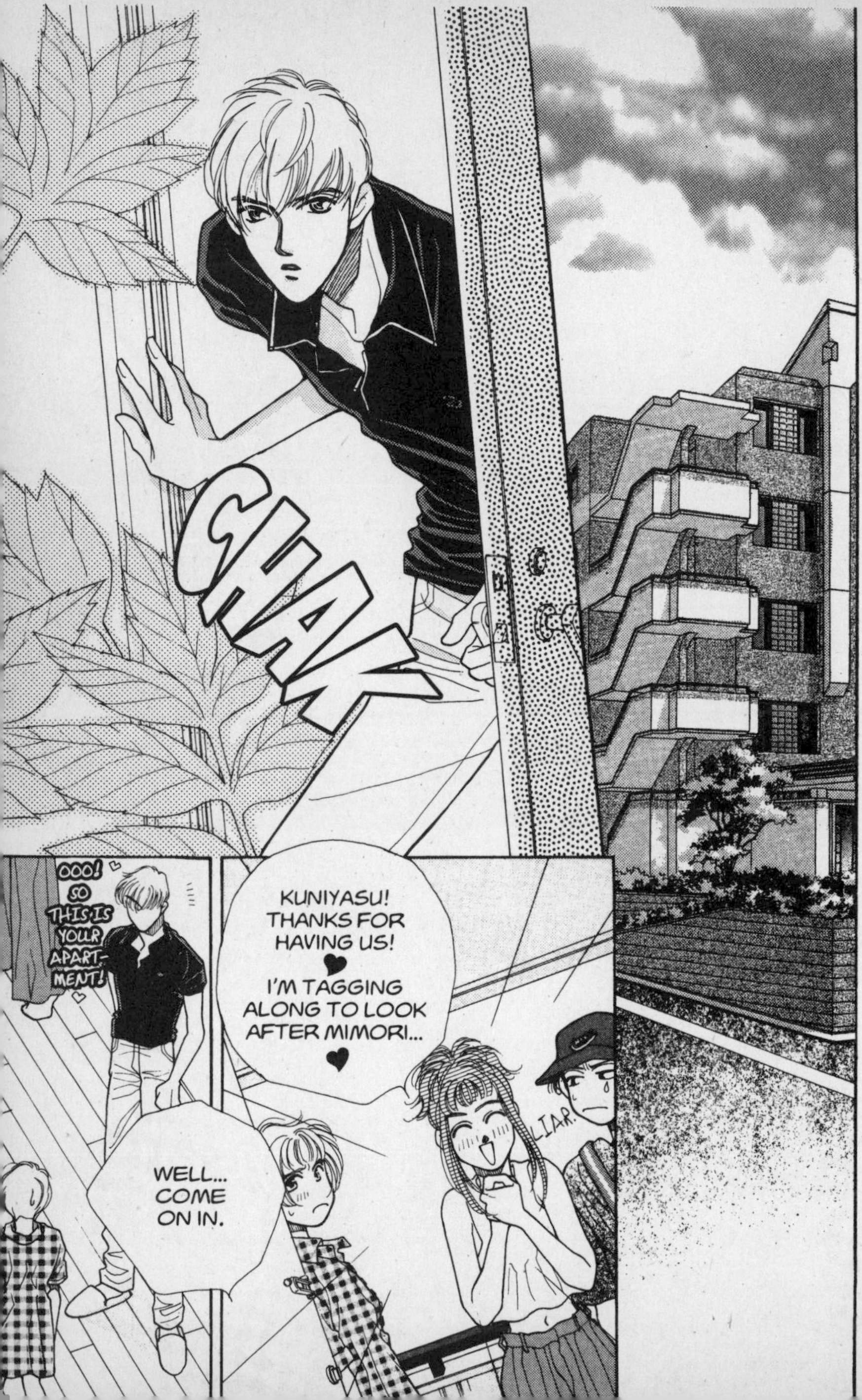
CHAK
KUNIYASU! THANKS FOR HAVING US! ♥ I'M TAGGING ALONG TO LOOK AFTER MIMORI... ♥
LIAR.
WELL... COME ON IN.
OOO! SO THIS IS YOUR APART-MENT!

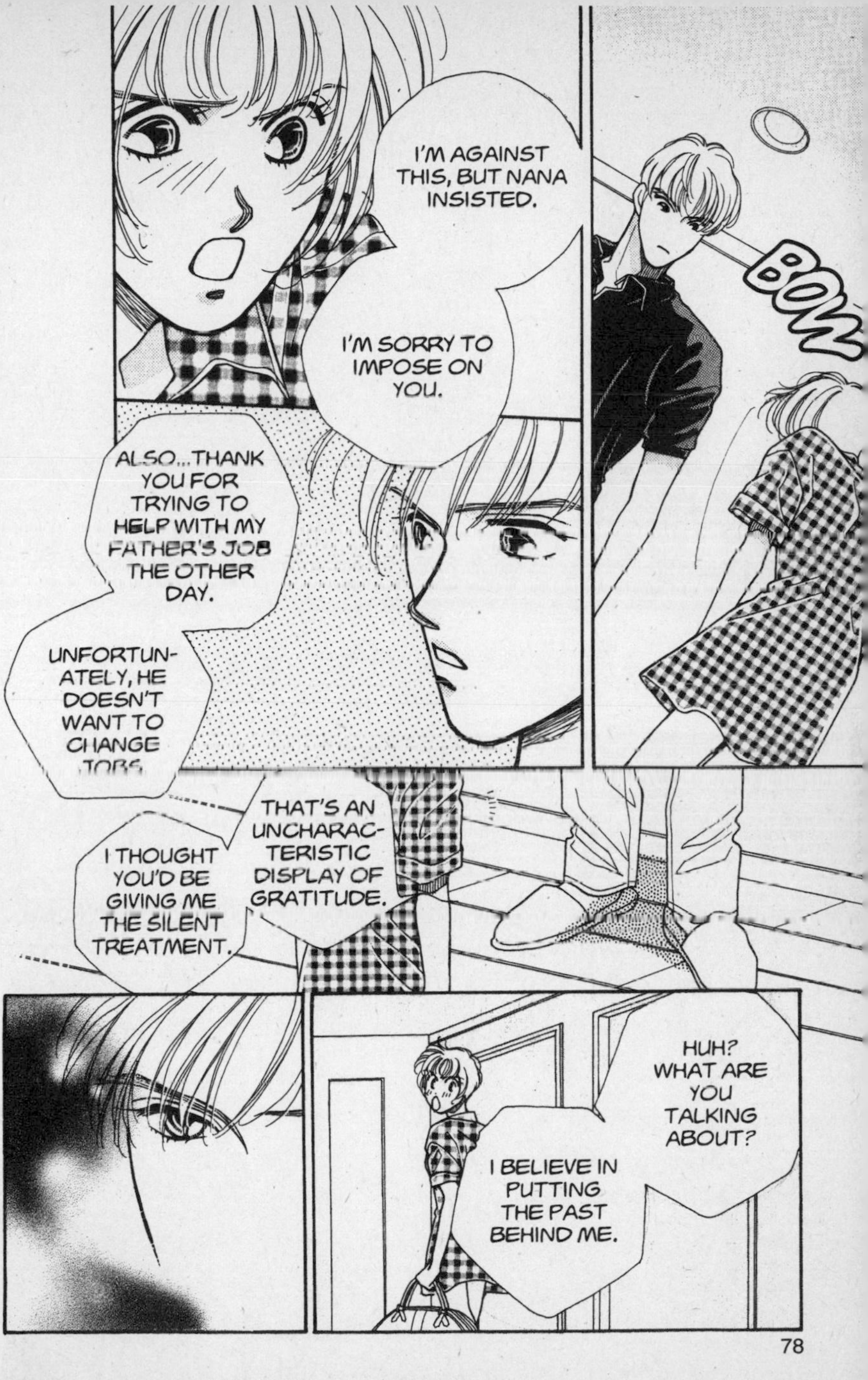
BOW
I'M AGAINST THIS, BUT NANA INSISTED.
I'M SORRY TO IMPOSE ON YOU.
ALSO...THANK YOU FOR TRYING TO HELP WITH MY FATHER'S JOB THE OTHER DAY.
UNFORTUN-ATELY, HE DOESN'T WANT TO CHANGE JOBS.
THAT'S AN UNCHARAC-TERISTIC DISPLAY OF GRATITUDE.
I THOUGHT YOU'D BE GIVING ME THE SILENT TREATMENT.
HUH? WHAT ARE YOU TALKING ABOUT?
I BELIEVE IN PUTTING THE PAST BEHIND ME.

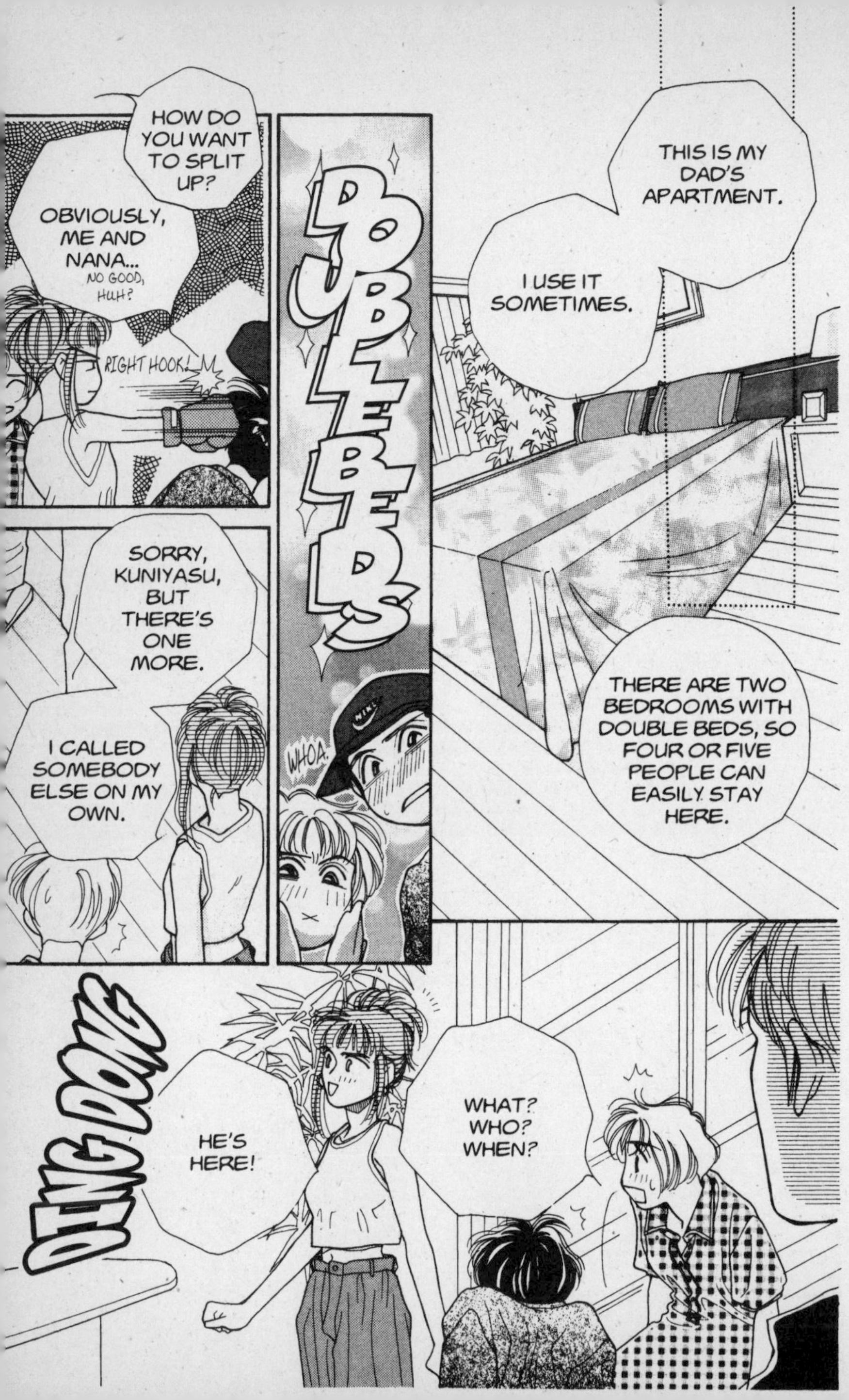
THIS IS MY DAD'S APARTMENT.
I USE IT SOMETIMES.
THERE ARE TWO BEDROOMS WITH DOUBLE BEDS, SO FOUR OR FIVE PEOPLE CAN EASILY STAY HERE.
DOUBLE BEDS
WHOA.
HOW DO YOU WANT TO SPLIT UP?
OBVIOUSLY, ME AND NANA...
NO GOOD, HUH?
RIGHT HOOK!
SORRY, KUNIYASU, BUT THERE'S ONE MORE.
I CALLED SOMEBODY ELSE ON MY OWN.
WHAT? WHO? WHEN?
HE'S HERE!
DING DONG

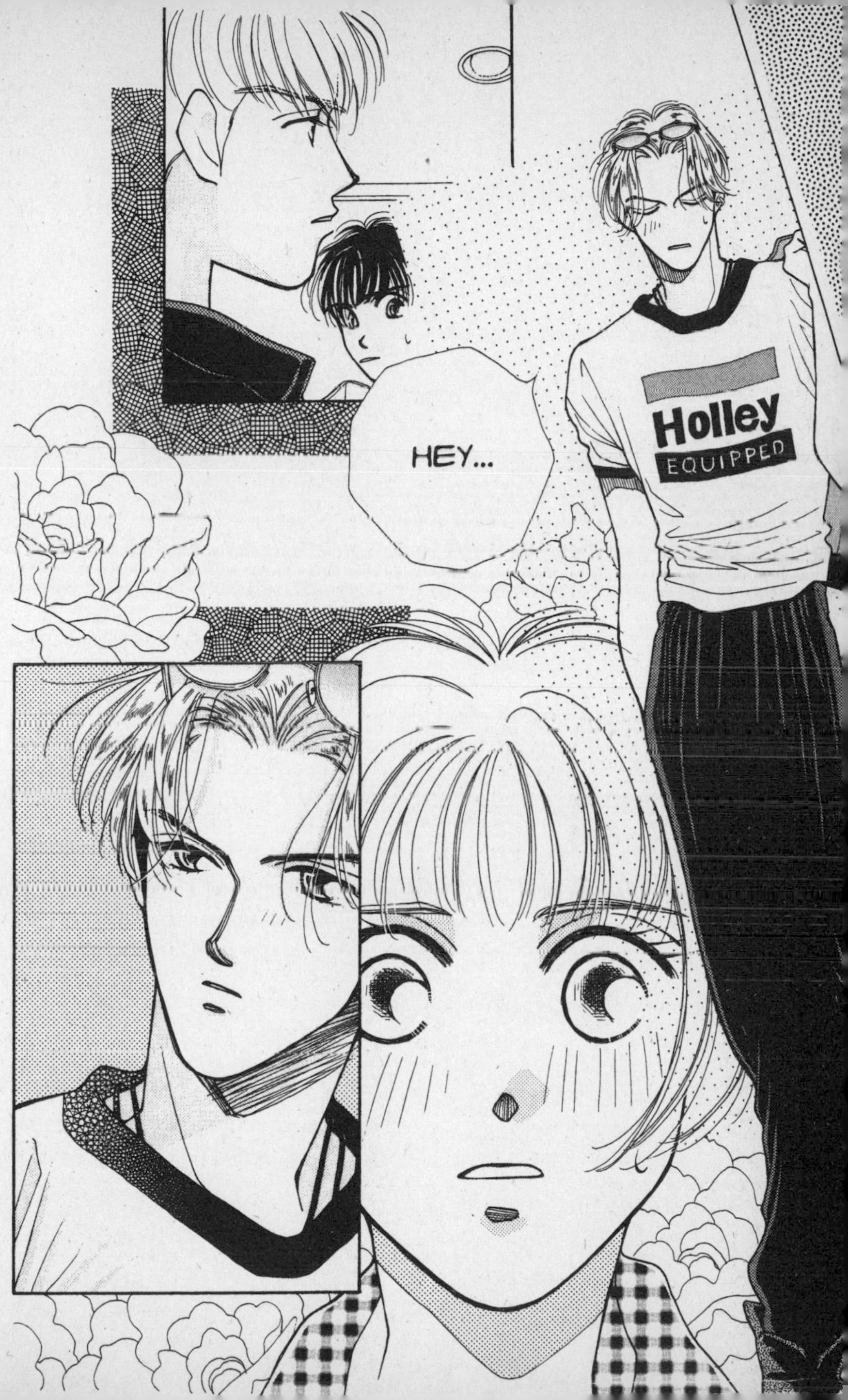
HEY...
Holley
EQUIPPED

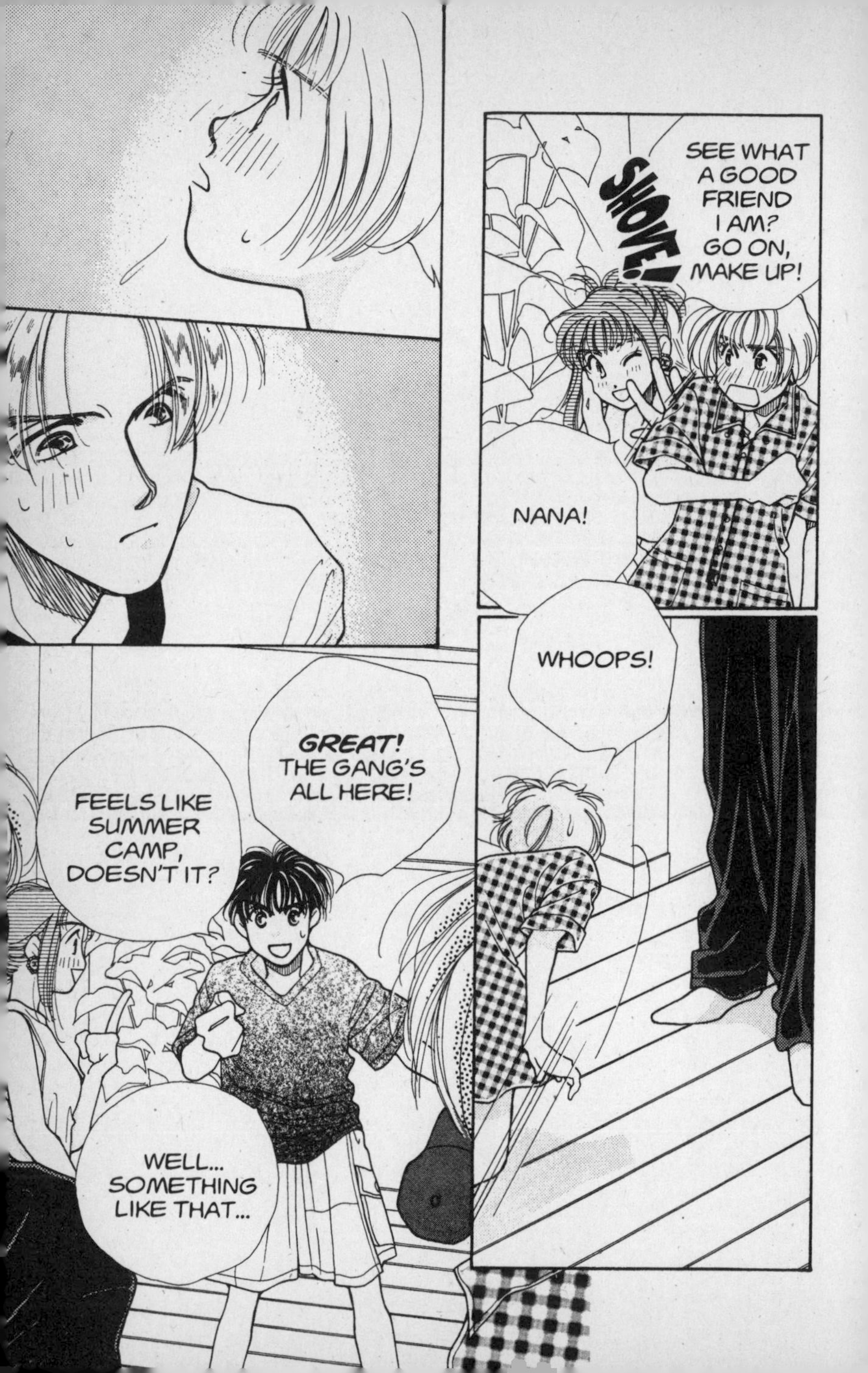
SEE WHAT A GOOD FRIEND I AM? GO ON, MAKE UP!
SHOVE!
NANA!
WHOOPS!
GREAT! THE GANG'S ALL HERE!
FEELS LIKE SUMMER CAMP, DOESN'T IT?
WELL... SOMETHING LIKE THAT...

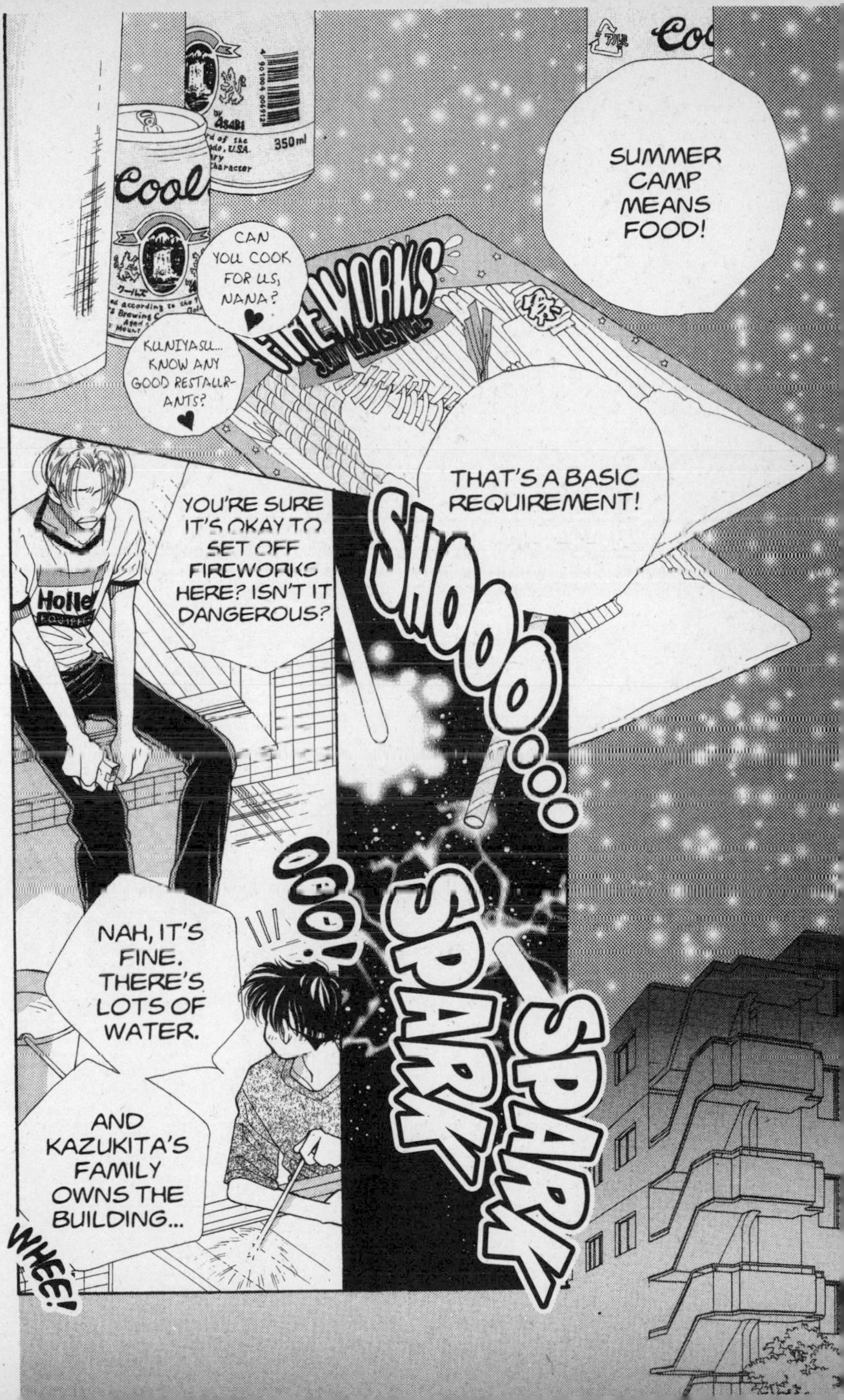
Cool
Cool
350ml
SUMMER CAMP MEANS FOOD!
THAT'S A BASIC REQUIREMENT!
CAN YOU COOK FOR US, NANA? ♥
KUNIYASU... KNOW ANY GOOD RESTAURANTS? ♥
FIREWORKS
SHOOOO...
SPARK SPARK
YOU'RE SURE IT'S OKAY TO SET OFF FIREWORKS HERE? ISN'T IT DANGEROUS?
OOOO!
NAH, IT'S FINE. THERE'S LOTS OF WATER.
AND KAZUKITA'S FAMILY OWNS THE BUILDING...
WHEE!

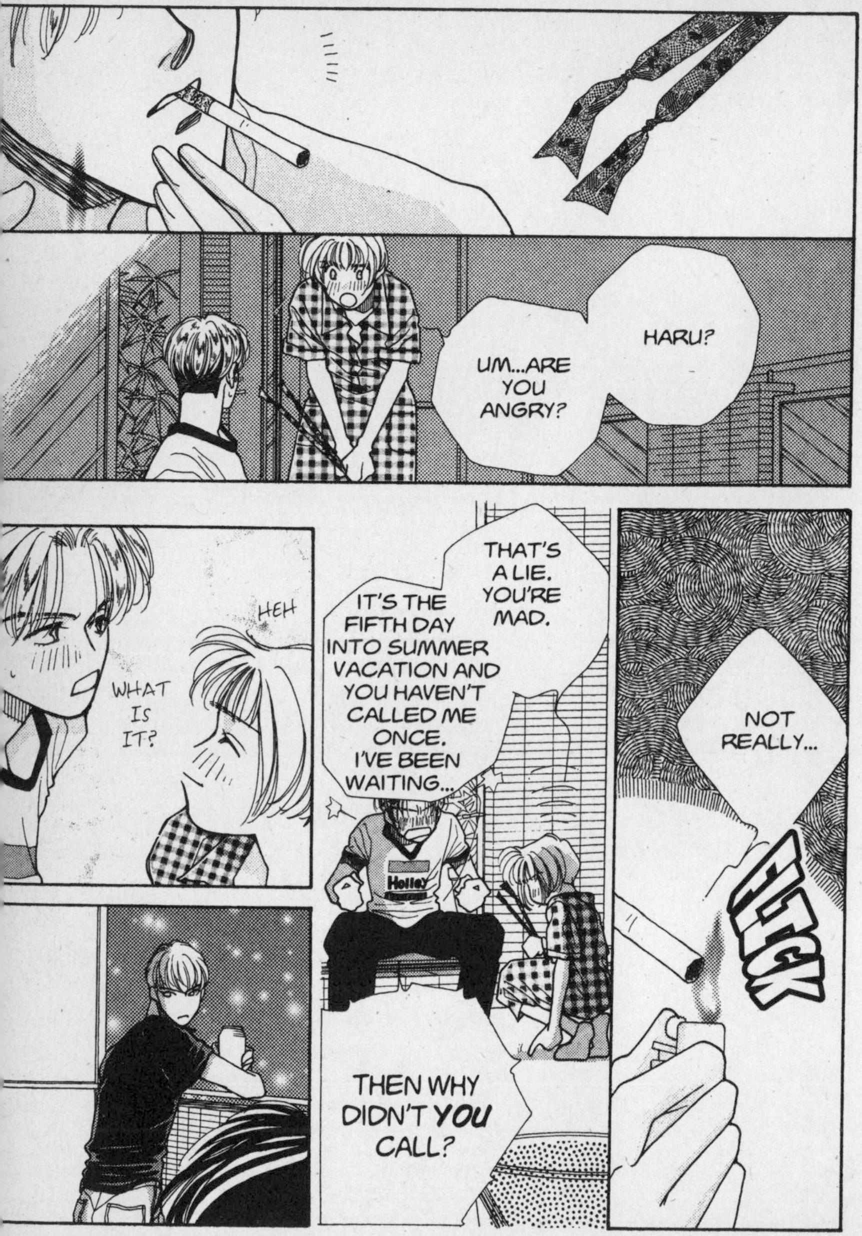
HARU?
UM...ARE YOU ANGRY?
NOT REALLY...
FLICK
THAT'S A LIE. YOU'RE MAD.
IT'S THE FIFTH DAY INTO SUMMER VACATION AND YOU HAVEN'T CALLED ME ONCE. I'VE BEEN WAITING...
THEN WHY DIDN'T YOU CALL?
HEH
WHAT IS IT?

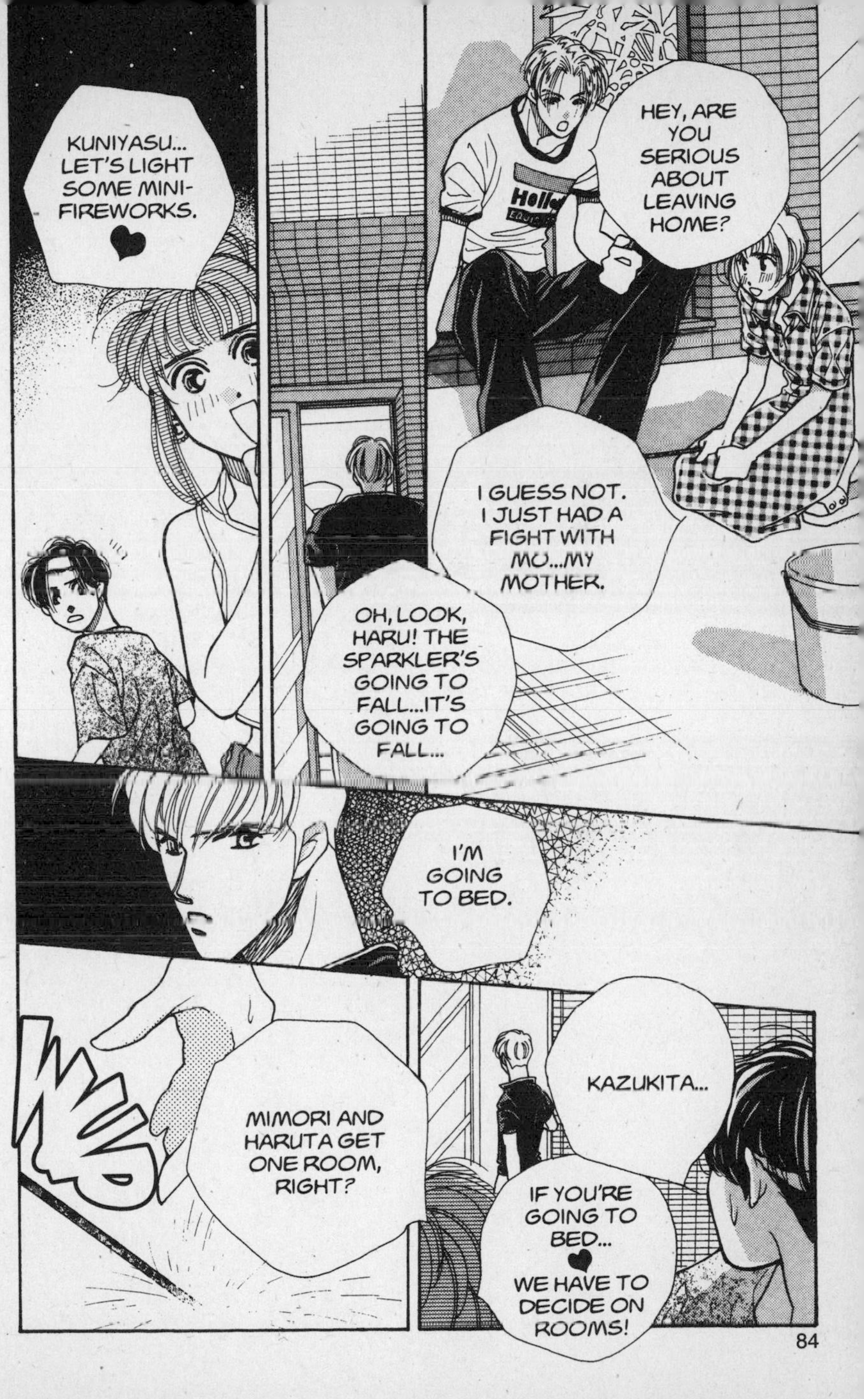
HEY, ARE YOU SERIOUS ABOUT LEAVING HOME?
I GUESS NOT. I JUST HAD A FIGHT WITH MO...MY MOTHER.
OH, LOOK, HARU! THE SPARKLER'S GOING TO FALL...IT'S GOING TO FALL...
KUNIYASU... LET'S LIGHT SOME MINI-FIREWORKS. ♥
I'M GOING TO BED.
KAZUKITA...
IF YOU'RE GOING TO BED... ♥ WE HAVE TO DECIDE ON ROOMS!
WHIP
MIMORI AND HARUTA GET ONE ROOM, RIGHT?

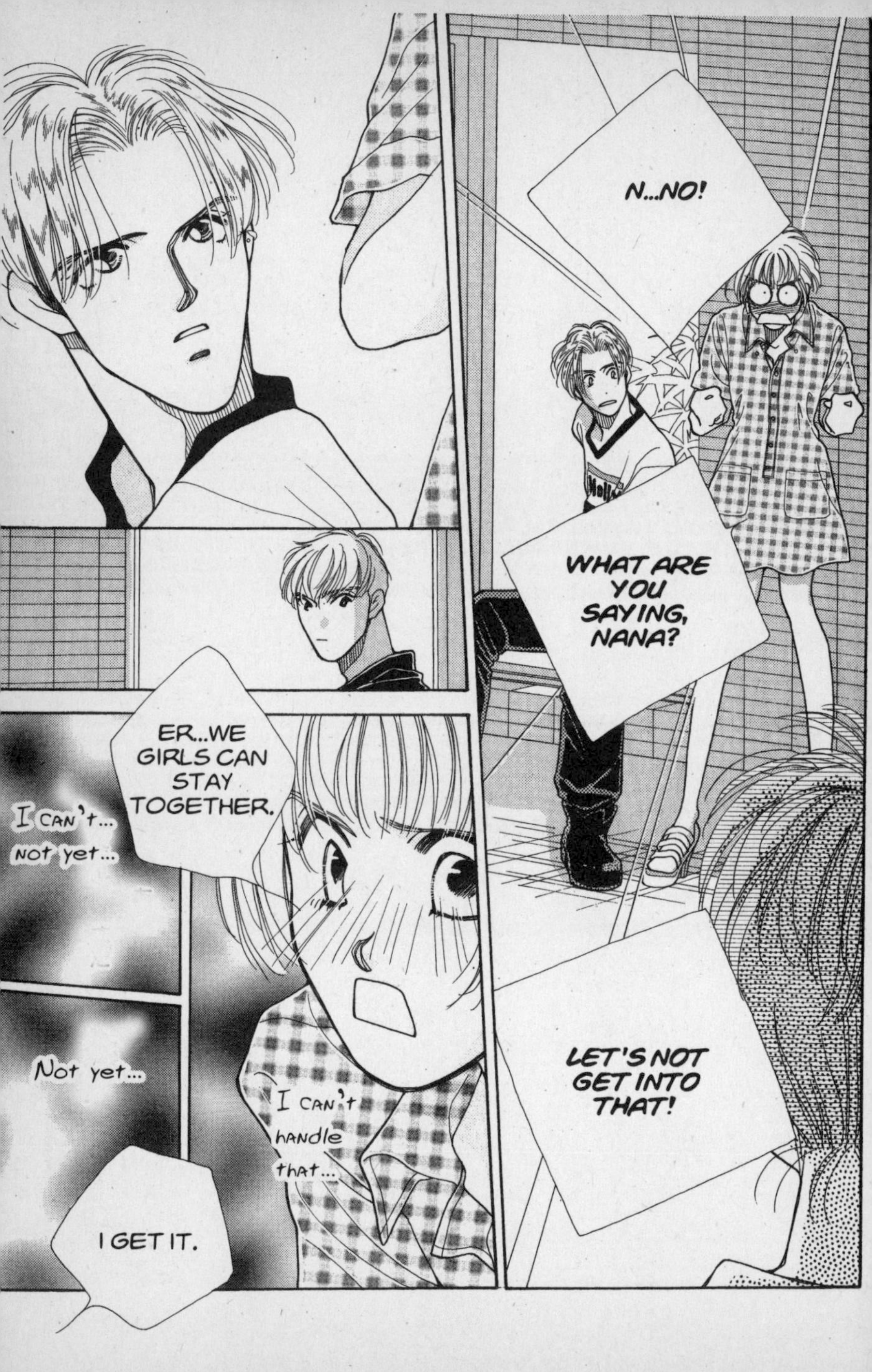
N...NO!
WHAT ARE YOU SAYING, NANA?
LET'S NOT GET INTO THAT!
ER...WE GIRLS CAN STAY TOGETHER.
I can't... not yet...
Not yet...
I can't handle that...
I GET IT.

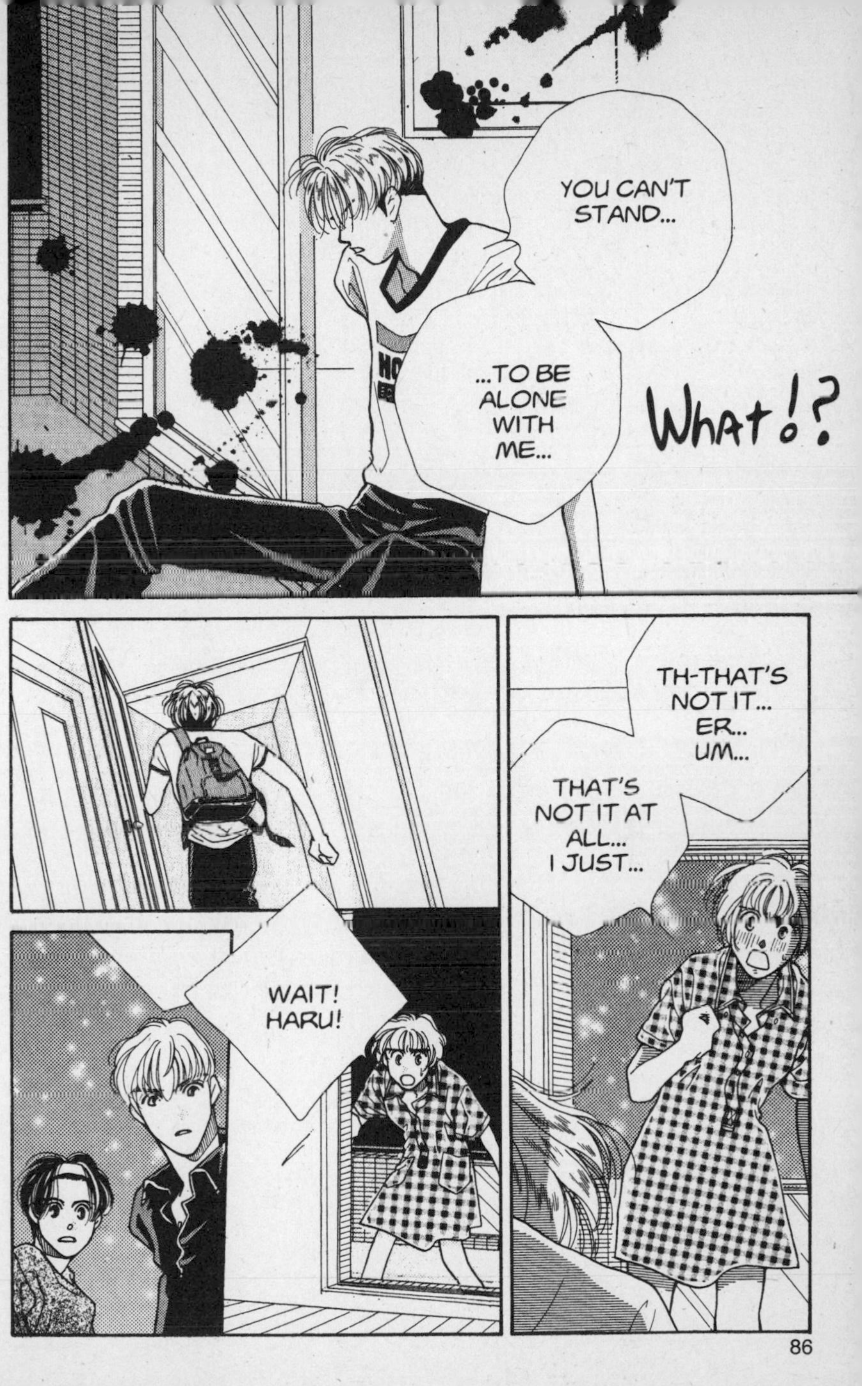
YOU CAN'T STAND...
...TO BE ALONE WITH ME...
What!?
TH-THAT'S NOT IT... ER... UM...
THAT'S NOT IT AT ALL... I JUST...
WAIT! HARU!

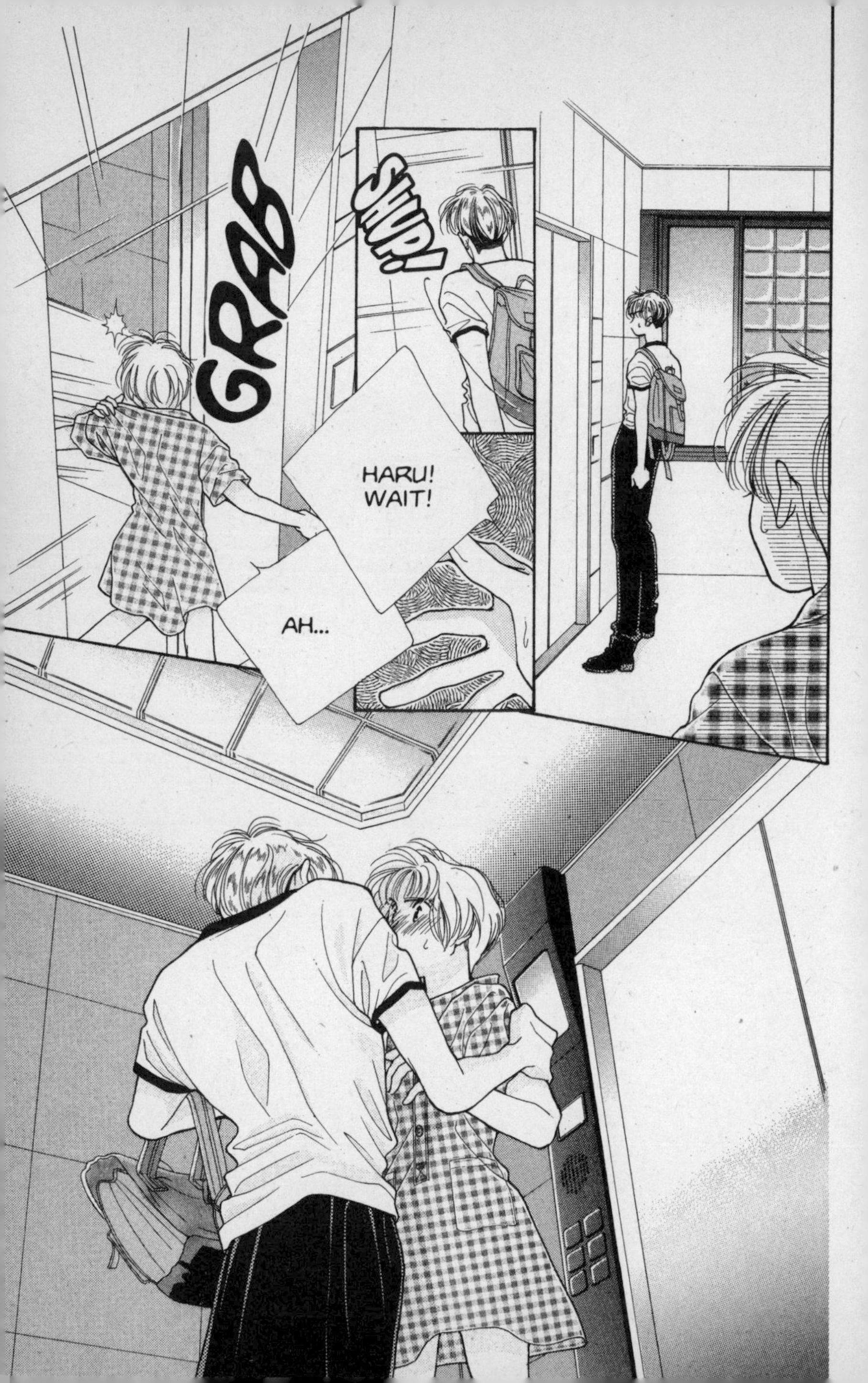
SHUP!
HARU! WAIT!
AH...
GRAB

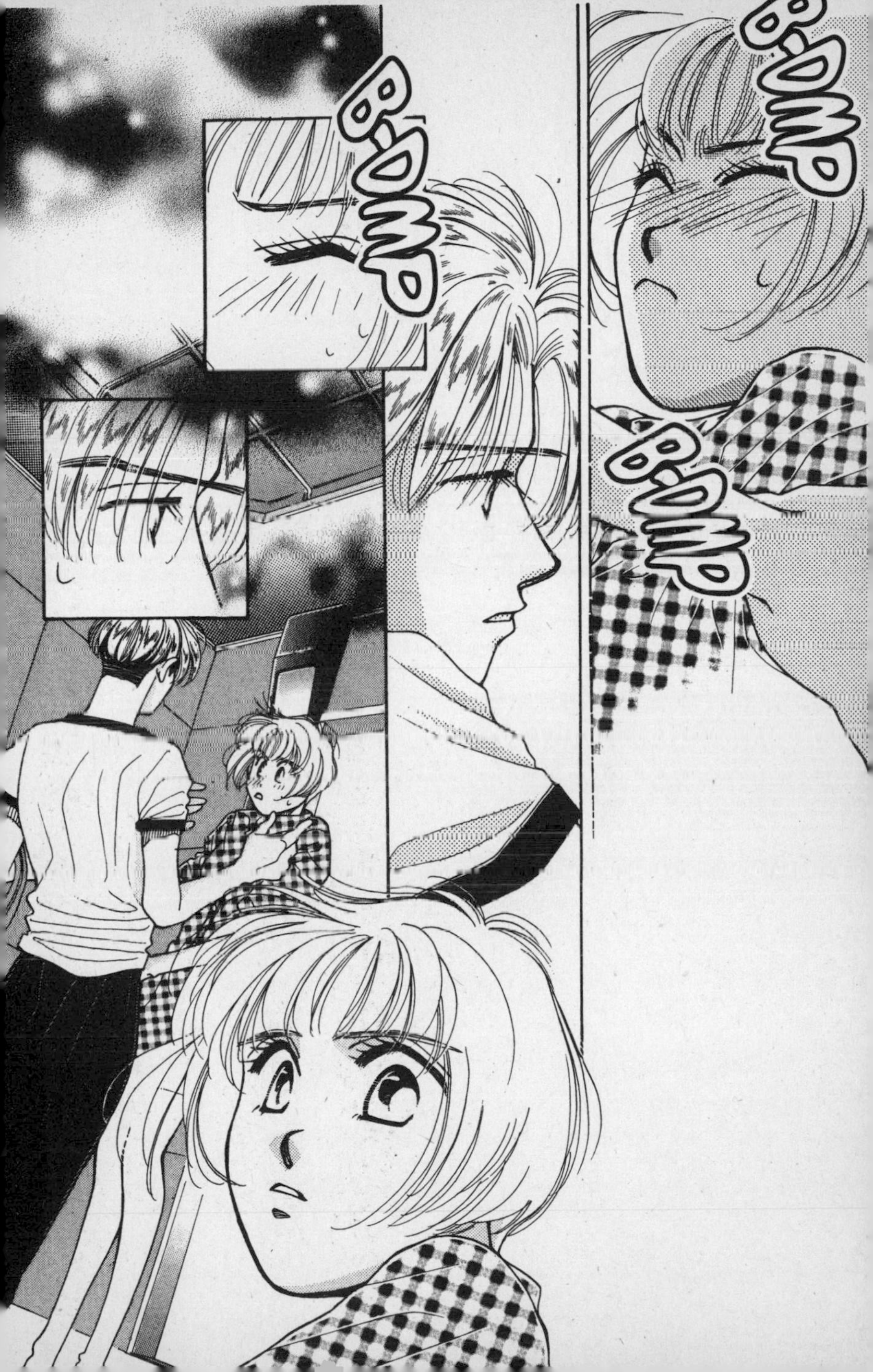
B-DMP
B-DMP
B-DMP

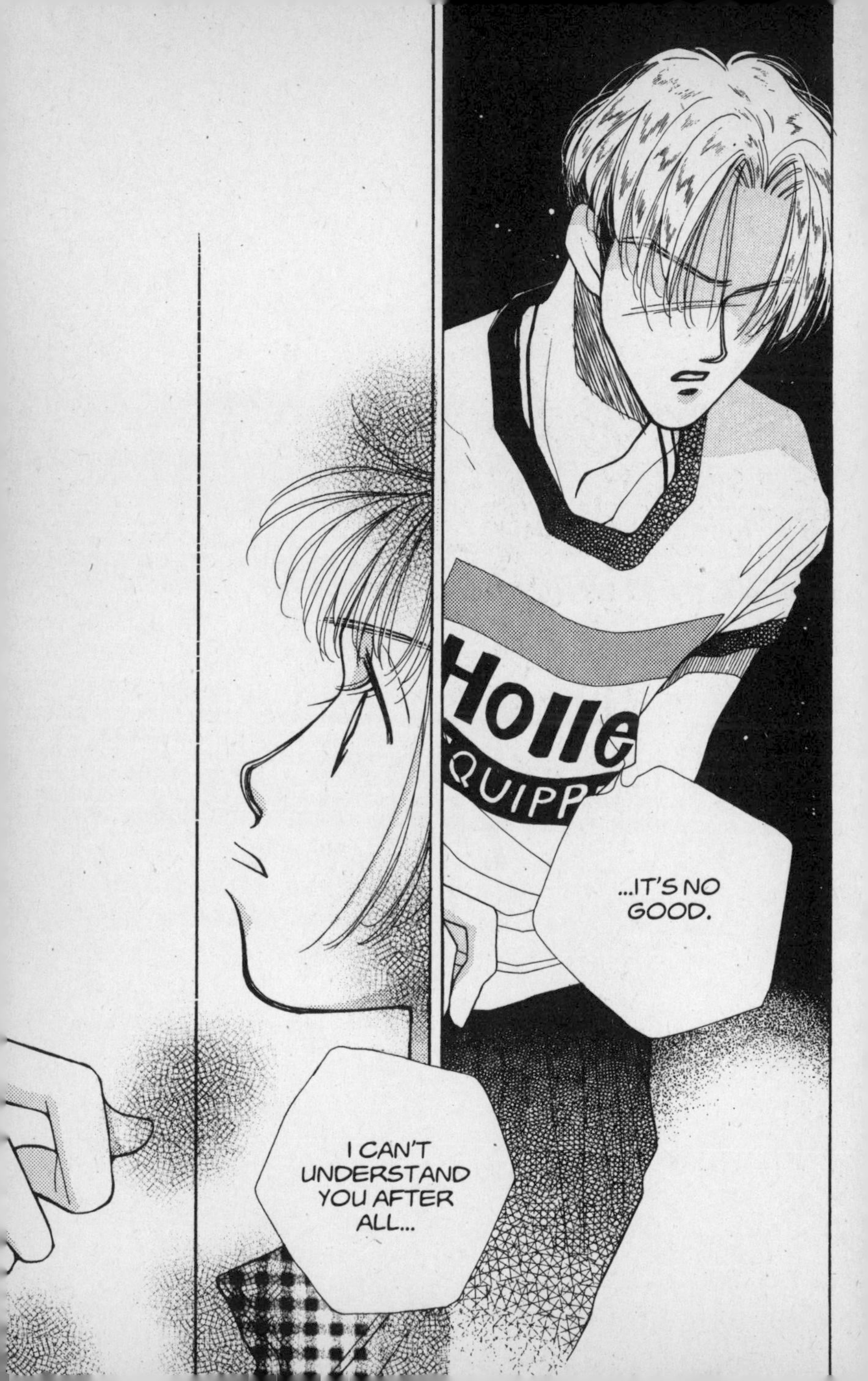
...IT'S NO GOOD.
I CAN'T UNDERSTAND YOU AFTER ALL...

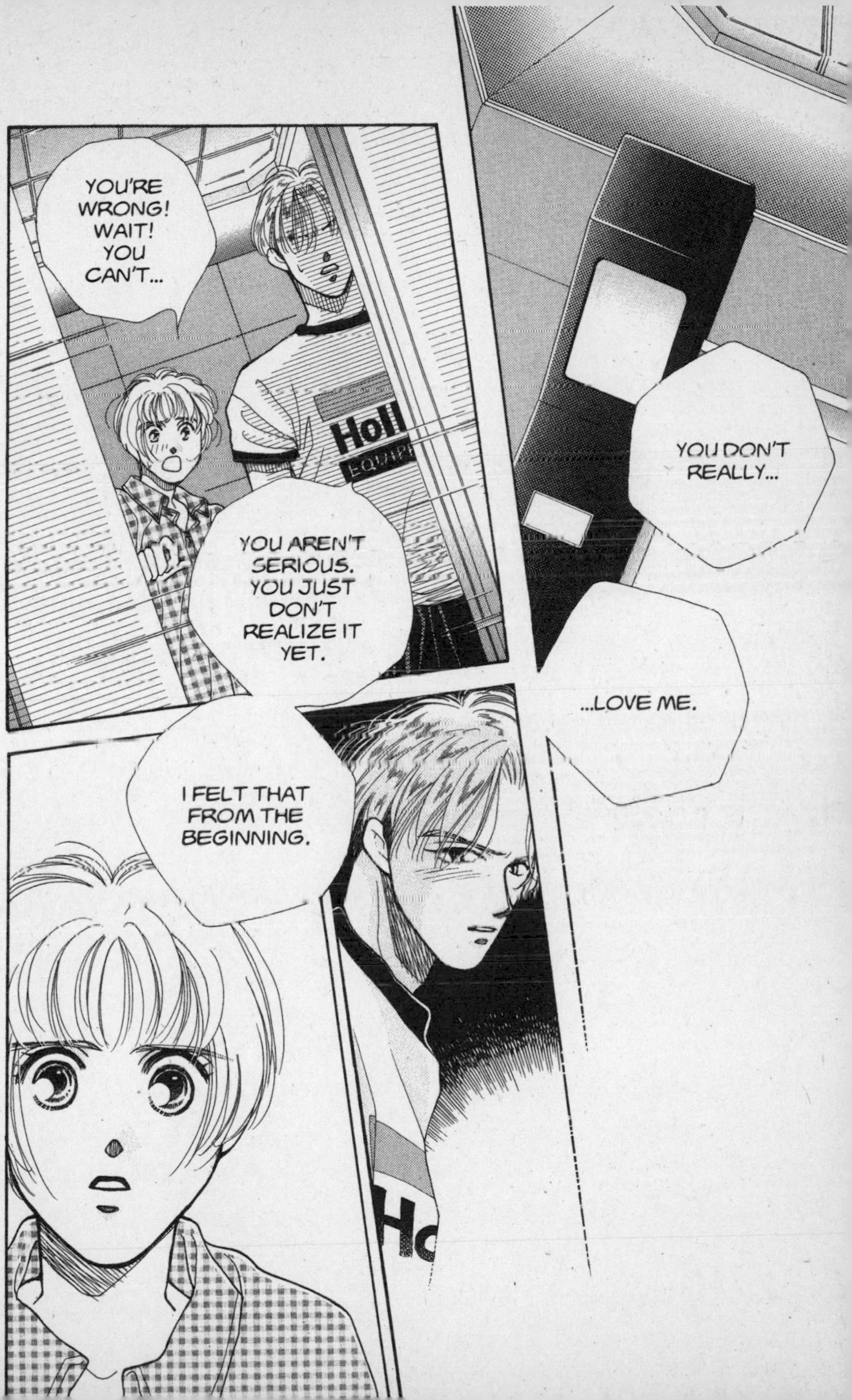
YOU DON'T REALLY...
...LOVE ME.
YOU'RE WRONG! WAIT! YOU CAN'T...
YOU AREN'T SERIOUS. YOU JUST DON'T REALIZE IT YET.
I FELT THAT FROM THE BEGINNING.

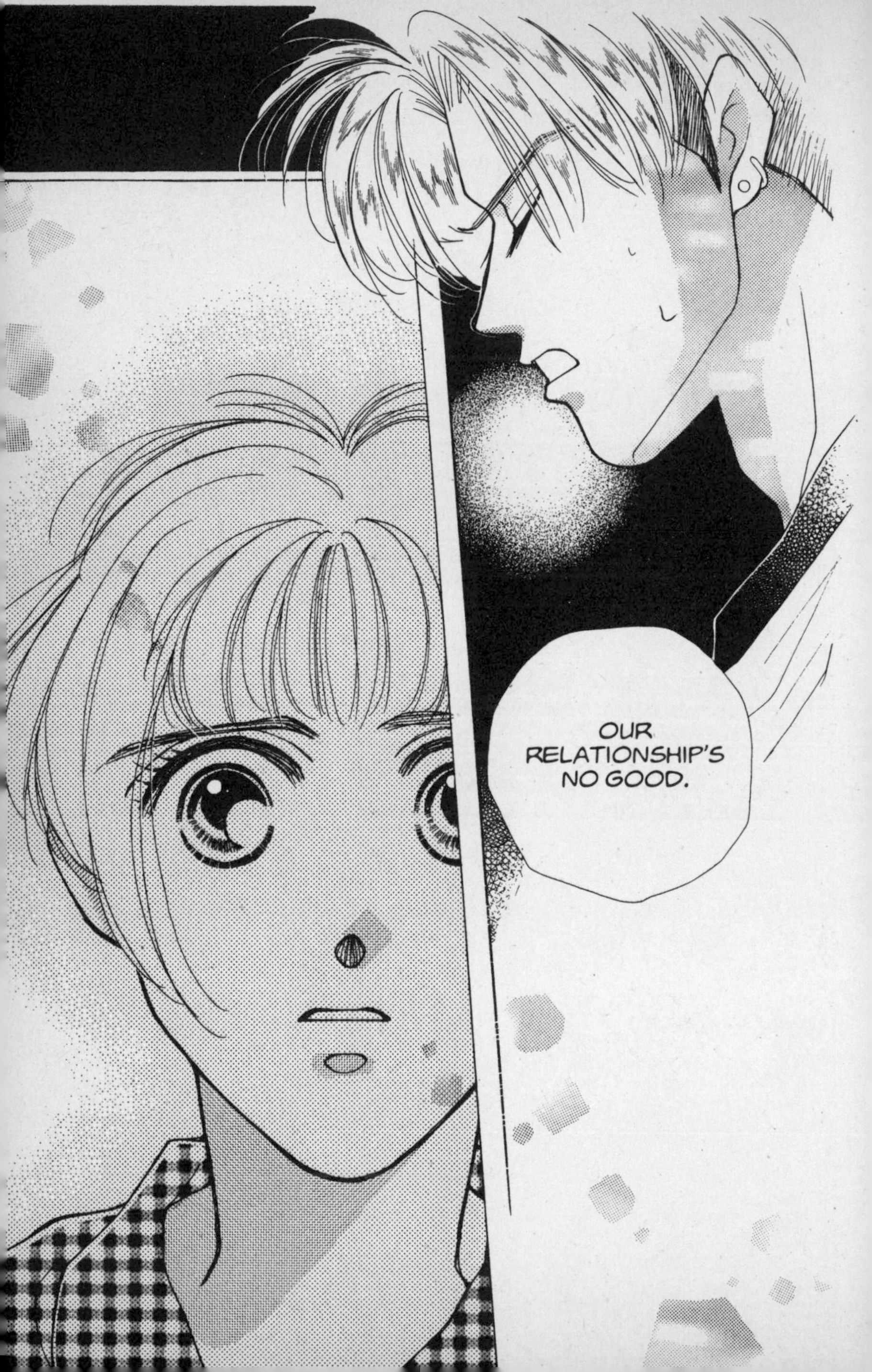
OUR RELATIONSHIP'S NO GOOD.

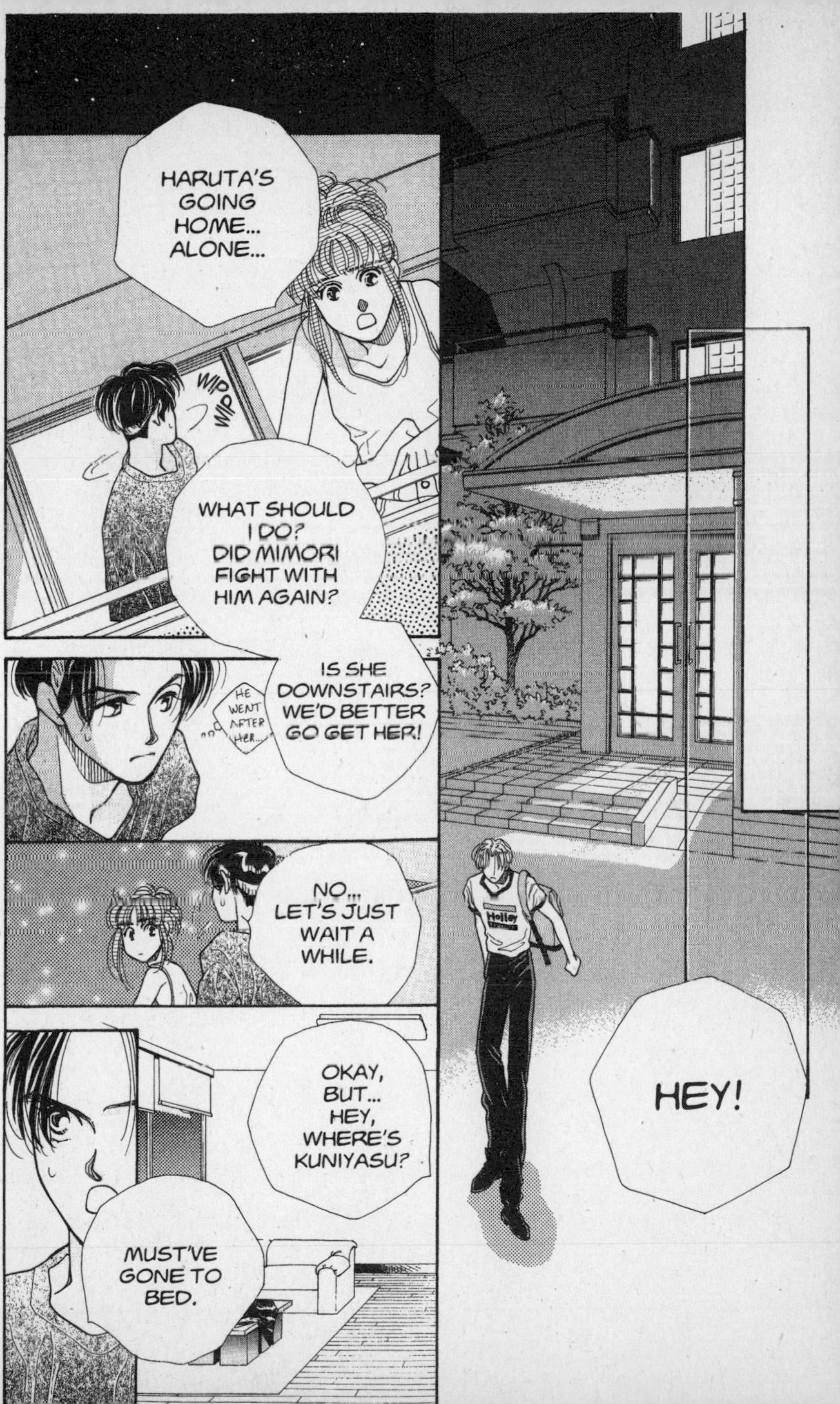
HEY!
HARUTA'S GOING HOME... ALONE...
WIP WIP
WHAT SHOULD I DO? DID MIMORI FIGHT WITH HIM AGAIN?
IS SHE DOWNSTAIRS? WE'D BETTER GO GET HER!
HE WENT AFTER HER...
NO... LET'S JUST WAIT A WHILE.
OKAY, BUT... HEY, WHERE'S KUNIYASU?
MUST'VE GONE TO BED.

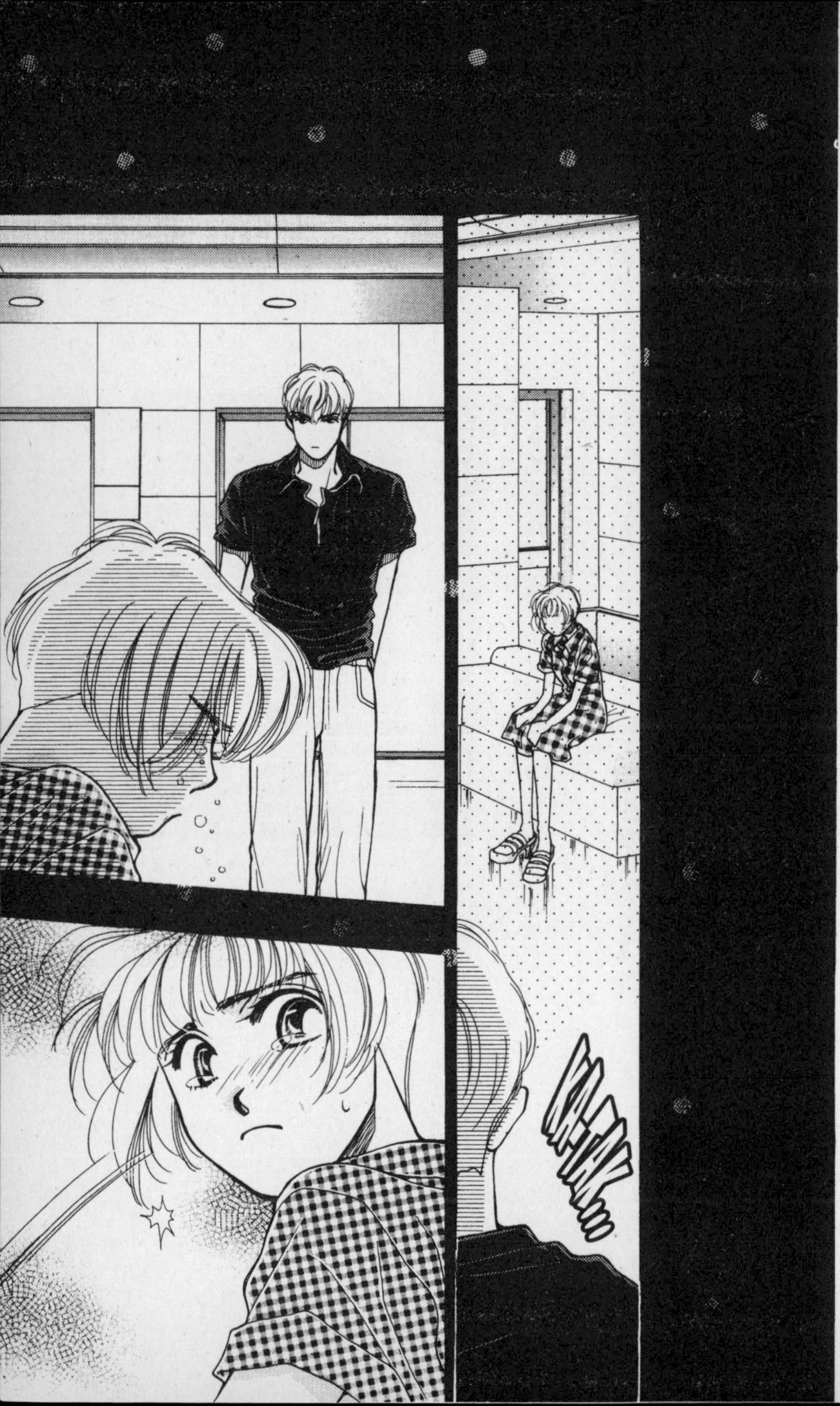

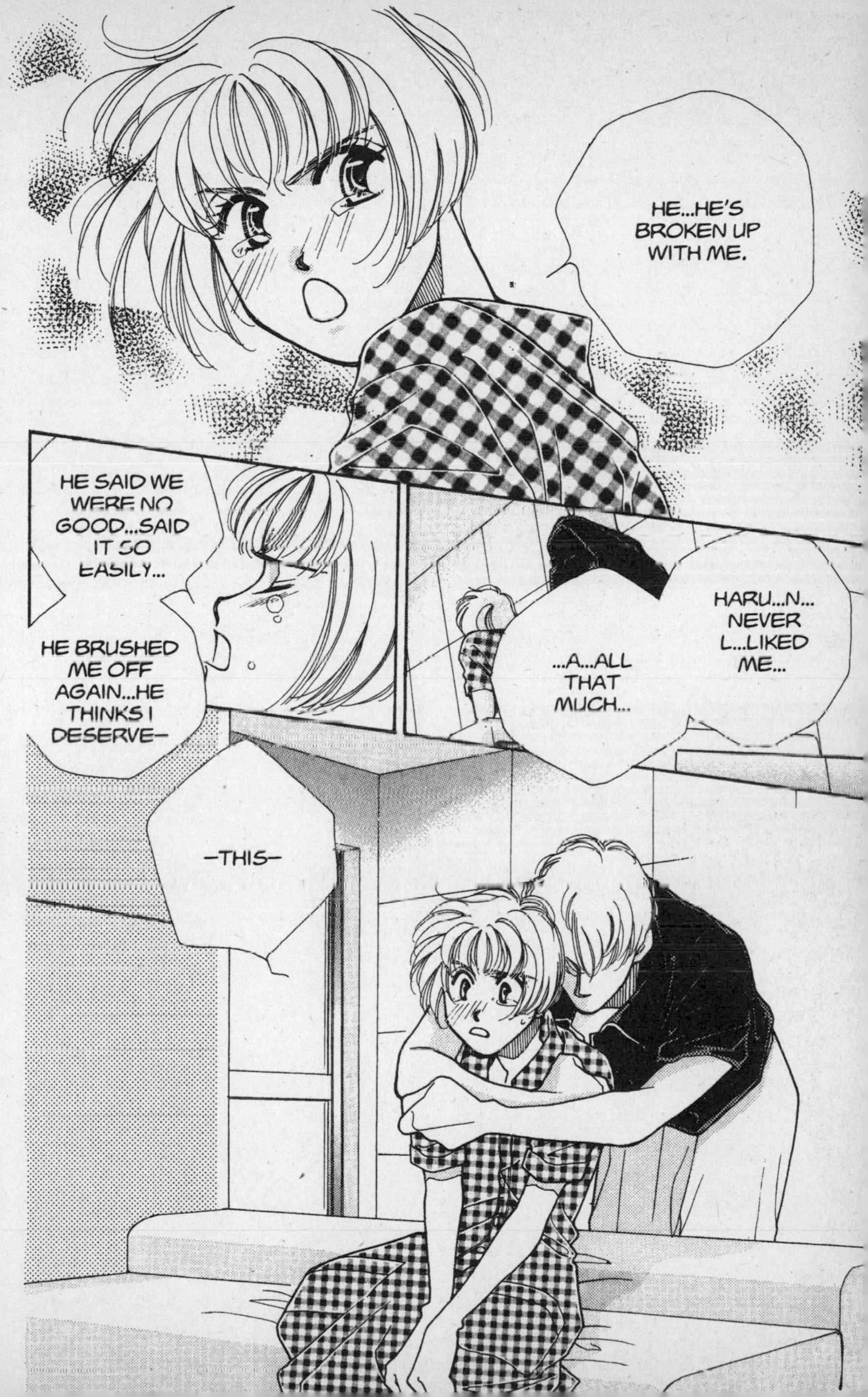
HE...HE'S BROKEN UP WITH ME.
HARU...N... NEVER L...LIKED ME...
...A...ALL THAT MUCH...
HE SAID WE WERE NO GOOD...SAID IT SO EASILY...
HE BRUSHED ME OFF AGAIN...HE THINKS I DESERVE—
—THIS—

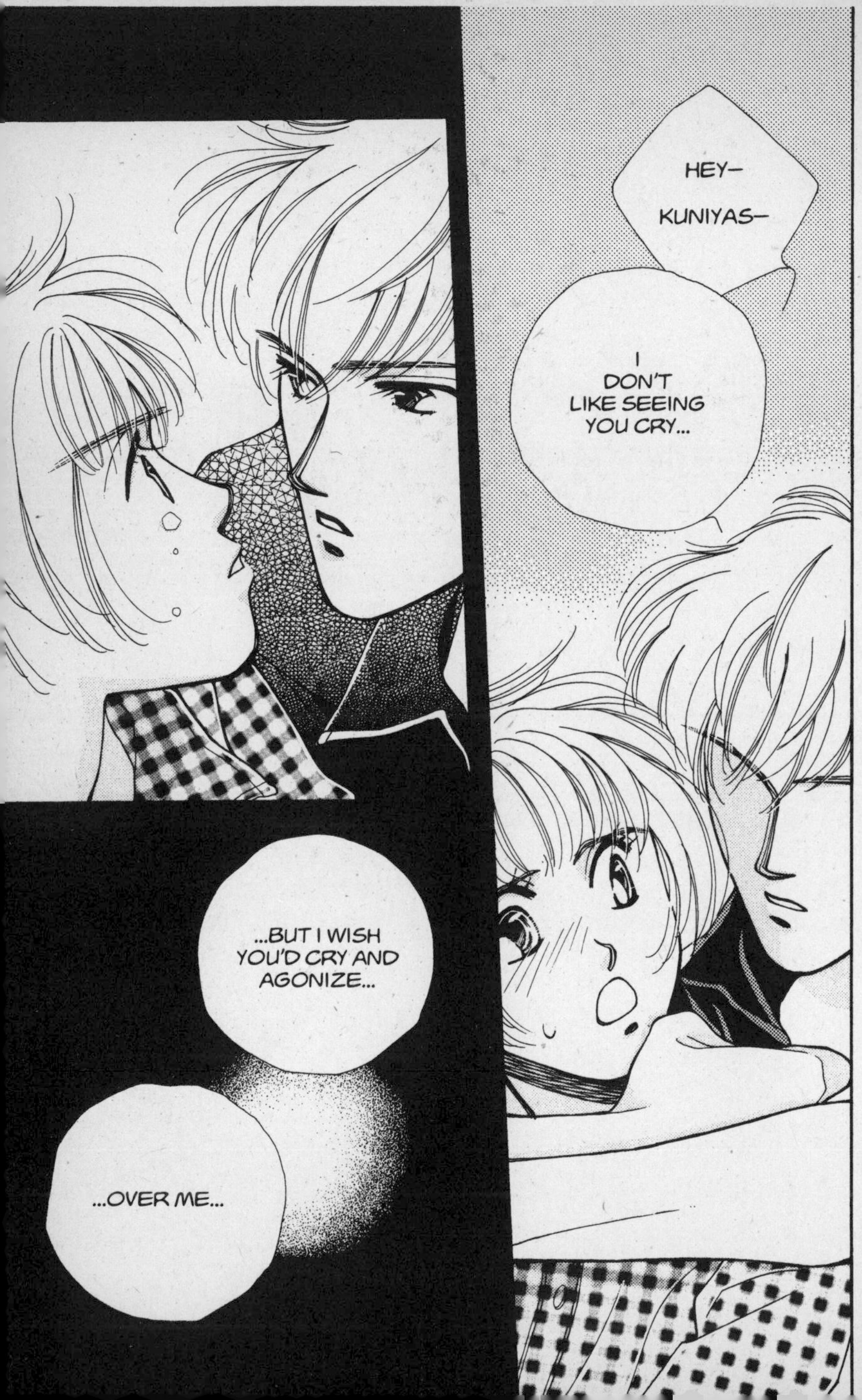
HEY—
KUNIYAS—
I DON'T LIKE SEEING YOU CRY...
...BUT I WISH YOU'D CRY AND AGONIZE...
...OVER ME...

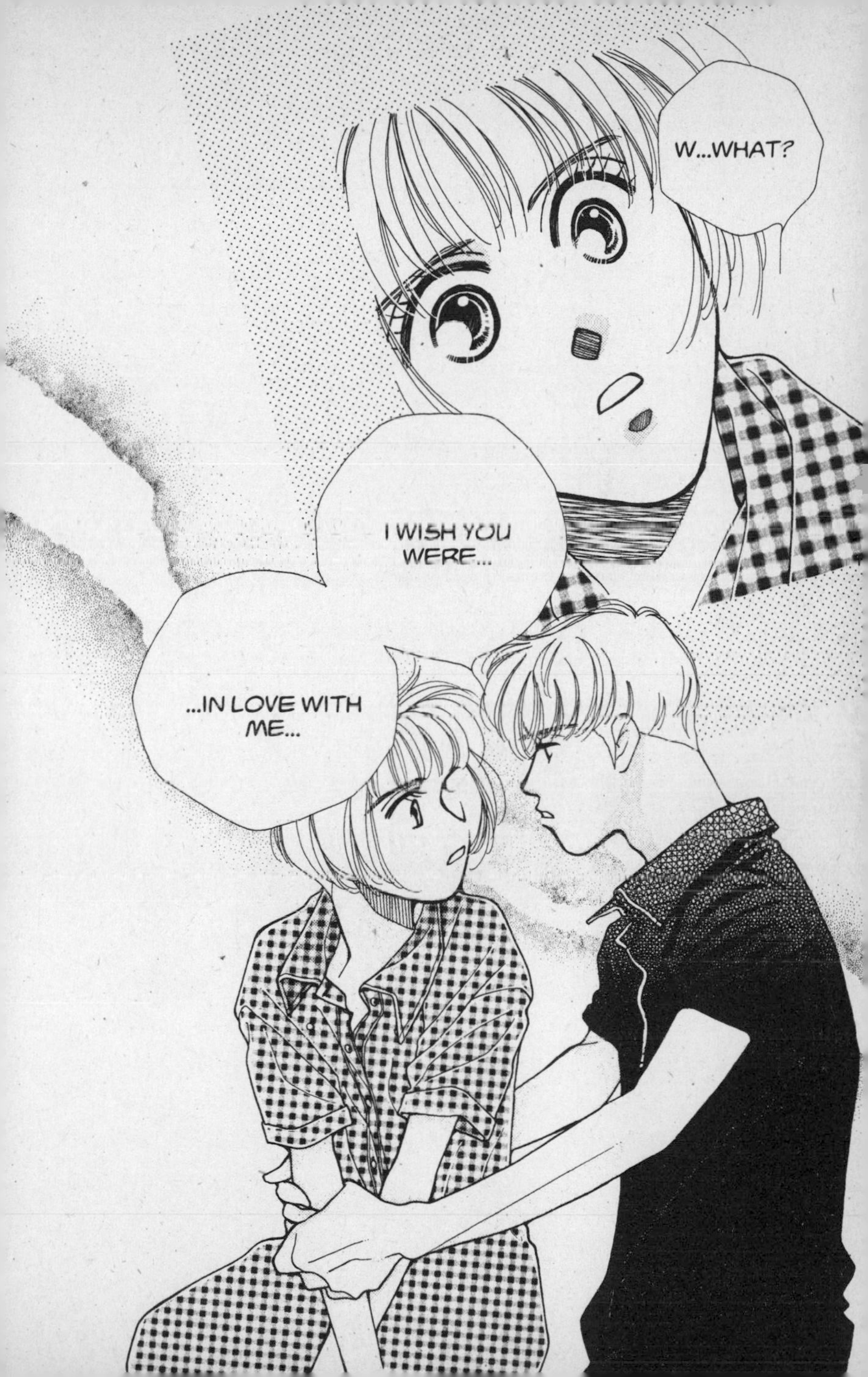
W...WHAT?
I WISH YOU WERE...
...IN LOVE WITH ME...

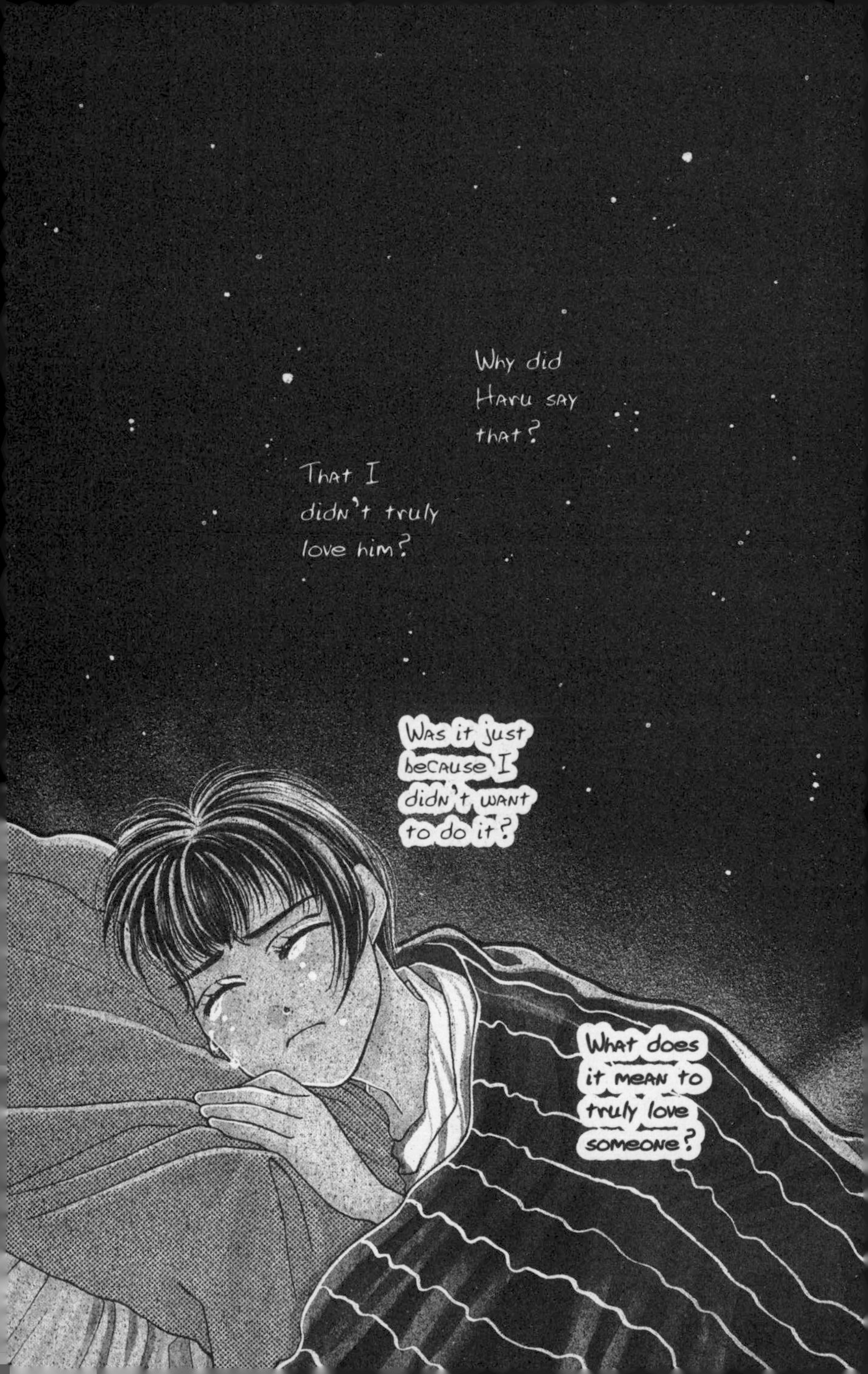
Why did Haru say that?
That I didn't truly love him?
Was it just because I didn't want to do it?
What does it mean to truly love someone?

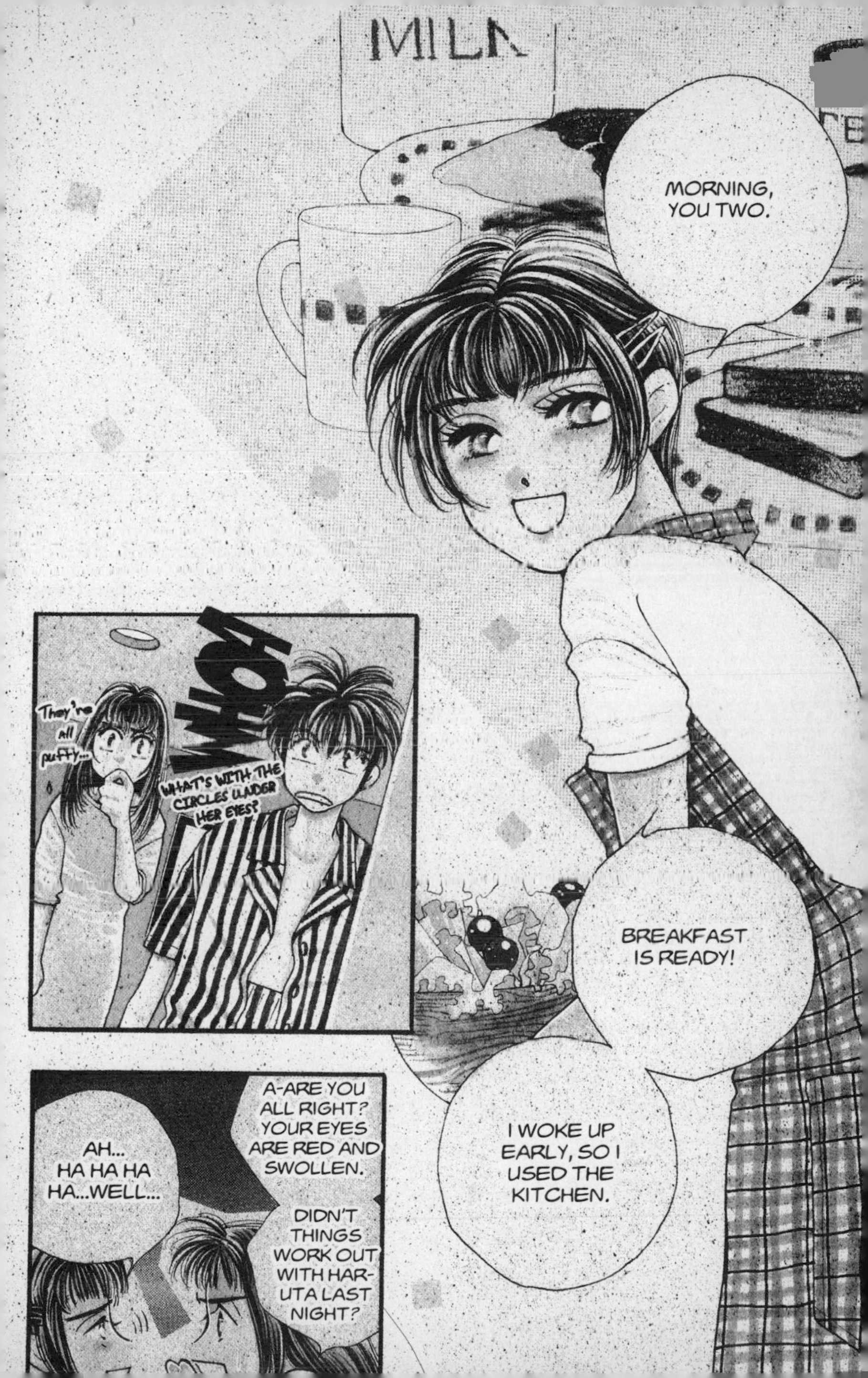
MILK
MORNING, YOU TWO.
BREAKFAST IS READY!
I WOKE UP EARLY, SO I USED THE KITCHEN.
WHOA
WHAT'S WITH THE CIRCLES UNDER HER EYES?
They're all puffy...
A-ARE YOU ALL RIGHT? YOUR EYES ARE RED AND SWOLLEN.
DIDN'T THINGS WORK OUT WITH HAR-UTA LAST NIGHT?
AH... HA HA HA HA...WELL...

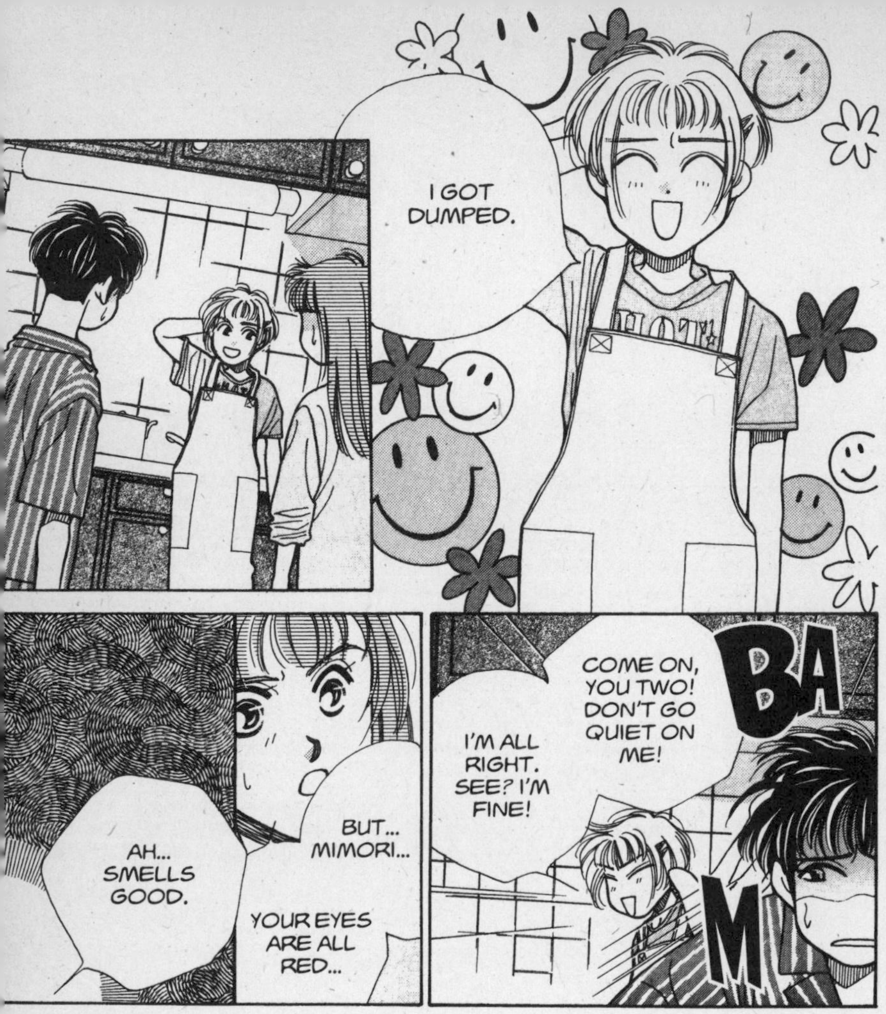
I GOT DUMPED.
COME ON, YOU TWO! DON'T GO QUIET ON ME!
I'M ALL RIGHT. SEE? I'M FINE!
BAM
BUT... MIMORI...
YOUR EYES ARE ALL RED...
AH... SMELLS GOOD.

Question Corner

*By Atsushi Haruta

Part Two

Question: "Why did Haruta wear his hair bobbed in elementary school?"

Answer:

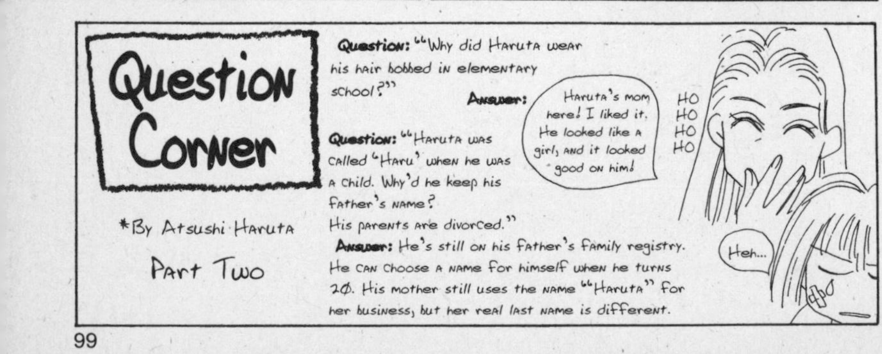
Haruta's mom here! I liked it. He looked like a girl, and it looked good on him!
HO HO HO HO
Heh...

Question: "Haruta was called 'Haru' when he was a child. Why'd he keep his father's name? His parents are divorced."

Answer: He's still on his father's family registry. He can choose a name for himself when he turns 20. His mother still uses the name "Haruta" for her business, but her real last name is different.

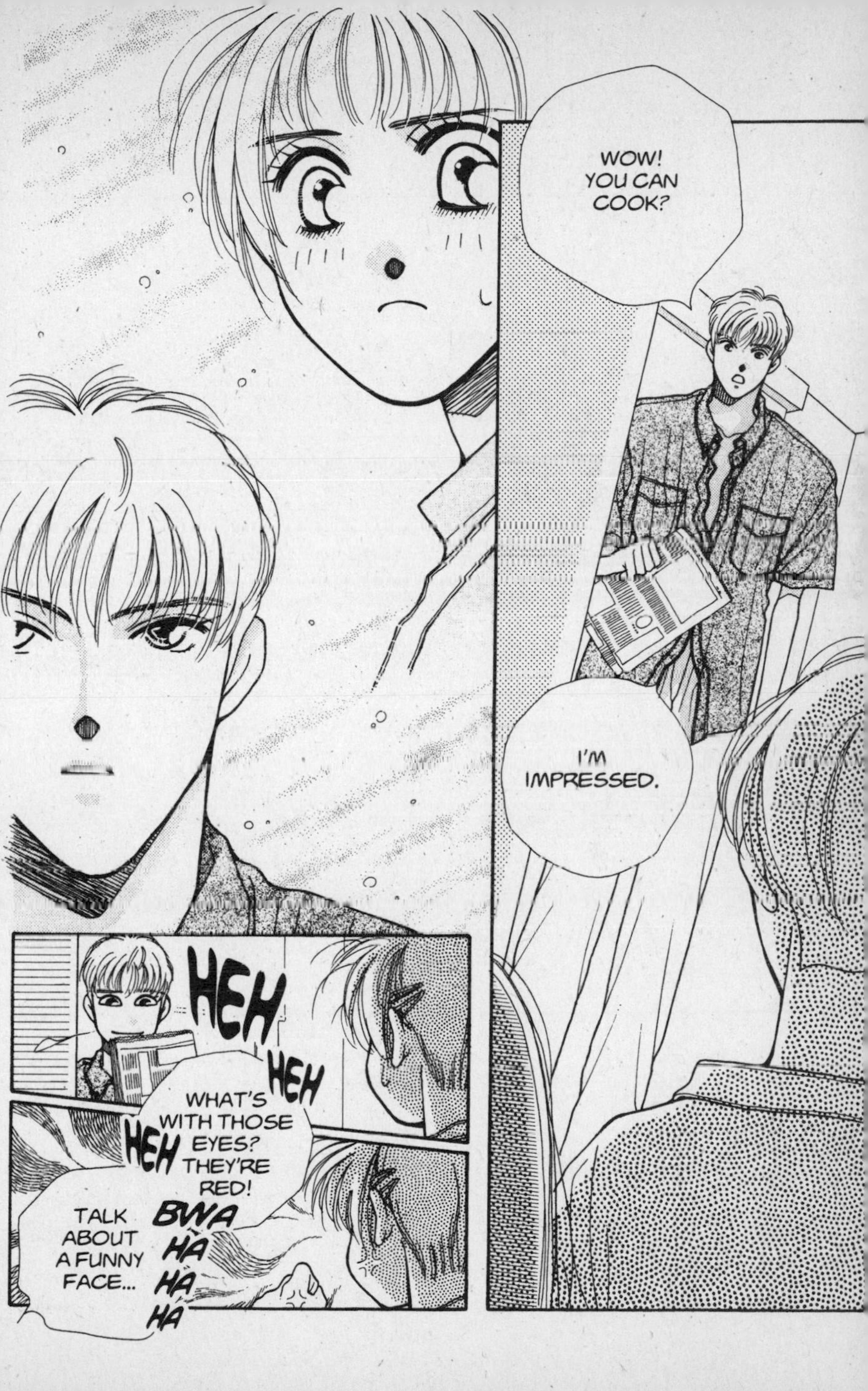
WOW! YOU CAN COOK?
I'M IMPRESSED.
HEH HEH HEH
WHAT'S WITH THOSE EYES? THEY'RE RED!
BWA HA HA HA
TALK ABOUT A FUNNY FACE...

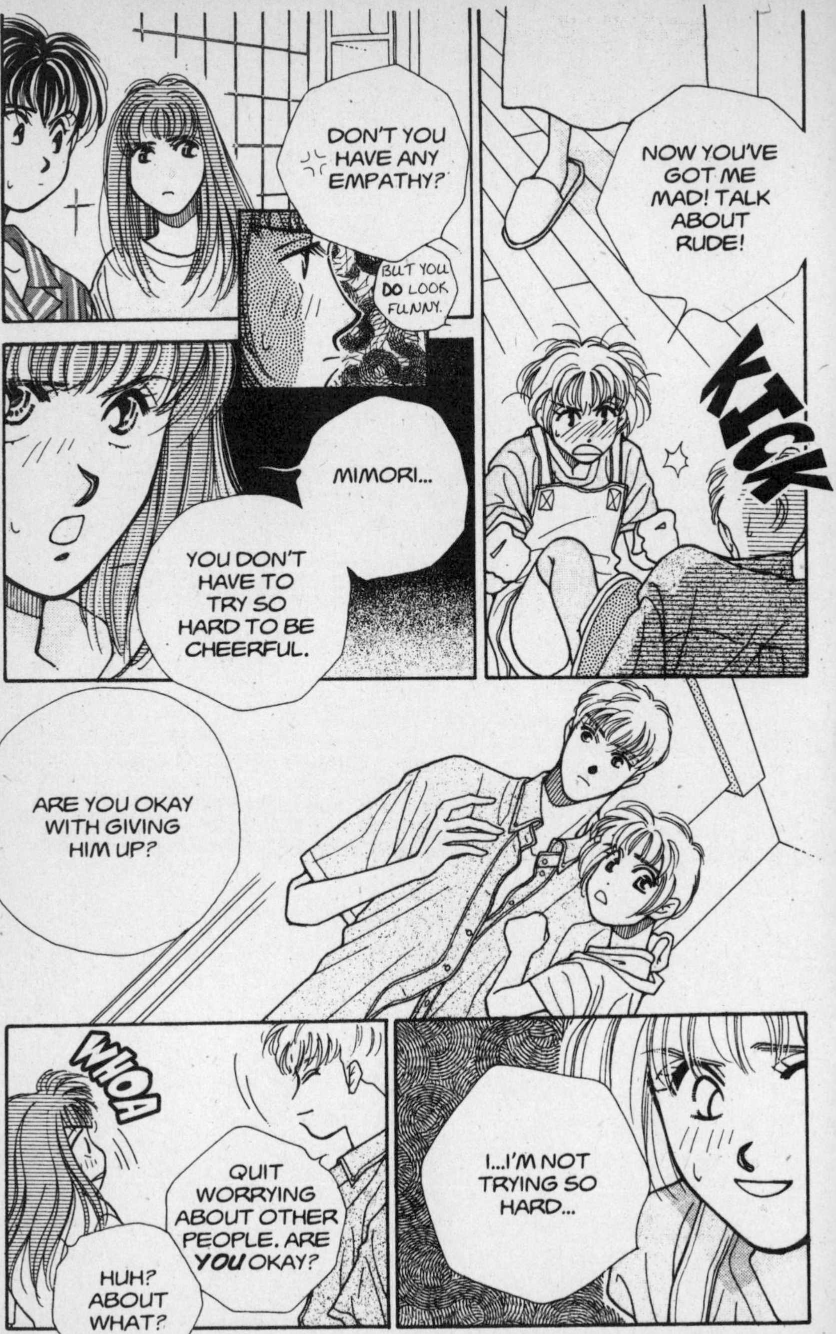
BUT YOU DO LOOK FUNNY.
DON'T YOU HAVE ANY EMPATHY?
NOW YOU'VE GOT ME MAD! TALK ABOUT RUDE!
KICK
MIMORI...
YOU DON'T HAVE TO TRY SO HARD TO BE CHEERFUL.
ARE YOU OKAY WITH GIVING HIM UP?
WHOA
QUIT WORRYING ABOUT OTHER PEOPLE. ARE ***YOU*** OKAY?
HUH? ABOUT WHAT?
I...I'M NOT TRYING SO HARD...

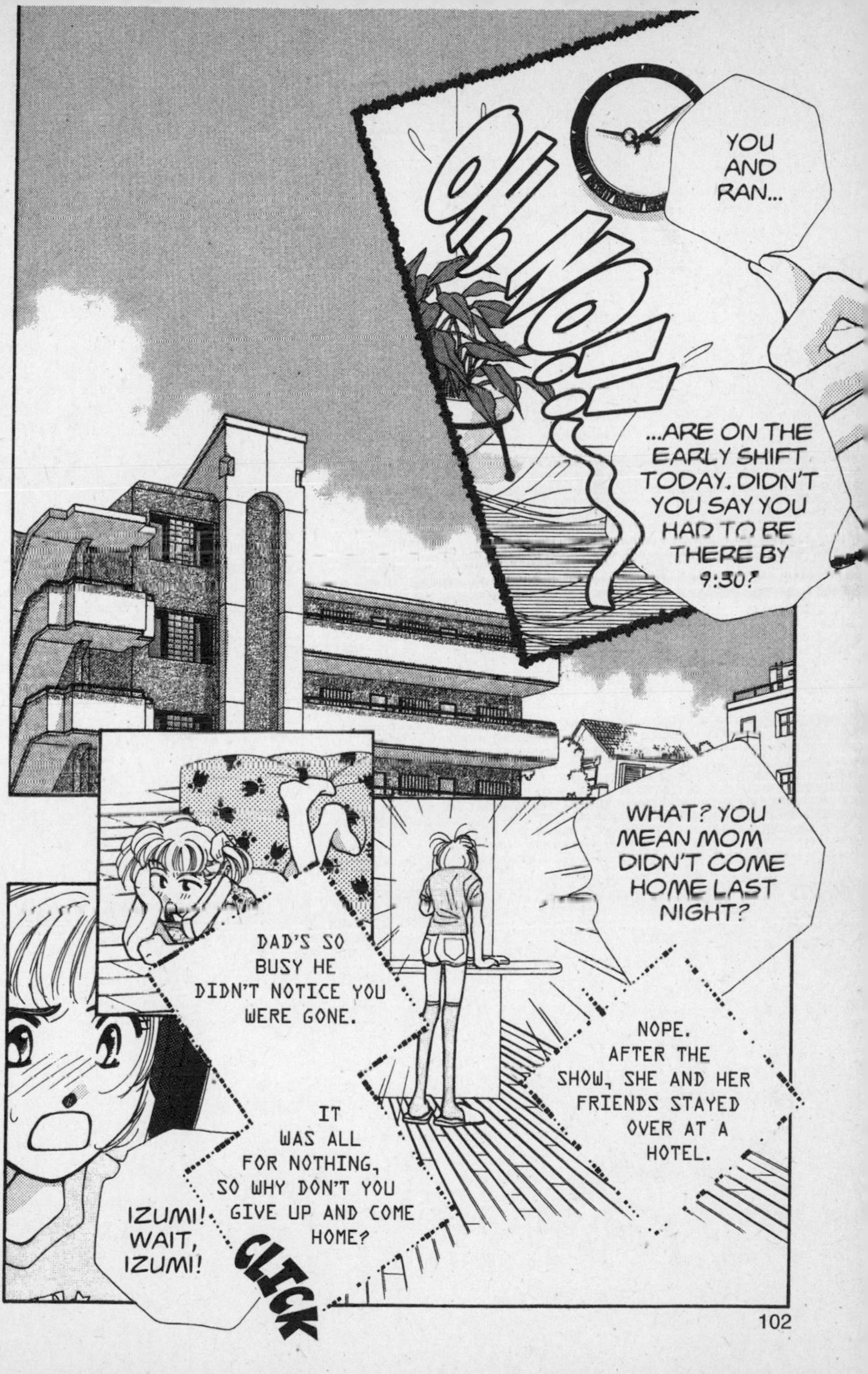
YOU AND RAN...
OH, NO!!...
...ARE ON THE EARLY SHIFT TODAY. DIDN'T YOU SAY YOU HAD TO BE THERE BY 9:30?
WHAT? YOU MEAN MOM DIDN'T COME HOME LAST NIGHT?
NOPE. AFTER THE SHOW, SHE AND HER FRIENDS STAYED OVER AT A HOTEL.
DAD'S SO BUSY HE DIDN'T NOTICE YOU WERE GONE.
IT WAS ALL FOR NOTHING, SO WHY DON'T YOU GIVE UP AND COME HOME?
IZUMI! WAIT, IZUMI!
CLICK

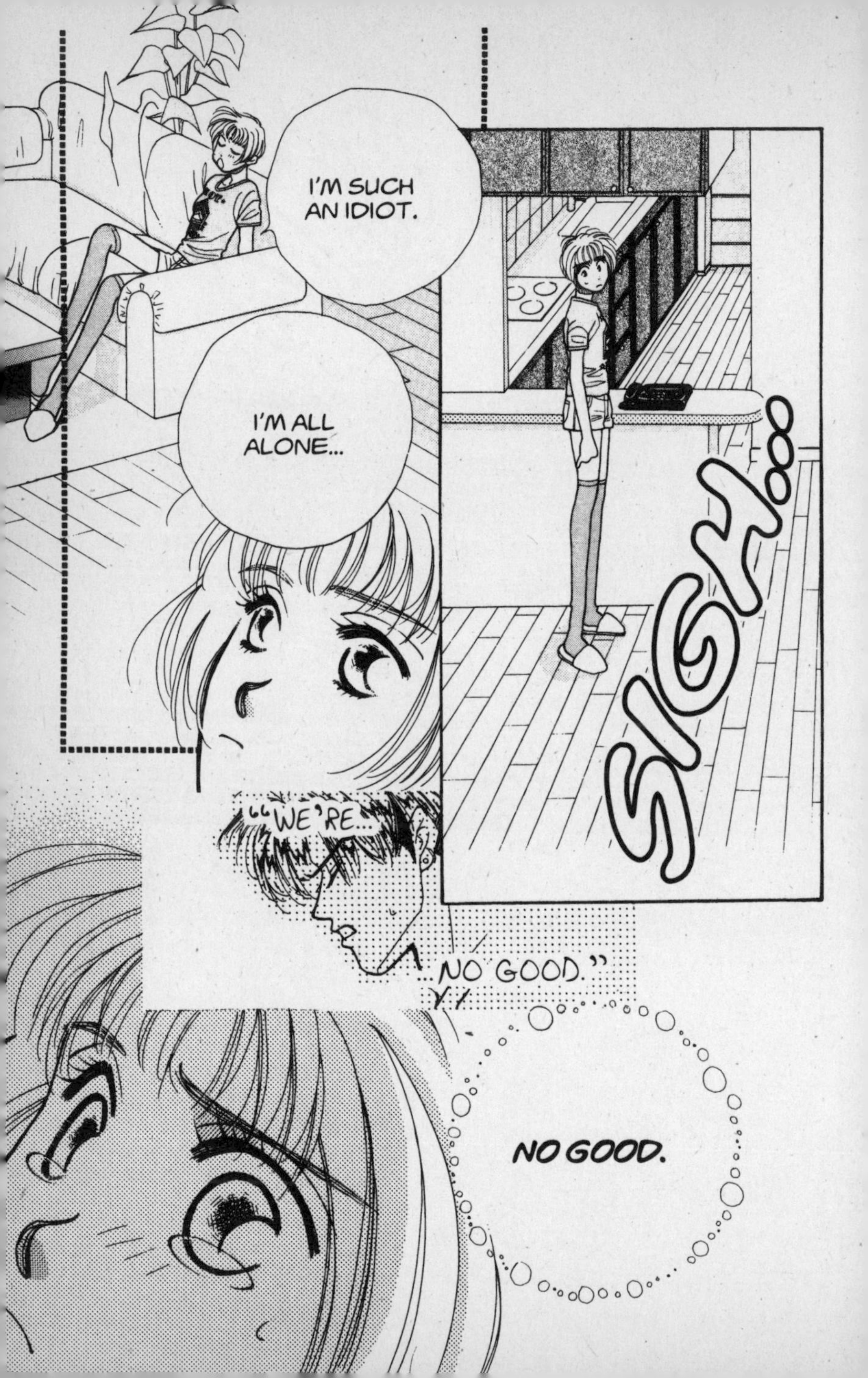
SIGH...
I'M SUCH AN IDIOT.
I'M ALL ALONE...
"WE'RE...
...NO GOOD."
NO GOOD.

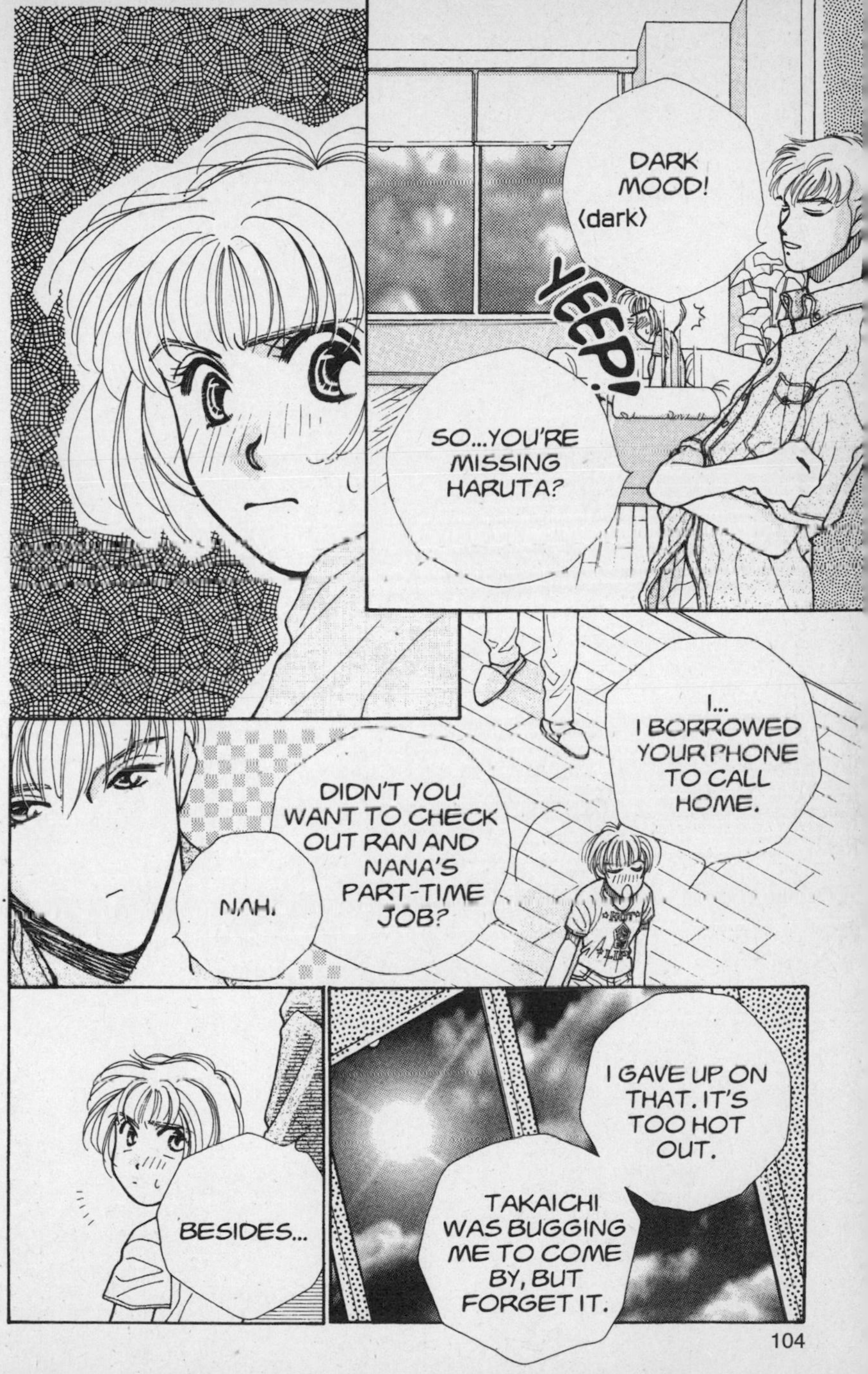
DARK MOOD!
〈dark〉
YEEP!
SO...YOU'RE MISSING HARUTA?
I... I BORROWED YOUR PHONE TO CALL HOME.
DIDN'T YOU WANT TO CHECK OUT RAN AND NANA'S PART-TIME JOB?
NAH.
I GAVE UP ON THAT. IT'S TOO HOT OUT.
TAKAICHI WAS BUGGING ME TO COME BY, BUT FORGET IT.
BESIDES...

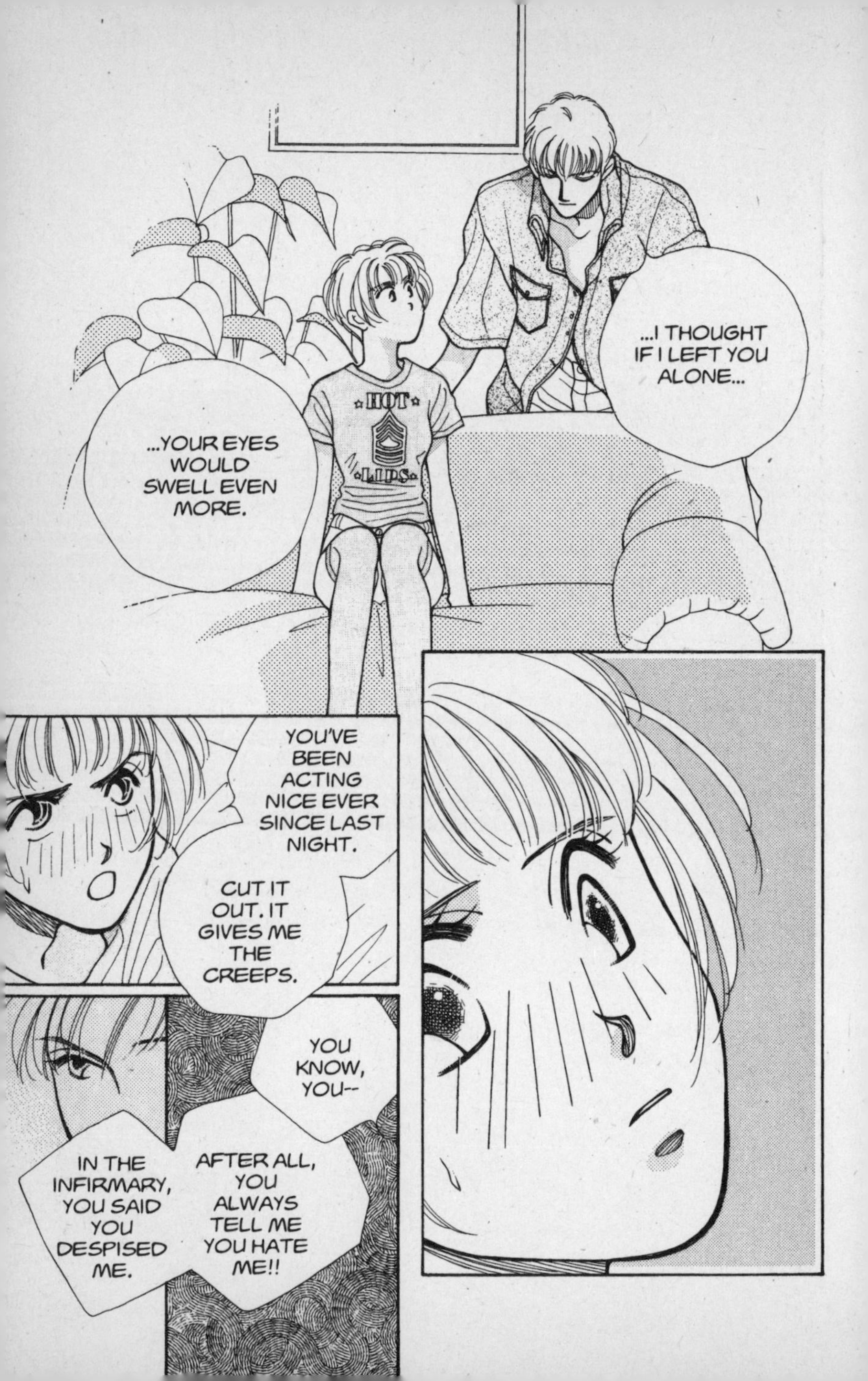
...I THOUGHT IF I LEFT YOU ALONE...
...YOUR EYES WOULD SWELL EVEN MORE.
HOT LIPS
YOU'VE BEEN ACTING NICE EVER SINCE LAST NIGHT.
CUT IT OUT. IT GIVES ME THE CREEPS.
YOU KNOW, YOU--
AFTER ALL, YOU ALWAYS TELL ME YOU HATE ME!!
IN THE INFIRMARY, YOU SAID YOU DESPISED ME.

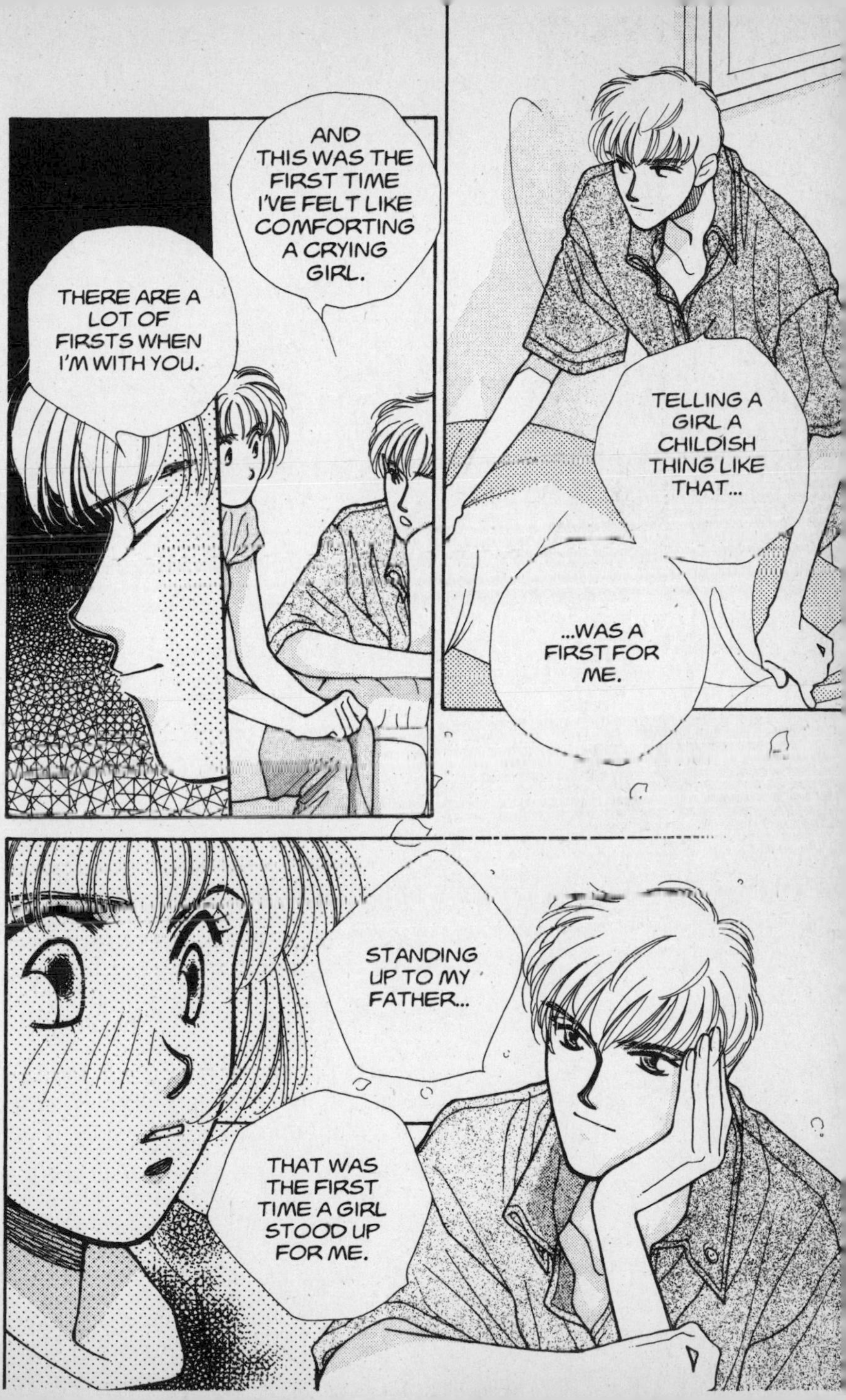
TELLING A GIRL A CHILDISH THING LIKE THAT...
...WAS A FIRST FOR ME.
AND THIS WAS THE FIRST TIME I'VE FELT LIKE COMFORTING A CRYING GIRL.
THERE ARE A LOT OF FIRSTS WHEN I'M WITH YOU.
STANDING UP TO MY FATHER...
THAT WAS THE FIRST TIME A GIRL STOOD UP FOR ME.

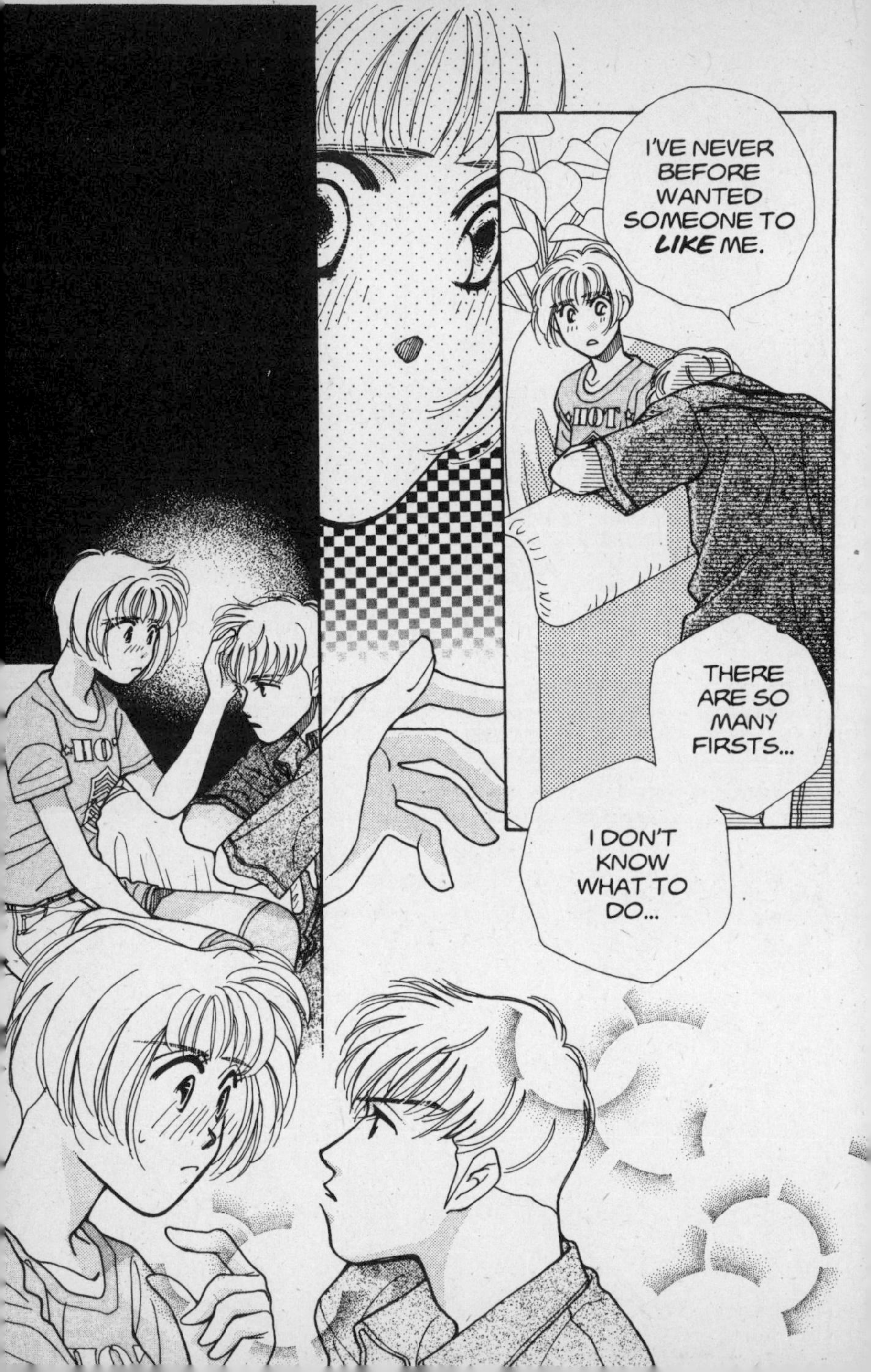
I'VE NEVER BEFORE WANTED SOMEONE TO **LIKE** ME.
THERE ARE SO MANY FIRSTS...
I DON'T KNOW WHAT TO DO...
HOT
HO

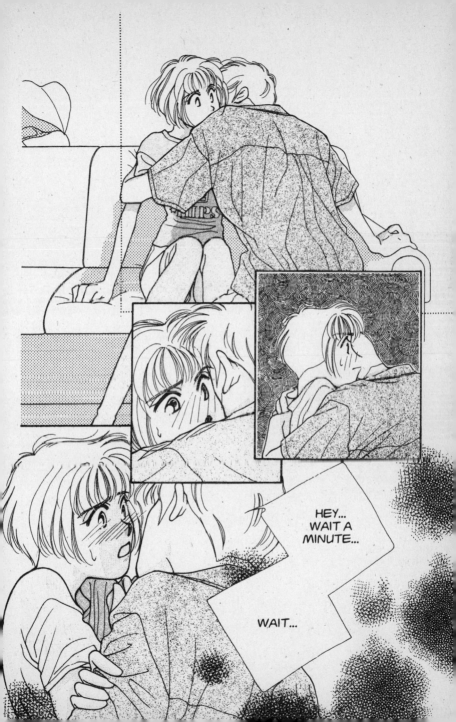

HEY...
WAIT A
MINUTE...

WAIT...

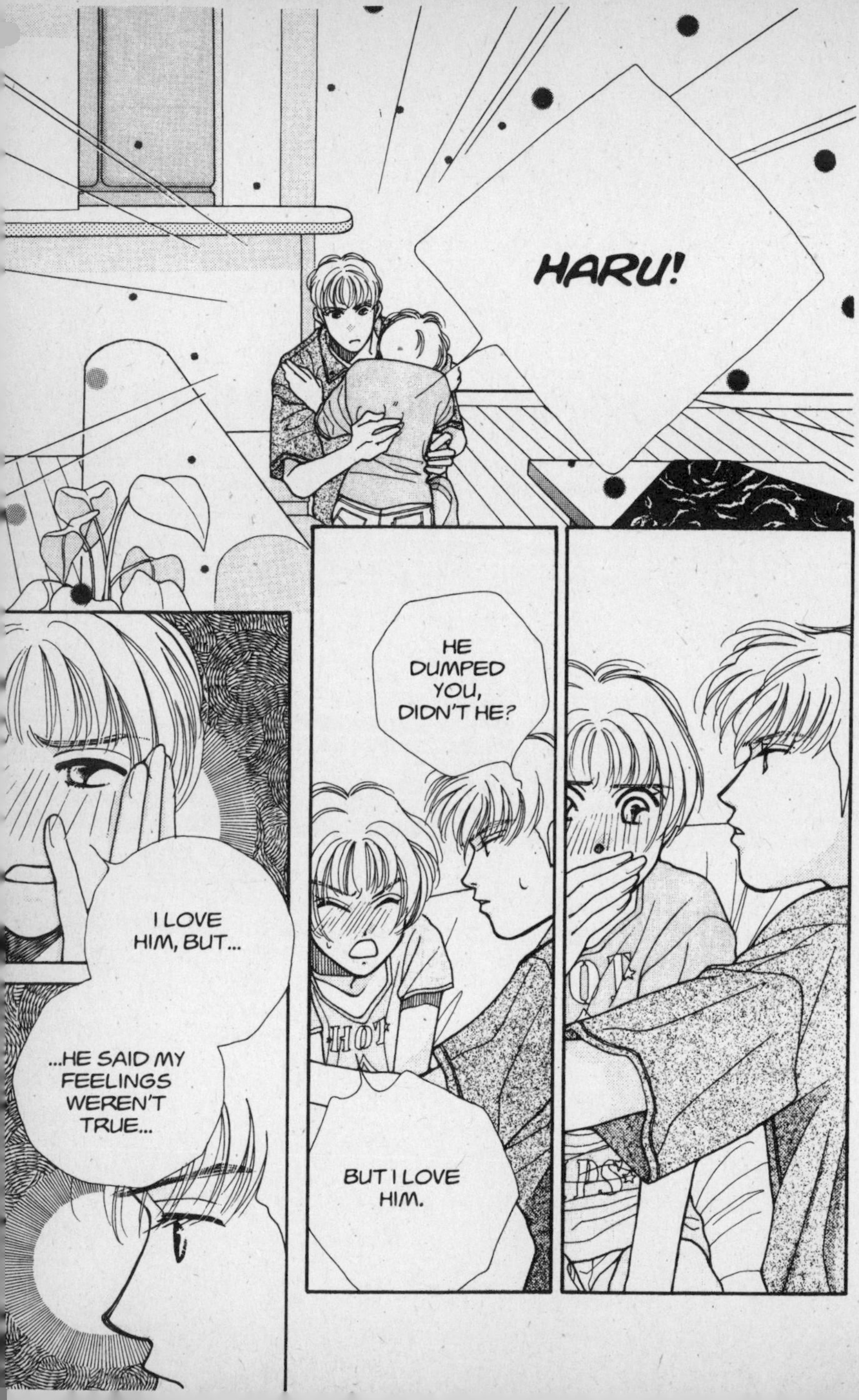
HARU!
HE DUMPED YOU, DIDN'T HE?
BUT I LOVE HIM.
I LOVE HIM, BUT...
...HE SAID MY FEELINGS WEREN'T TRUE...

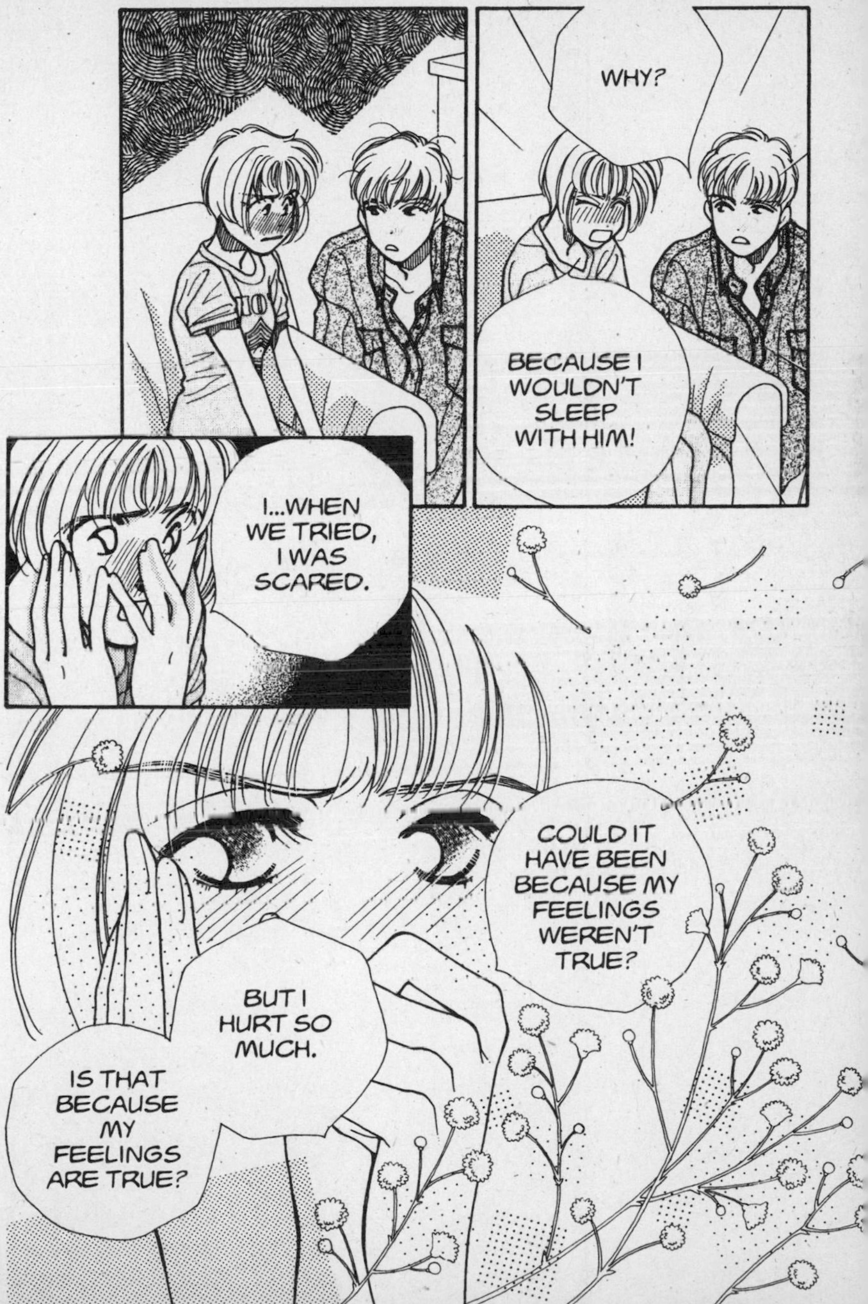
WHY?
BECAUSE I WOULDN'T SLEEP WITH HIM!
I...WHEN WE TRIED, I WAS SCARED.
COULD IT HAVE BEEN BECAUSE MY FEELINGS WEREN'T TRUE?
BUT I HURT SO MUCH.
IS THAT BECAUSE MY FEELINGS ARE TRUE?

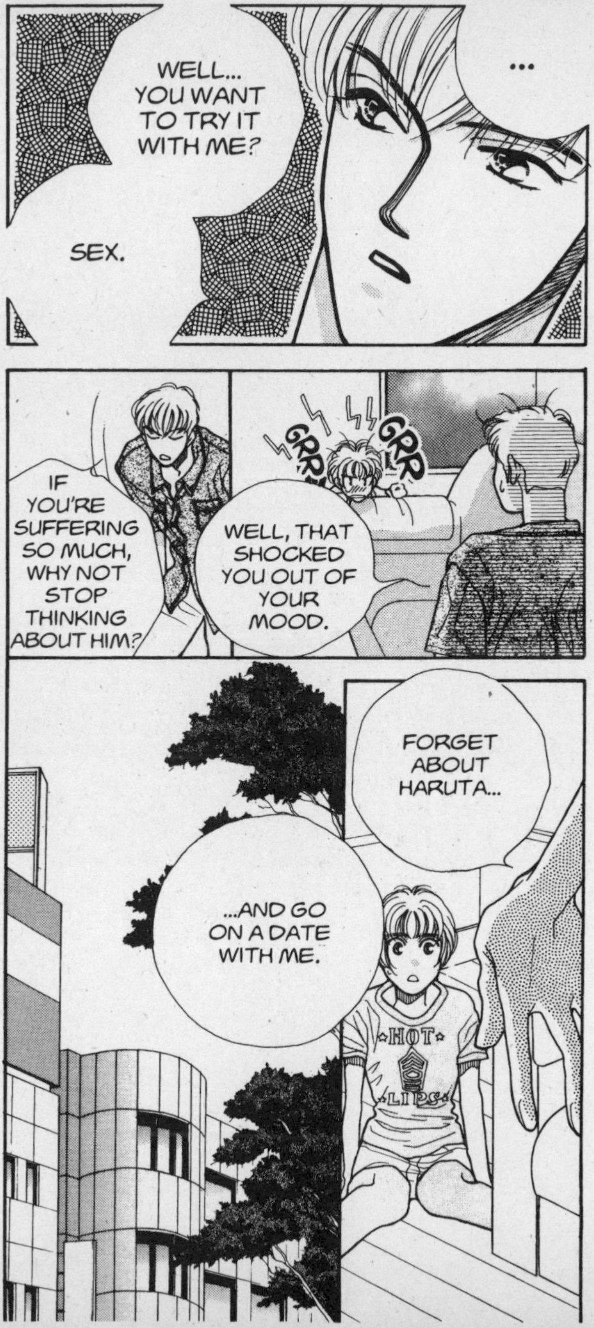
...
WELL... YOU WANT TO TRY IT WITH ME?
SEX.
GRR
GRR
WELL, THAT SHOCKED YOU OUT OF YOUR MOOD.
IF YOU'RE SUFFERING SO MUCH, WHY NOT STOP THINKING ABOUT HIM?
FORGET ABOUT HARUTA...
...AND GO ON A DATE WITH ME.
HOT
LIPS

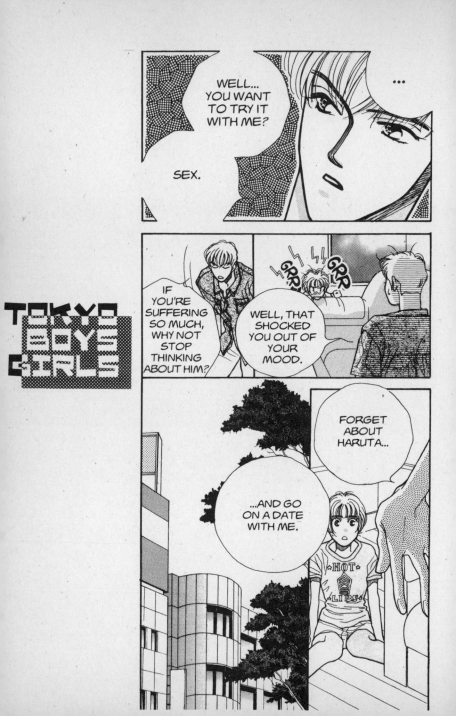

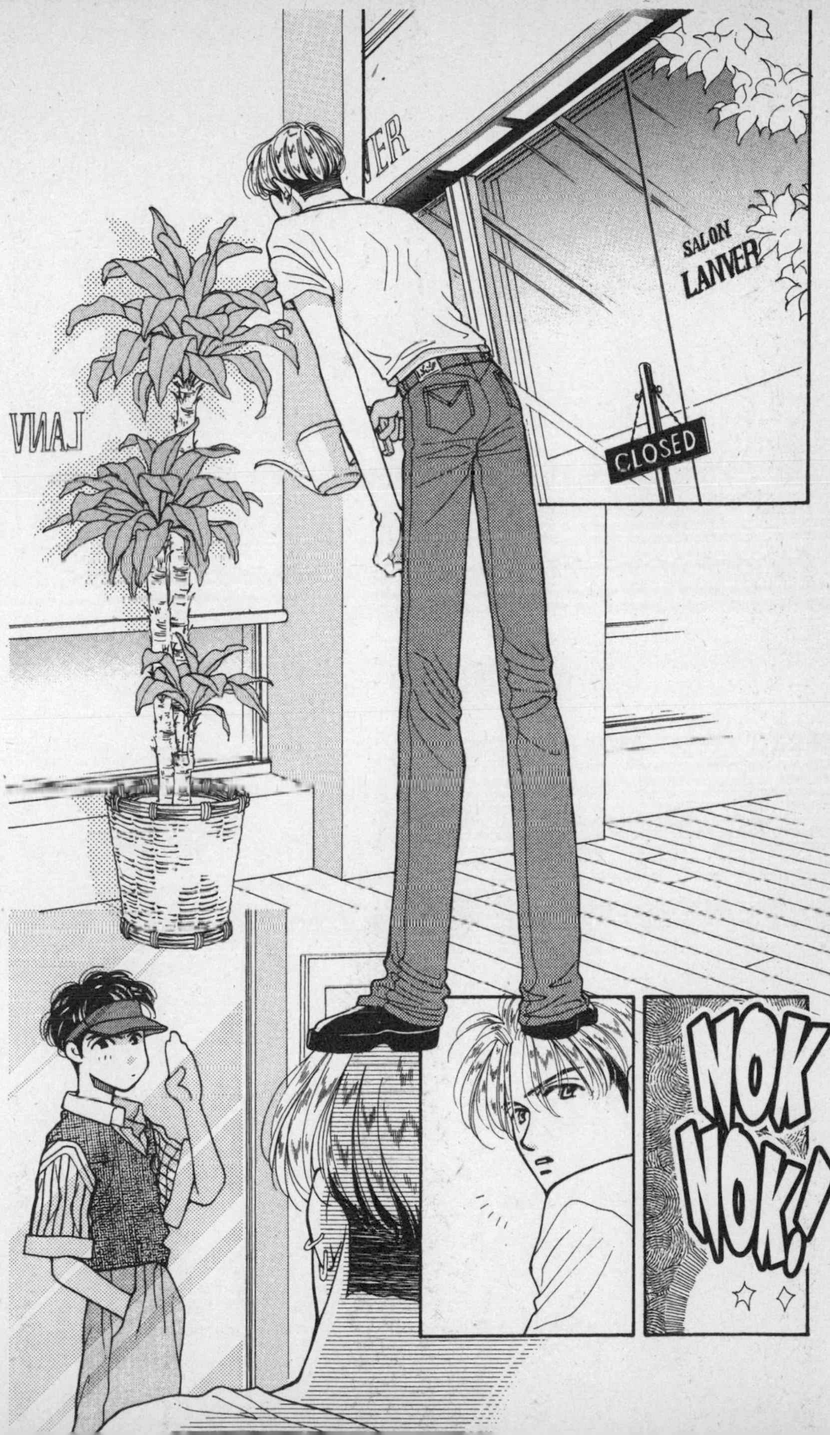
SALON
LANVER
CLOSED
NOK NOK!

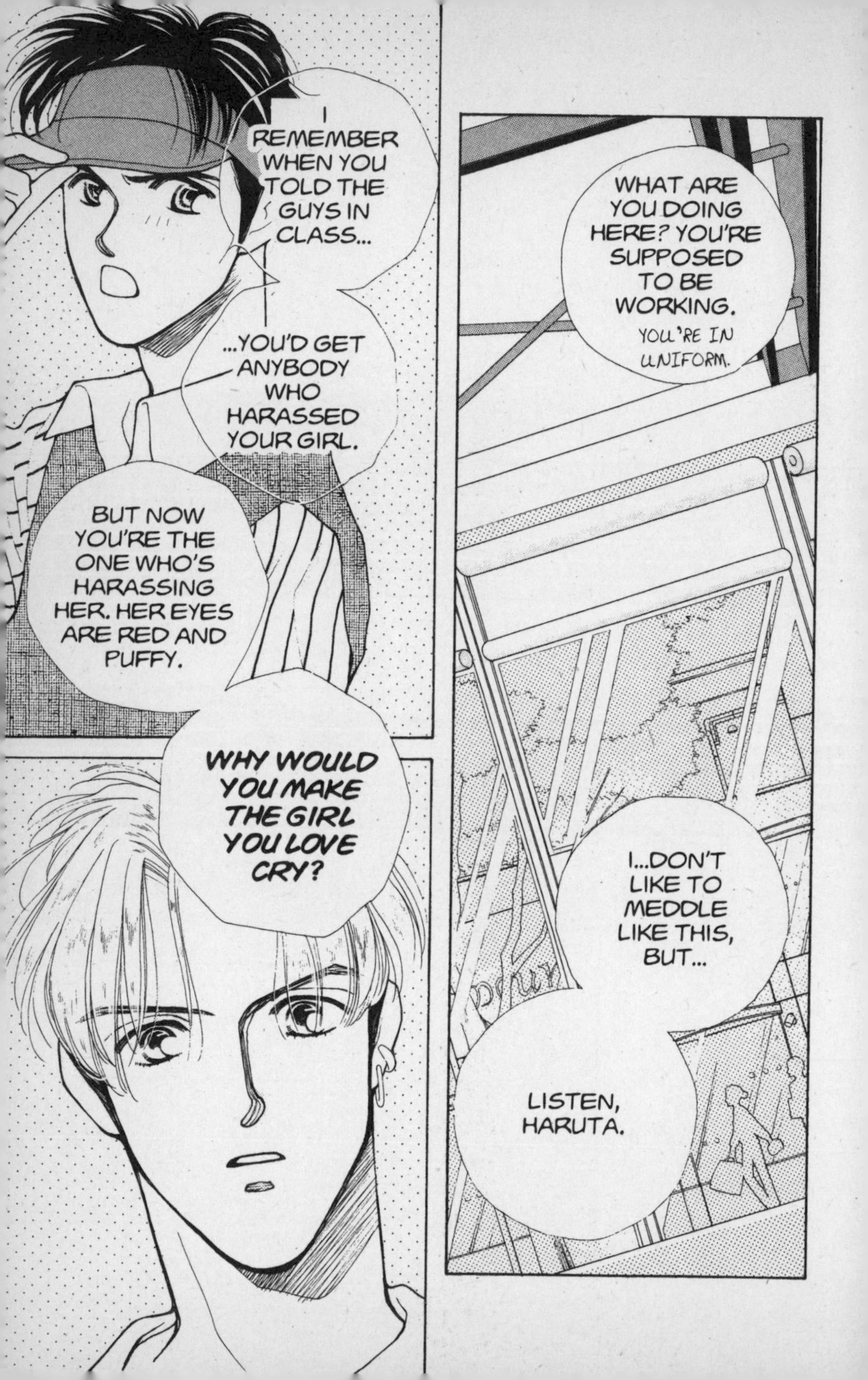
WHAT ARE YOU DOING HERE? YOU'RE SUPPOSED TO BE WORKING.
YOU'RE IN UNIFORM.
I...DON'T LIKE TO MEDDLE LIKE THIS, BUT...
LISTEN, HARUTA.
I REMEMBER WHEN YOU TOLD THE GUYS IN CLASS...
...YOU'D GET ANYBODY WHO HARASSED YOUR GIRL.
BUT NOW YOU'RE THE ONE WHO'S HARASSING HER. HER EYES ARE RED AND PUFFY.
WHY WOULD YOU MAKE THE GIRL YOU LOVE CRY?

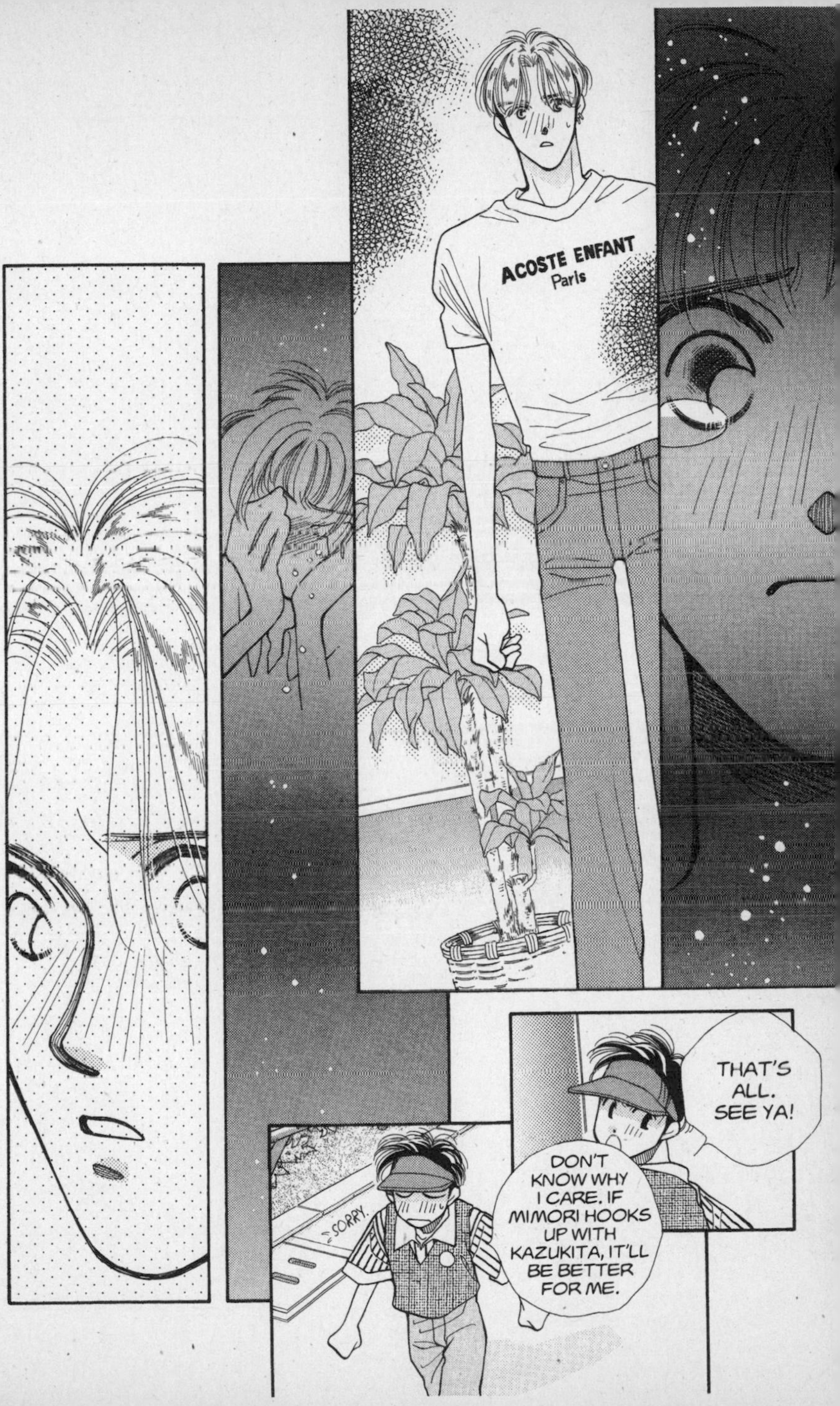
ACOSTE ENFANT
Paris
THAT'S ALL. SEE YA!
DON'T KNOW WHY I CARE. IF MIMORI HOOKS UP WITH KAZUKITA, IT'LL BE BETTER FOR ME.
SORRY.

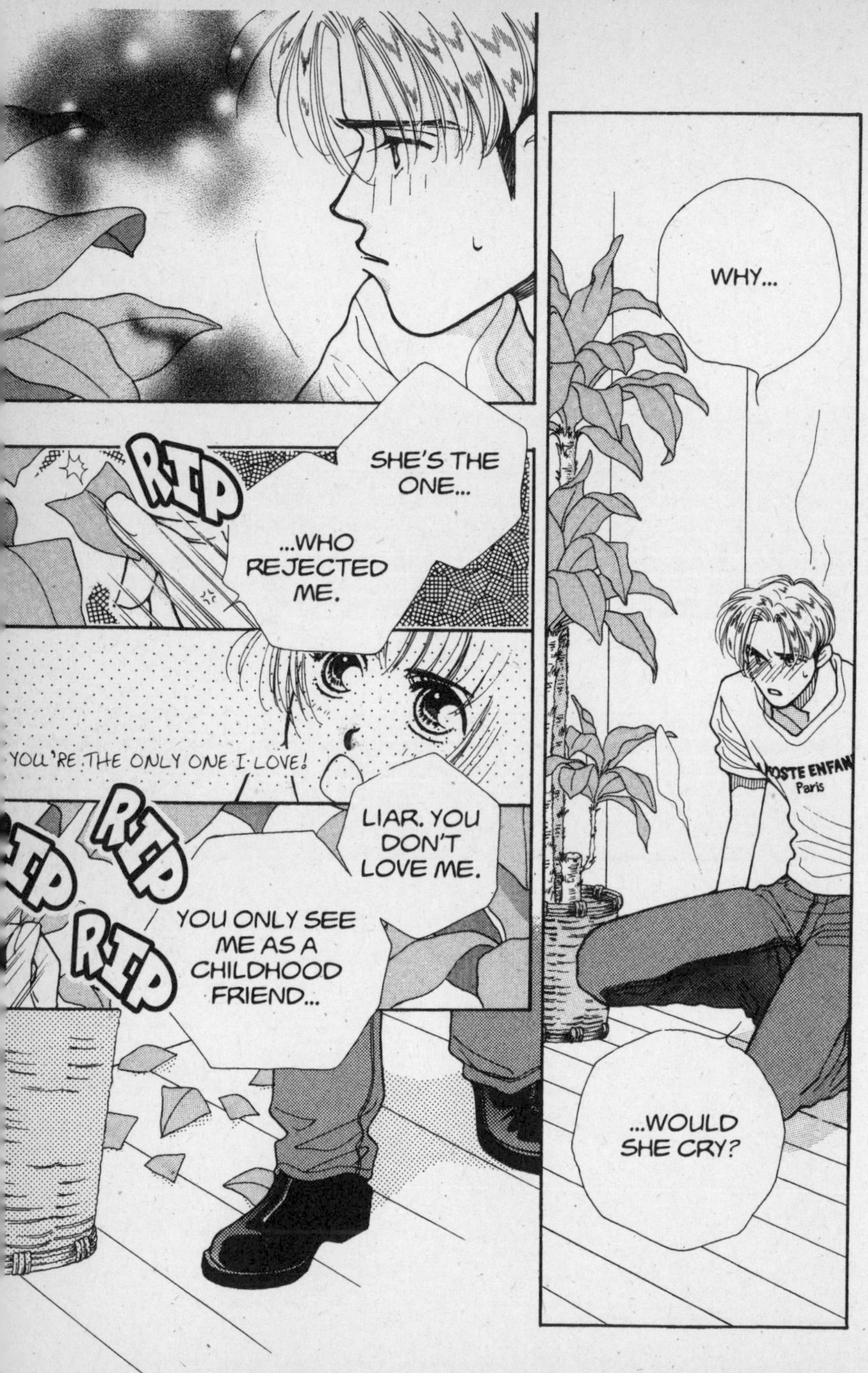
WHY...
...WOULD SHE CRY?
SHE'S THE ONE...
...WHO REJECTED ME.
RIP
YOU'RE THE ONLY ONE I LOVE!
LIAR. YOU DON'T LOVE ME.
RIP
RIP
RIP
YOU ONLY SEE ME AS A CHILDHOOD FRIEND...
POSTE ENFAN
Paris

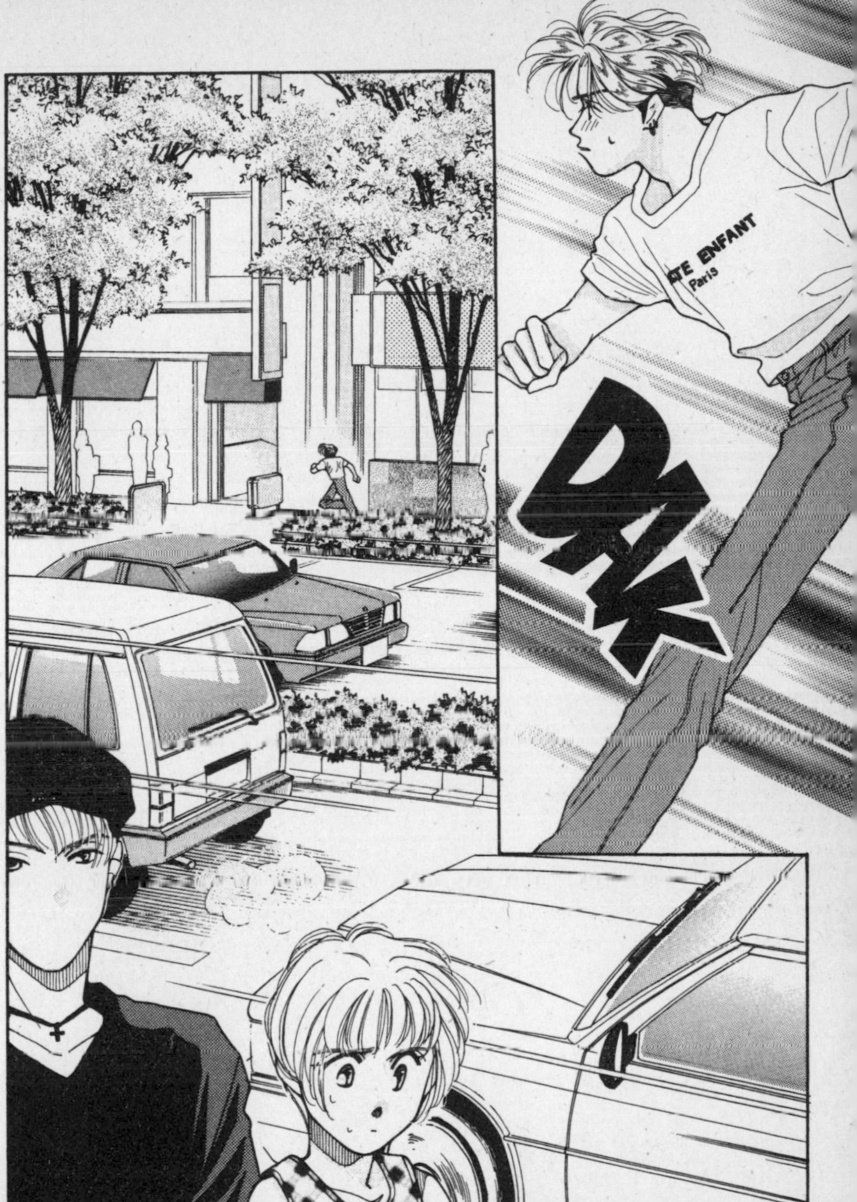
DAK
TE ENFANT
Paris

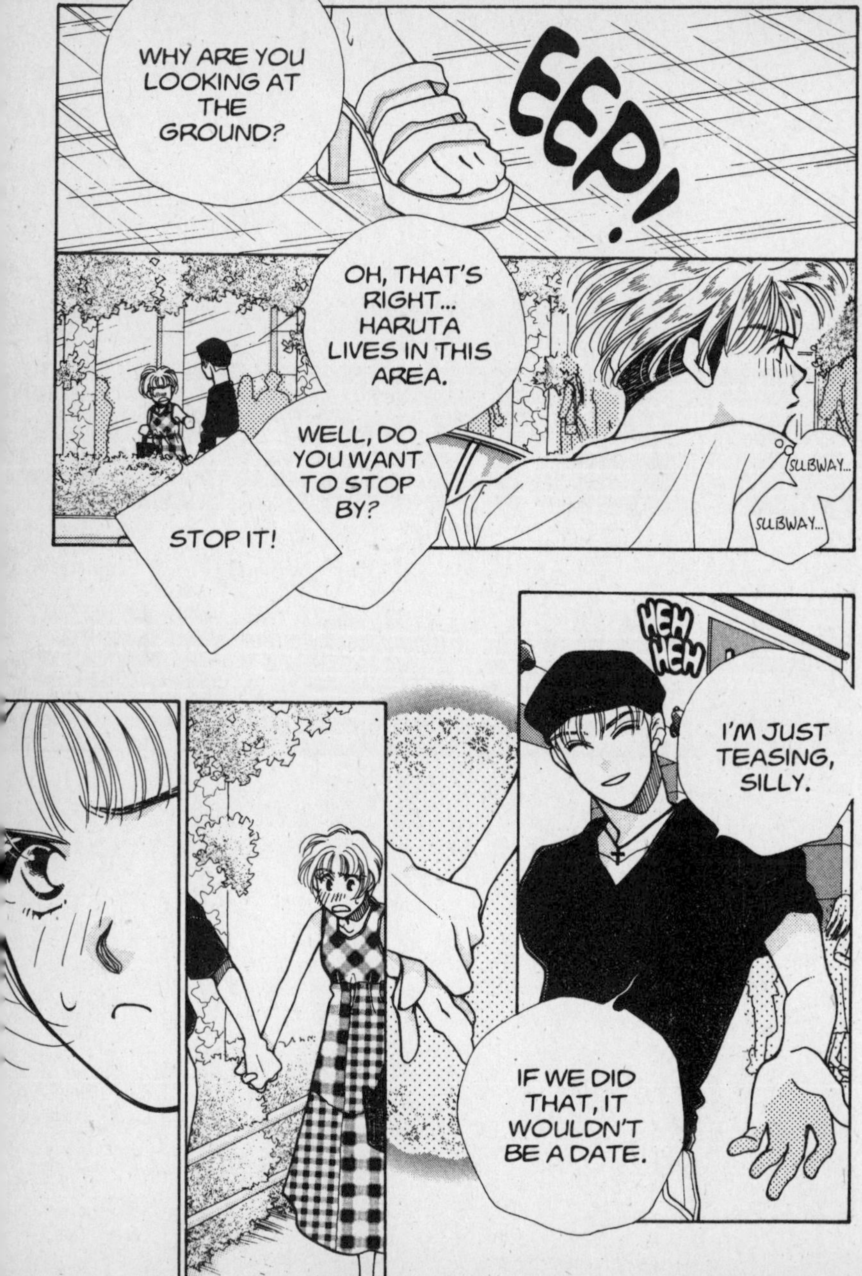
EEP!
WHY ARE YOU LOOKING AT THE GROUND?
SUBWAY...
SUBWAY...
OH, THAT'S RIGHT... HARUTA LIVES IN THIS AREA.
WELL, DO YOU WANT TO STOP BY?
STOP IT!
HEH HEH
I'M JUST TEASING, SILLY.
IF WE DID THAT, IT WOULDN'T BE A DATE.

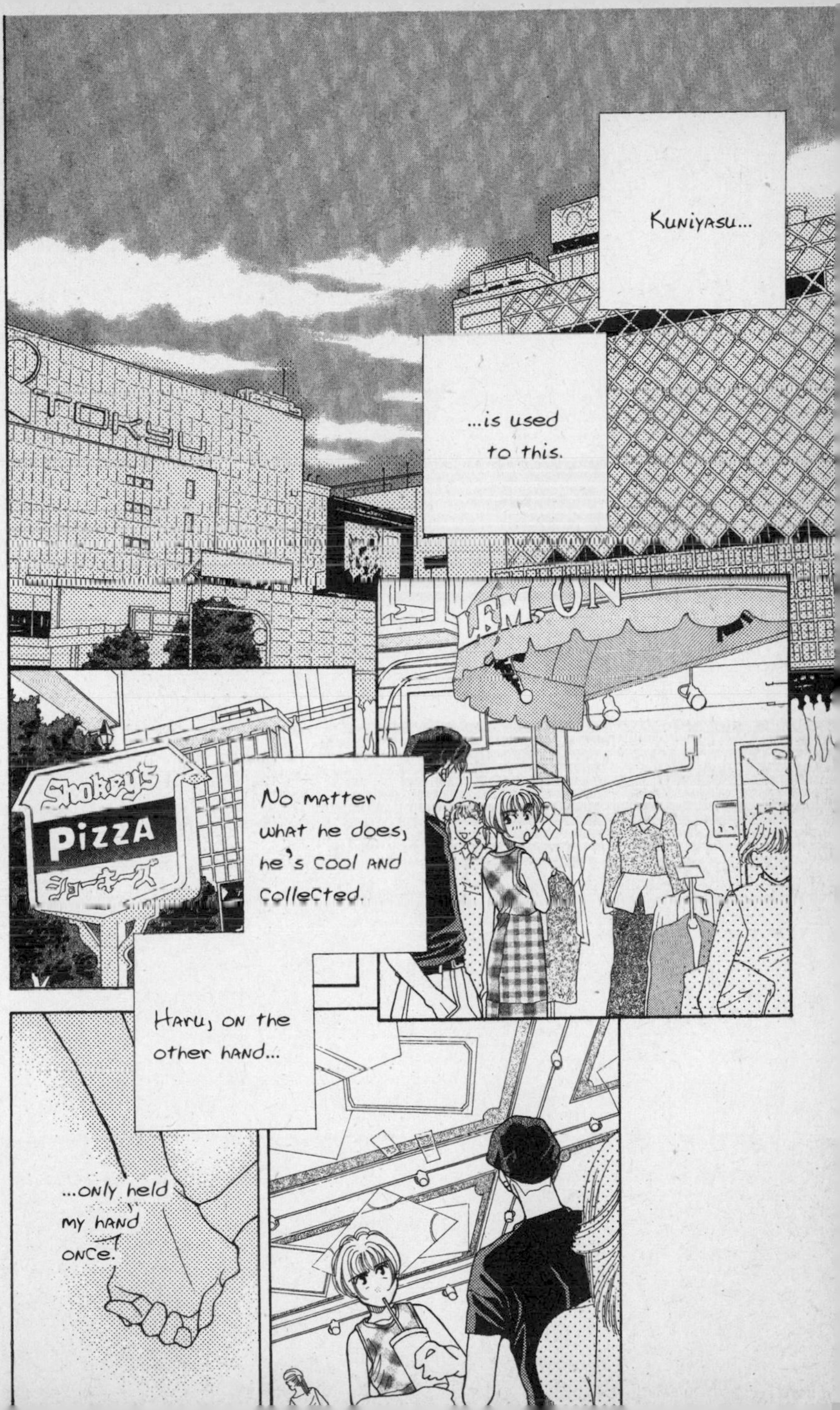
Kuniyasu...
...is used to this.
TOKYU
LEM.ON
No matter what he does, he's cool and collected.
Shokey's
PIZZA
ショーキーズ
Haru, on the other hand...
...only held my hand once.

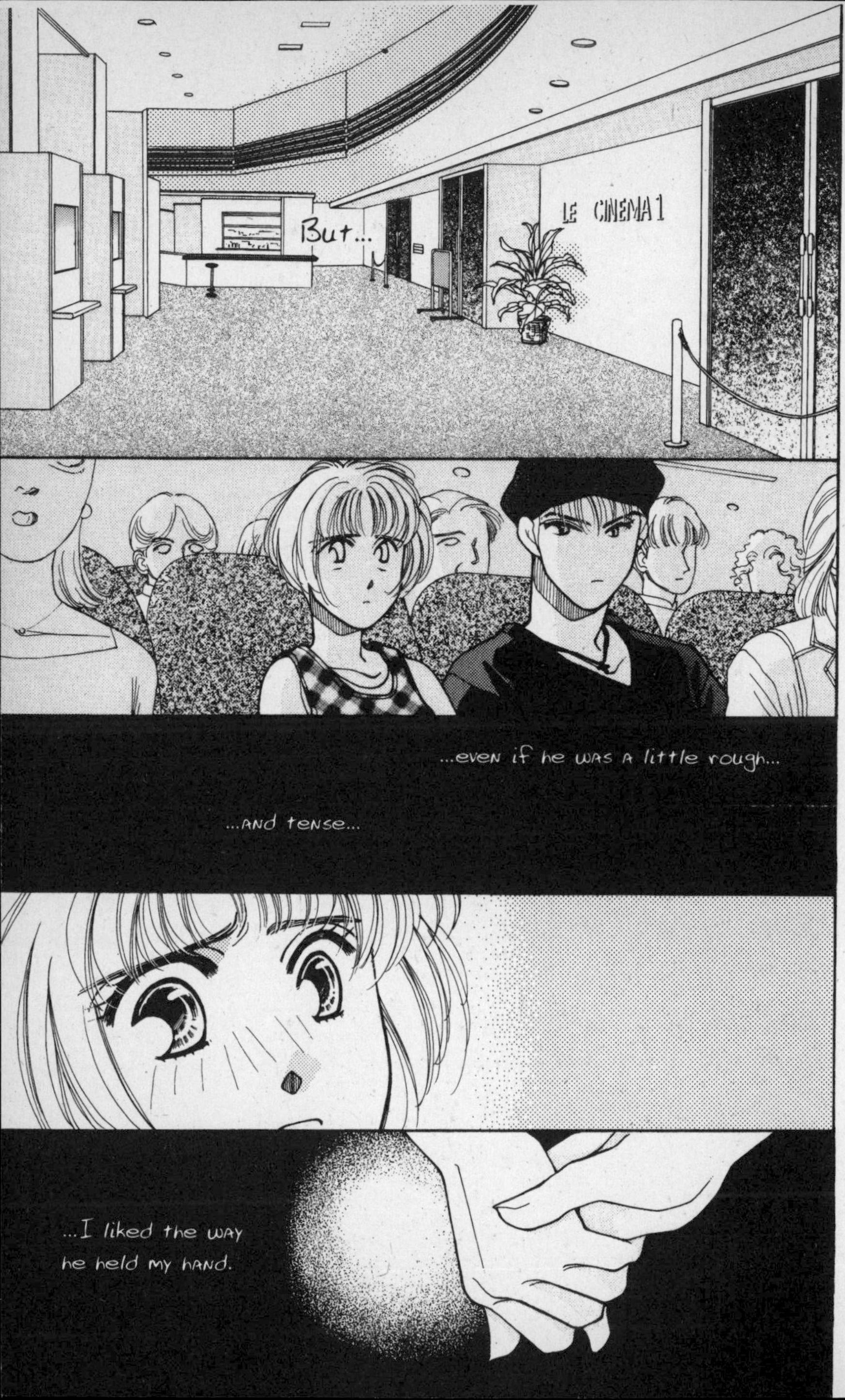
LE CINEMA 1
But...
...even if he was a little rough...
...and tense...
...I liked the way
he held my hand.

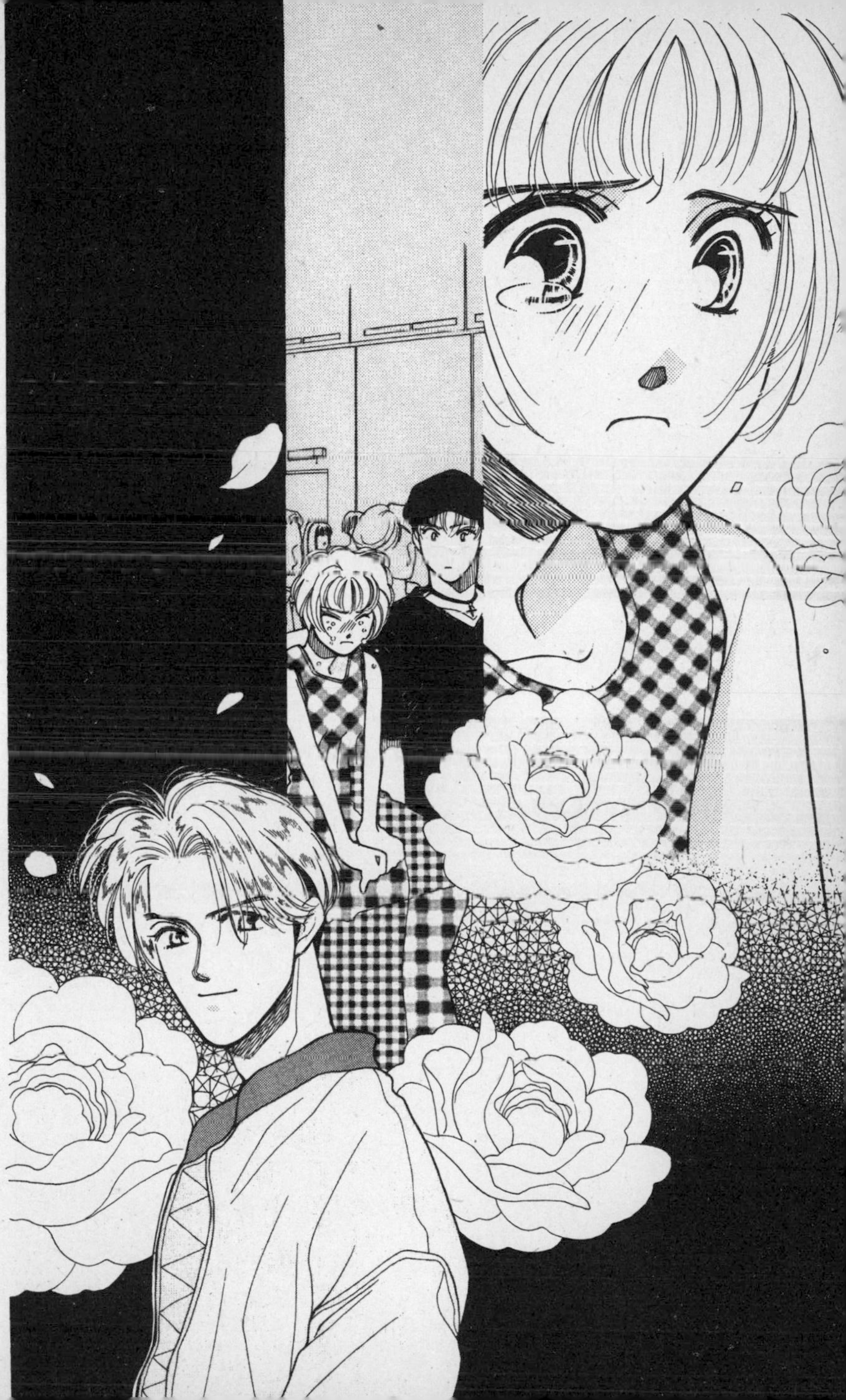

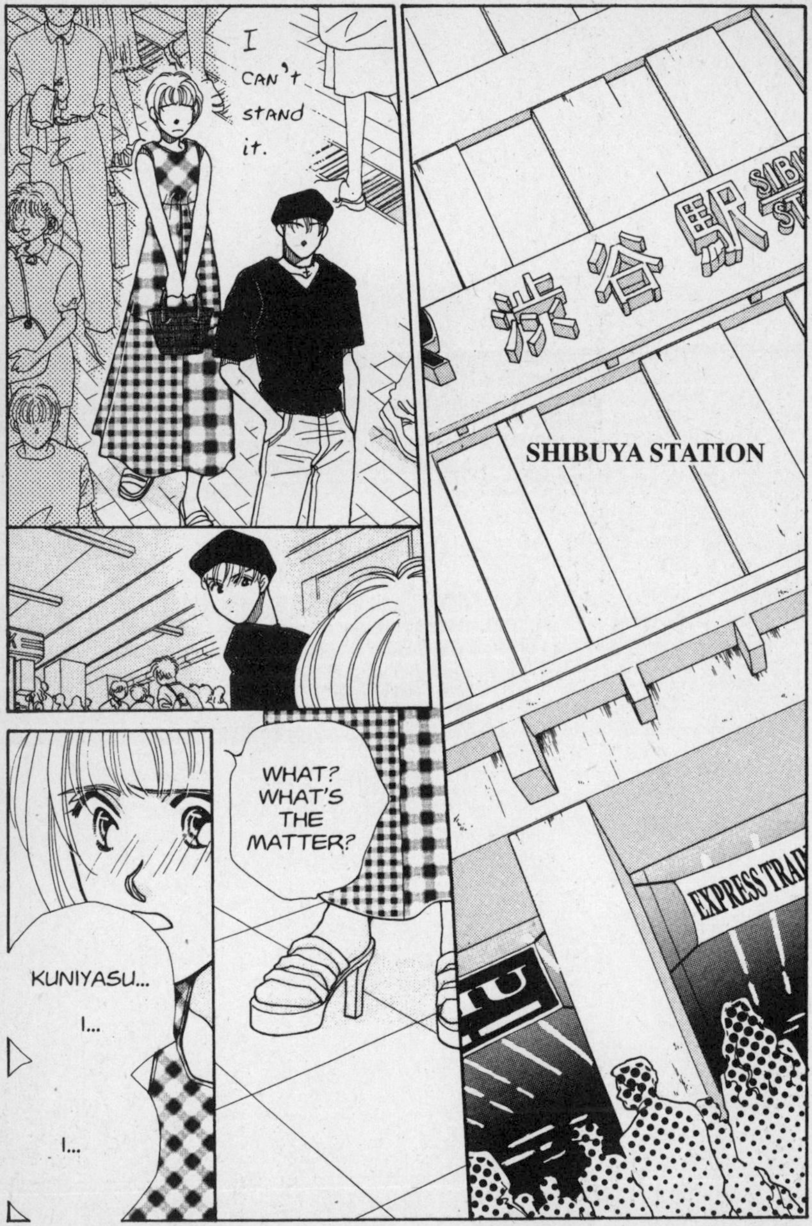
渋谷駅
SHIBUYA STATION
I can't stand it.
WHAT? WHAT'S THE MATTER?
KUNIYASU...
I...
I...

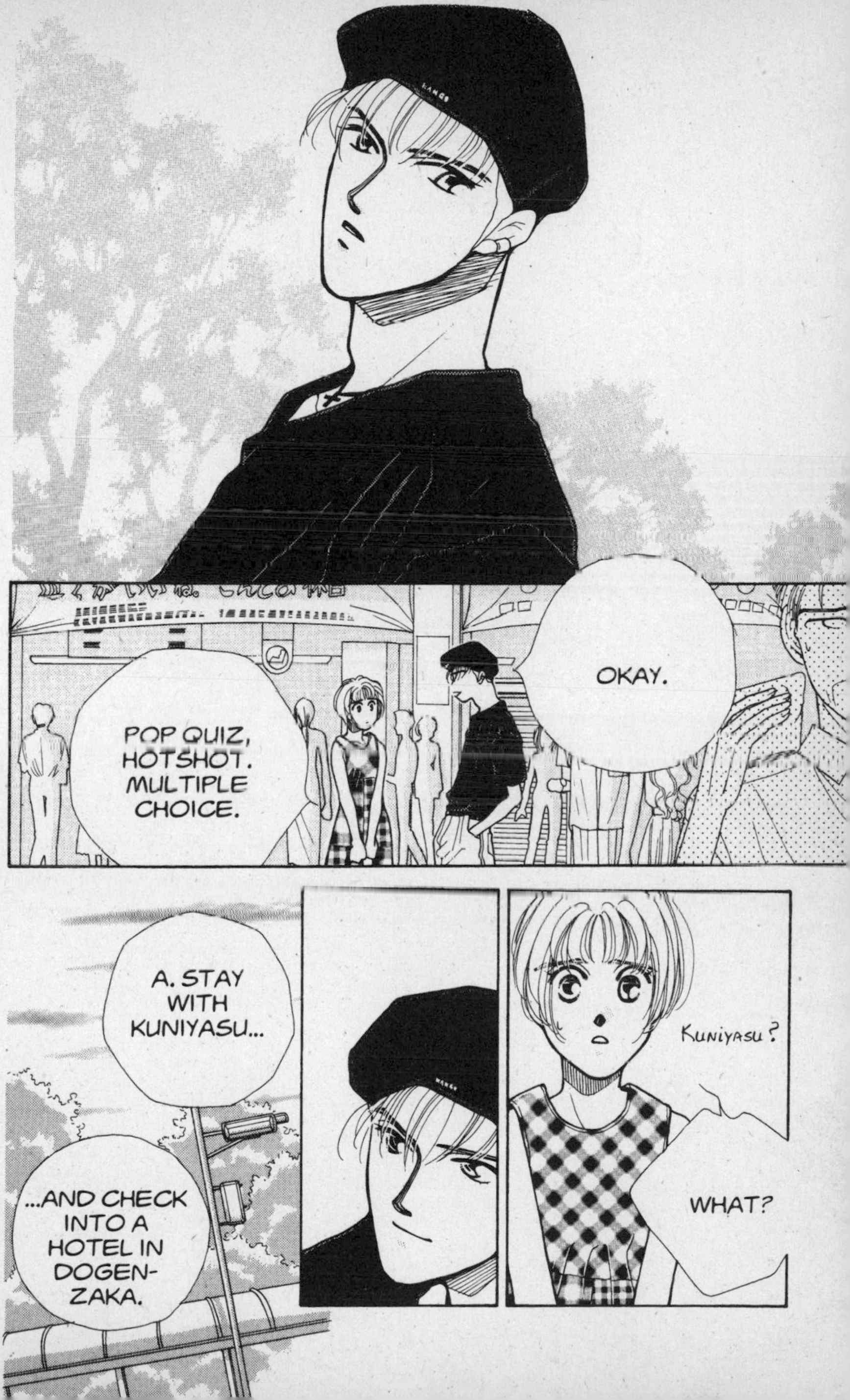
OKAY.
POP QUIZ, HOTSHOT. MULTIPLE CHOICE.
Kuniyasu?
WHAT?
A. STAY WITH KUNIYASU...
...AND CHECK INTO A HOTEL IN DOGEN-ZAKA.

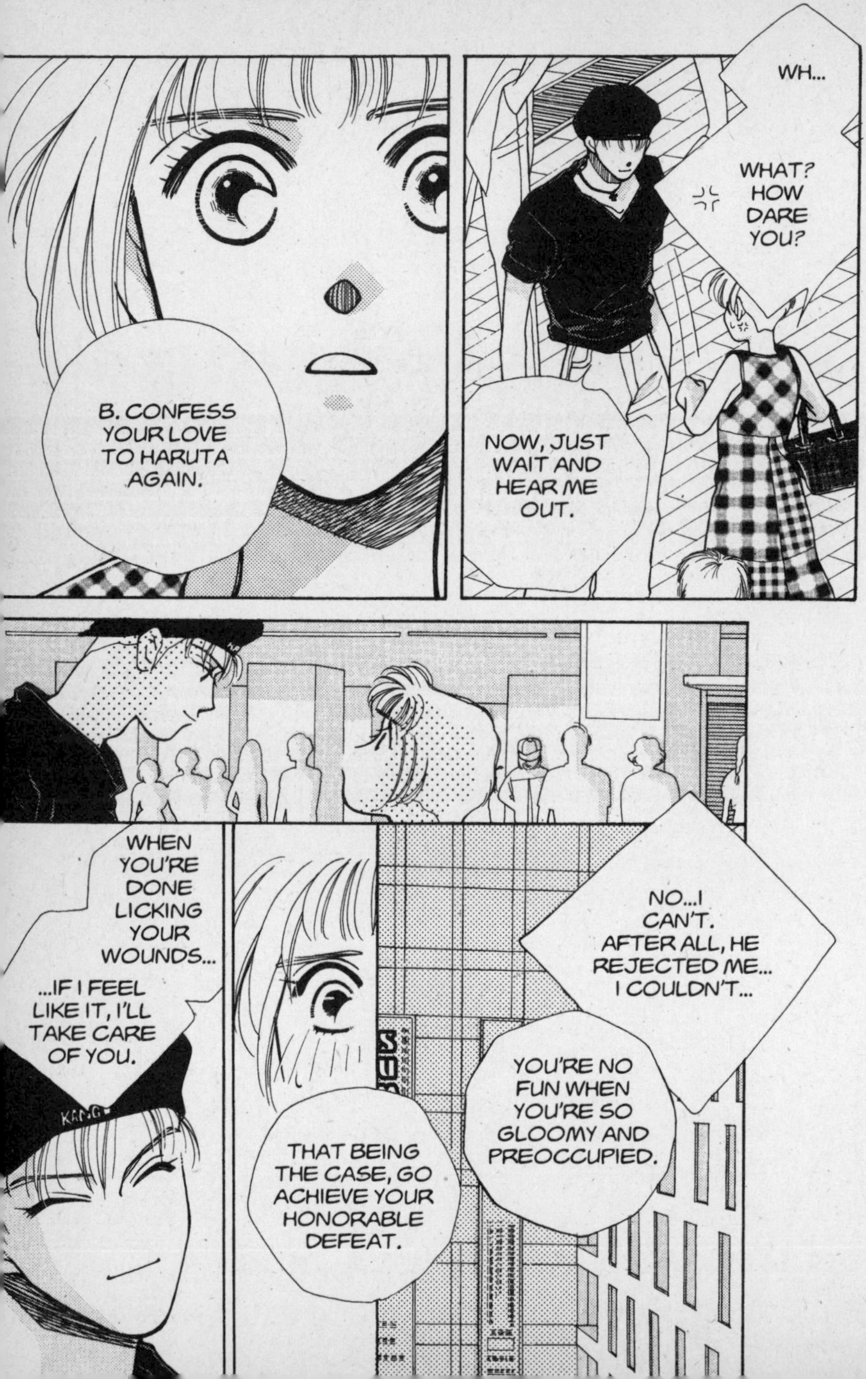
WH...
WHAT? HOW DARE YOU?
NOW, JUST WAIT AND HEAR ME OUT.
B. CONFESS YOUR LOVE TO HARUTA AGAIN.
NO...I CAN'T. AFTER ALL, HE REJECTED ME... I COULDN'T...
YOU'RE NO FUN WHEN YOU'RE SO GLOOMY AND PREOCCUPIED.
THAT BEING THE CASE, GO ACHIEVE YOUR HONORABLE DEFEAT.
WHEN YOU'RE DONE LICKING YOUR WOUNDS...
...IF I FEEL LIKE IT, I'LL TAKE CARE OF YOU.
KANG

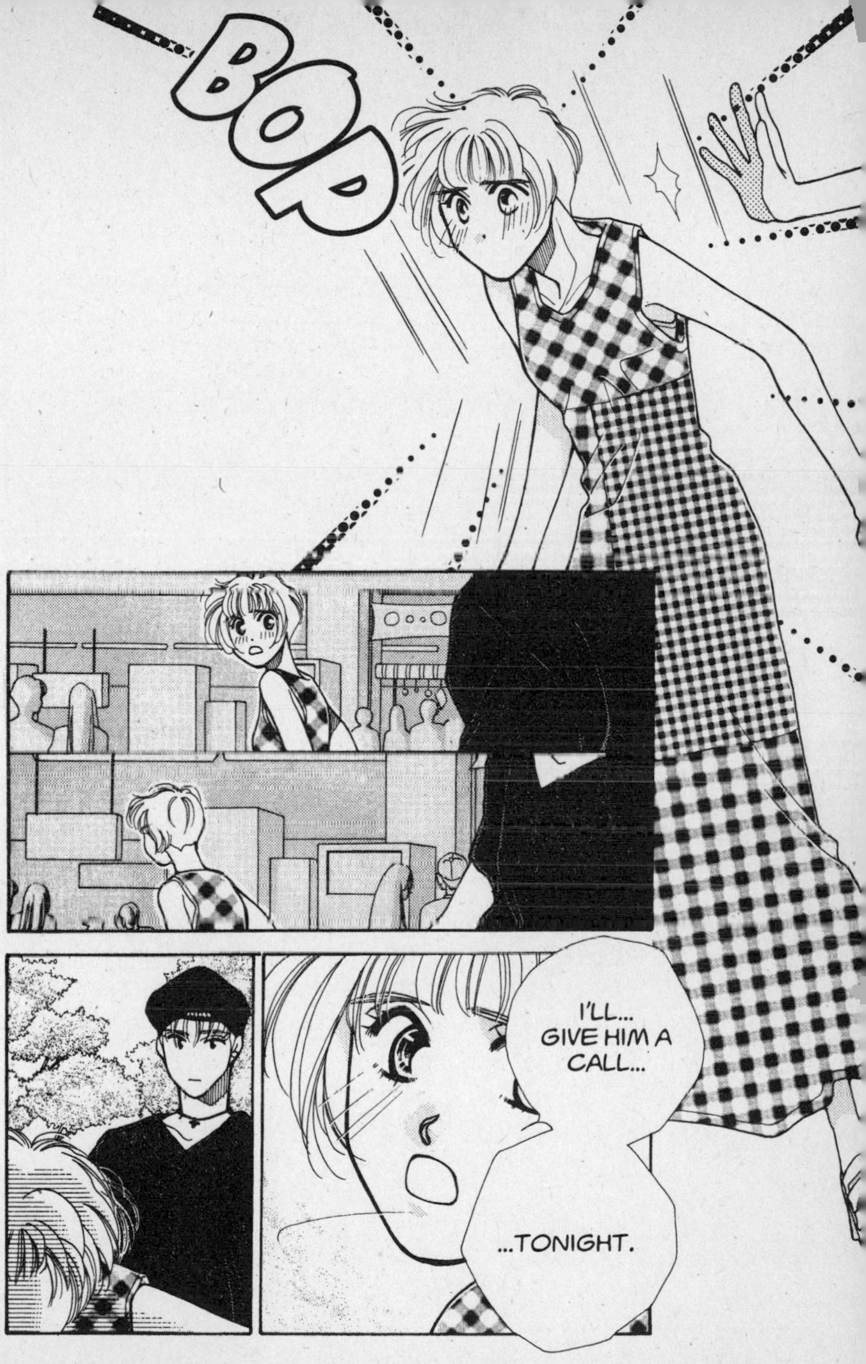
BOP
I'LL... GIVE HIM A CALL...
...TONIGHT.

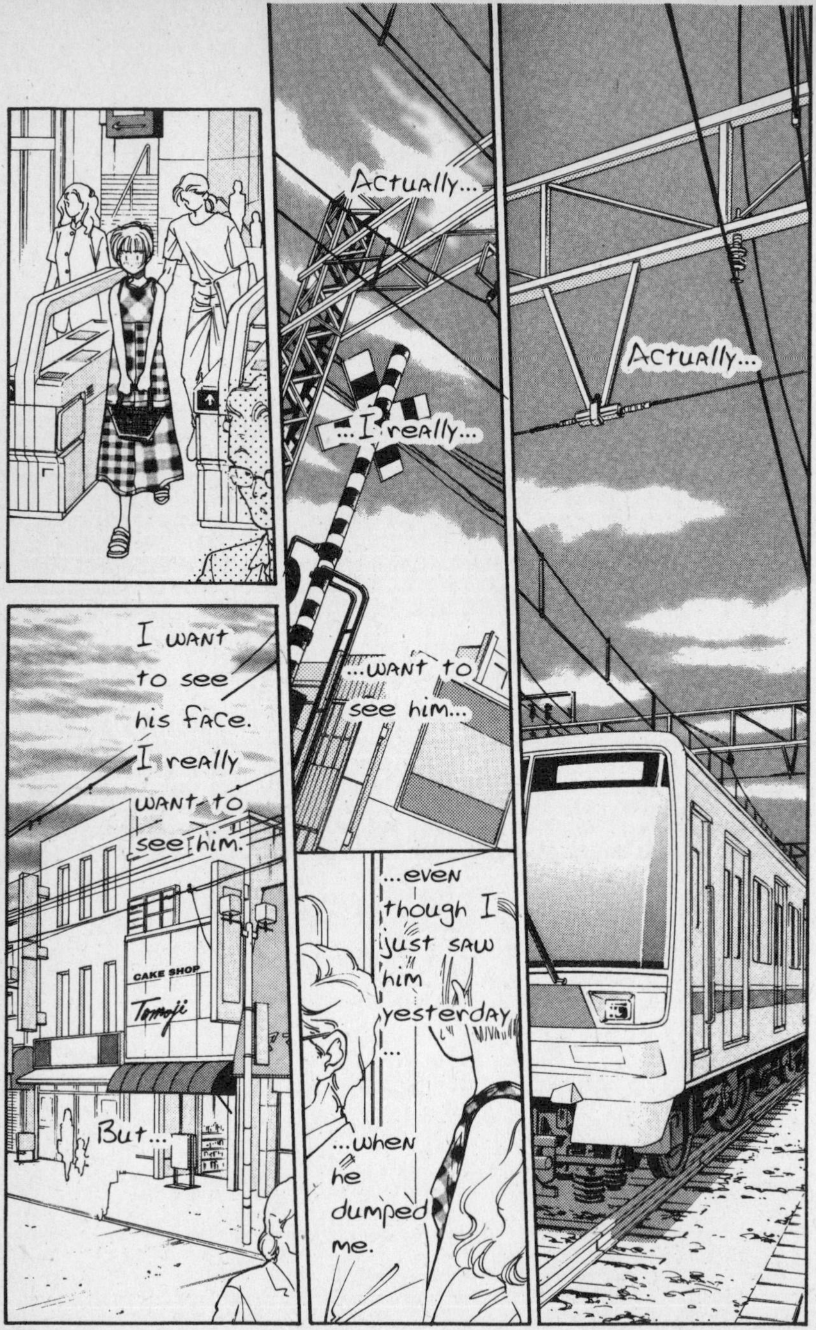
Actually...
Actually...
...I really...
...want to see him...
...even though I just saw him yesterday...
...when he dumped me.
I want to see his face. I really want to see him.
But...
CAKE SHOP
Tomoji

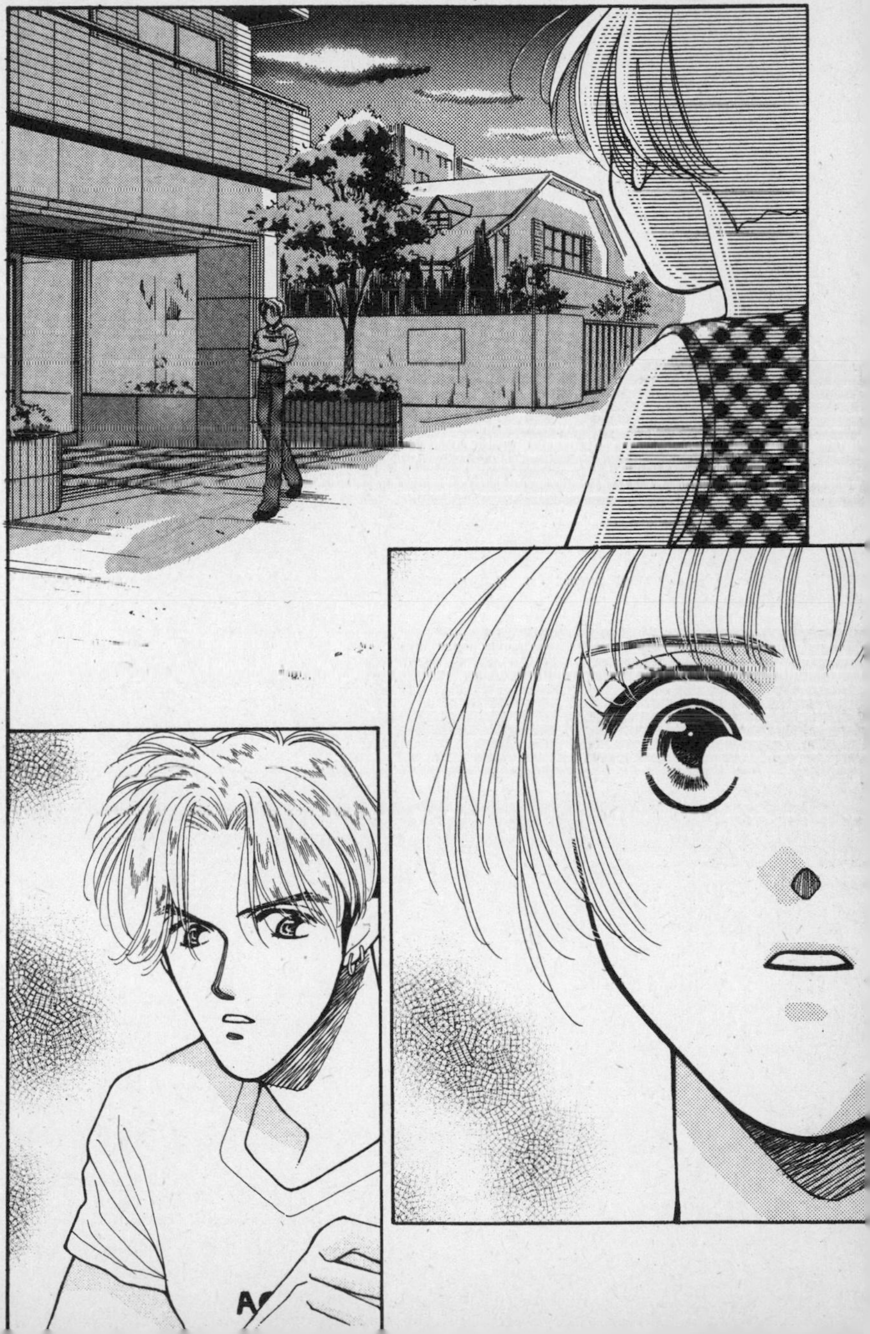

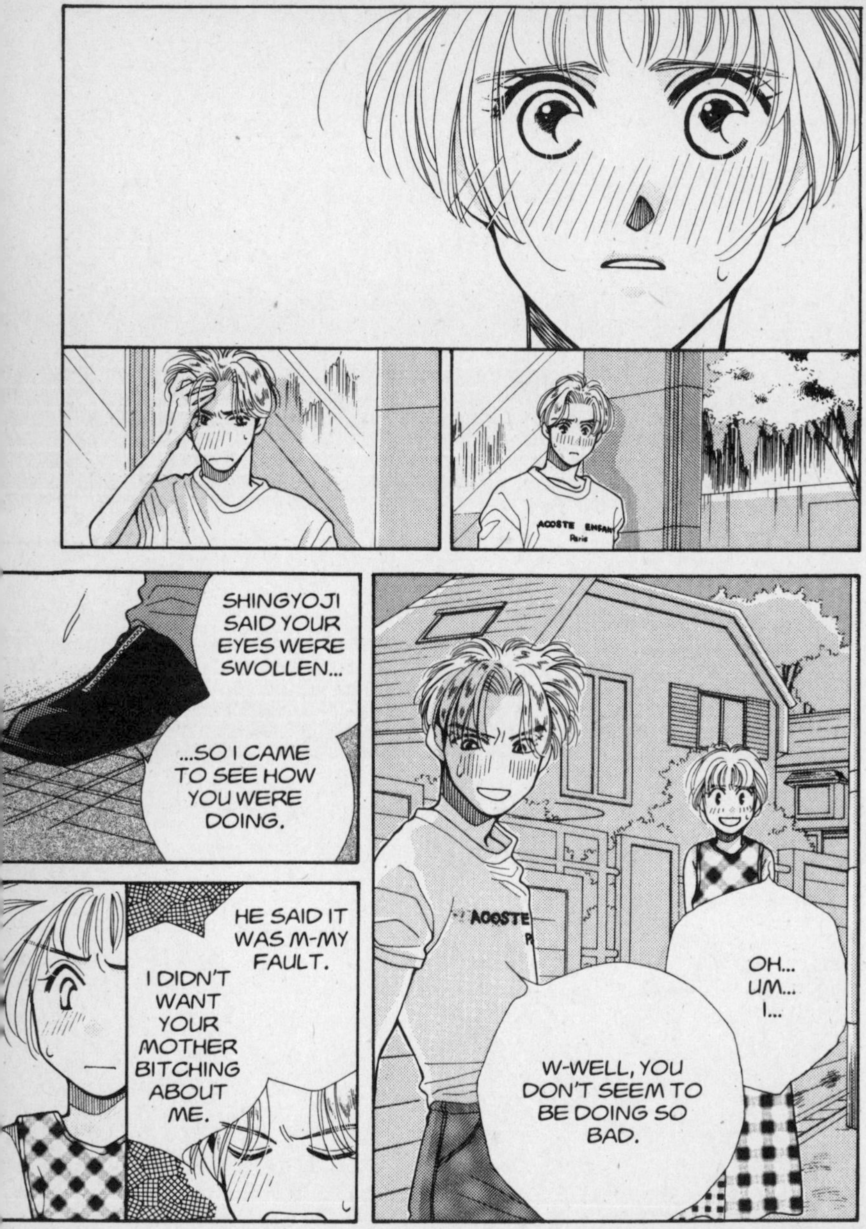
OH... UM... I...
W-WELL, YOU DON'T SEEM TO BE DOING SO BAD.
SHINGYOJI SAID YOUR EYES WERE SWOLLEN...
...SO I CAME TO SEE HOW YOU WERE DOING.
HE SAID IT WAS M-MY FAULT.
I DIDN'T WANT YOUR MOTHER BITCHING ABOUT ME.

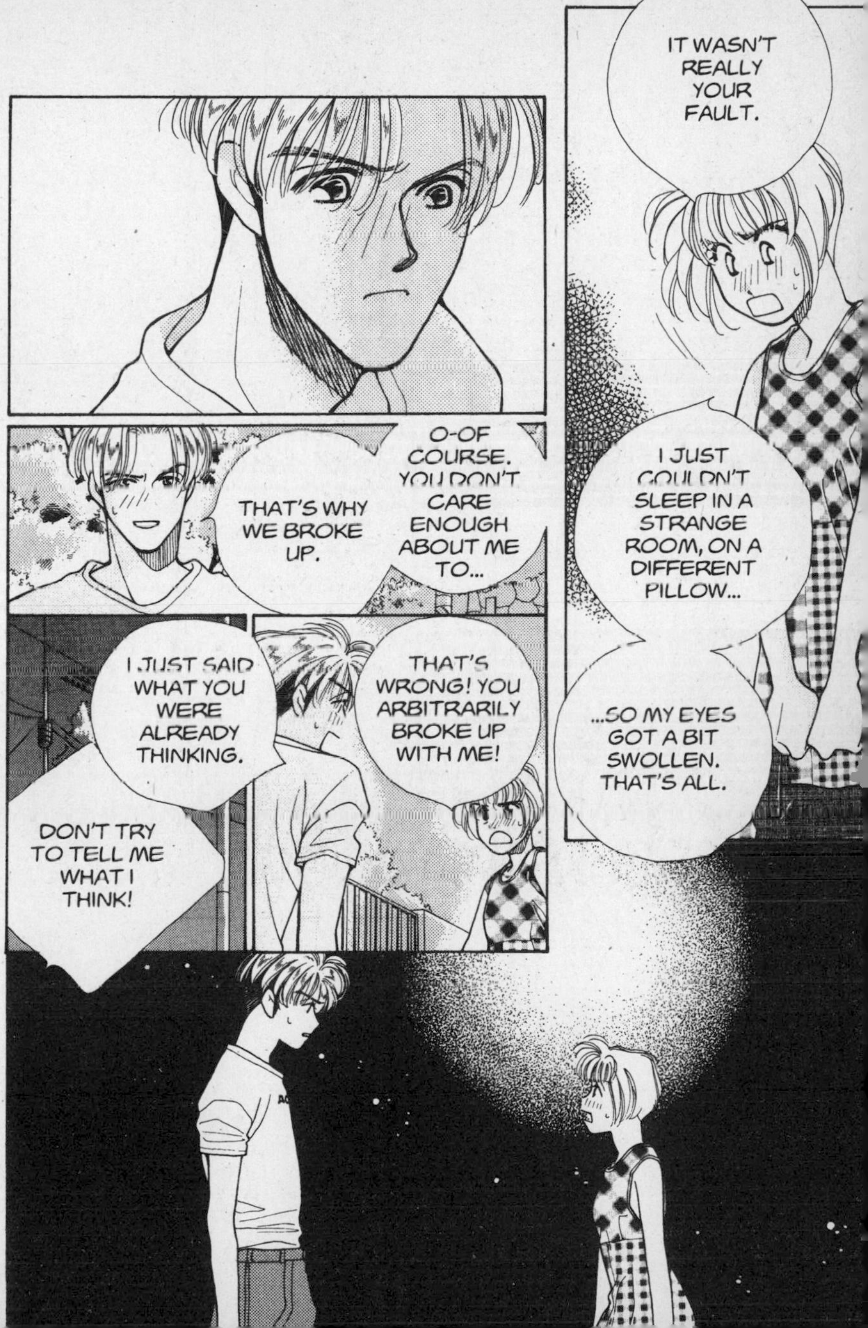
IT WASN'T REALLY YOUR FAULT.
I JUST COULDN'T SLEEP IN A STRANGE ROOM, ON A DIFFERENT PILLOW...
...SO MY EYES GOT A BIT SWOLLEN. THAT'S ALL.
O-OF COURSE. YOU DON'T CARE ENOUGH ABOUT ME TO...
THAT'S WHY WE BROKE UP.
THAT'S WRONG! YOU ARBITRARILY BROKE UP WITH ME!
I JUST SAID WHAT YOU WERE ALREADY THINKING.
DON'T TRY TO TELL ME WHAT I THINK!

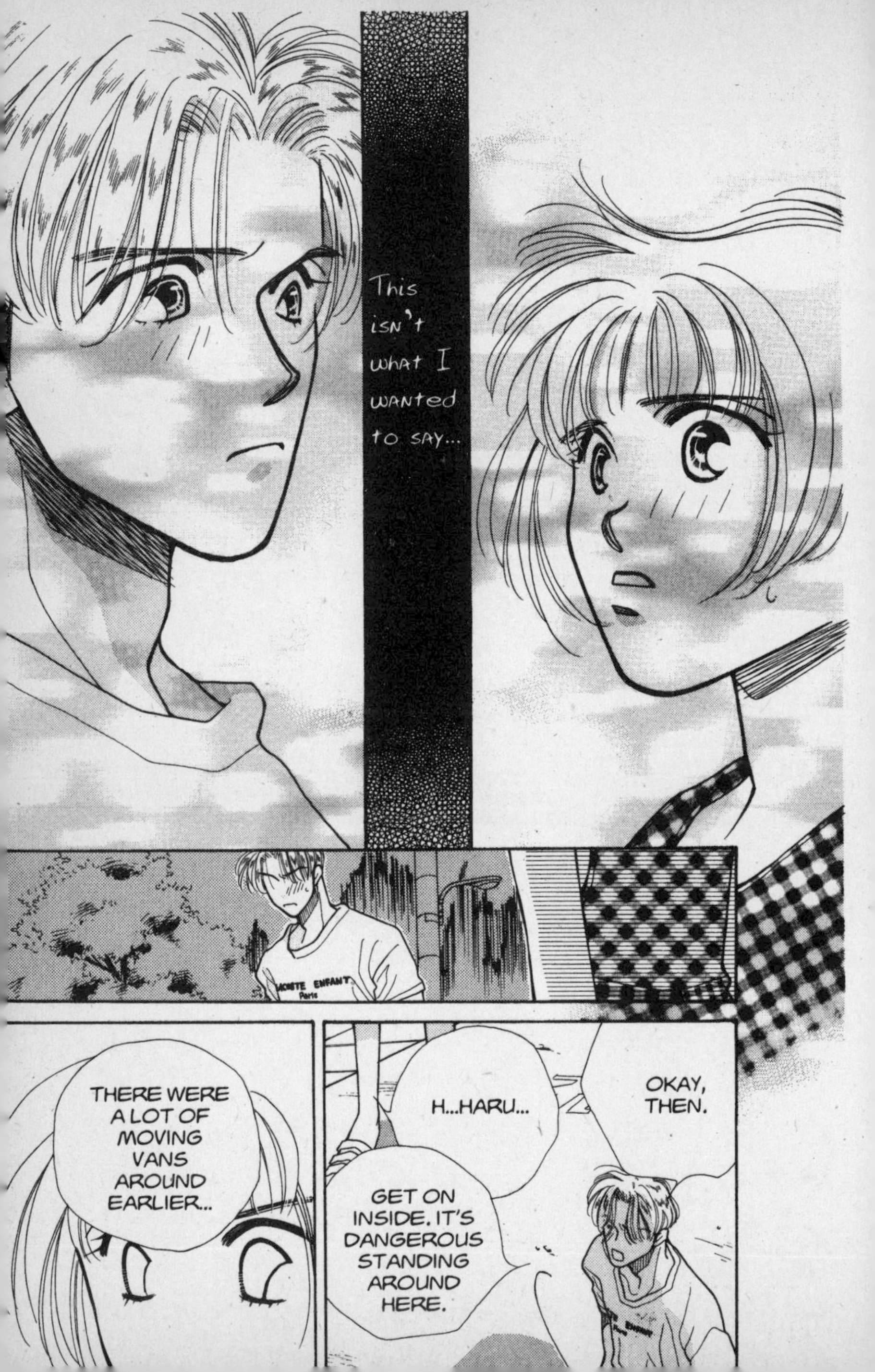
This isn't what I wanted to say...
OKAY, THEN.
H...HARU...
GET ON INSIDE. IT'S DANGEROUS STANDING AROUND HERE.
THERE WERE A LOT OF MOVING VANS AROUND EARLIER...

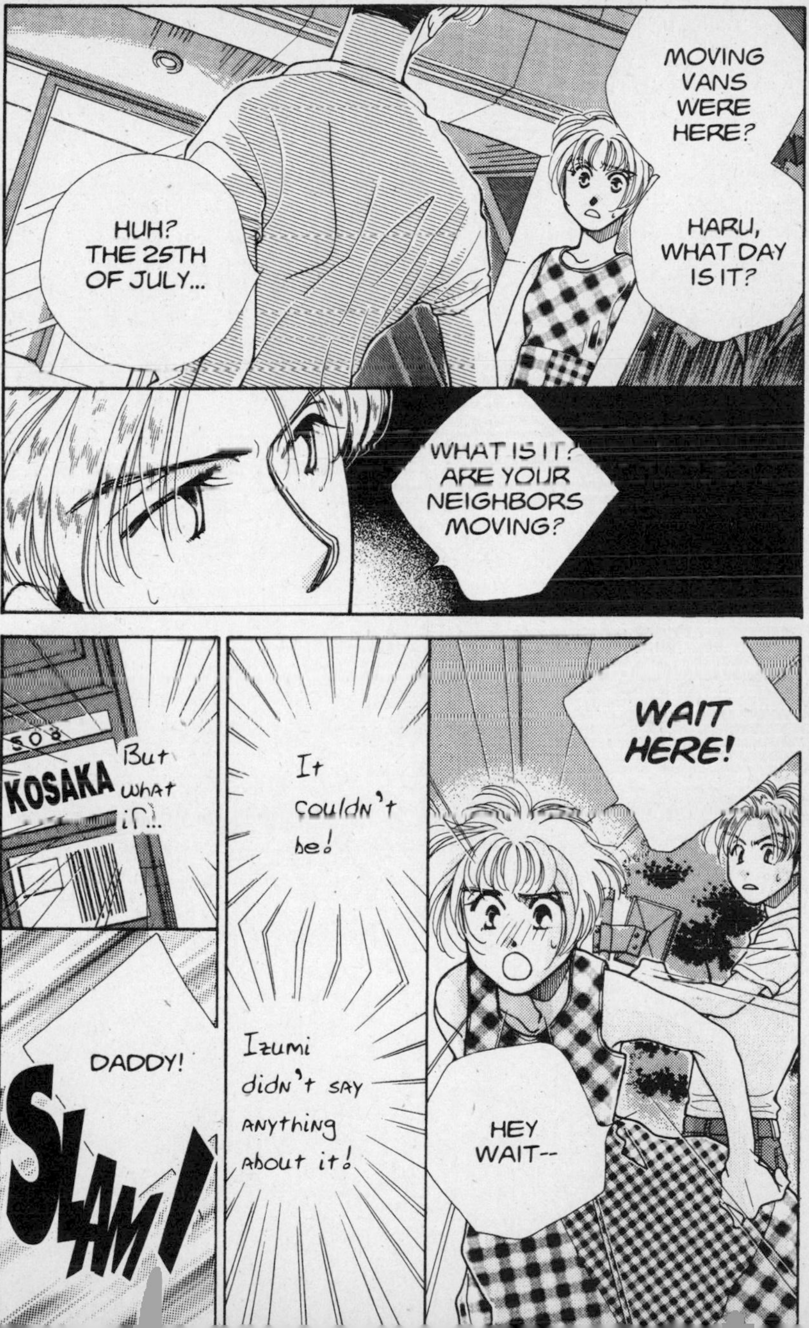
MOVING VANS WERE HERE?
HARU, WHAT DAY IS IT?
HUH? THE 25TH OF JULY...
WHAT IS IT? ARE YOUR NEIGHBORS MOVING?
WAIT HERE!
HEY WAIT--
It couldn't be!
Izumi didn't say anything about it!
503
KOSAKA
But what if...
DADDY!
SLAM!

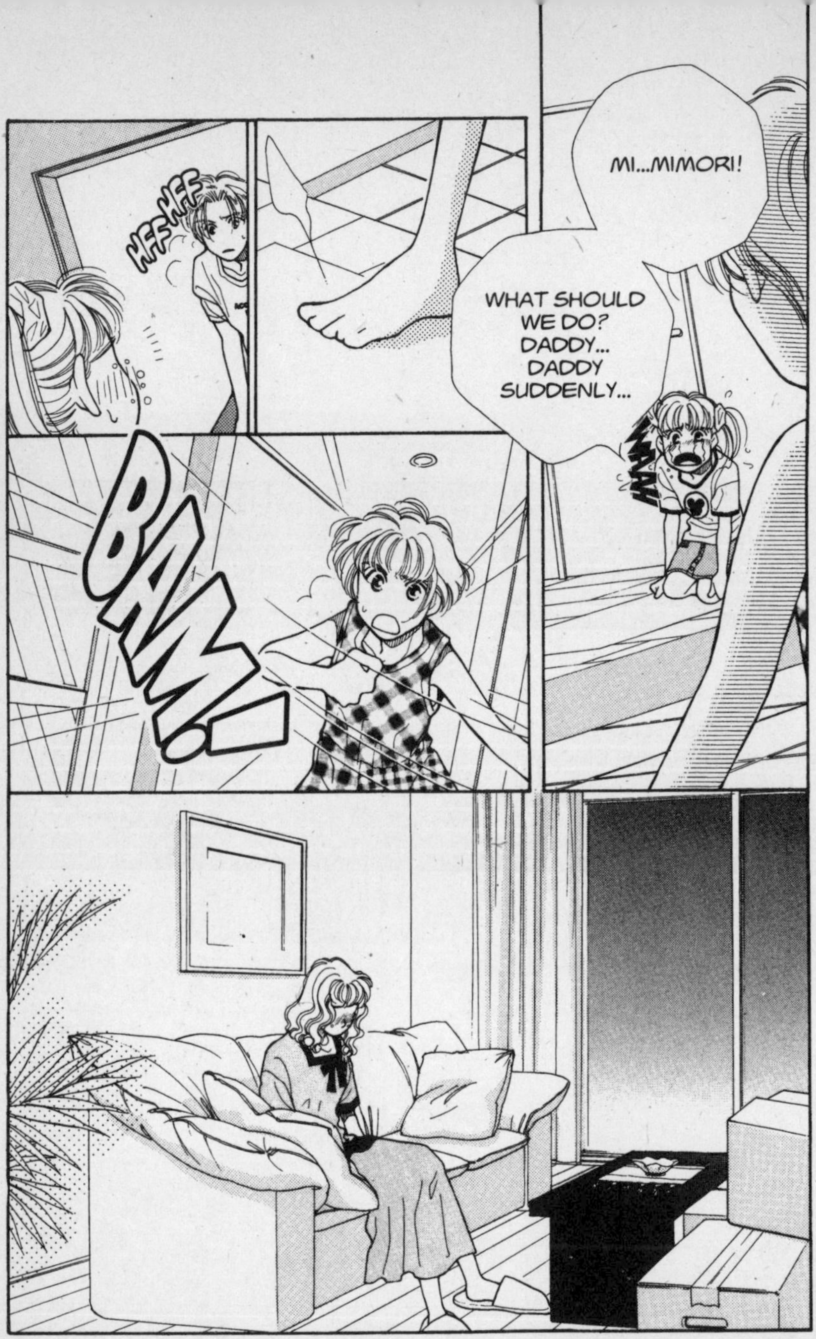
MI...MIMORI!
WHAT SHOULD WE DO? DADDY... DADDY SUDDENLY...
HFF HFF
BAM!

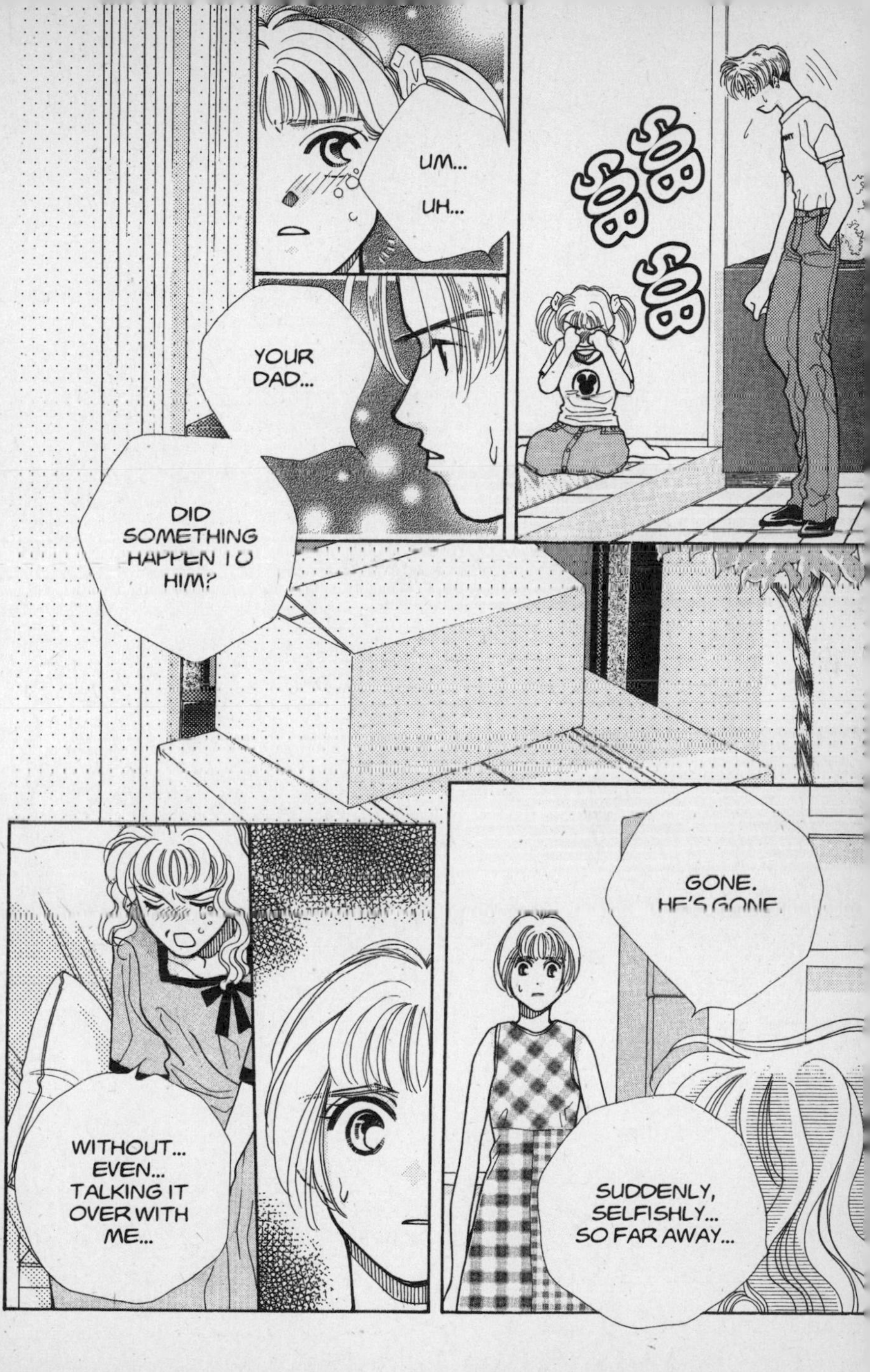
SOB SOB SOB SOB
UM...
UH...
YOUR DAD...
DID SOMETHING HAPPEN TO HIM?
GONE. HE'S GONE.
SUDDENLY, SELFISHLY... SO FAR AWAY...
WITHOUT... EVEN... TALKING IT OVER WITH ME...

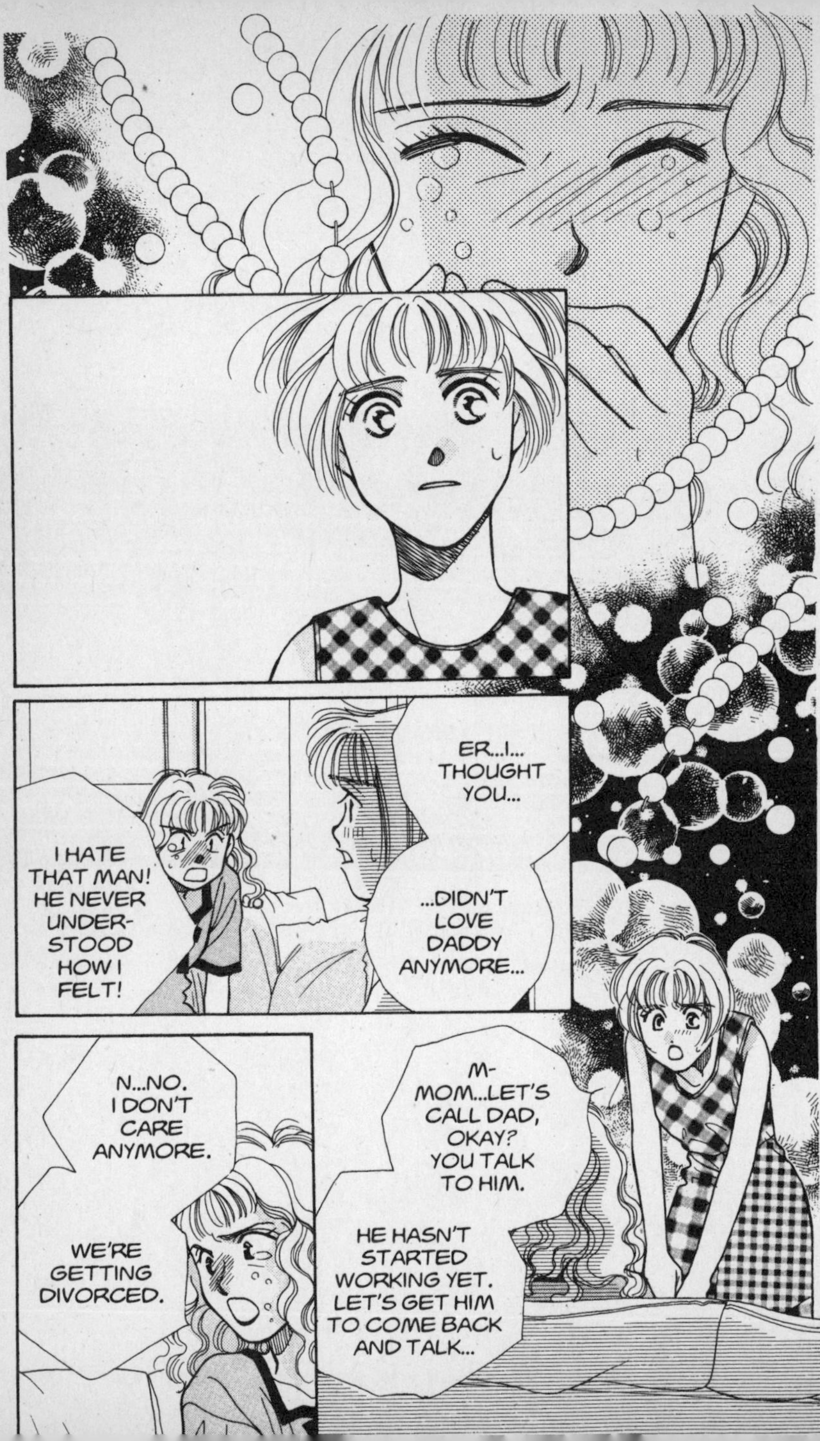
ER...I... THOUGHT YOU...
...DIDN'T LOVE DADDY ANYMORE...
I HATE THAT MAN! HE NEVER UNDER-STOOD HOW I FELT!
M-MOM...LET'S CALL DAD, OKAY? YOU TALK TO HIM.
HE HASN'T STARTED WORKING YET. LET'S GET HIM TO COME BACK AND TALK...
N...NO. I DON'T CARE ANYMORE.
WE'RE GETTING DIVORCED.

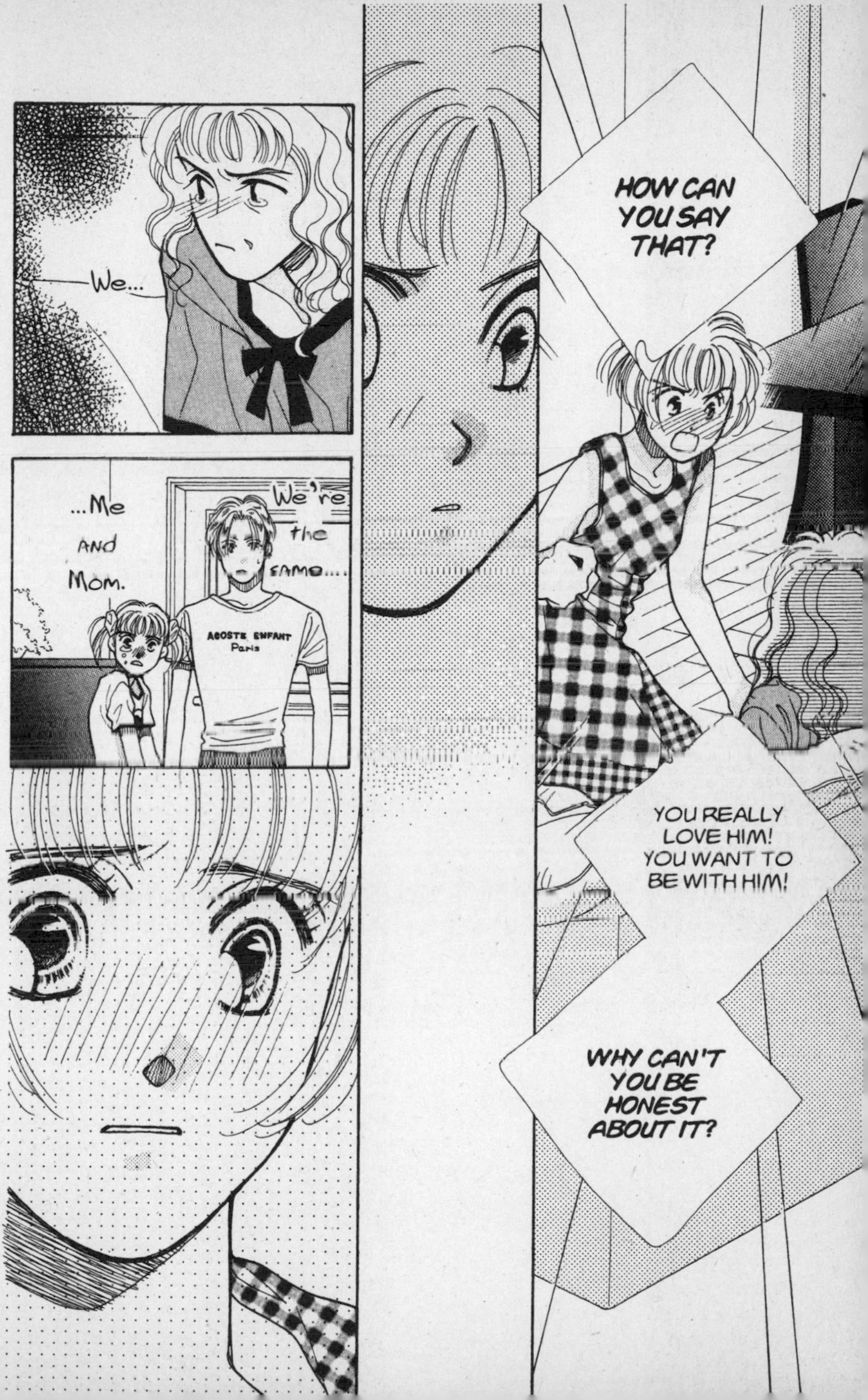
HOW CAN YOU SAY THAT?
YOU REALLY LOVE HIM! YOU WANT TO BE WITH HIM!
WHY CAN'T YOU BE HONEST ABOUT IT?
We...
We're the same....
...Me and Mom.
AGOSTE ENFANT Paris

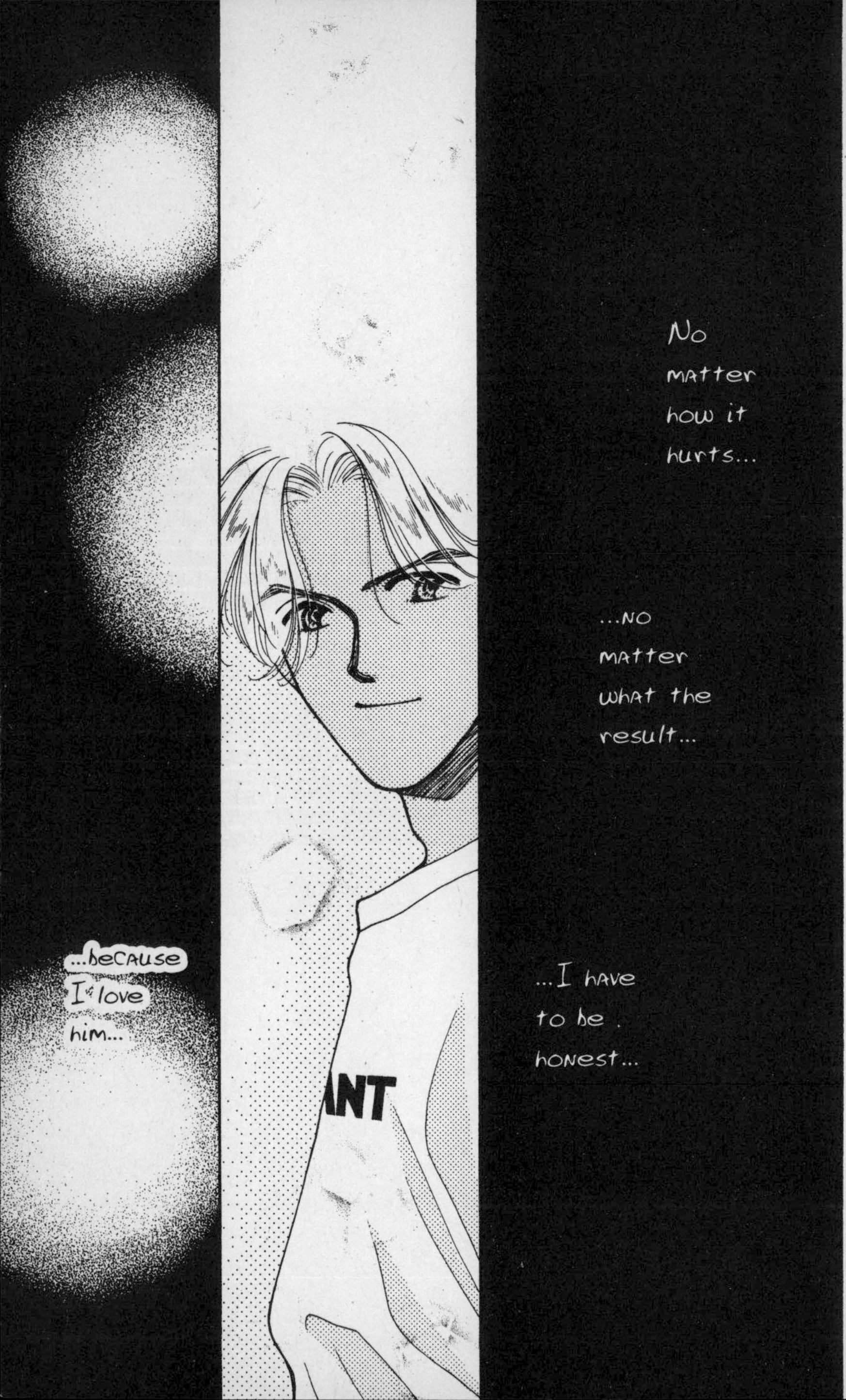
No matter how it hurts...
...no matter what the result...
...I have to be honest...
ANT
...because I love him...

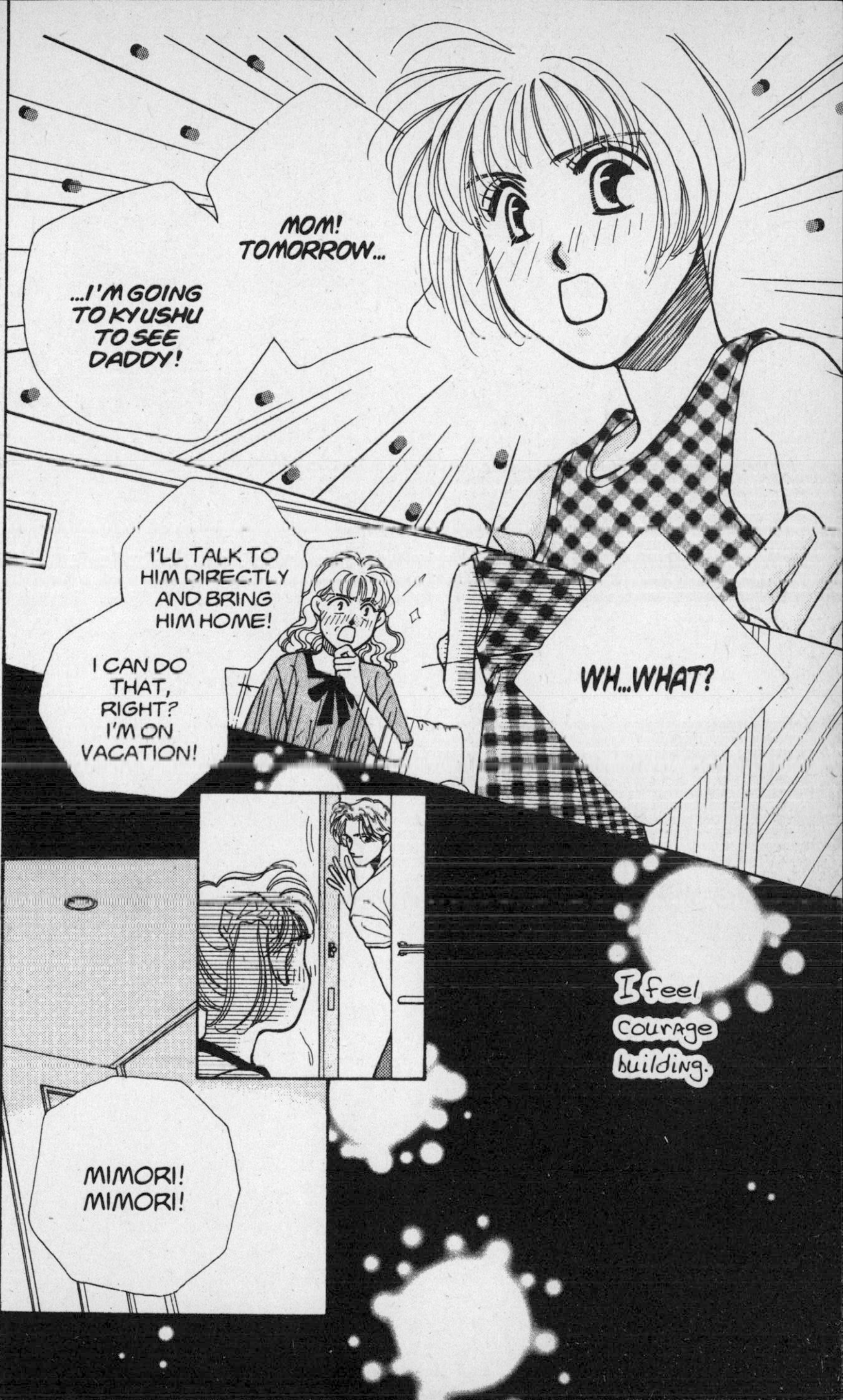
MOM! TOMORROW...
...I'M GOING TO KYUSHU TO SEE DADDY!
WH...WHAT?
I'LL TALK TO HIM DIRECTLY AND BRING HIM HOME!
I CAN DO THAT, RIGHT? I'M ON VACATION!
I feel courage building.
MIMORI! MIMORI!

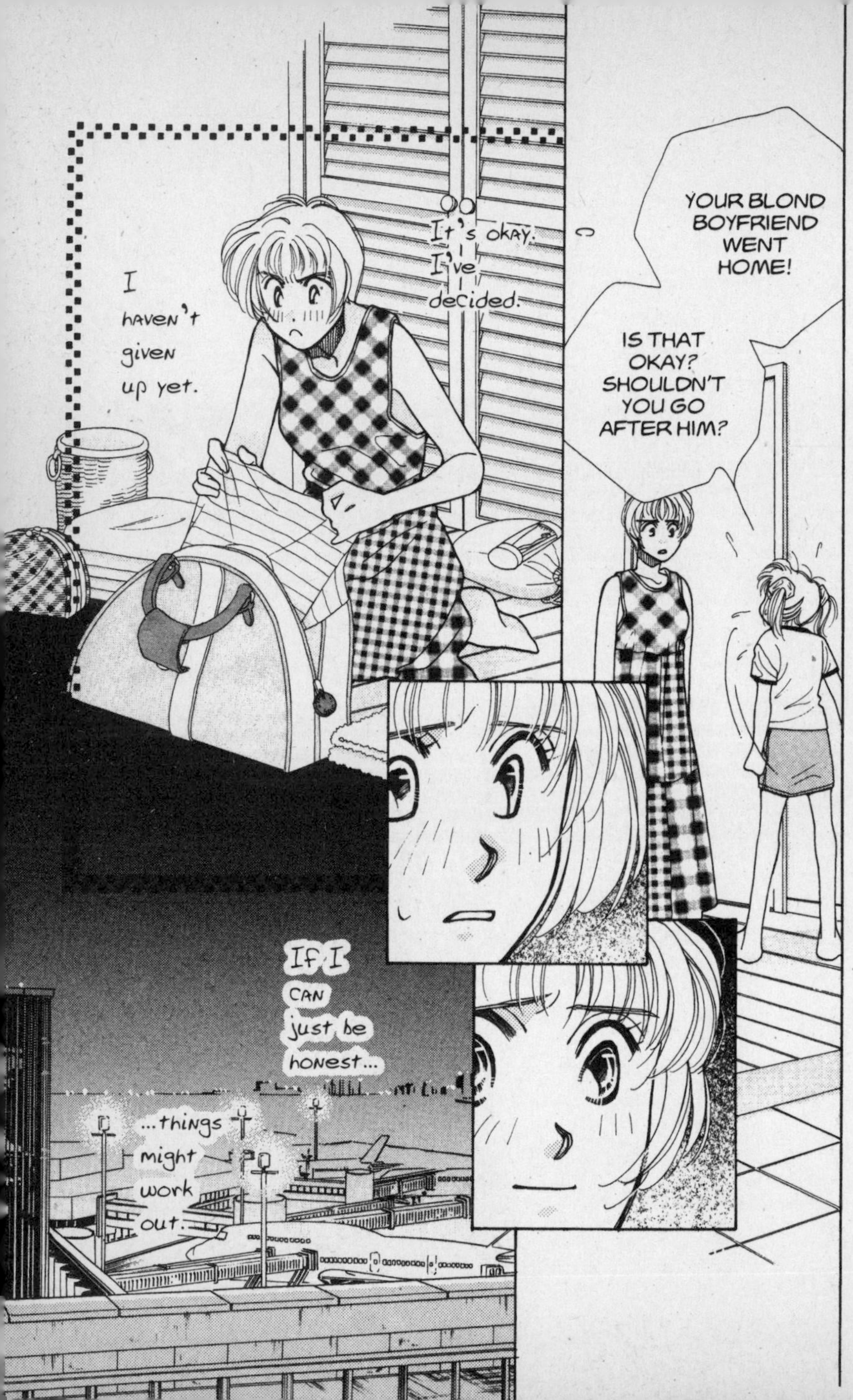
YOUR BLOND BOYFRIEND WENT HOME!
IS THAT OKAY? SHOULDN'T YOU GO AFTER HIM?
It's okay. I've decided.
I haven't given up yet.
If I can just be honest...
...things might work out.

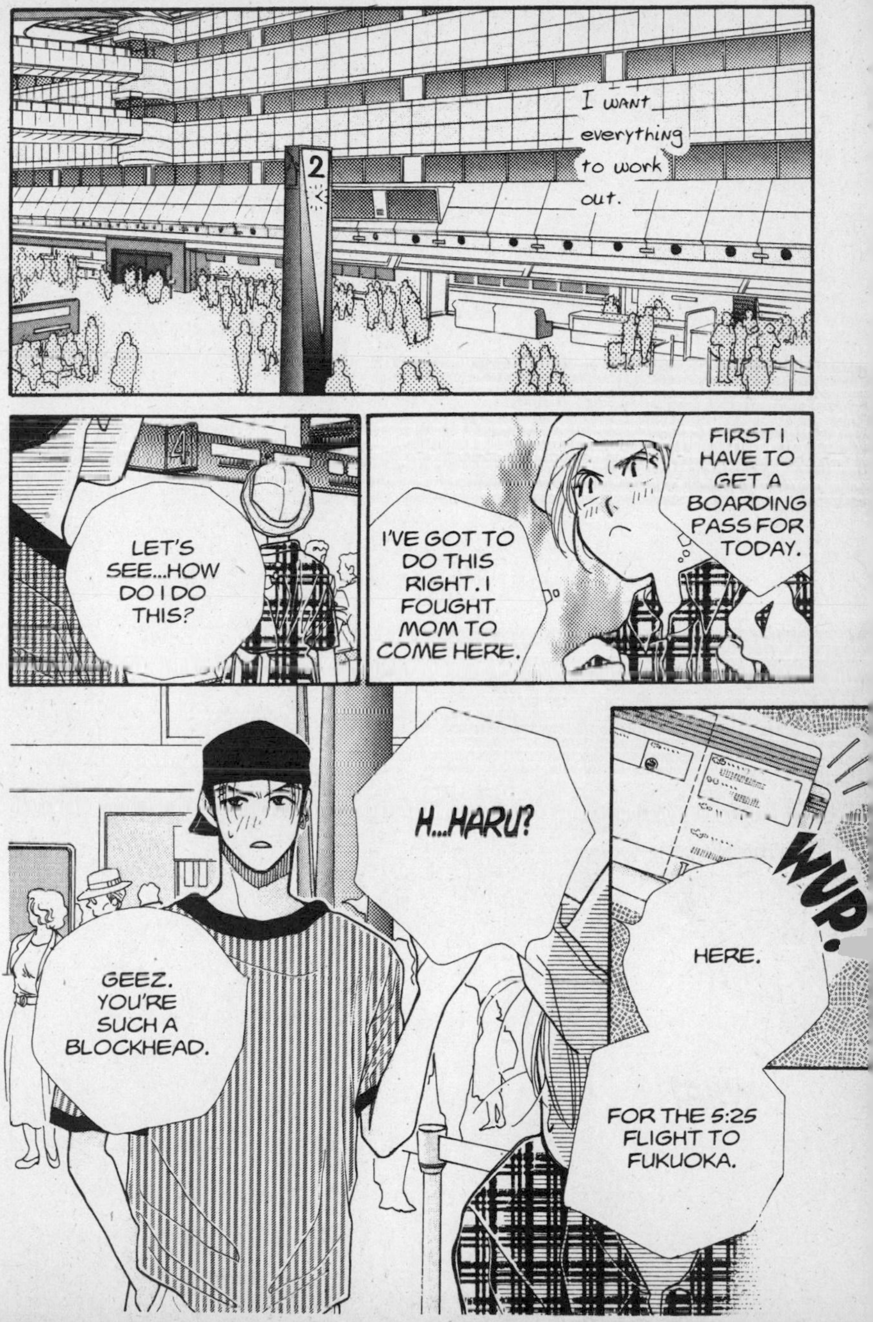
I want everything to work out.
FIRST I HAVE TO GET A BOARDING PASS FOR TODAY.
I'VE GOT TO DO THIS RIGHT. I FOUGHT MOM TO COME HERE.
LET'S SEE...HOW DO I DO THIS?
WUP.
HERE.
FOR THE 5:25 FLIGHT TO FUKUOKA.
H...HARU?
GEEZ. YOU'RE SUCH A BLOCKHEAD.

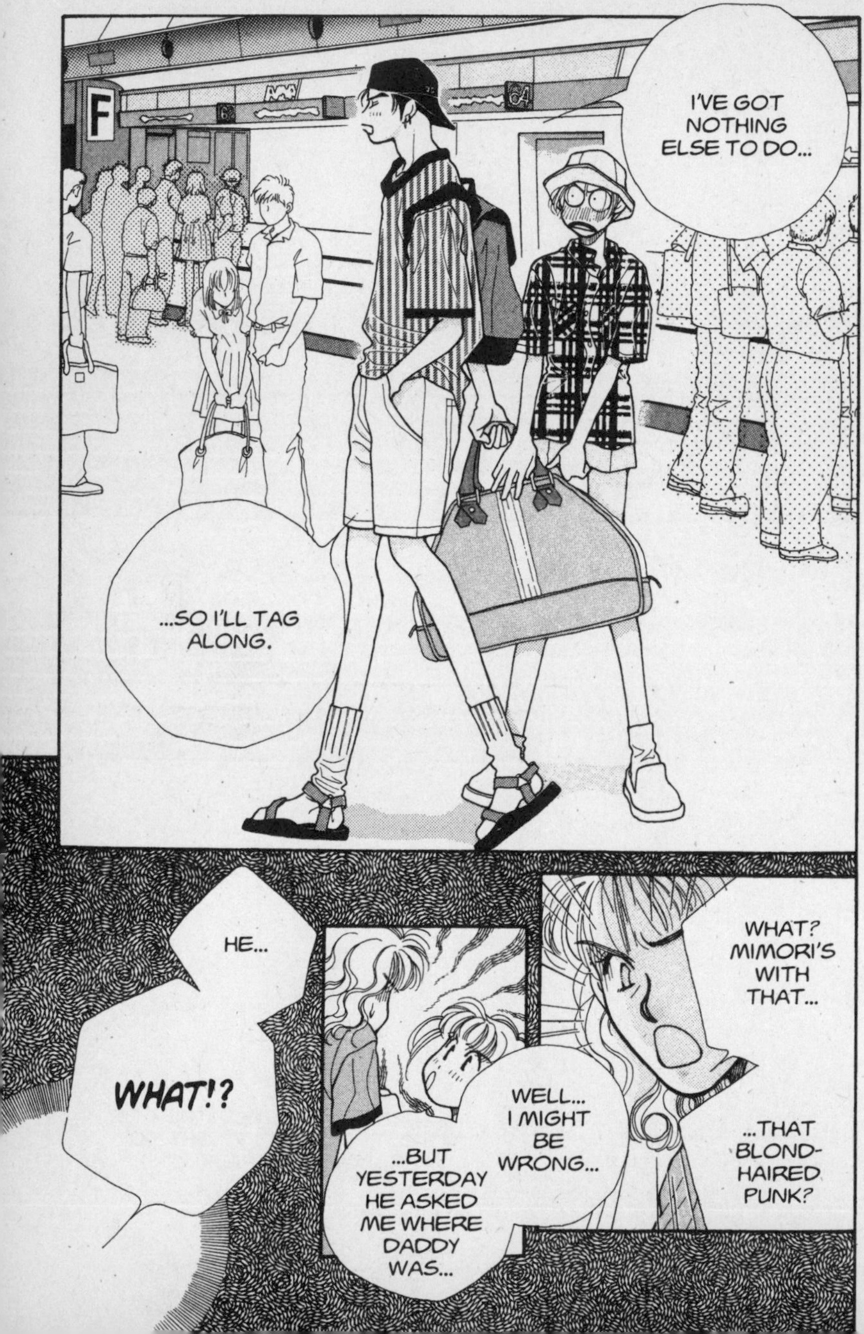
I'VE GOT NOTHING ELSE TO DO...
...SO I'LL TAG ALONG.
WHAT? MIMORI'S WITH THAT...
...THAT BLOND-HAIRED PUNK?
WELL... I MIGHT BE WRONG...
...BUT YESTERDAY HE ASKED ME WHERE DADDY WAS...
HE...
WHAT!?

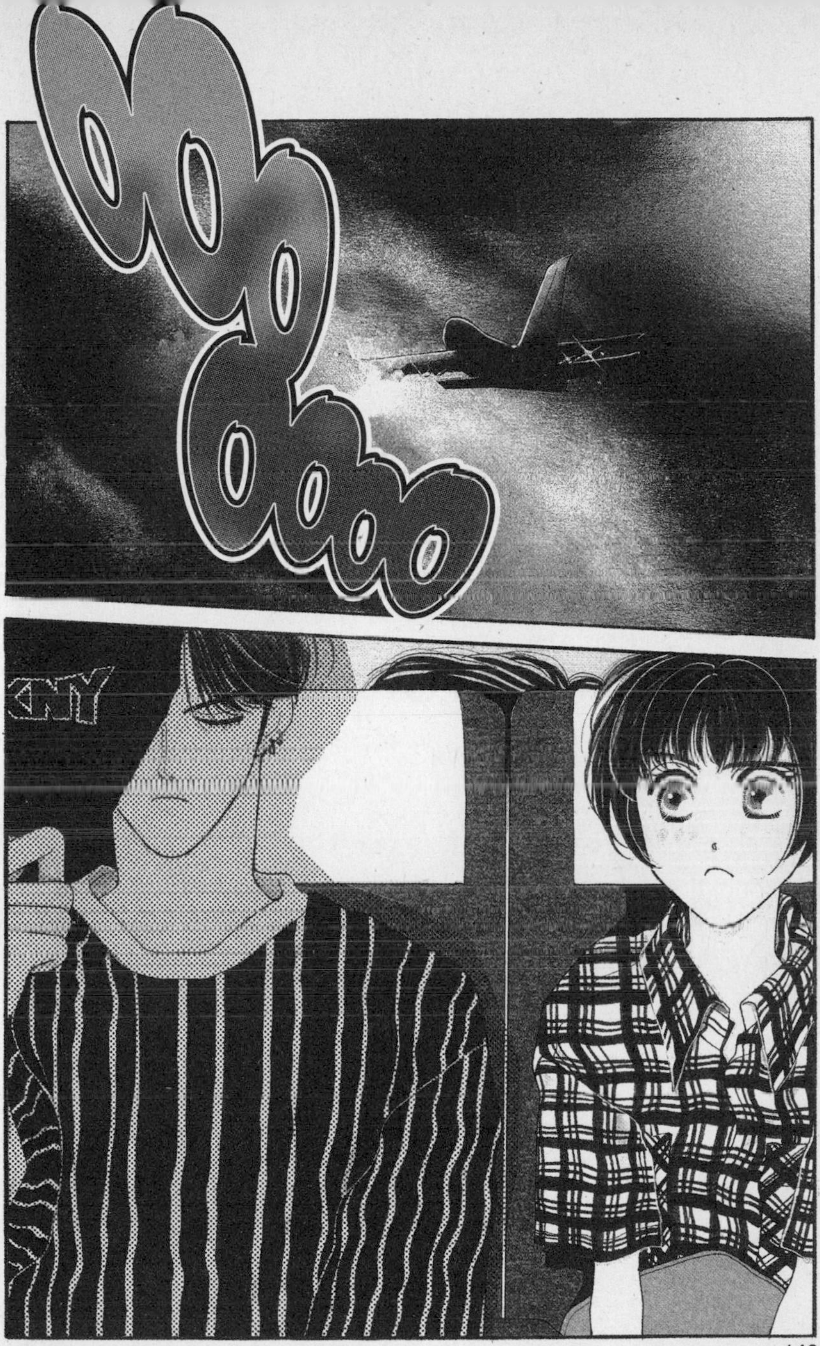

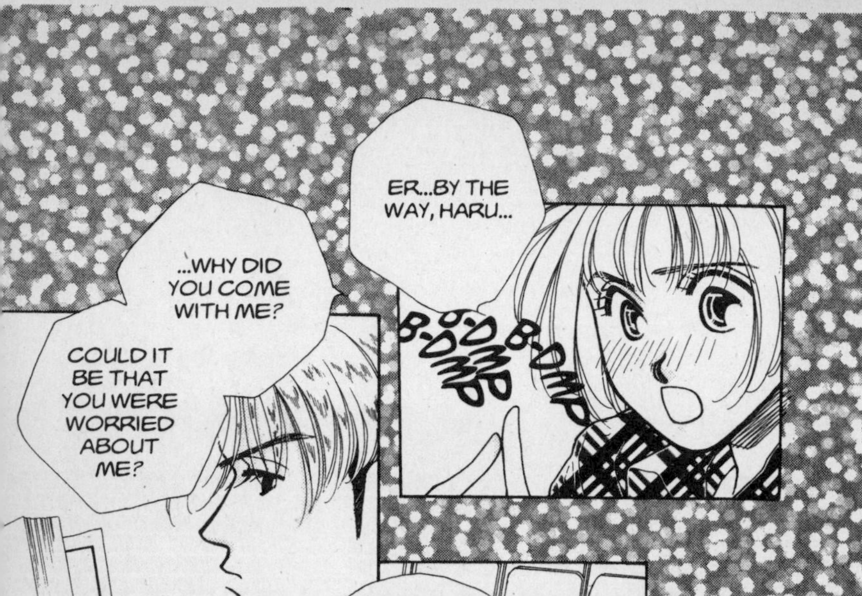
ER...BY THE WAY, HARU...
B-DMP B-DMP B-DMP
...WHY DID YOU COME WITH ME?
COULD IT BE THAT YOU WERE WORRIED ABOUT ME?
IDIOT! THINK YOU'RE ALL THAT?
I'M GOING TO THE DOME TO CATCH SOME BASEBALL.
HMPH
SHONEN HOP
FIRST 60 PAGES IN COLOR!

Question Corner

*Kuniyasu and Shingyoji

No. 3

Q. "Ran and Kazukita are childhood friends, but what were they like back then?"

A. They lived in the same neighborhood, so they've known each other since elementary school. They weren't always friends. They were in class together in junior high. After fighting over the same girl, they became close. Kazukita doesn't seem to care about most things, but he treasures Ran's friendship. Ran considers Kazukita a playboy, but thinks he's charming.

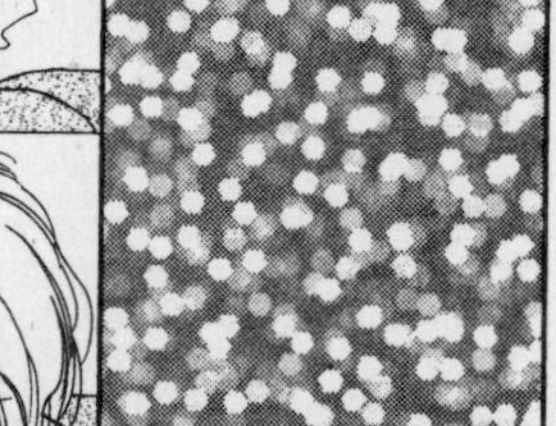

THE TWO OF THEM IN JUNIOR HIGH.

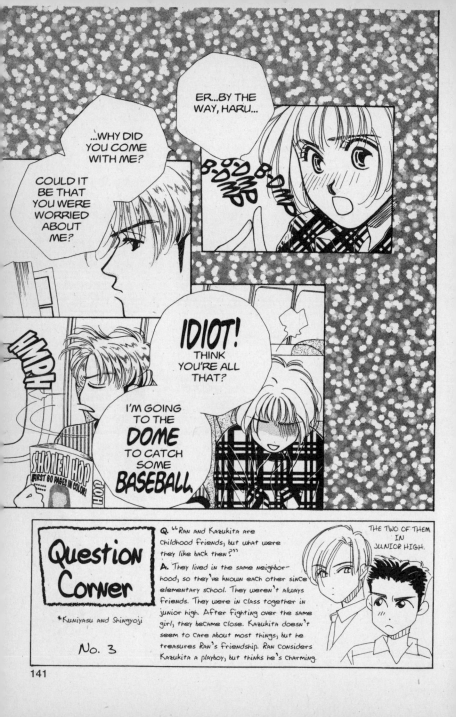

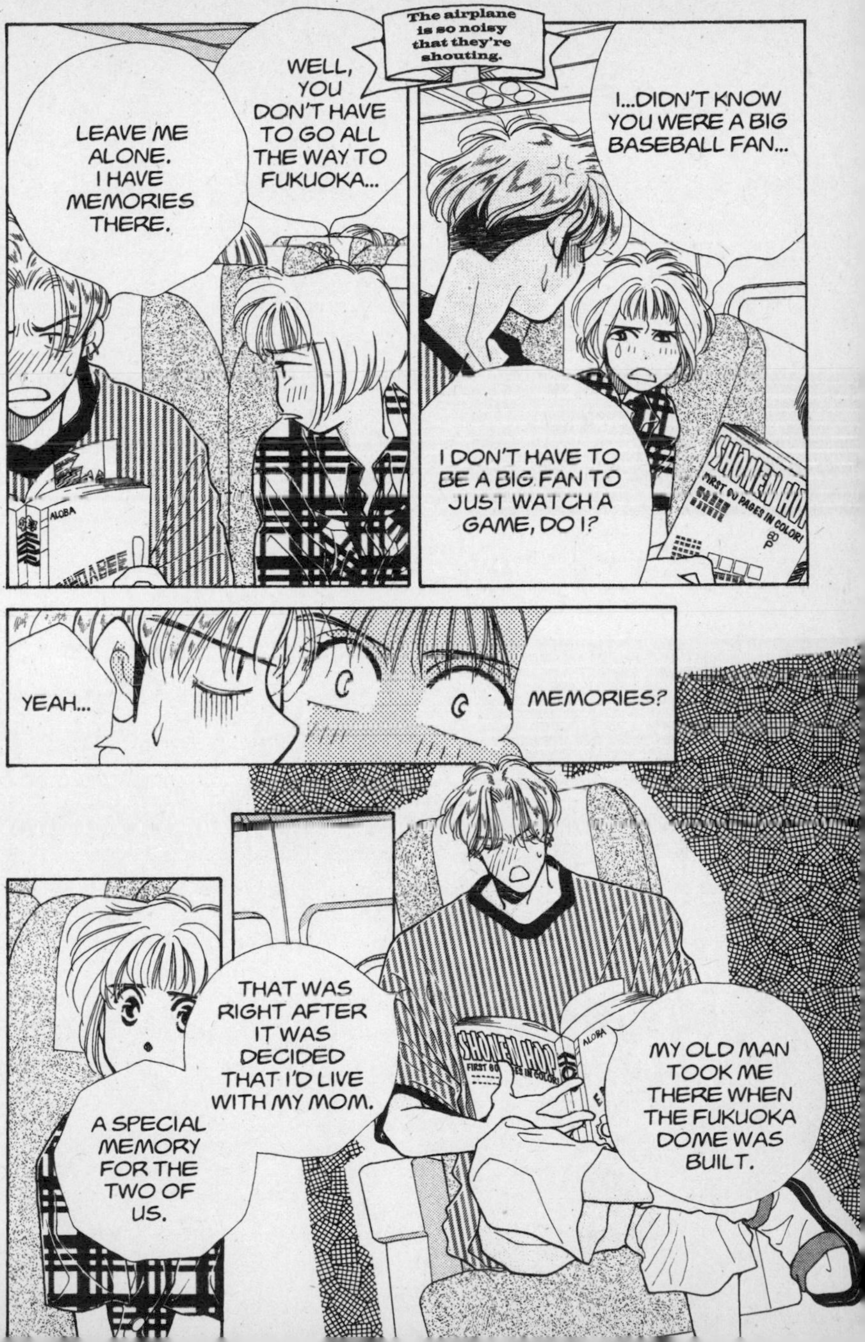
The airplane is so noisy that they're shouting.
I...DIDN'T KNOW YOU WERE A BIG BASEBALL FAN...
I DON'T HAVE TO BE A BIG FAN TO JUST WATCH A GAME, DO I?
WELL, YOU DON'T HAVE TO GO ALL THE WAY TO FUKUOKA...
LEAVE ME ALONE. I HAVE MEMORIES THERE.
MEMORIES?
YEAH...
MY OLD MAN TOOK ME THERE WHEN THE FUKUOKA DOME WAS BUILT.
THAT WAS RIGHT AFTER IT WAS DECIDED THAT I'D LIVE WITH MY MOM.
A SPECIAL MEMORY FOR THE TWO OF US.

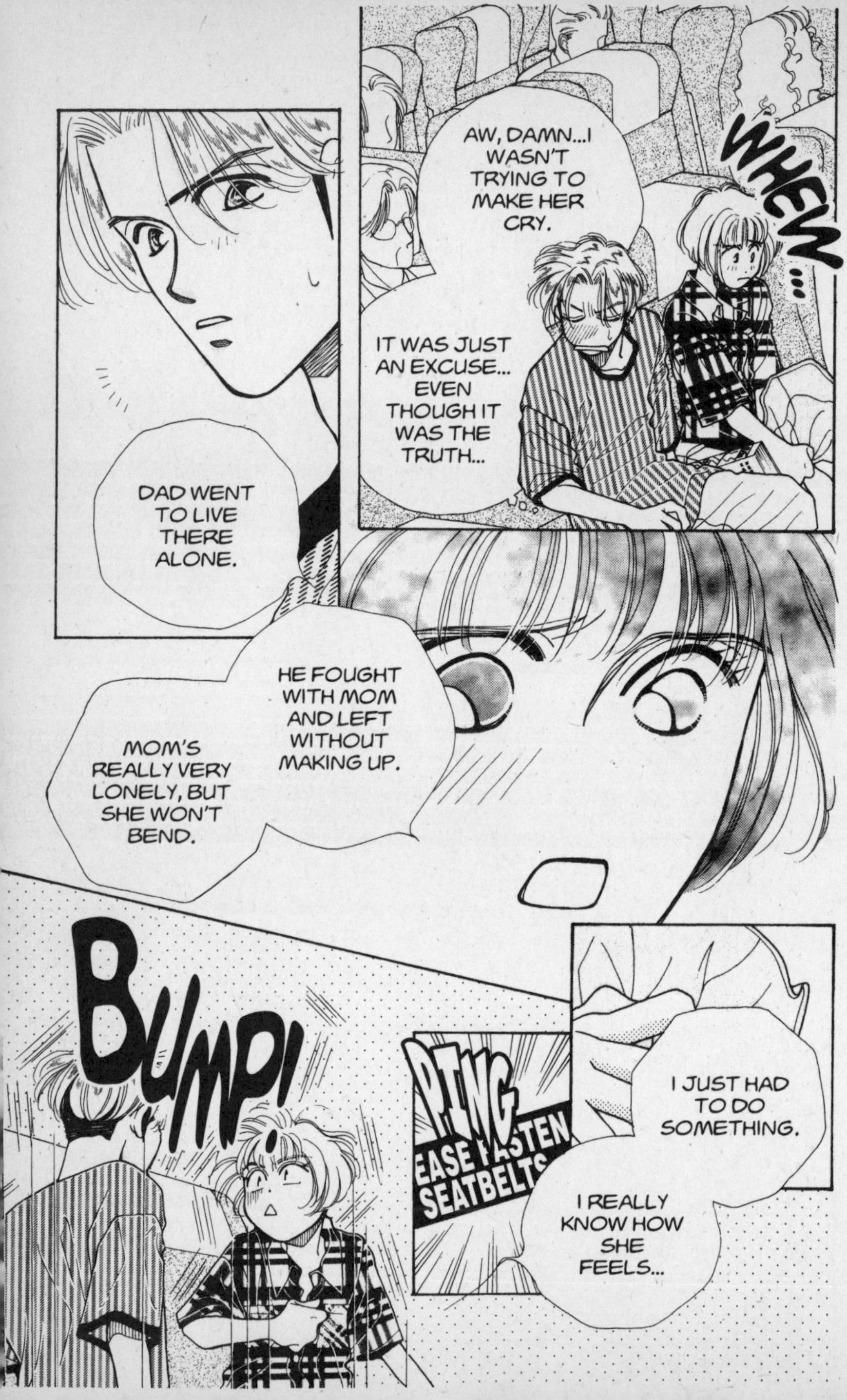
WHEW...
AW, DAMN...I WASN'T TRYING TO MAKE HER CRY.
IT WAS JUST AN EXCUSE... EVEN THOUGH IT WAS THE TRUTH...
DAD WENT TO LIVE THERE ALONE.
HE FOUGHT WITH MOM AND LEFT WITHOUT MAKING UP.
MOM'S REALLY VERY LONELY, BUT SHE WON'T BEND.
I JUST HAD TO DO SOMETHING.
I REALLY KNOW HOW SHE FEELS...
PING
EASE FASTEN SEATBELTS
BUMP!

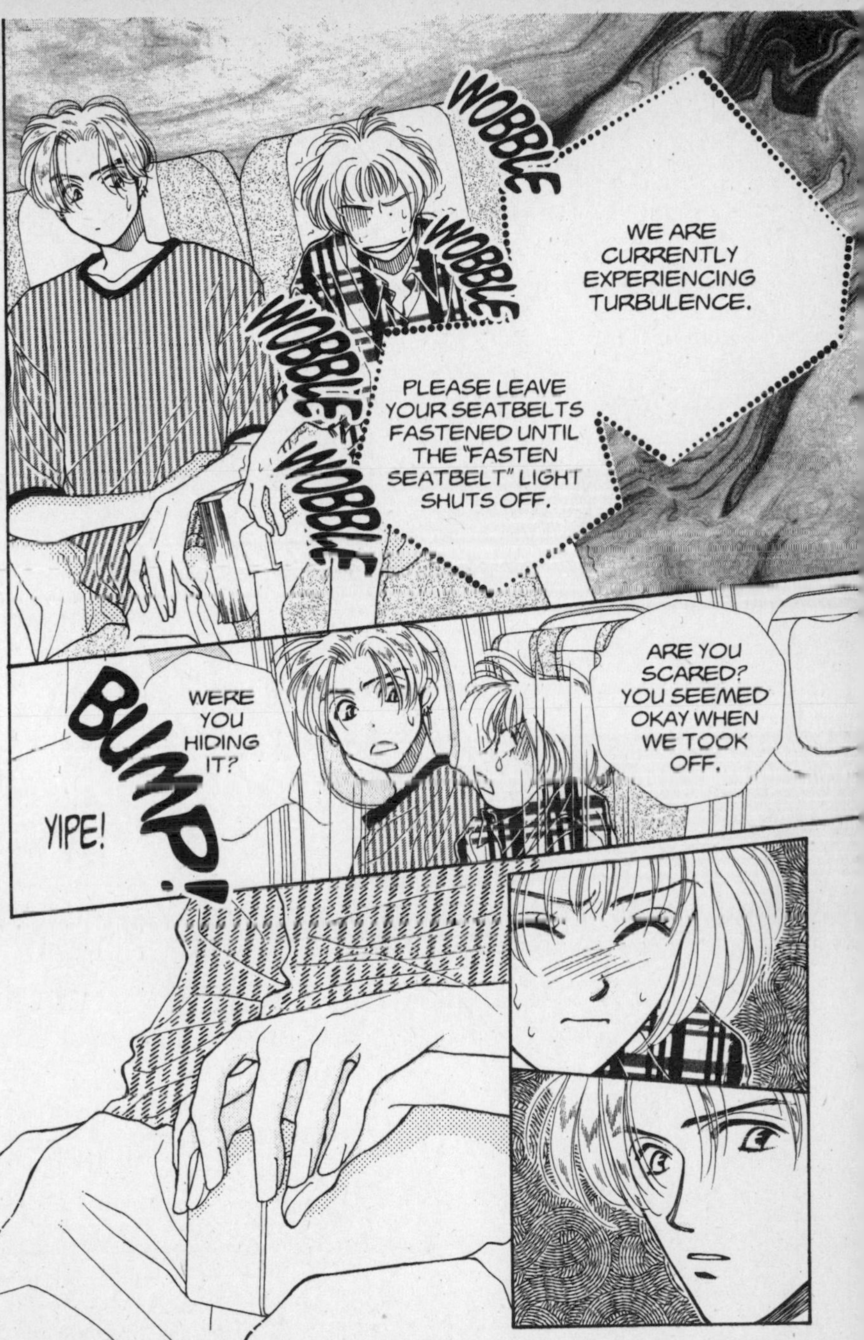
WE ARE CURRENTLY EXPERIENCING TURBULENCE.
PLEASE LEAVE YOUR SEATBELTS FASTENED UNTIL THE "FASTEN SEATBELT" LIGHT SHUTS OFF.
WOBBLE
WOBBLE
WOBBLE
WOBBLE
ARE YOU SCARED? YOU SEEMED OKAY WHEN WE TOOK OFF.
WERE YOU HIDING IT?
BUMP!!
YIPE!

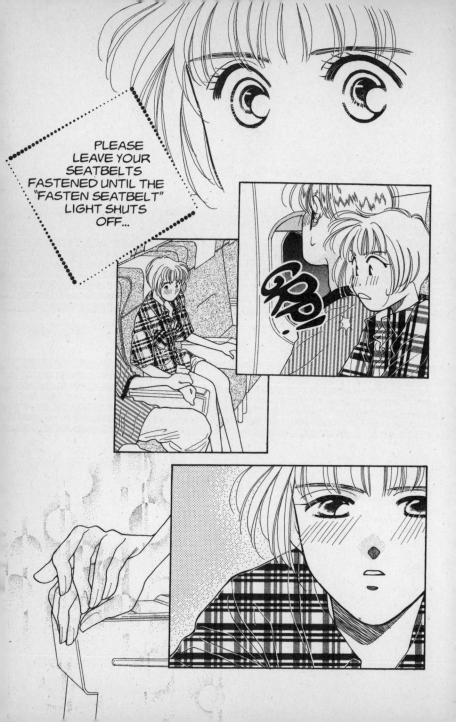

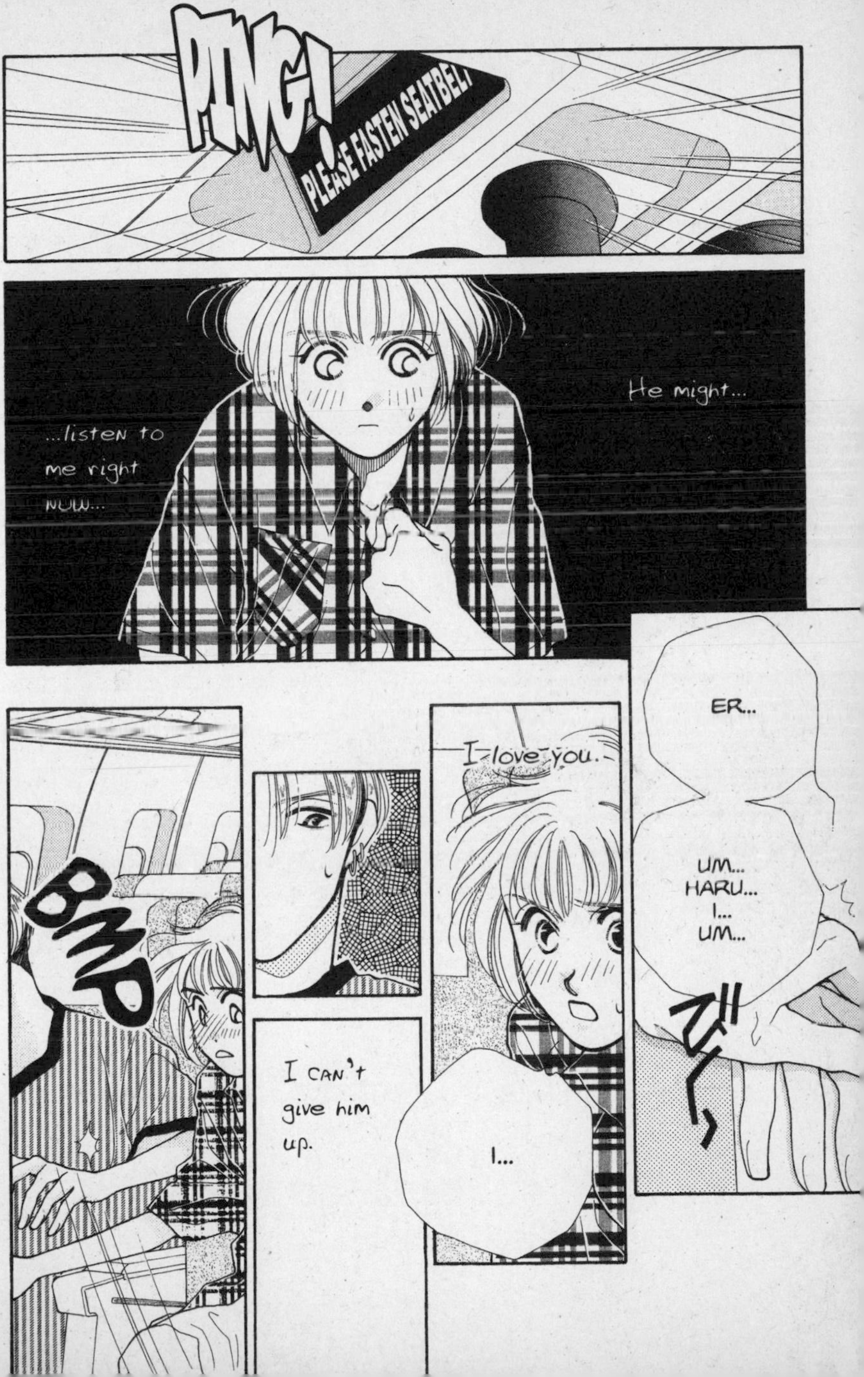
PING!
PLEASE FASTEN SEATBEL
He might...
...listen to me right now...
ER...
UM... HARU... I... UM...
I love you.
I...
I can't give him up.
BMP

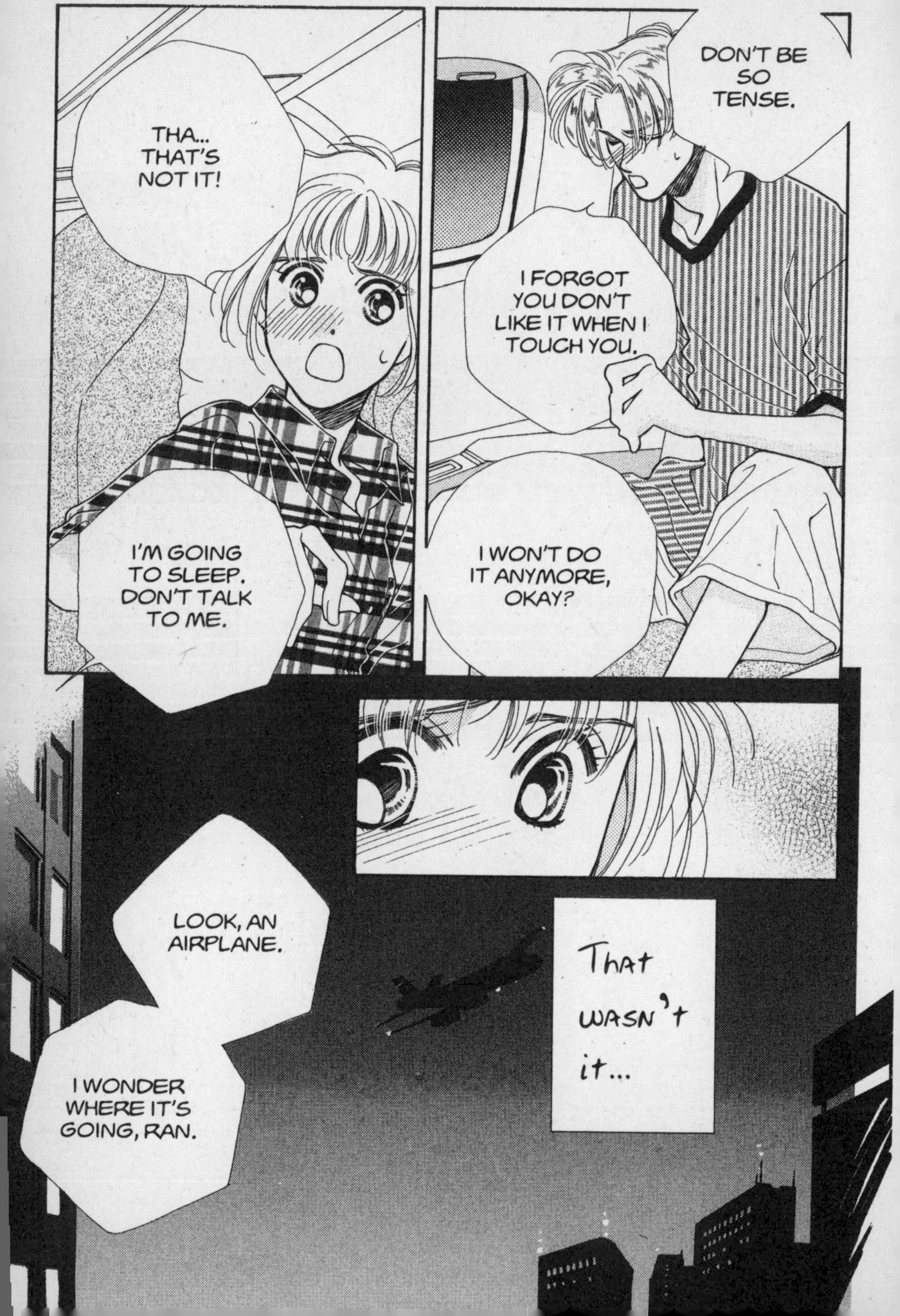
DON'T BE SO TENSE.
I FORGOT YOU DON'T LIKE IT WHEN I TOUCH YOU.
I WON'T DO IT ANYMORE, OKAY?
THA... THAT'S NOT IT!
I'M GOING TO SLEEP. DON'T TALK TO ME.
That wasn't it...
LOOK, AN AIRPLANE.
I WONDER WHERE IT'S GOING, RAN.

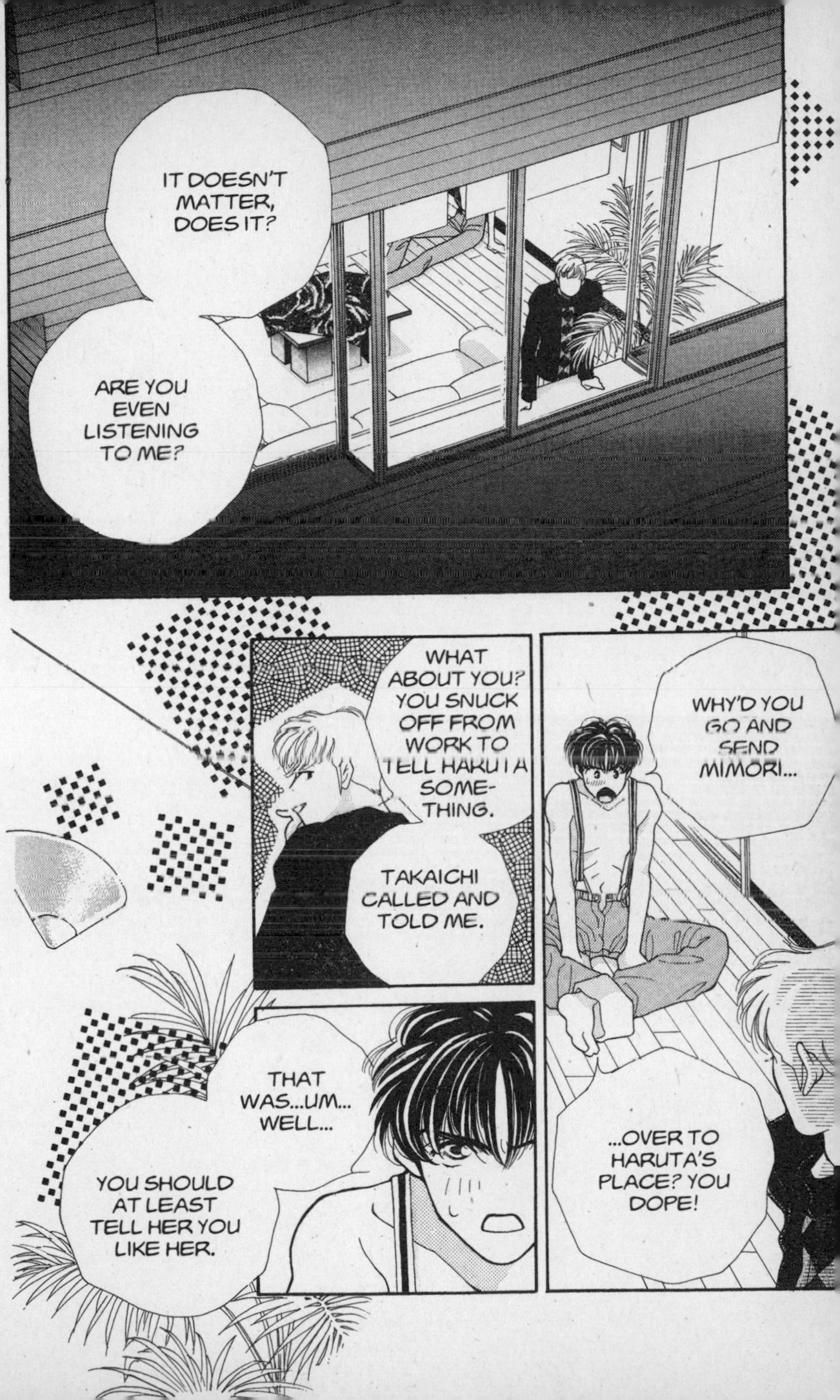
IT DOESN'T MATTER, DOES IT?
ARE YOU EVEN LISTENING TO ME?
WHY'D YOU GO AND SEND MIMORI...
...OVER TO HARUTA'S PLACE? YOU DOPE!
WHAT ABOUT YOU? YOU SNUCK OFF FROM WORK TO TELL HARUTA SOMETHING.
TAKAICHI CALLED AND TOLD ME.
THAT WAS...UM... WELL...
YOU SHOULD AT LEAST TELL HER YOU LIKE HER.

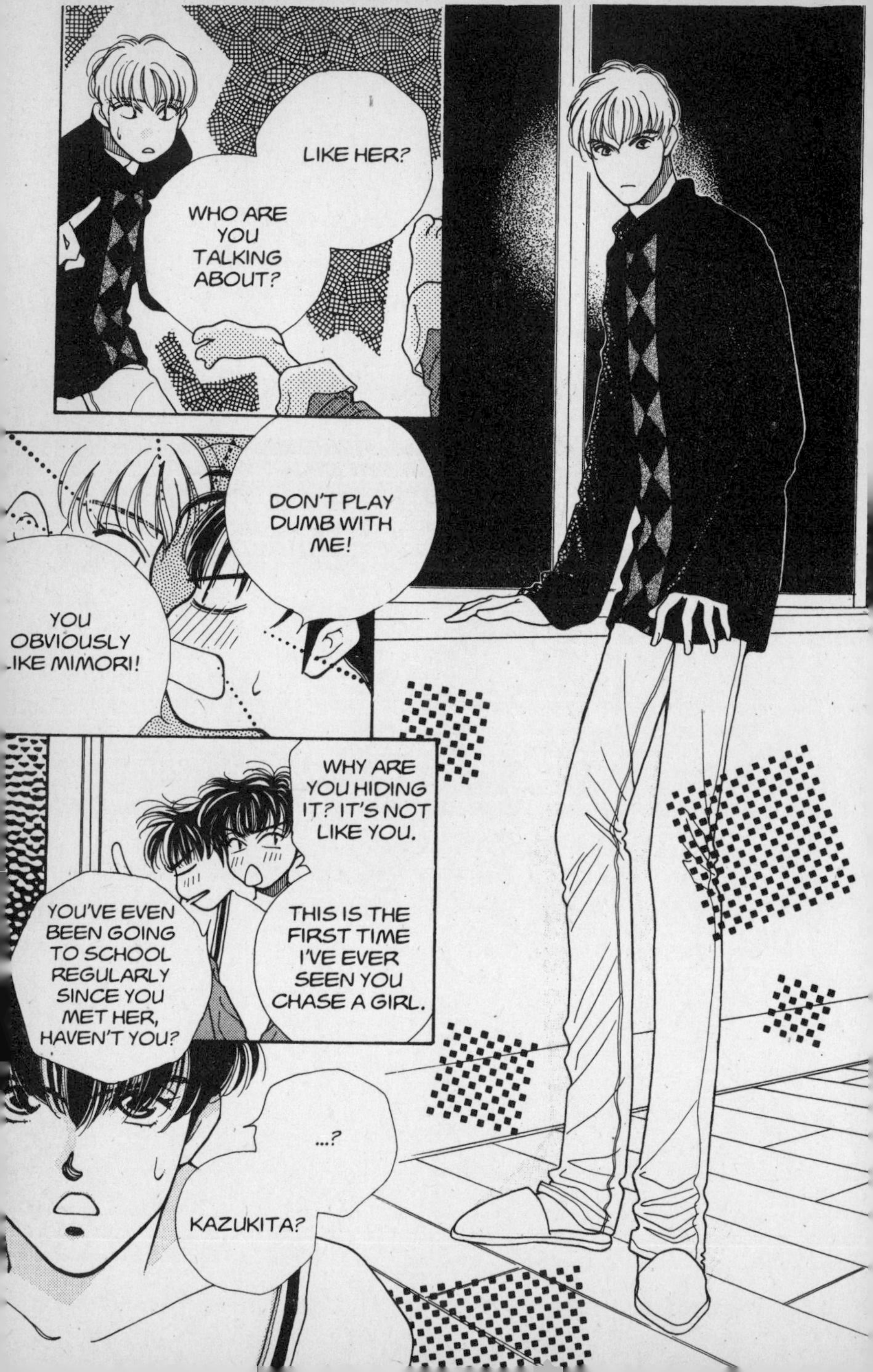
LIKE HER?
WHO ARE YOU TALKING ABOUT?
DON'T PLAY DUMB WITH ME!
YOU OBVIOUSLY LIKE MIMORI!
WHY ARE YOU HIDING IT? IT'S NOT LIKE YOU.
THIS IS THE FIRST TIME I'VE EVER SEEN YOU CHASE A GIRL.
YOU'VE EVEN BEEN GOING TO SCHOOL REGULARLY SINCE YOU MET HER, HAVEN'T YOU?
...?
KAZUKITA?

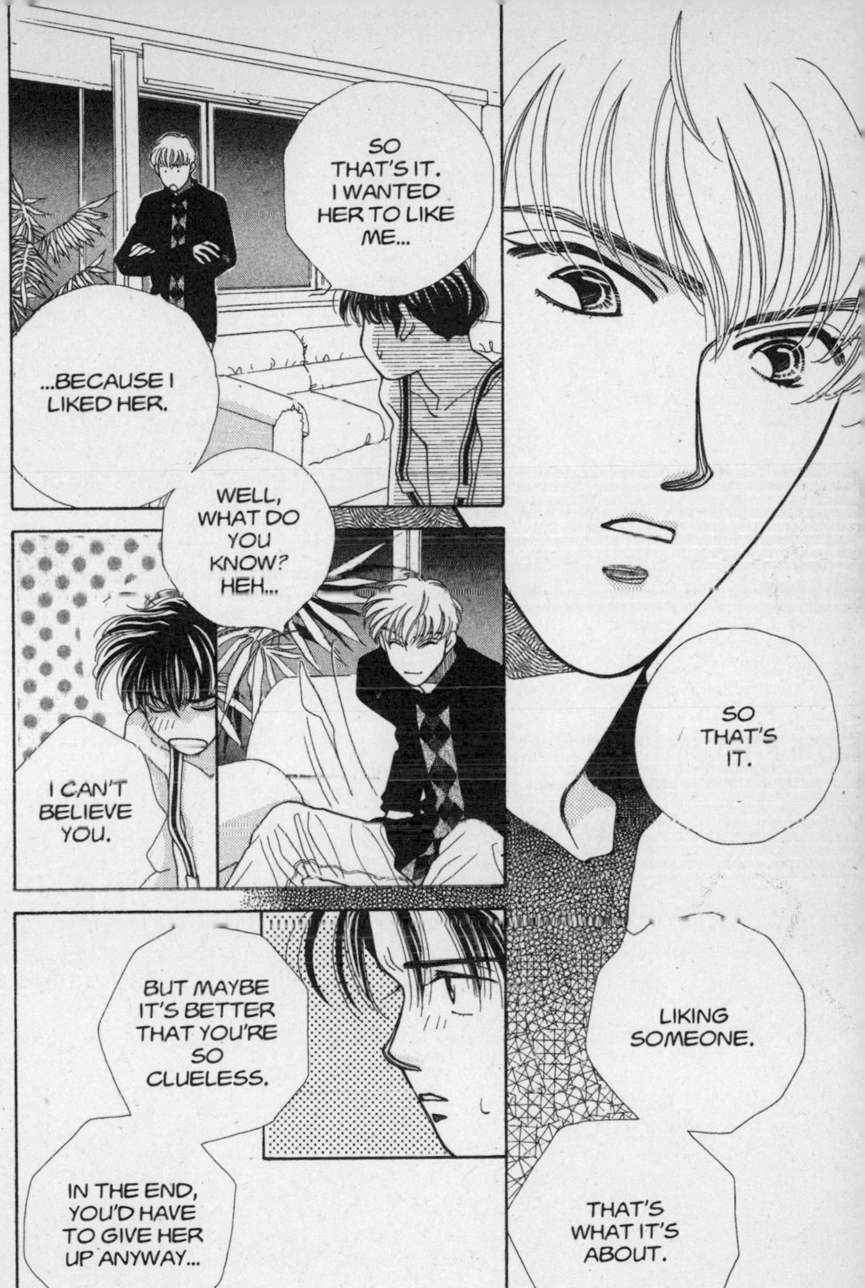
SO THAT'S IT.
LIKING SOMEONE.
THAT'S WHAT IT'S ABOUT.
SO THAT'S IT. I WANTED HER TO LIKE ME...
...BECAUSE I LIKED HER.
WELL, WHAT DO YOU KNOW? HEH...
I CAN'T BELIEVE YOU.
BUT MAYBE IT'S BETTER THAT YOU'RE SO CLUELESS.
IN THE END, YOU'D HAVE TO GIVE HER UP ANYWAY...

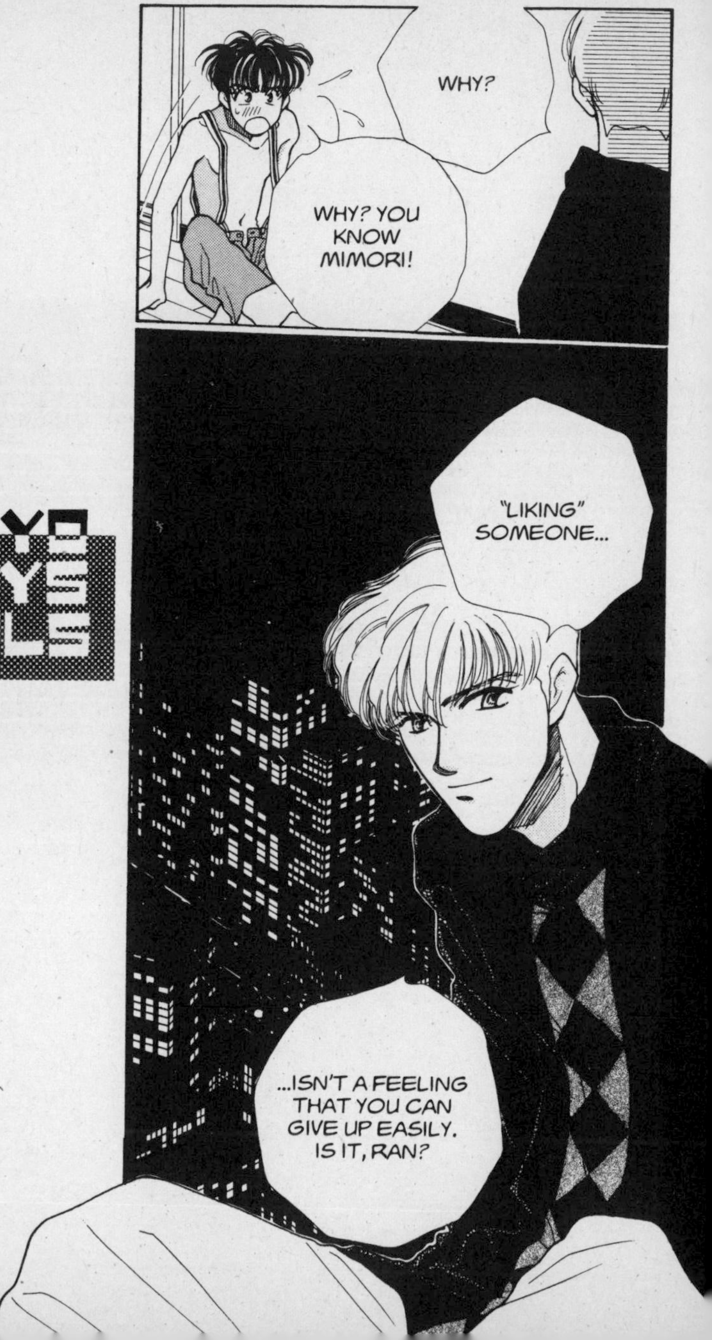
WHY?
WHY? YOU KNOW MIMORI!
"LIKING" SOMEONE...
...ISN'T A FEELING THAT YOU CAN GIVE UP EASILY. IS IT, RAN?

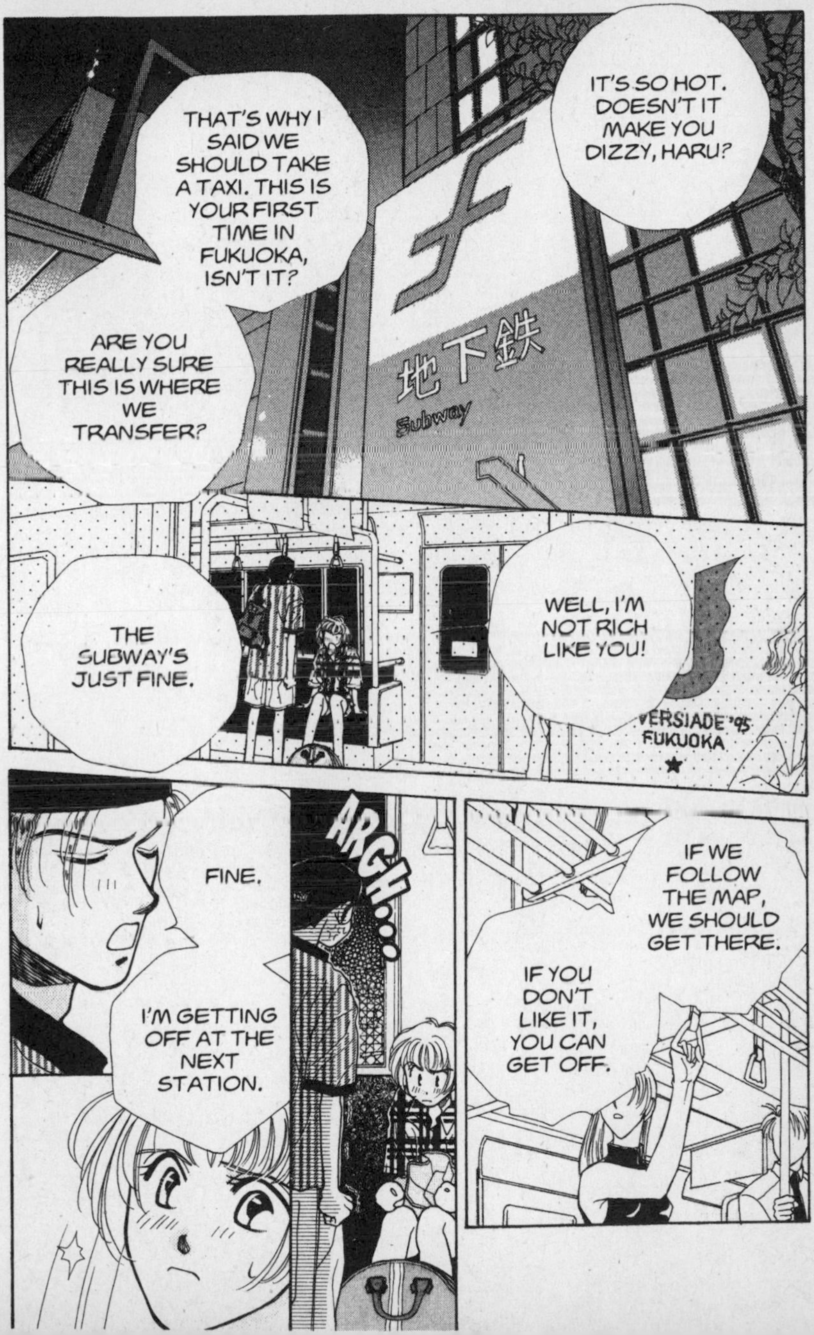
IT'S SO HOT. DOESN'T IT MAKE YOU DIZZY, HARU?
THAT'S WHY I SAID WE SHOULD TAKE A TAXI. THIS IS YOUR FIRST TIME IN FUKUOKA, ISN'T IT?
地下鉄
Subway
ARE YOU REALLY SURE THIS IS WHERE WE TRANSFER?
WELL, I'M NOT RICH LIKE YOU!
VERSIADE '95 FUKUOKA
THE SUBWAY'S JUST FINE.
IF WE FOLLOW THE MAP, WE SHOULD GET THERE.
IF YOU DON'T LIKE IT, YOU CAN GET OFF.
ARGH...
FINE.
I'M GETTING OFF AT THE NEXT STATION.

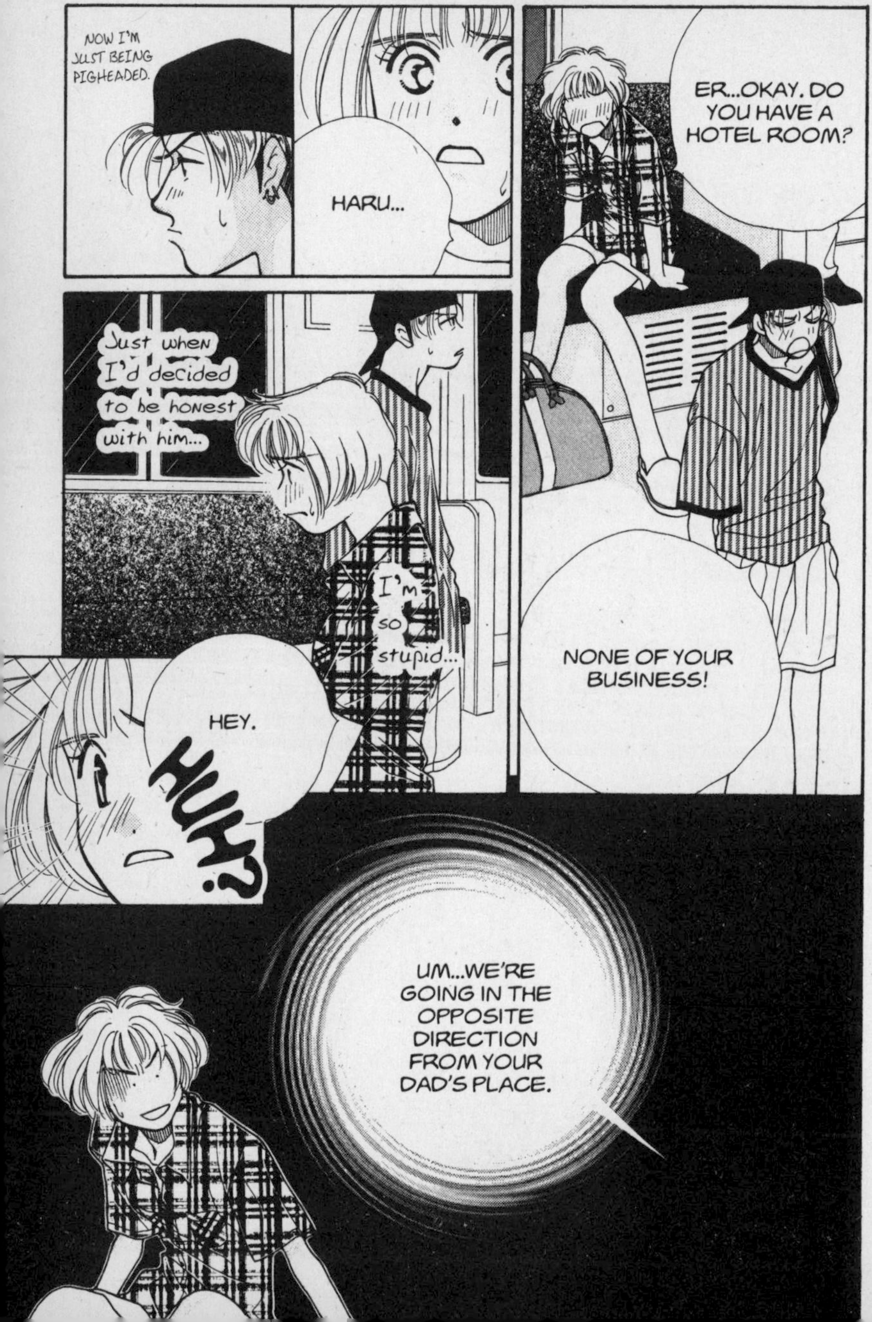
ER...OKAY. DO YOU HAVE A HOTEL ROOM?
NONE OF YOUR BUSINESS!
HARU...
NOW I'M JUST BEING PIGHEADED.
Just when I'd decided to be honest with him...
I'm so stupid...
HEY.
HUH?!
UM...WE'RE GOING IN THE OPPOSITE DIRECTION FROM YOUR DAD'S PLACE.

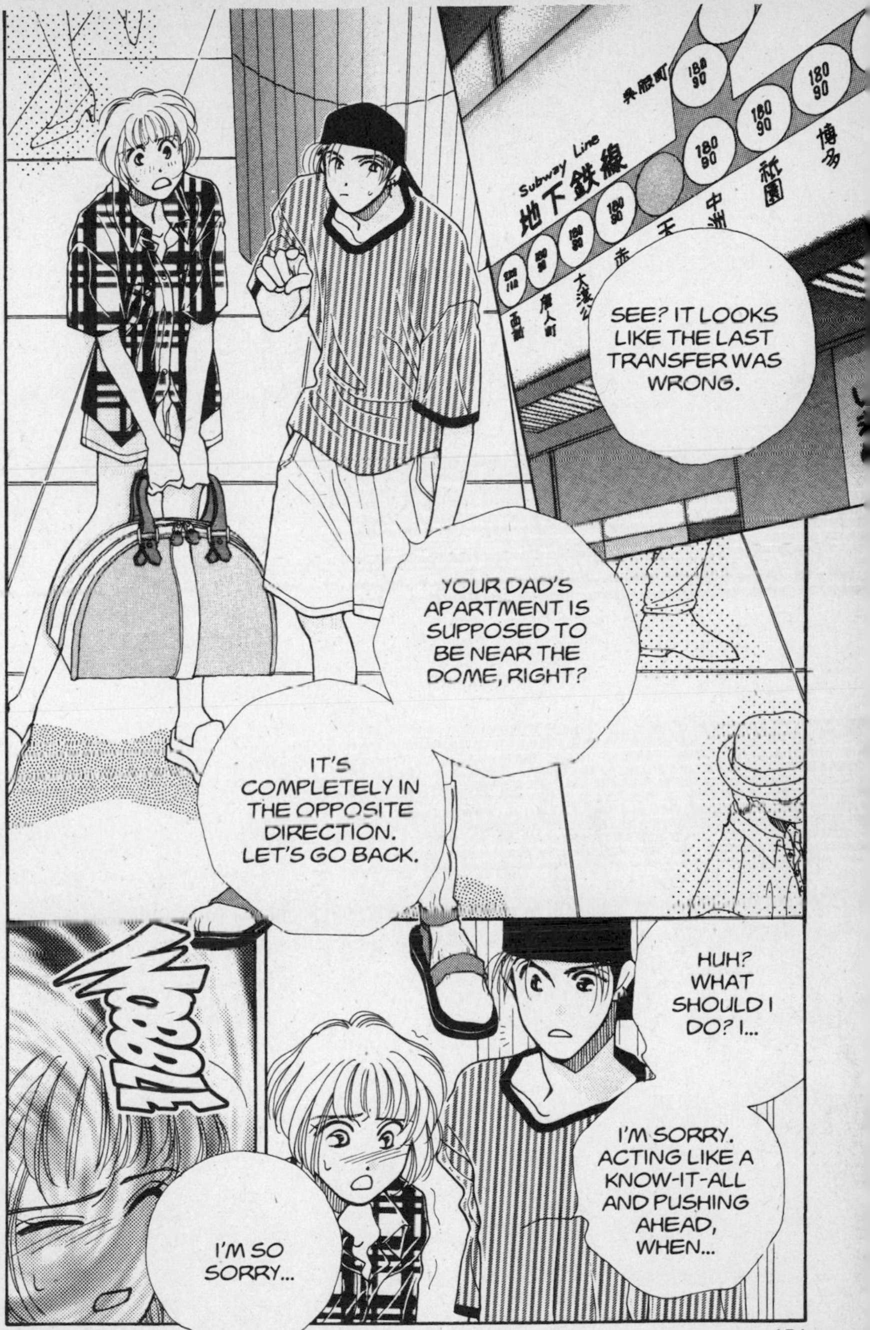
Subway Line
地下鉄線
呉服町
祇園
博多
SEE? IT LOOKS LIKE THE LAST TRANSFER WAS WRONG.
YOUR DAD'S APARTMENT IS SUPPOSED TO BE NEAR THE DOME, RIGHT?
IT'S COMPLETELY IN THE OPPOSITE DIRECTION. LET'S GO BACK.
HUH? WHAT SHOULD I DO? I...
I'M SORRY. ACTING LIKE A KNOW-IT-ALL AND PUSHING AHEAD, WHEN...
I'M SO SORRY...
WOBBLE

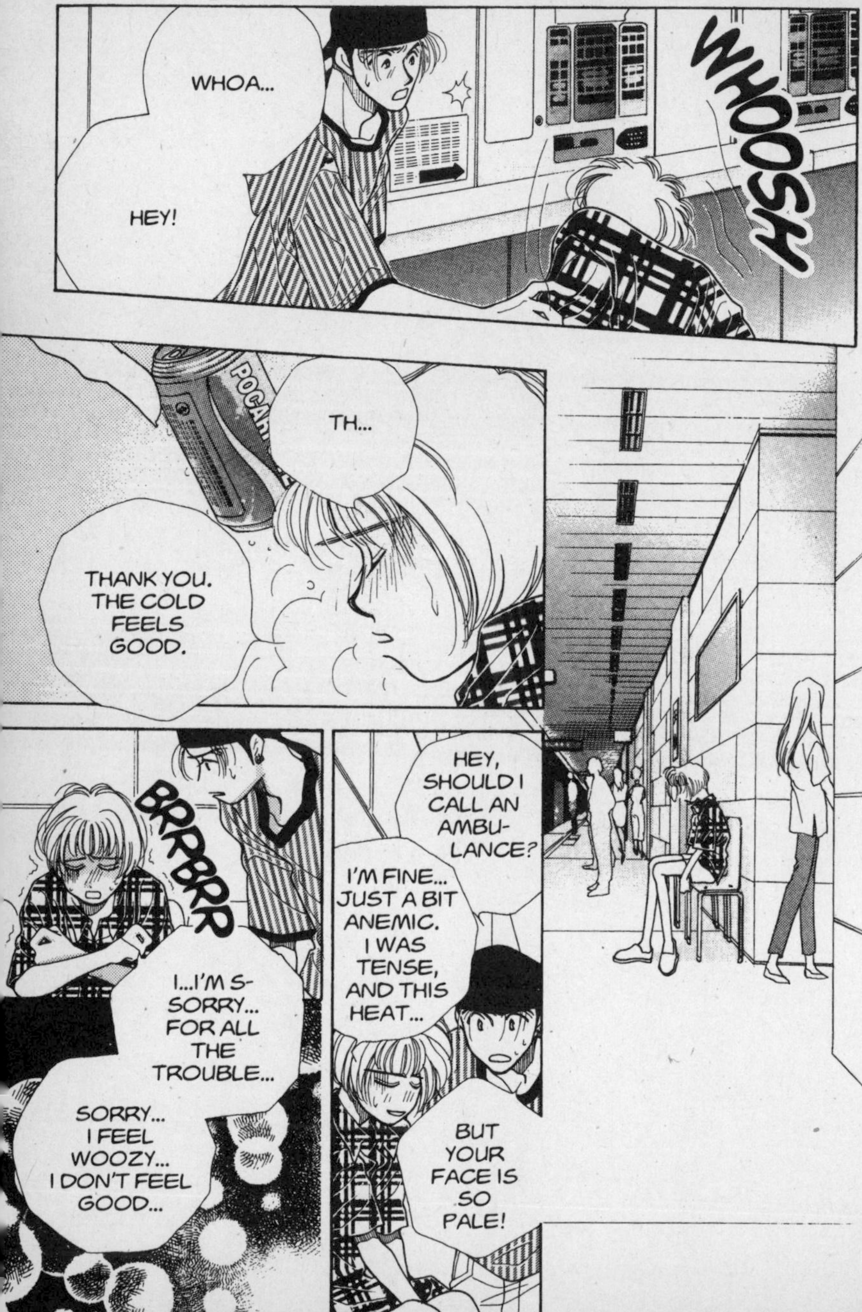
WHOOSH
WHOA...
HEY!
POCARI
TH...
THANK YOU. THE COLD FEELS GOOD.
HEY, SHOULD I CALL AN AMBU-LANCE?
I'M FINE... JUST A BIT ANEMIC. I WAS TENSE, AND THIS HEAT...
BUT YOUR FACE IS SO PALE!
BRRBRR
I...I'M S-SORRY... FOR ALL THE TROUBLE...
SORRY... I FEEL WOOZY... I DON'T FEEL GOOD...

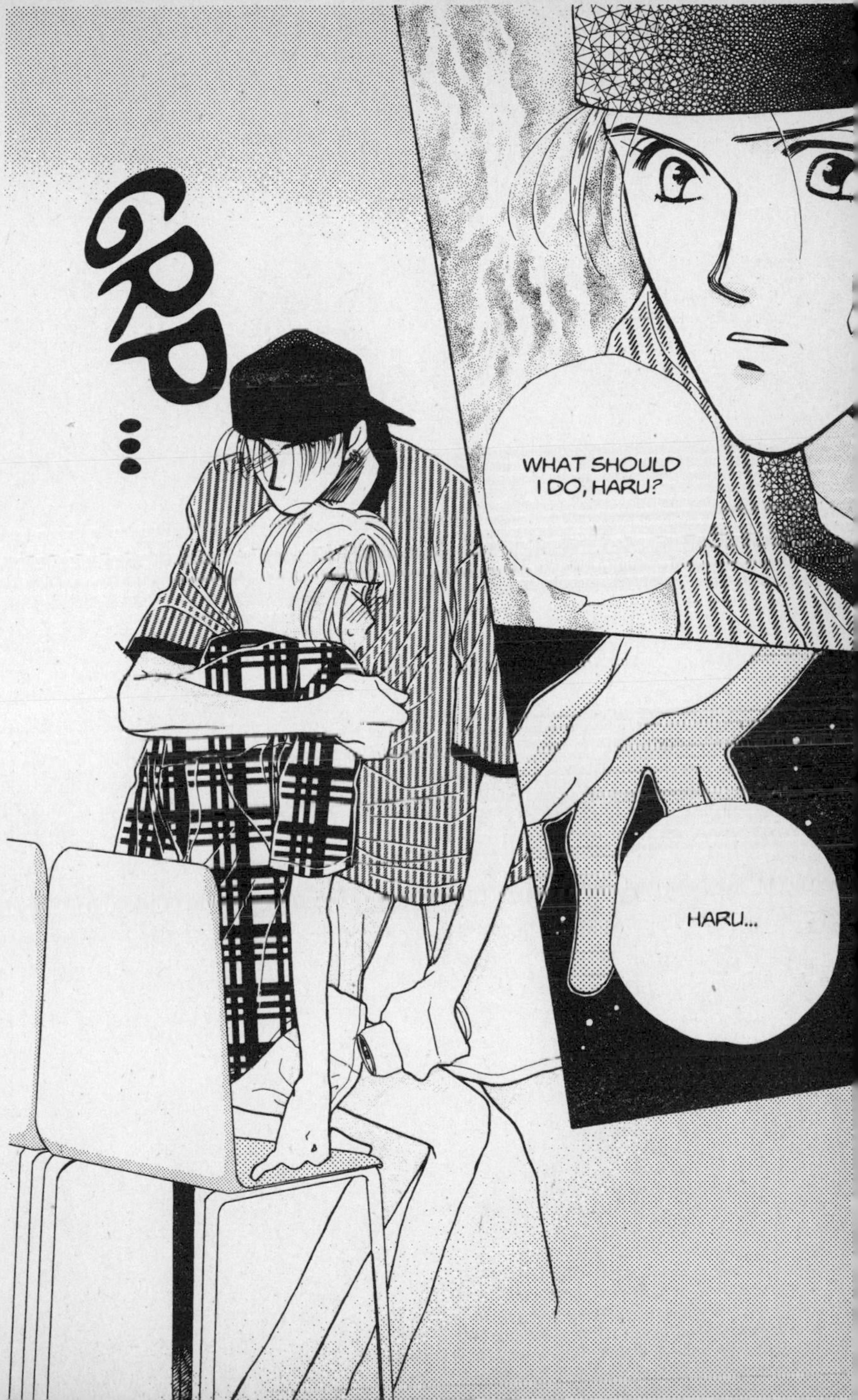
WHAT SHOULD I DO, HARU?
HARU...
GRP...

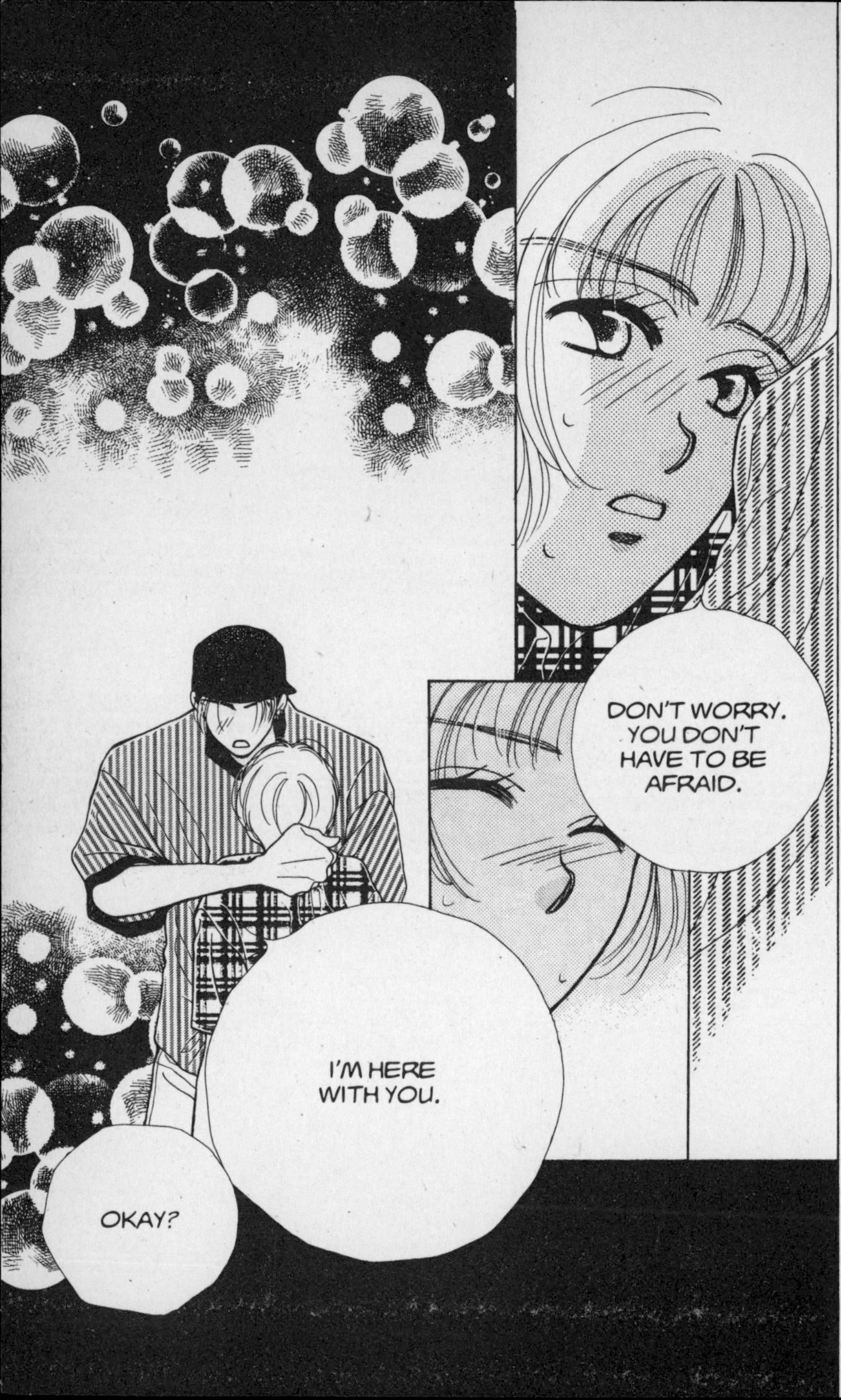
DON'T WORRY. YOU DON'T HAVE TO BE AFRAID.
I'M HERE WITH YOU.
OKAY?

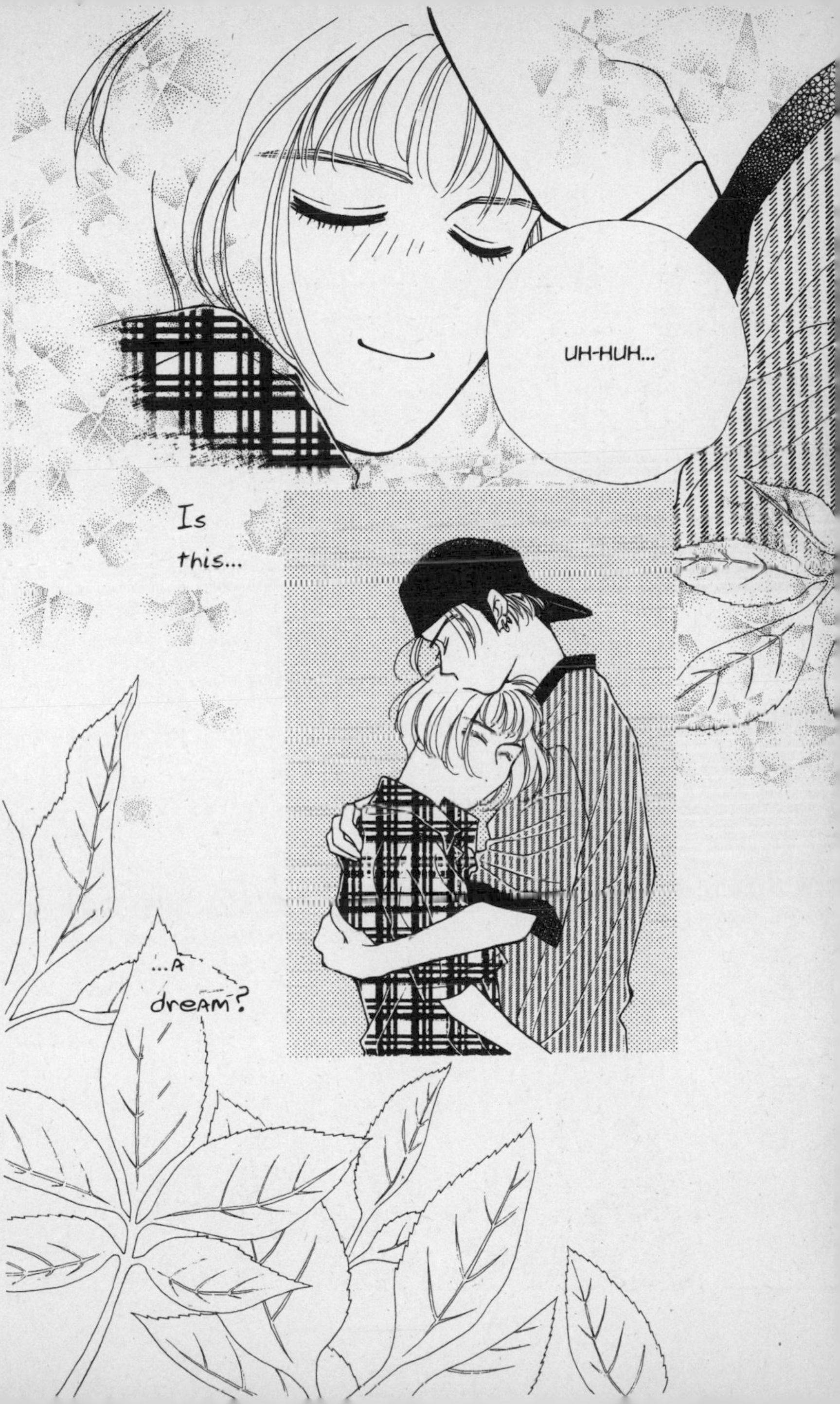
UH-HUH...
Is this...
...A dream?

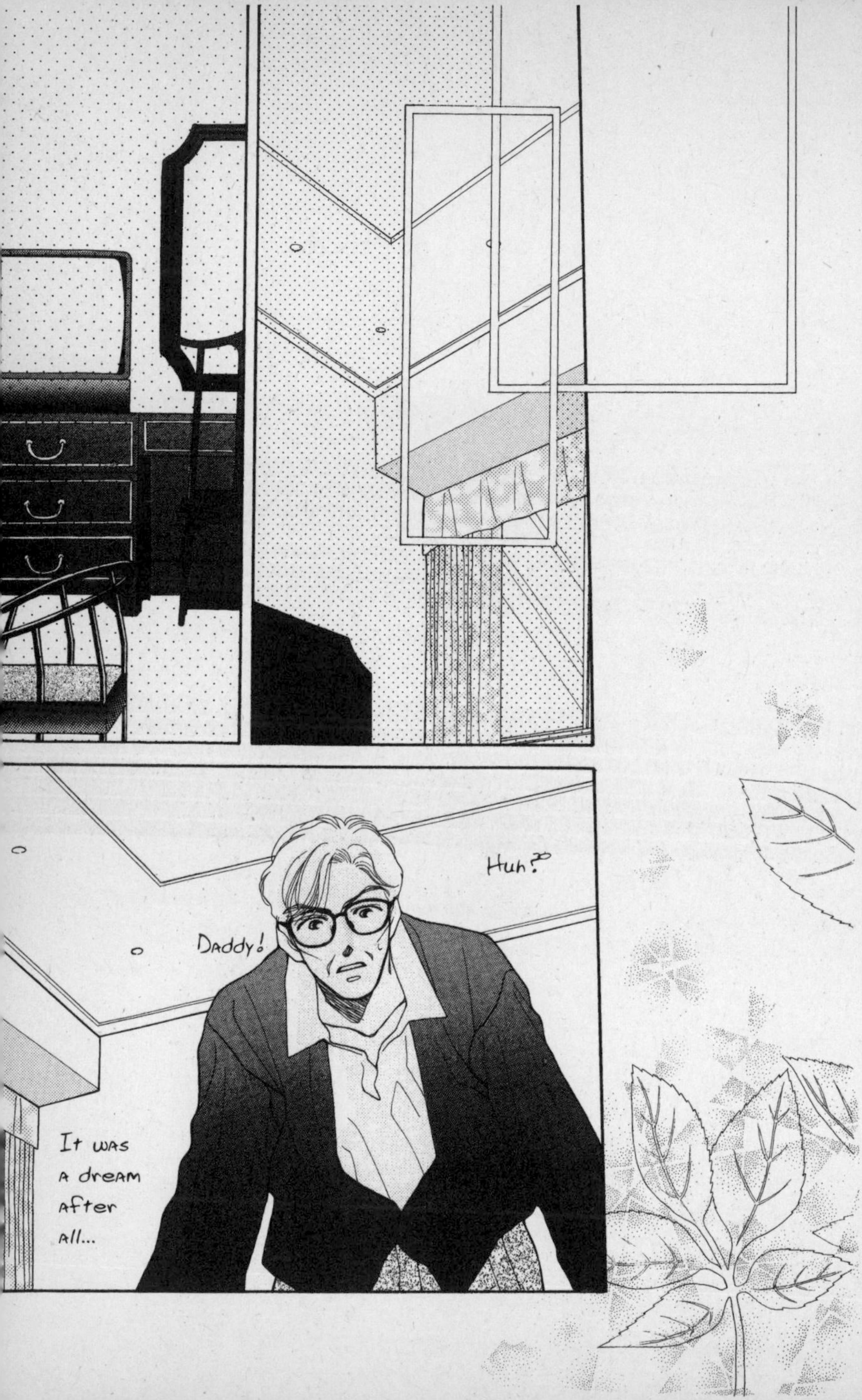
Huh?
Daddy!
It was a dream after all...

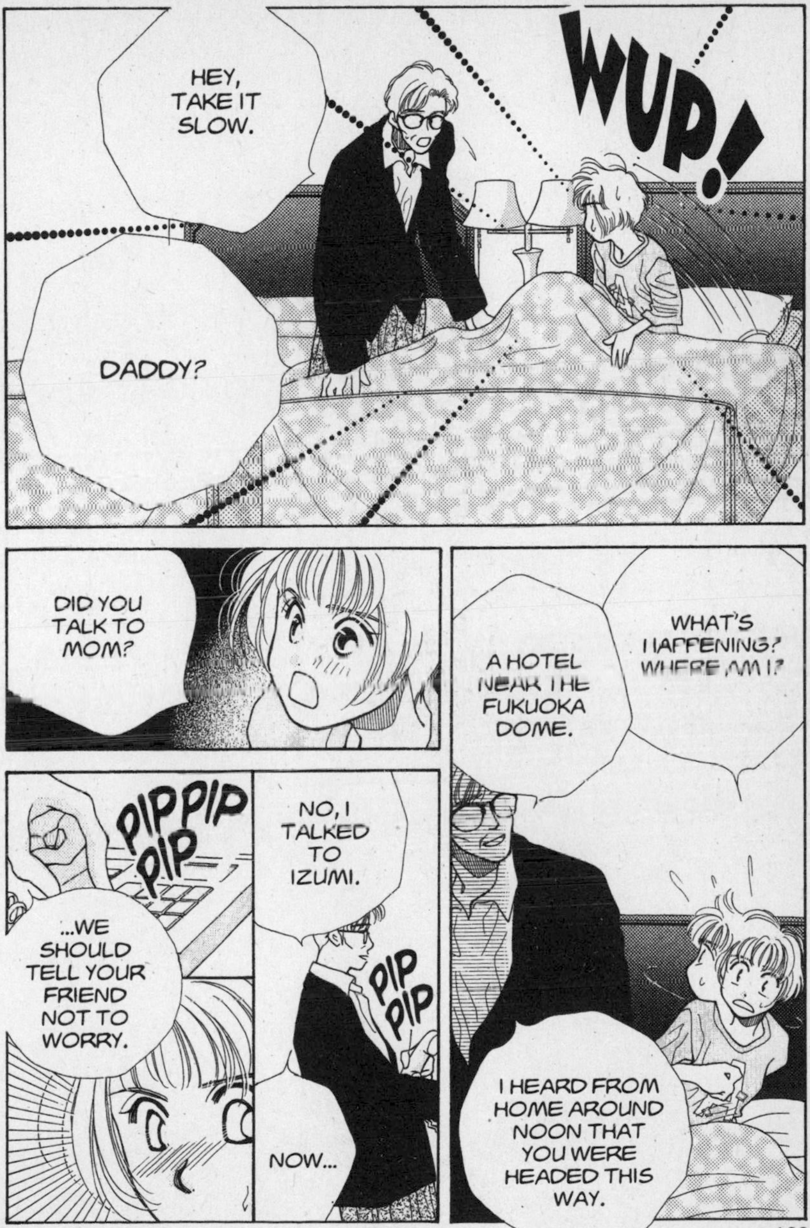
WUP!
HEY, TAKE IT SLOW.
DADDY?
WHAT'S HAPPENING? WHERE AM I?
A HOTEL NEAR THE FUKUOKA DOME.
I HEARD FROM HOME AROUND NOON THAT YOU WERE HEADED THIS WAY.
DID YOU TALK TO MOM?
NO, I TALKED TO IZUMI.
PIP PIP
NOW...
PIPPIP PIP
...WE SHOULD TELL YOUR FRIEND NOT TO WORRY.

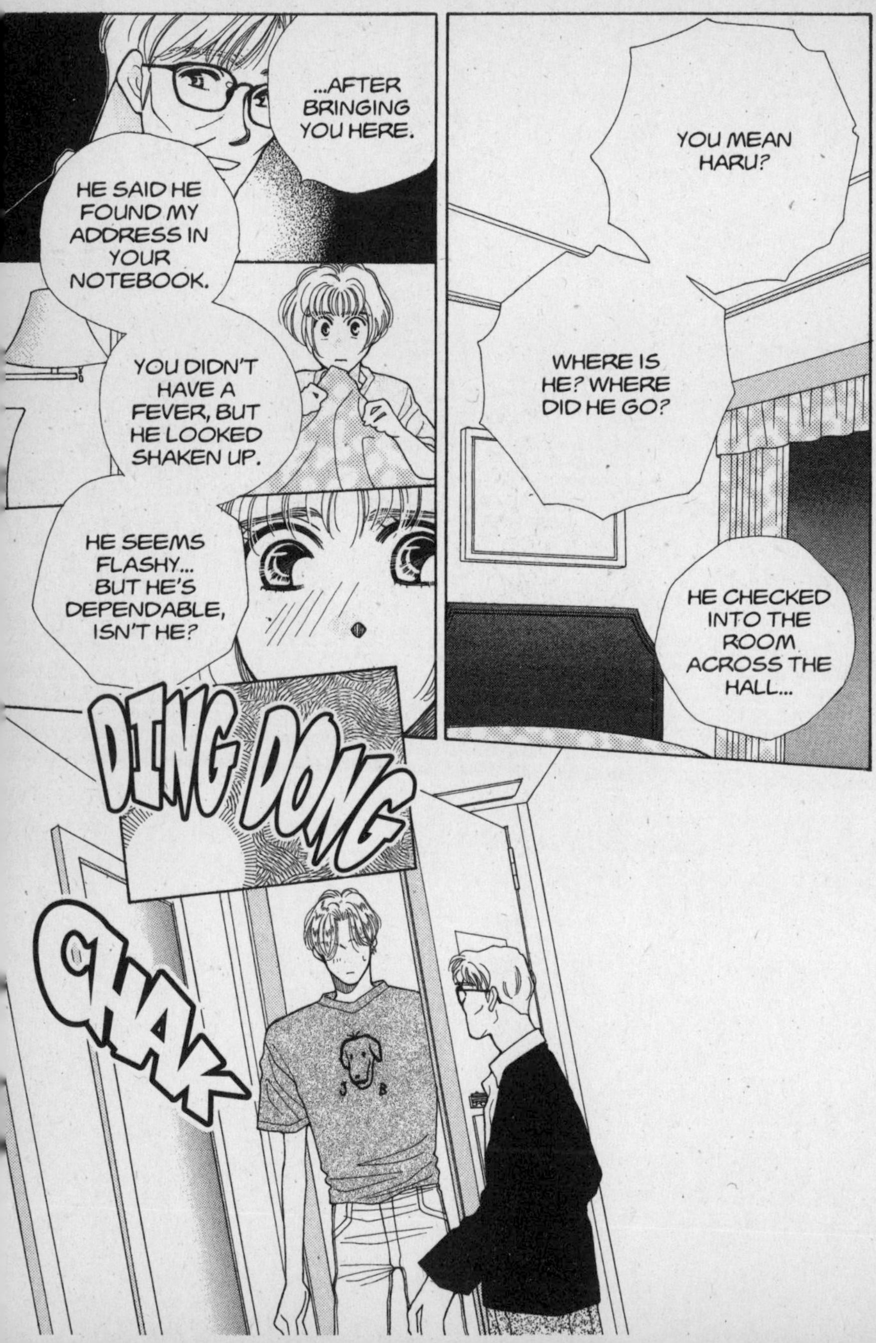
YOU MEAN HARU?
WHERE IS HE? WHERE DID HE GO?
HE CHECKED INTO THE ROOM ACROSS THE HALL...
...AFTER BRINGING YOU HERE.
HE SAID HE FOUND MY ADDRESS IN YOUR NOTEBOOK.
YOU DIDN'T HAVE A FEVER, BUT HE LOOKED SHAKEN UP.
HE SEEMS FLASHY... BUT HE'S DEPENDABLE, ISN'T HE?
DING DONG
CHAK

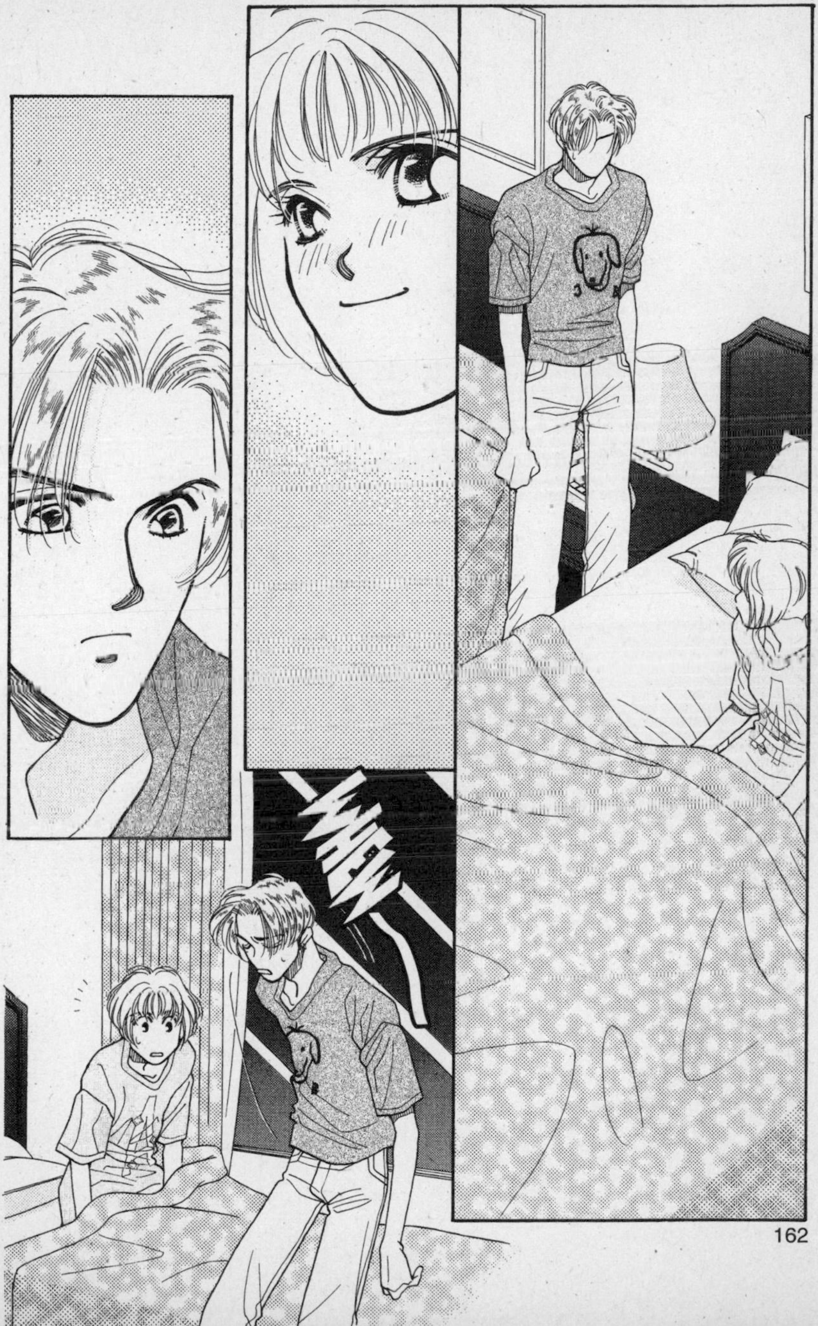
WHEW

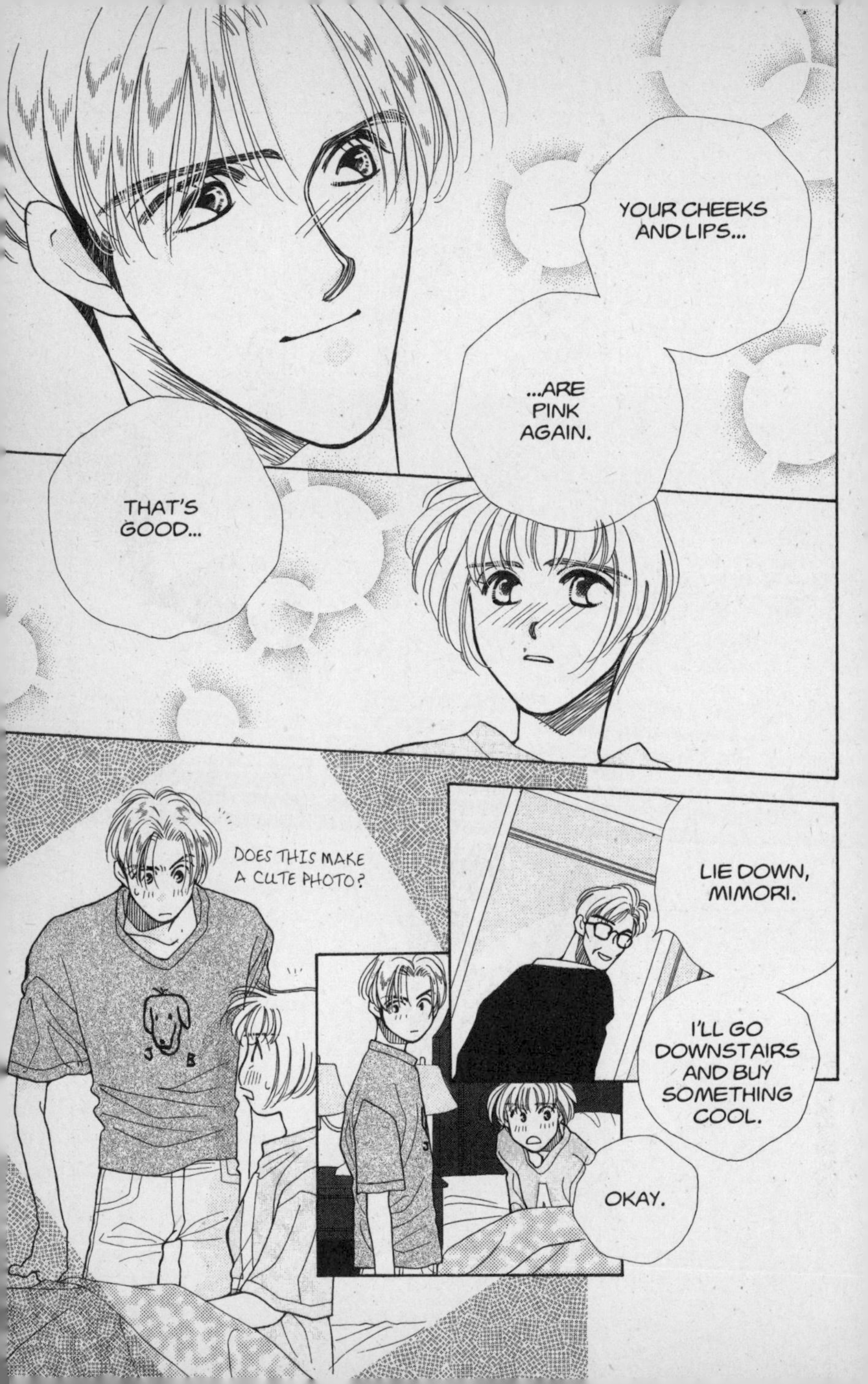
YOUR CHEEKS AND LIPS...
...ARE PINK AGAIN.
THAT'S GOOD...
LIE DOWN, MIMORI.
I'LL GO DOWNSTAIRS AND BUY SOMETHING COOL.
OKAY.
DOES THIS MAKE A CUTE PHOTO?

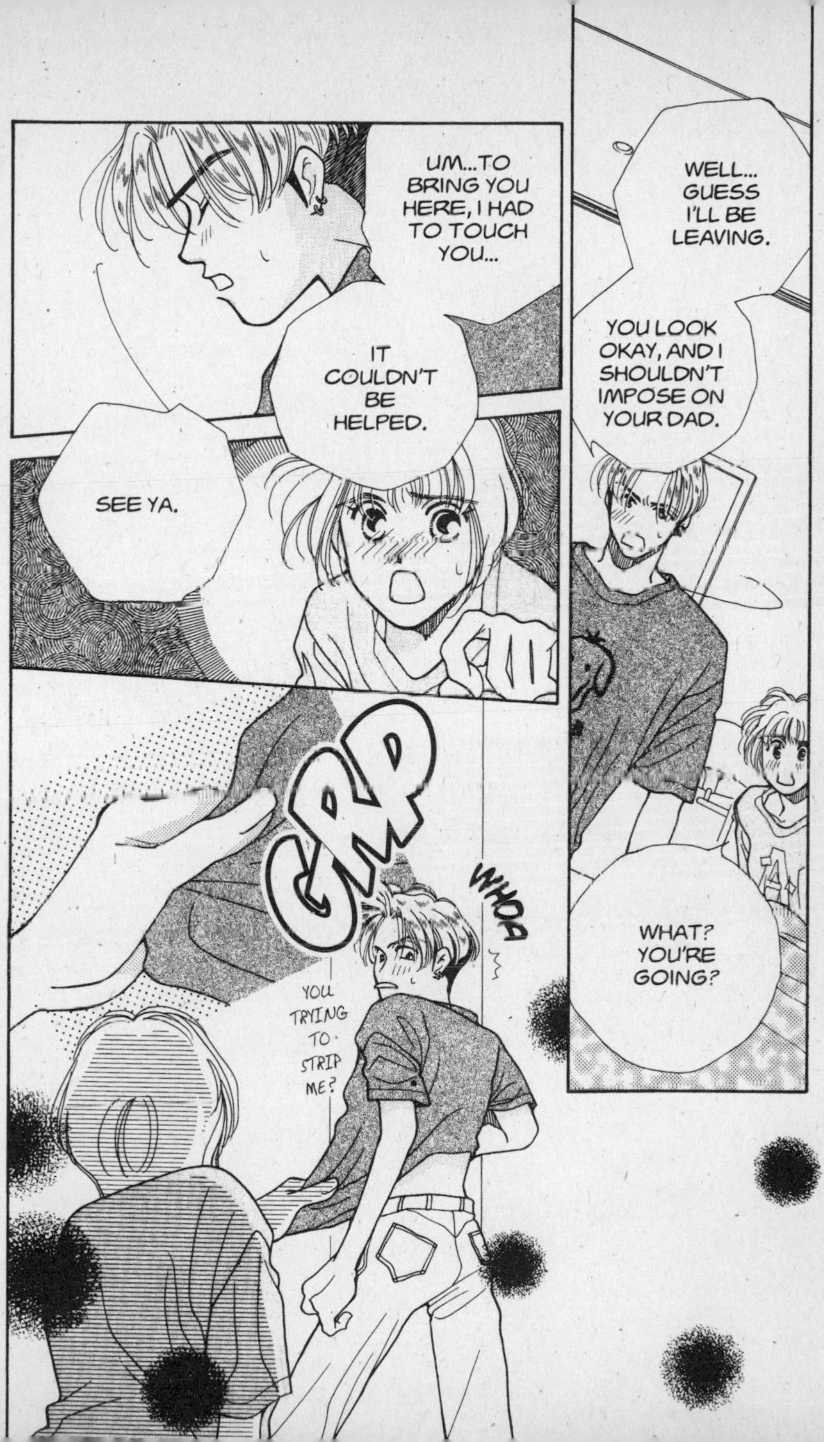
WELL... GUESS I'LL BE LEAVING.
YOU LOOK OKAY, AND I SHOULDN'T IMPOSE ON YOUR DAD.
WHAT? YOU'RE GOING?
UM...TO BRING YOU HERE, I HAD TO TOUCH YOU...
IT COULDN'T BE HELPED.
SEE YA.
GRP
WHOA
YOU TRYING TO STRIP ME?

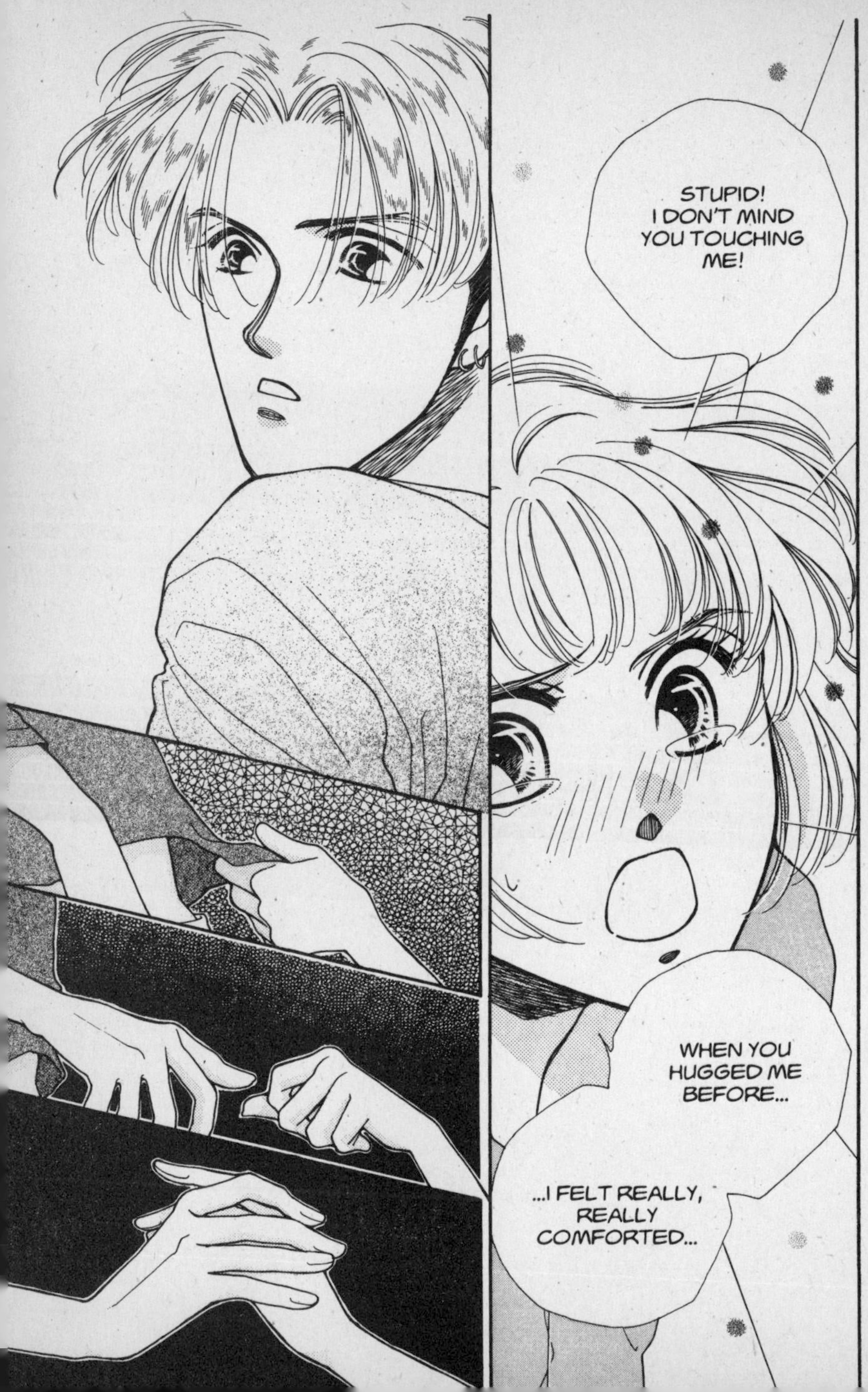
STUPID! I DON'T MIND YOU TOUCHING ME!
WHEN YOU HUGGED ME BEFORE...
...I FELT REALLY, REALLY COMFORTED...

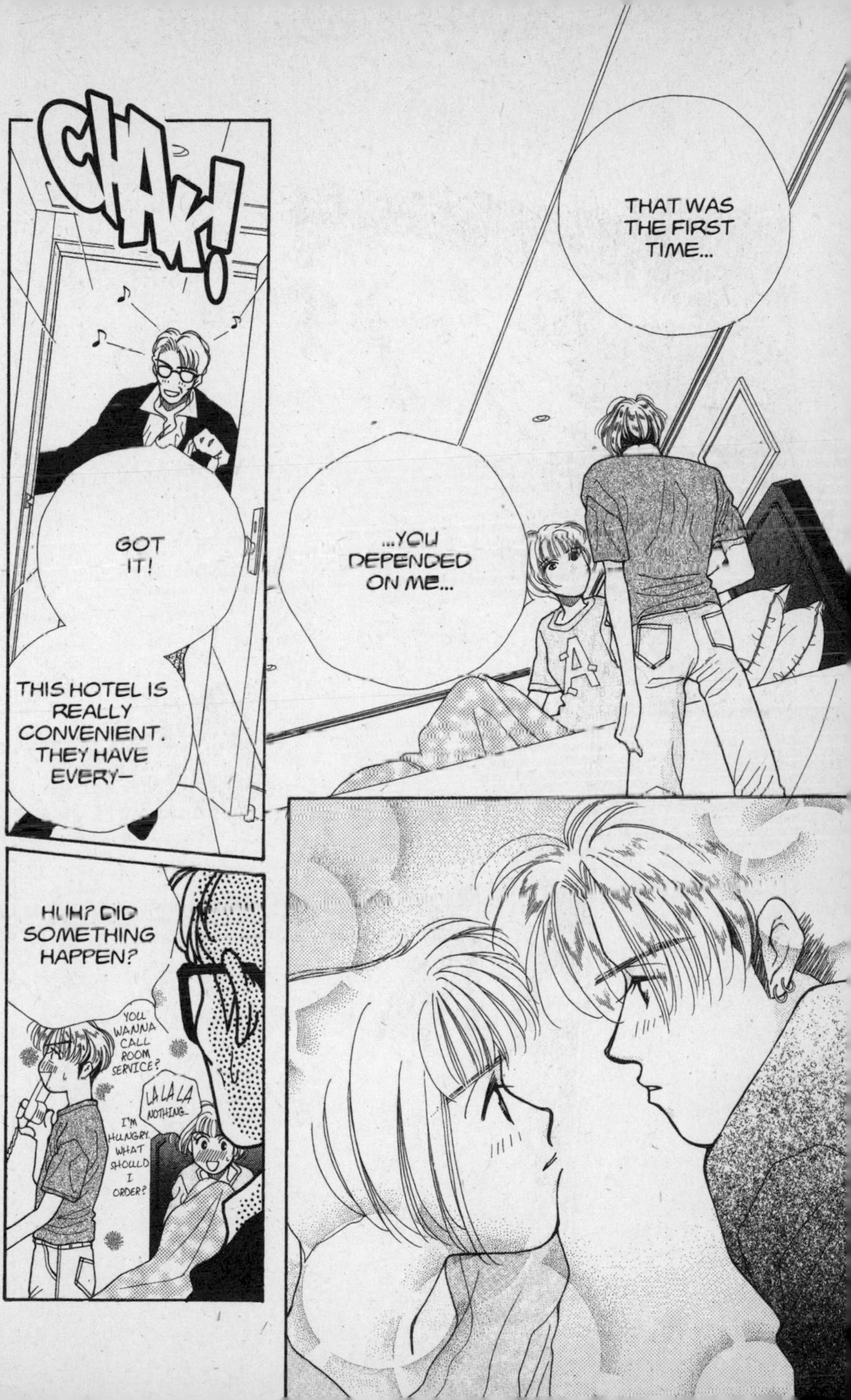
THAT WAS THE FIRST TIME...
...YOU DEPENDED ON ME...
CHAK!
GOT IT!
THIS HOTEL IS REALLY CONVENIENT. THEY HAVE EVERY—
HUH? DID SOMETHING HAPPEN?
YOU WANNA CALL ROOM SERVICE?
LA LA LA NOTHING...
I'M HUNGRY. WHAT SHOULD I ORDER?

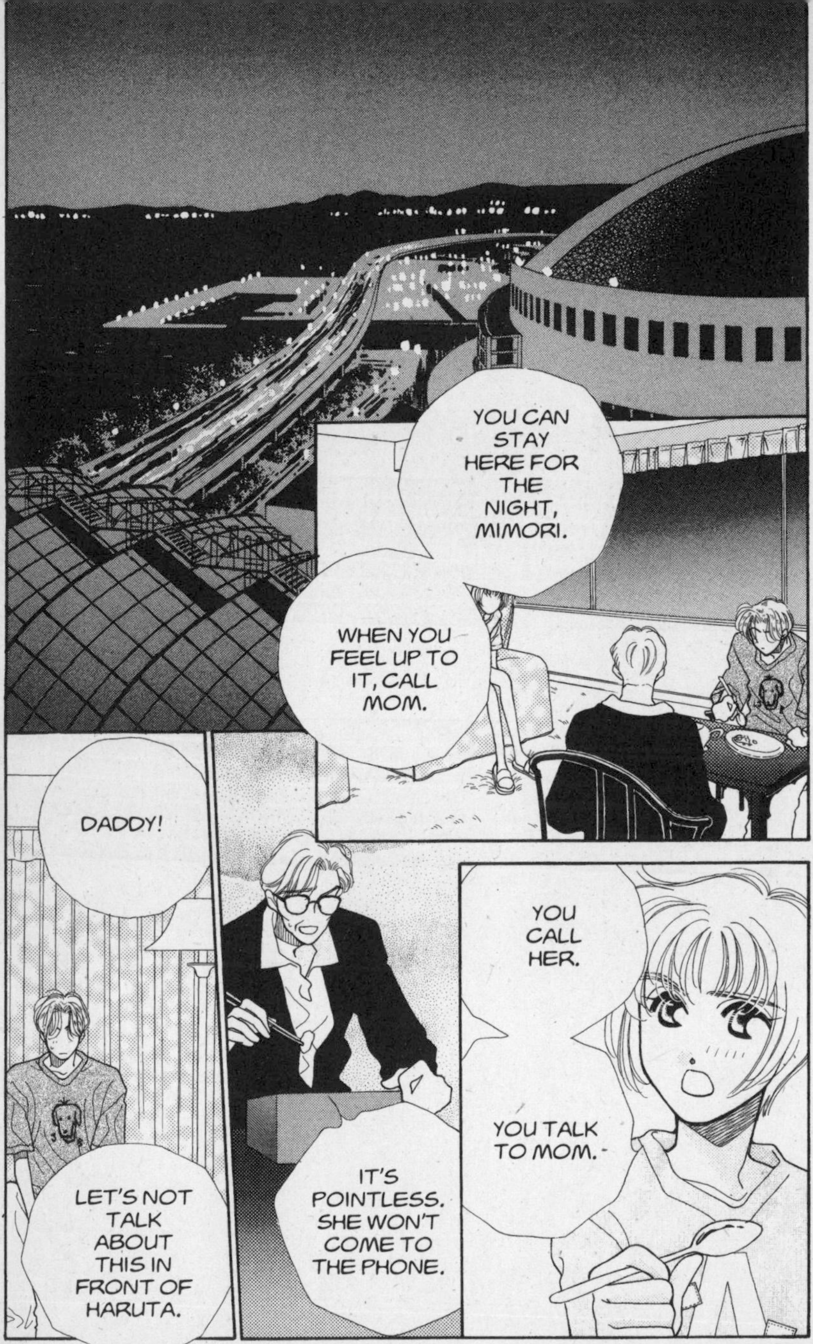
YOU CAN STAY HERE FOR THE NIGHT, MIMORI.
WHEN YOU FEEL UP TO IT, CALL MOM.
YOU CALL HER.
YOU TALK TO MOM.
IT'S POINTLESS. SHE WON'T COME TO THE PHONE.
DADDY!
LET'S NOT TALK ABOUT THIS IN FRONT OF HARUTA.

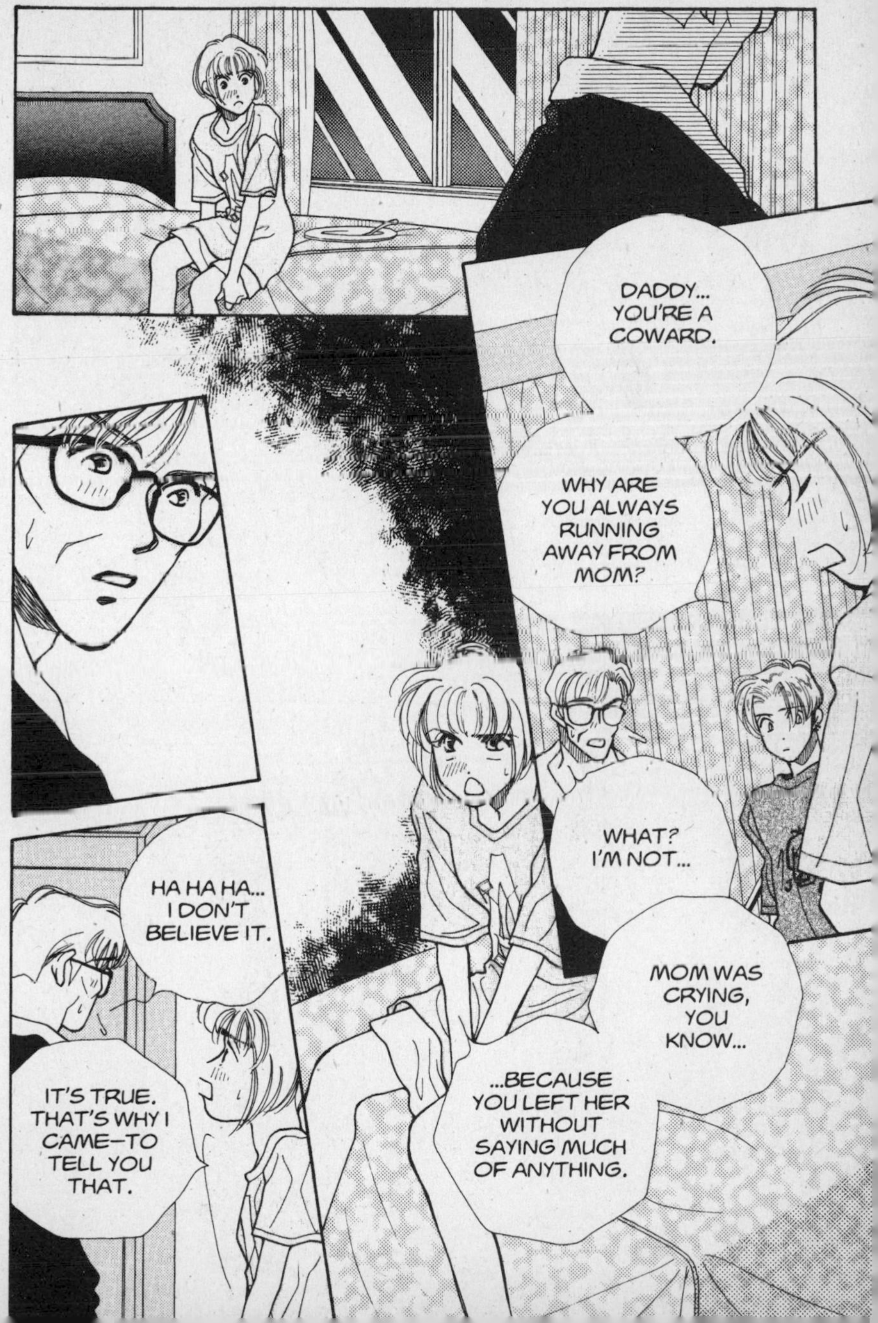
DADDY... YOU'RE A COWARD.
WHY ARE YOU ALWAYS RUNNING AWAY FROM MOM?
WHAT? I'M NOT...
MOM WAS CRYING, YOU KNOW...
...BECAUSE YOU LEFT HER WITHOUT SAYING MUCH OF ANYTHING.
HA HA HA... I DON'T BELIEVE IT.
IT'S TRUE. THAT'S WHY I CAME—TO TELL YOU THAT.

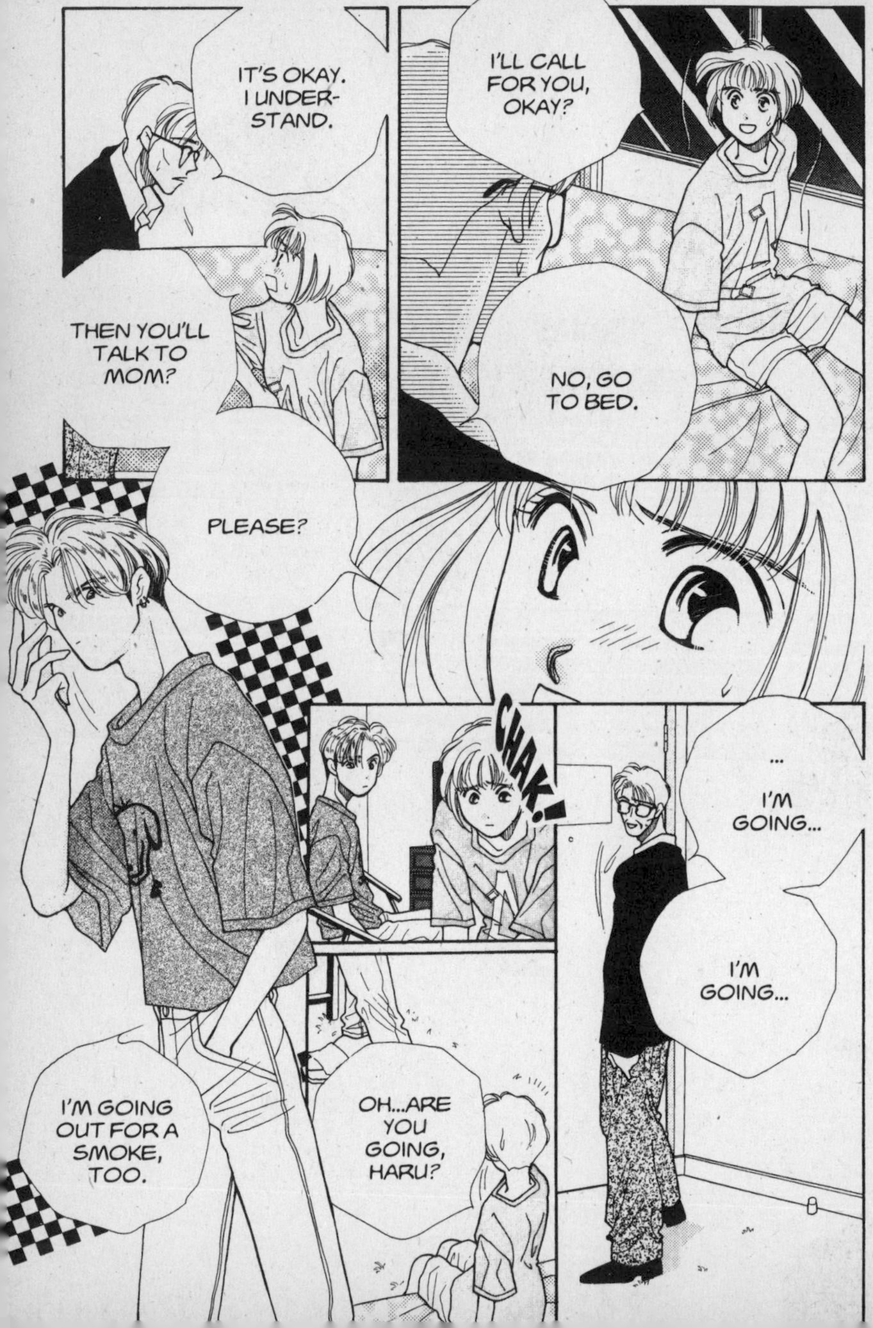
I'LL CALL FOR YOU, OKAY?
NO, GO TO BED.
IT'S OKAY. I UNDER-STAND.
THEN YOU'LL TALK TO MOM?
PLEASE?
CHAK!
... I'M GOING...
I'M GOING...
OH...ARE YOU GOING, HARU?
I'M GOING OUT FOR A SMOKE, TOO.

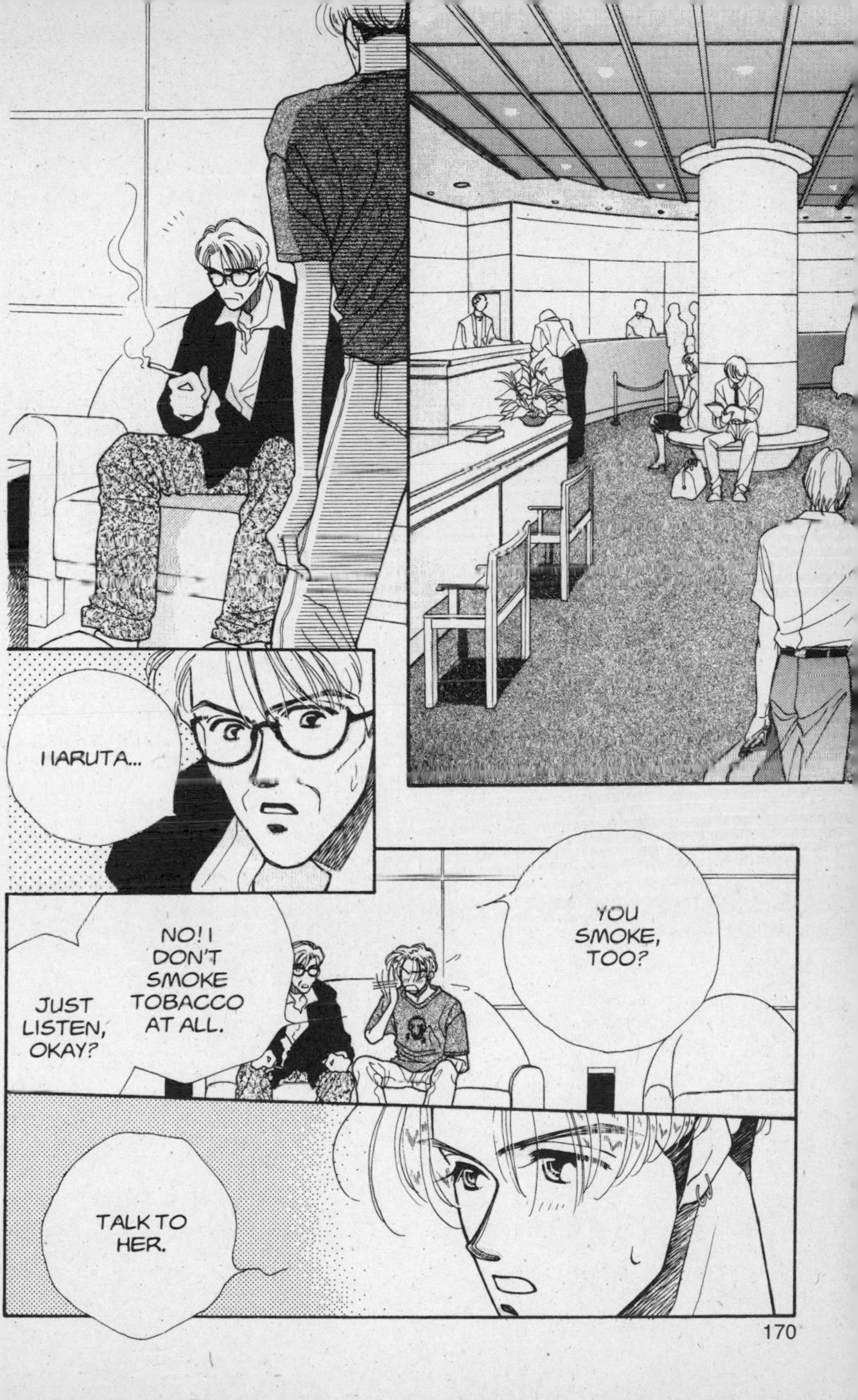
HARUTA...
YOU SMOKE, TOO?
NO! I DON'T SMOKE TOBACCO AT ALL.
JUST LISTEN, OKAY?
TALK TO HER.

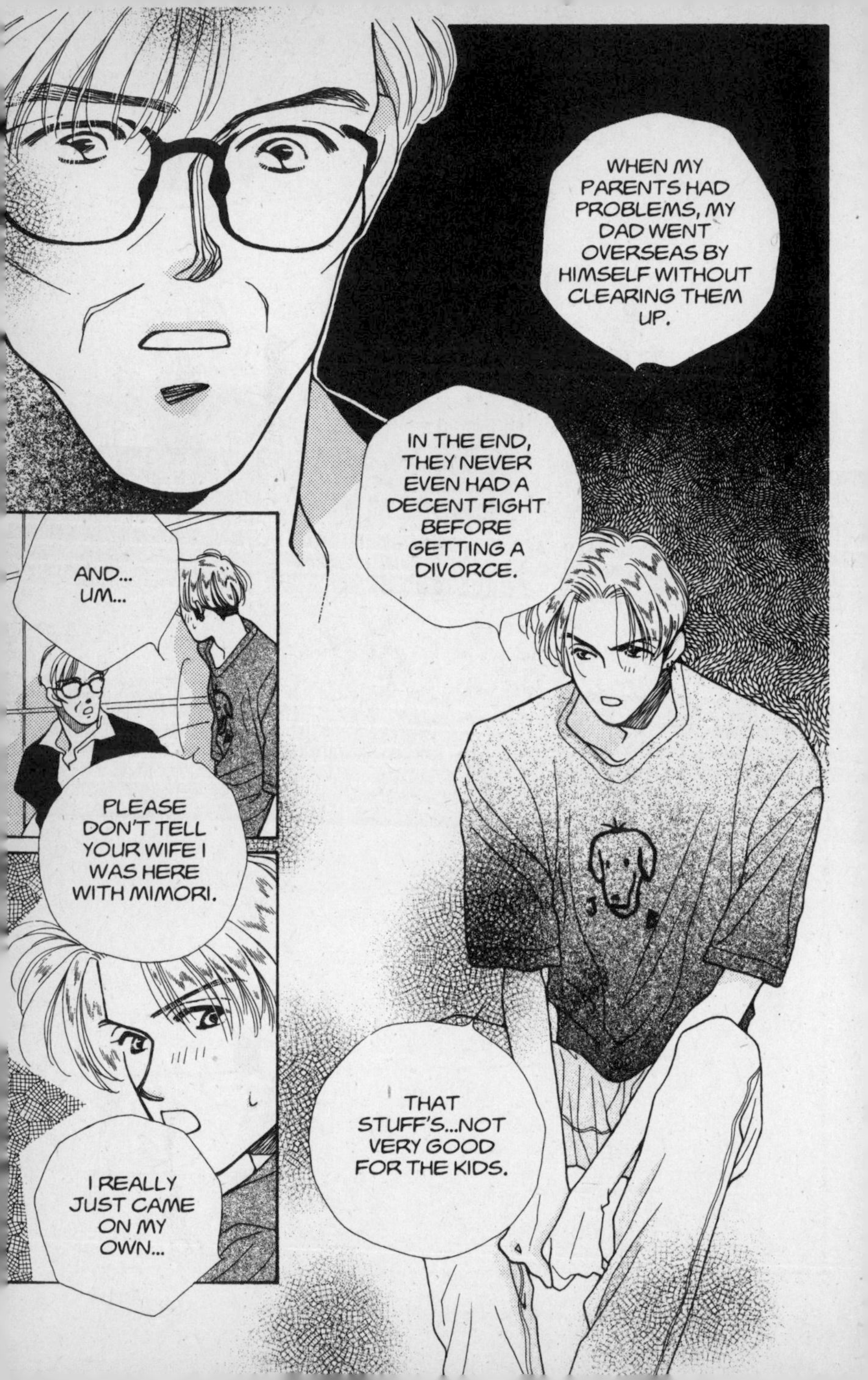
WHEN MY PARENTS HAD PROBLEMS, MY DAD WENT OVERSEAS BY HIMSELF WITHOUT CLEARING THEM UP.
IN THE END, THEY NEVER EVEN HAD A DECENT FIGHT BEFORE GETTING A DIVORCE.
THAT STUFF'S...NOT VERY GOOD FOR THE KIDS.
AND... UM...
PLEASE DON'T TELL YOUR WIFE I WAS HERE WITH MIMORI.
I REALLY JUST CAME ON MY OWN...

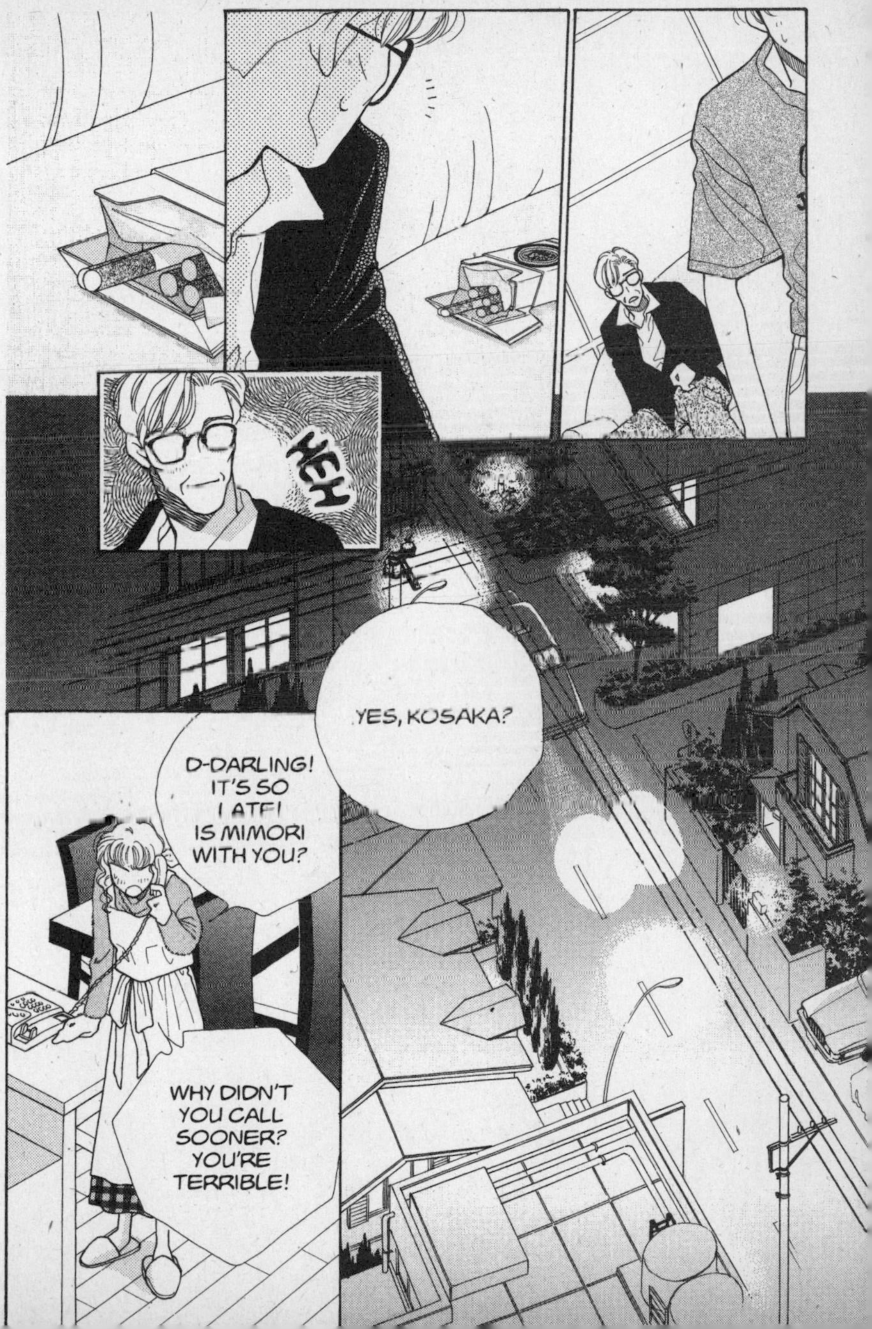
HEH
YES, KOSAKA?
D-DARLING! IT'S SO LATE! IS MIMORI WITH YOU?
WHY DIDN'T YOU CALL SOONER? YOU'RE TERRIBLE!

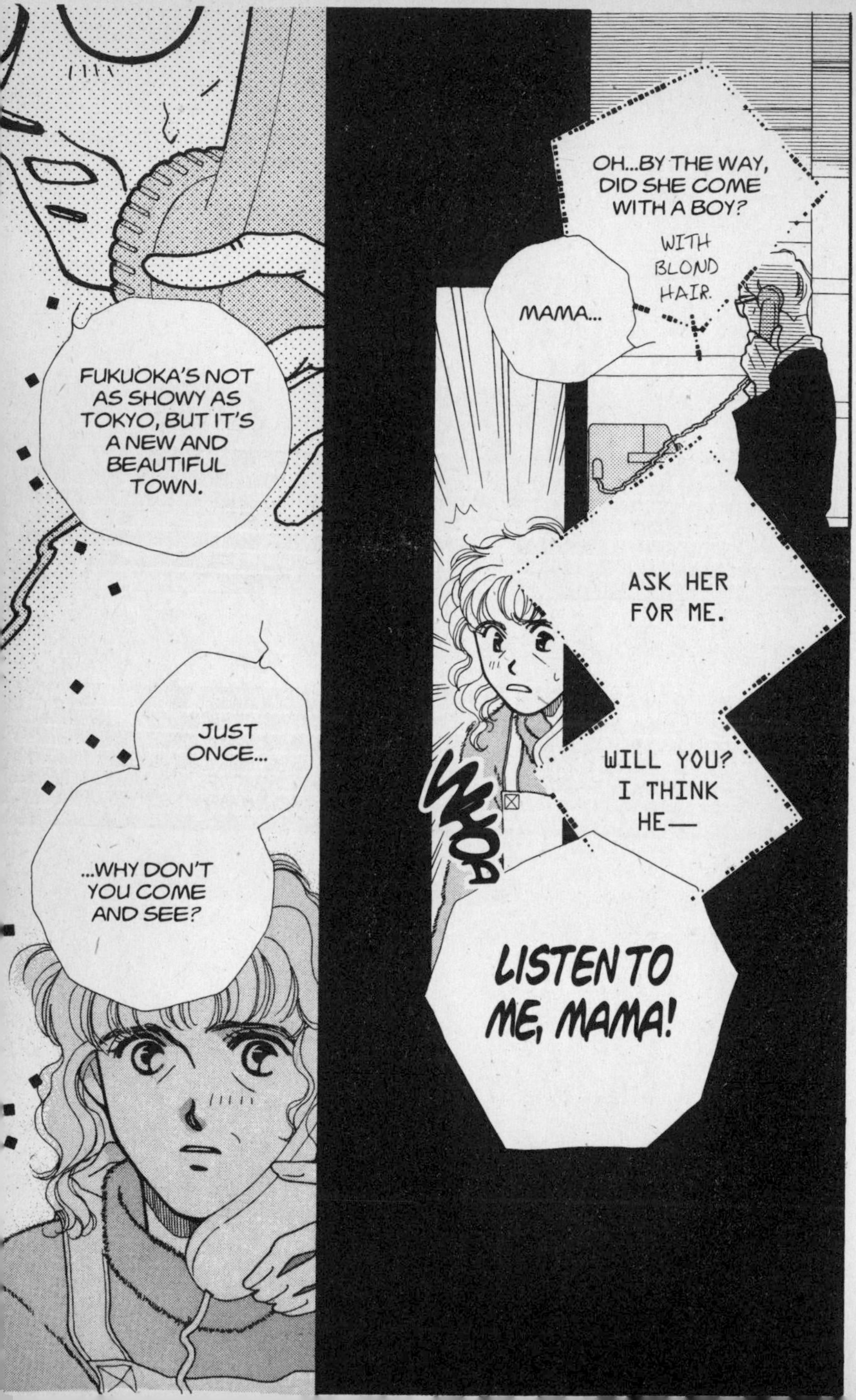
OH...BY THE WAY, DID SHE COME WITH A BOY?
WITH BLOND HAIR.
MAMA...
ASK HER FOR ME.
WILL YOU? I THINK HE—
WHOA
LISTEN TO ME, MAMA!
FUKUOKA'S NOT AS SHOWY AS TOKYO, BUT IT'S A NEW AND BEAUTIFUL TOWN.
JUST ONCE...
...WHY DON'T YOU COME AND SEE?

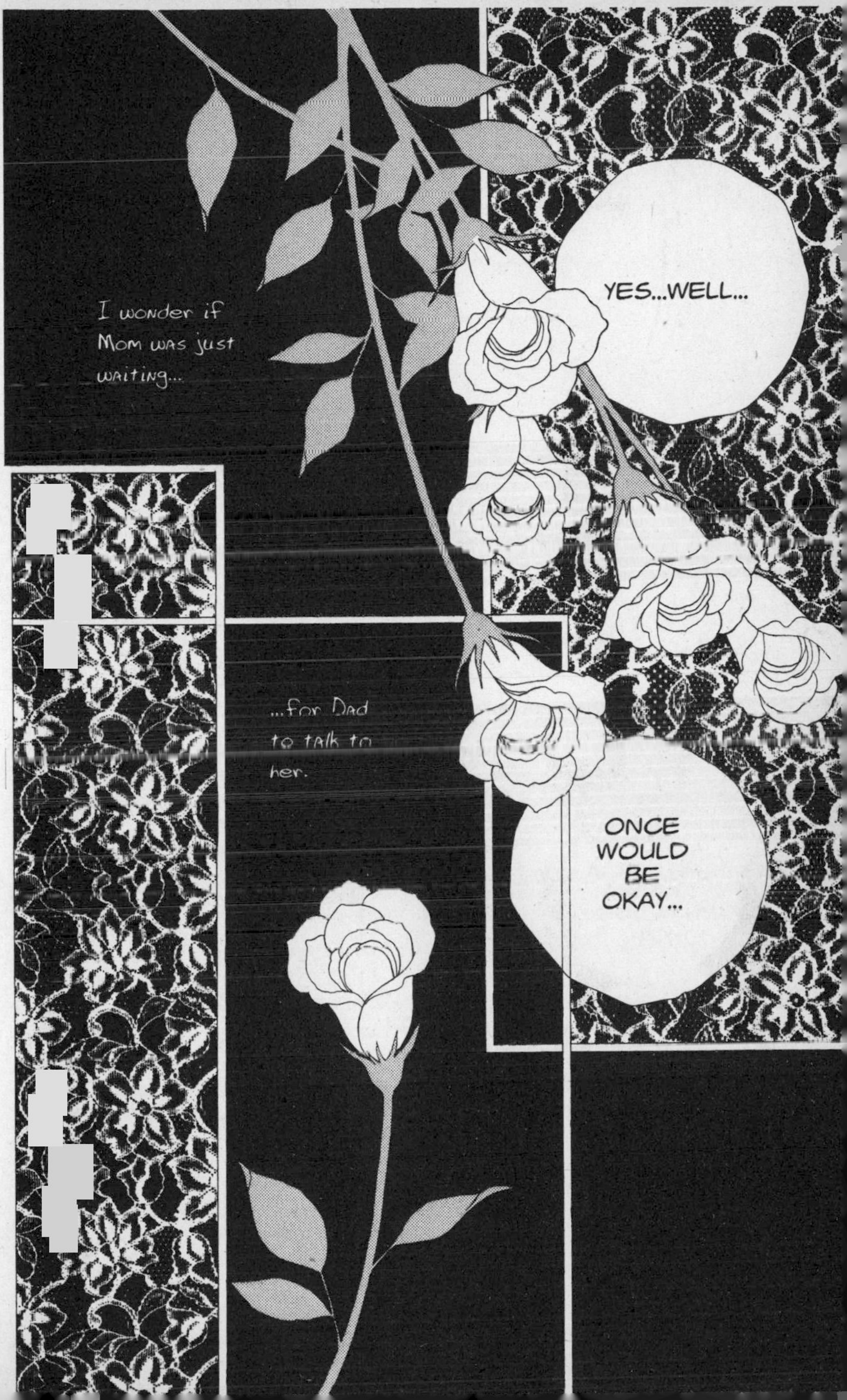
YES...WELL...
ONCE WOULD BE OKAY...
I wonder if Mom was just waiting...
...for Dad to talk to her.

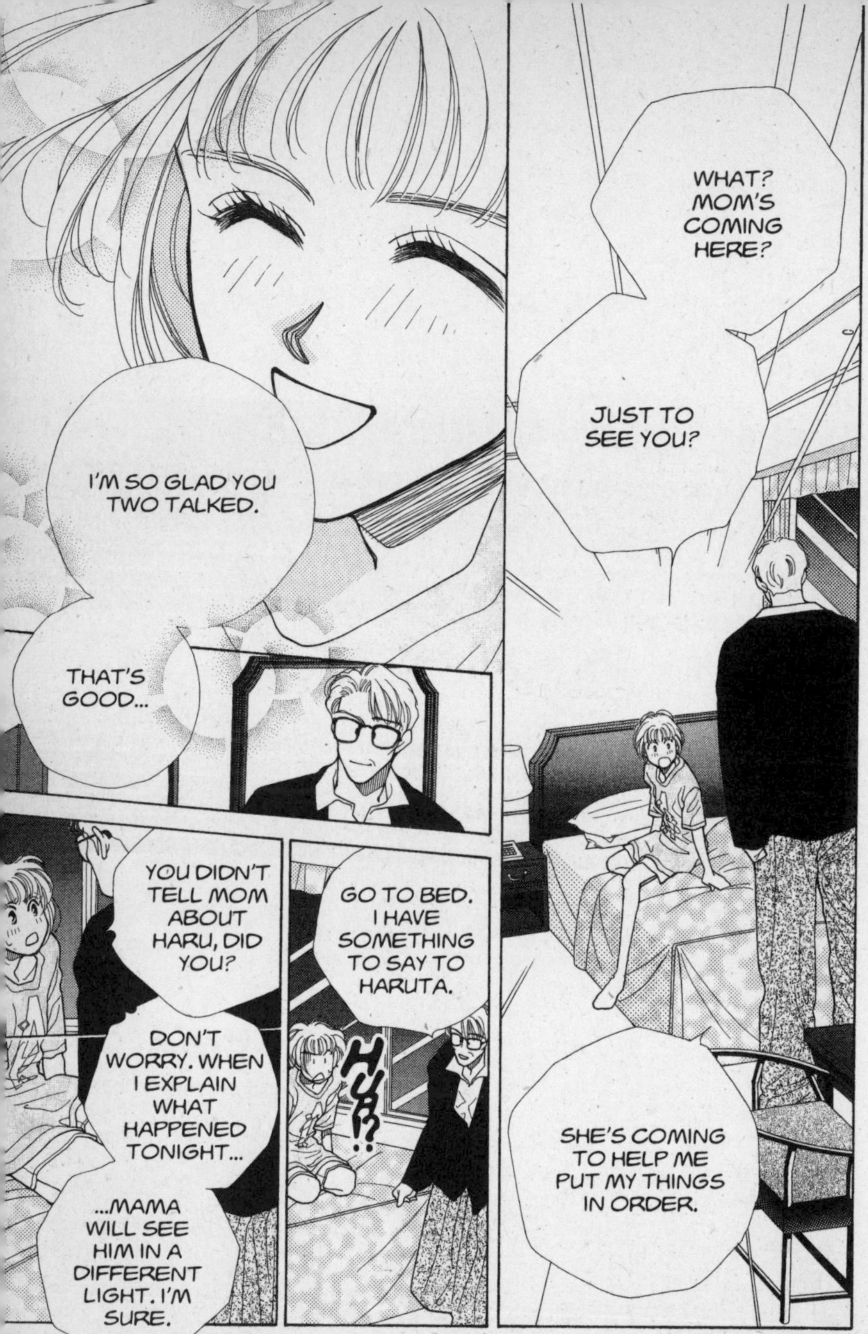
WHAT? MOM'S COMING HERE?
JUST TO SEE YOU?
SHE'S COMING TO HELP ME PUT MY THINGS IN ORDER.
I'M SO GLAD YOU TWO TALKED.
THAT'S GOOD...
GO TO BED. I HAVE SOMETHING TO SAY TO HARUTA.
HUH!?
YOU DIDN'T TELL MOM ABOUT HARU, DID YOU?
DON'T WORRY. WHEN I EXPLAIN WHAT HAPPENED TONIGHT...
...MAMA WILL SEE HIM IN A DIFFERENT LIGHT. I'M SURE.

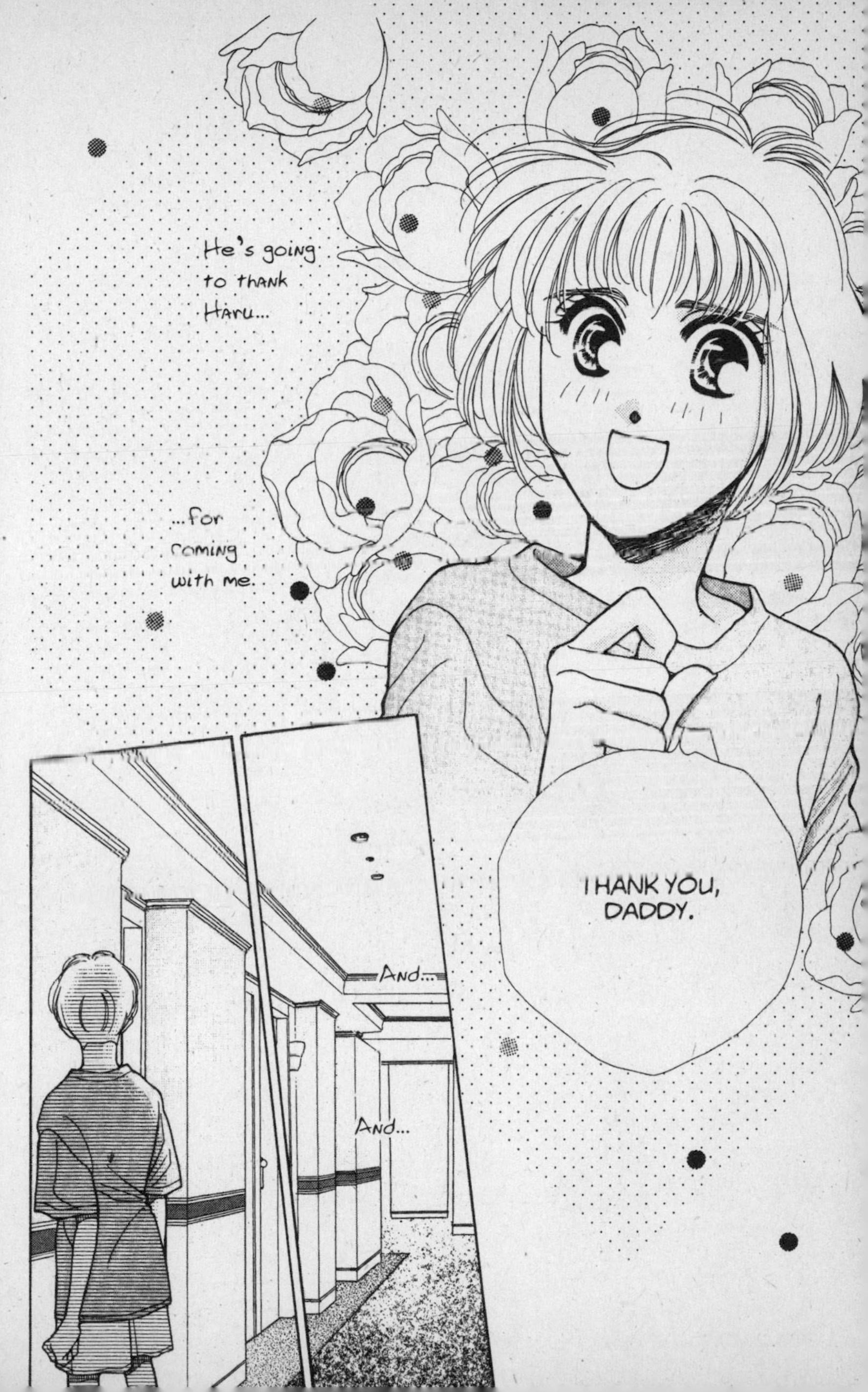
He's going to thank Haru...
...for coming with me.
THANK YOU, DADDY.
And...
And...

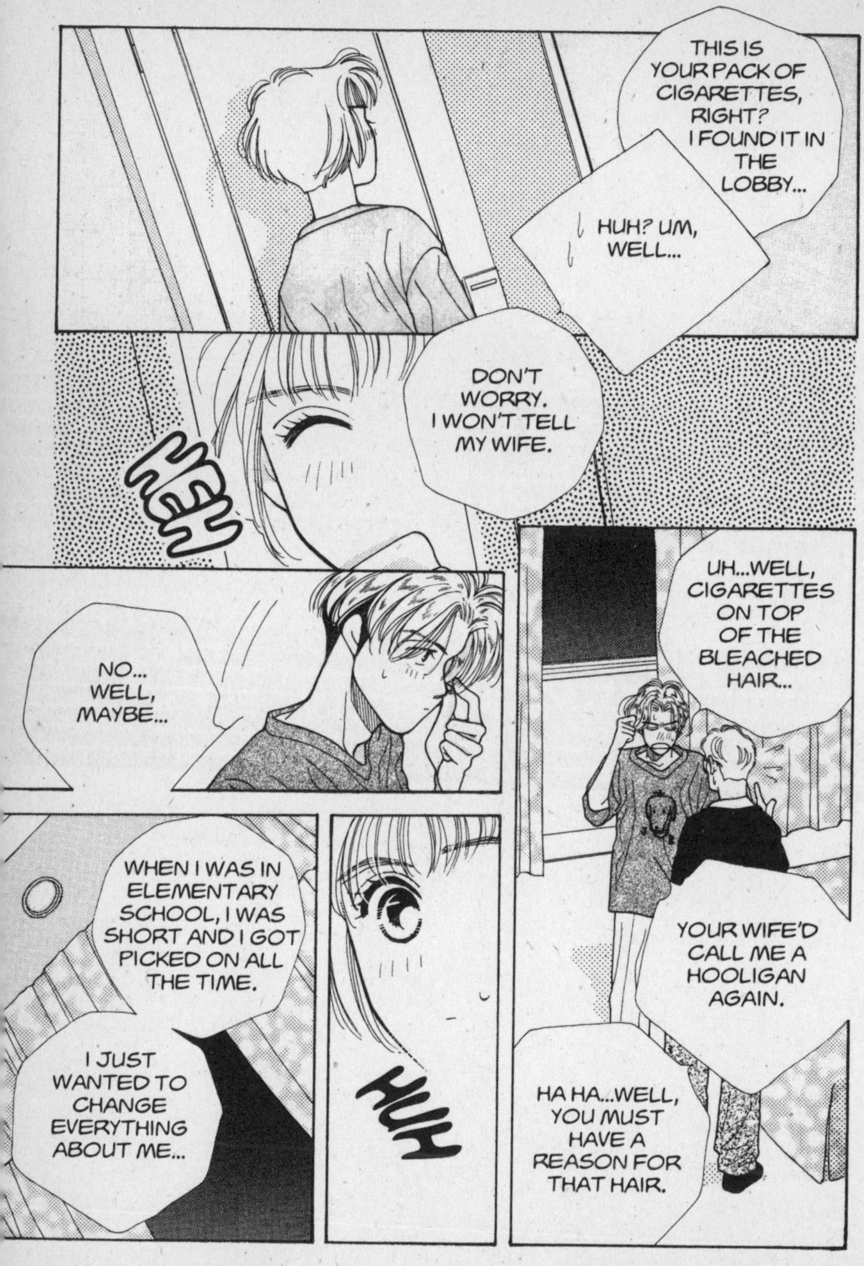
THIS IS YOUR PACK OF CIGARETTES, RIGHT? I FOUND IT IN THE LOBBY...
HUH? UM, WELL...
DON'T WORRY. I WON'T TELL MY WIFE.
HEH
UH...WELL, CIGARETTES ON TOP OF THE BLEACHED HAIR...
YOUR WIFE'D CALL ME A HOOLIGAN AGAIN.
HA HA...WELL, YOU MUST HAVE A REASON FOR THAT HAIR.
NO... WELL, MAYBE...
HUH
WHEN I WAS IN ELEMENTARY SCHOOL, I WAS SHORT AND I GOT PICKED ON ALL THE TIME.
I JUST WANTED TO CHANGE EVERYTHING ABOUT ME...

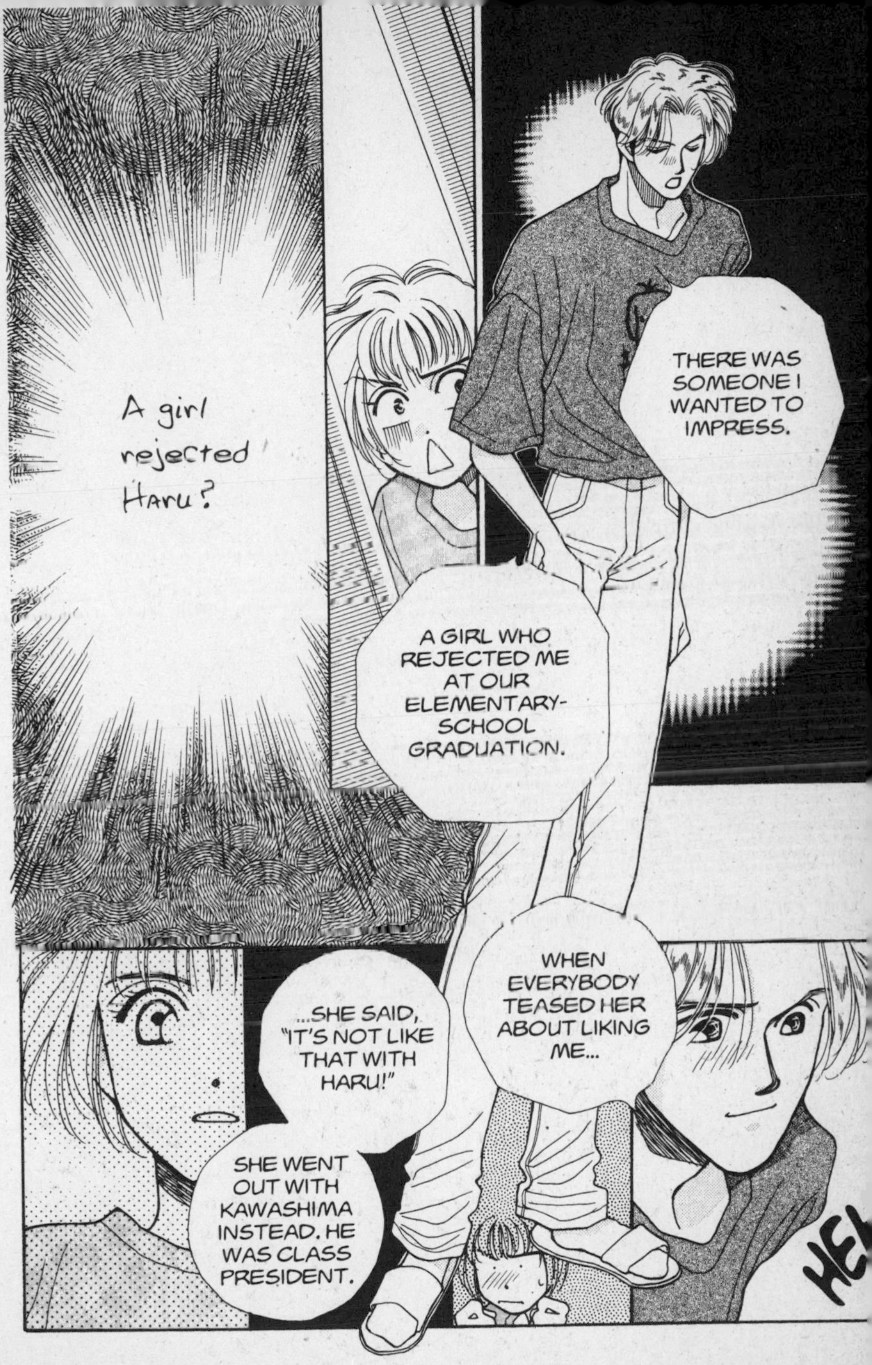
THERE WAS SOMEONE I WANTED TO IMPRESS.
A GIRL WHO REJECTED ME AT OUR ELEMENTARY-SCHOOL GRADUATION.
A girl rejected Haru?
WHEN EVERYBODY TEASED HER ABOUT LIKING ME...
...SHE SAID, "IT'S NOT LIKE THAT WITH HARU!"
SHE WENT OUT WITH KAWASHIMA INSTEAD. HE WAS CLASS PRESIDENT.

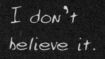

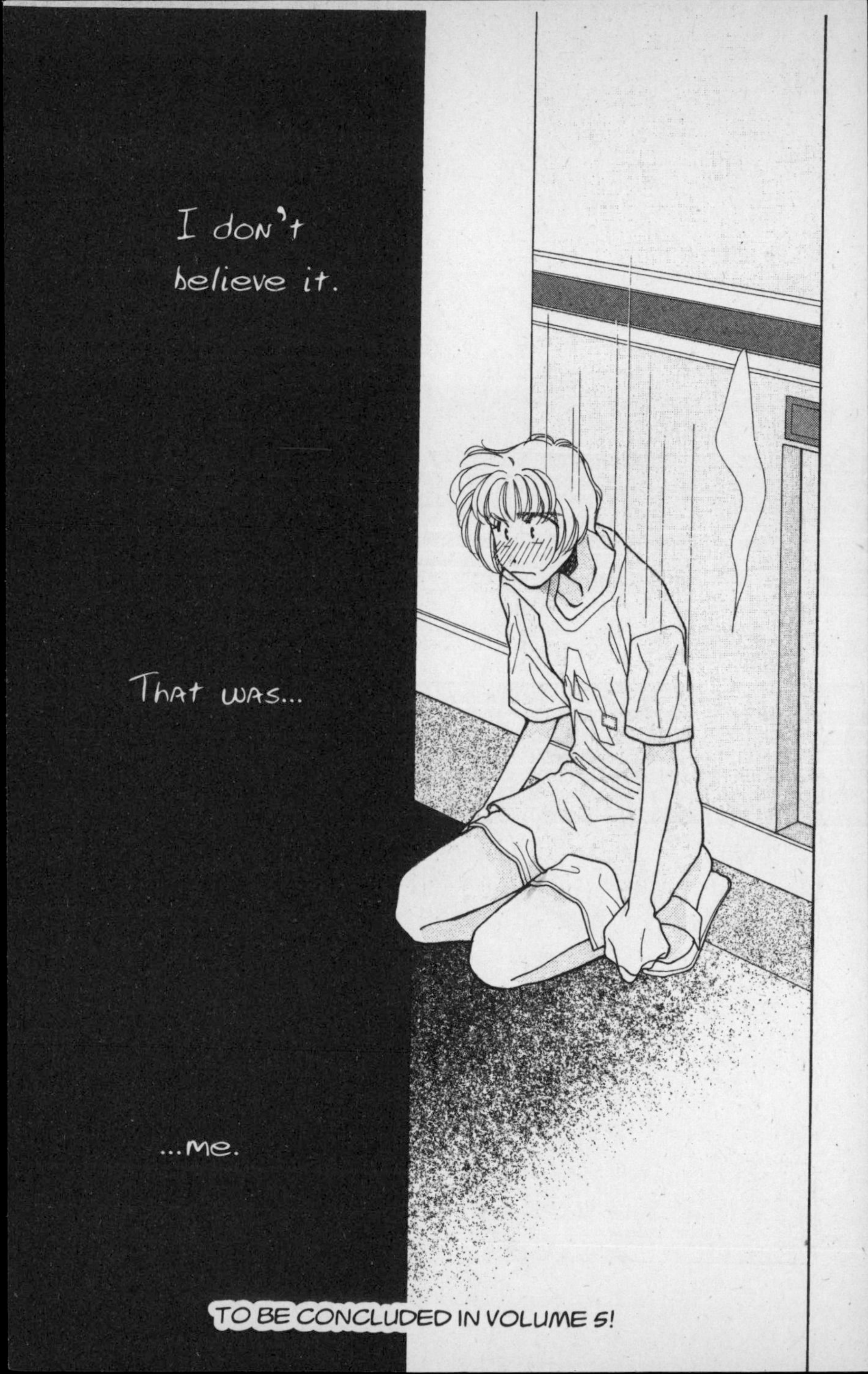

I don't
believe it.

That was...

...me.

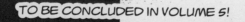

TO BE CONCLUDED IN VOLUME 5!

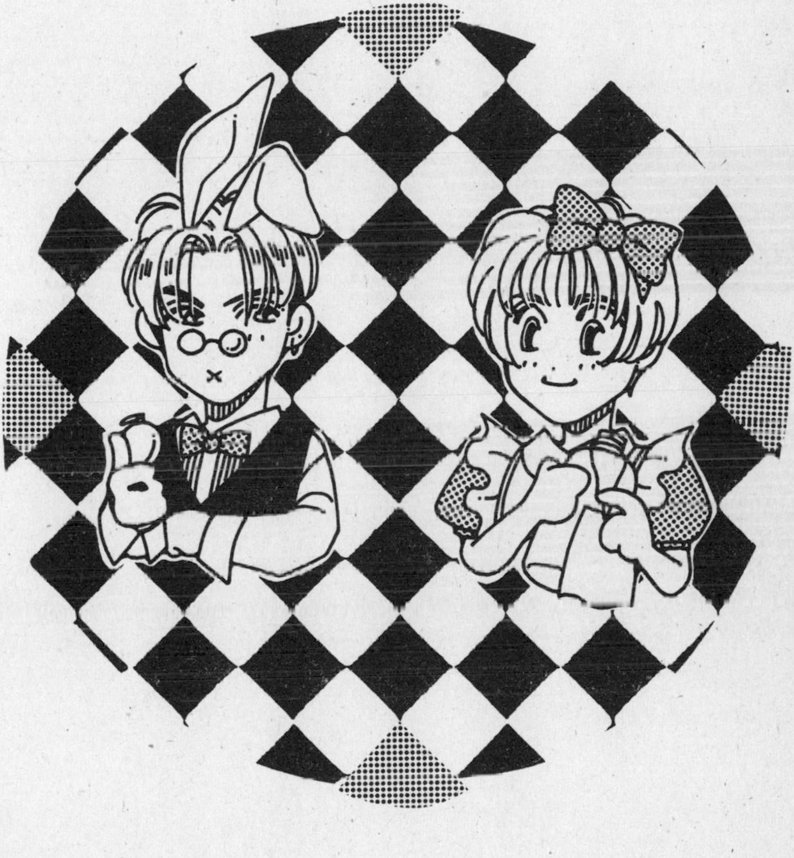

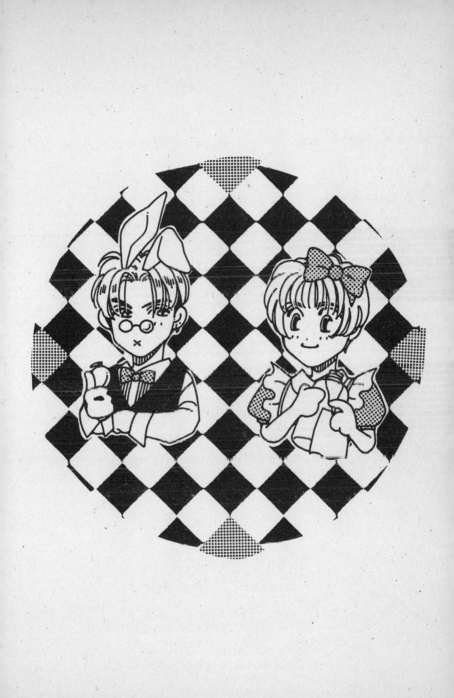

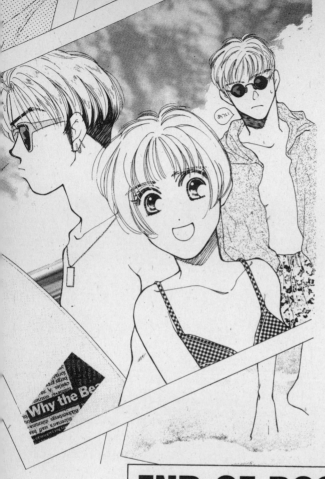

END-OF-BOOK
BONUS

1. AFTER-PUBLICATION COMICS...PAGE 182
WRITTEN BY MIKI AIHARA AND HER ASSISTANTS
2. ILLUSTRATION...PAGE 186
FROM THE BETSUCOMI COMICS FRONTISPIECE

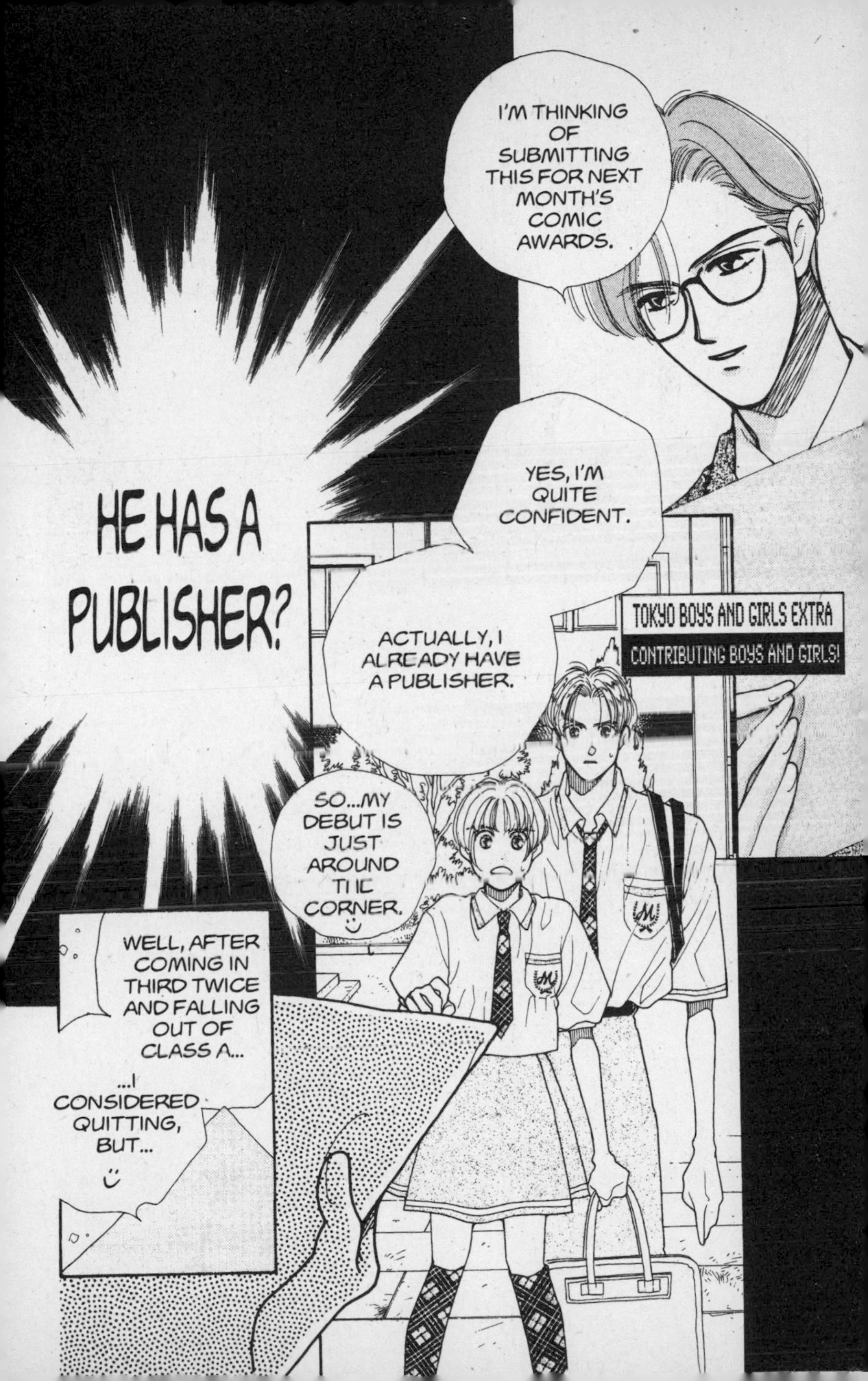
I'M THINKING OF SUBMITTING THIS FOR NEXT MONTH'S COMIC AWARDS.
YES, I'M QUITE CONFIDENT.
TOKYO BOYS AND GIRLS EXTRA
CONTRIBUTING BOYS AND GIRLS!
ACTUALLY, I ALREADY HAVE A PUBLISHER.
HE HAS A PUBLISHER?
SO...MY DEBUT IS JUST AROUND THE CORNER.
WELL, AFTER COMING IN THIRD TWICE AND FALLING OUT OF CLASS A...
...I CONSIDERED QUITTING, BUT...

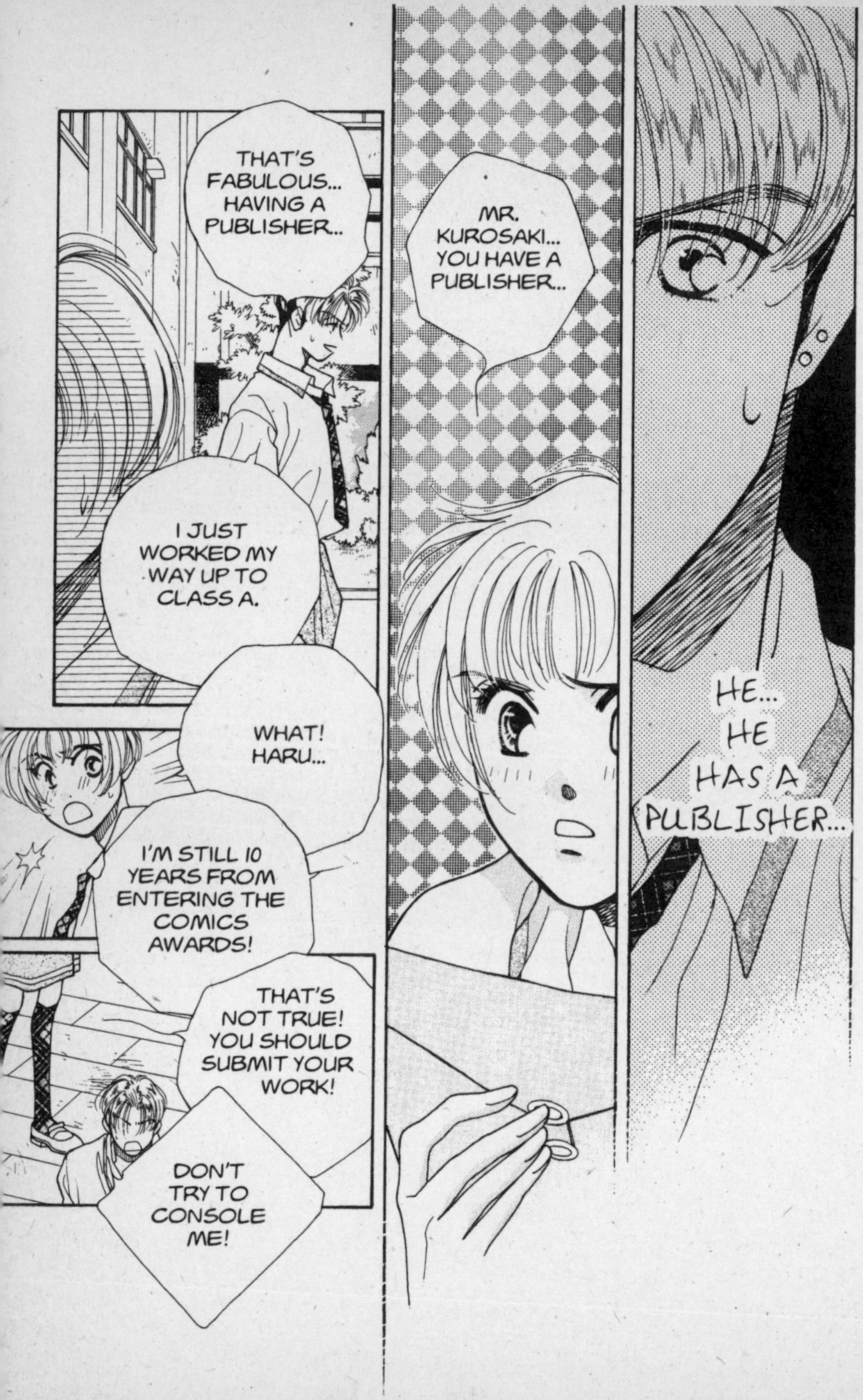
HE... HE HAS A PUBLISHER...
MR. KUROSAKI... YOU HAVE A PUBLISHER...
THAT'S FABULOUS... HAVING A PUBLISHER...
I JUST WORKED MY WAY UP TO CLASS A.
WHAT! HARU...
I'M STILL 10 YEARS FROM ENTERING THE COMICS AWARDS!
THAT'S NOT TRUE! YOU SHOULD SUBMIT YOUR WORK!
DON'T TRY TO CONSOLE ME!

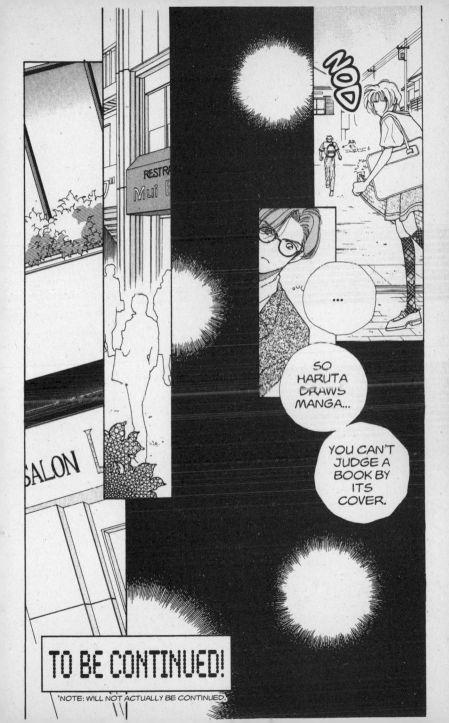

TOKYO
BOYS
GIRLS

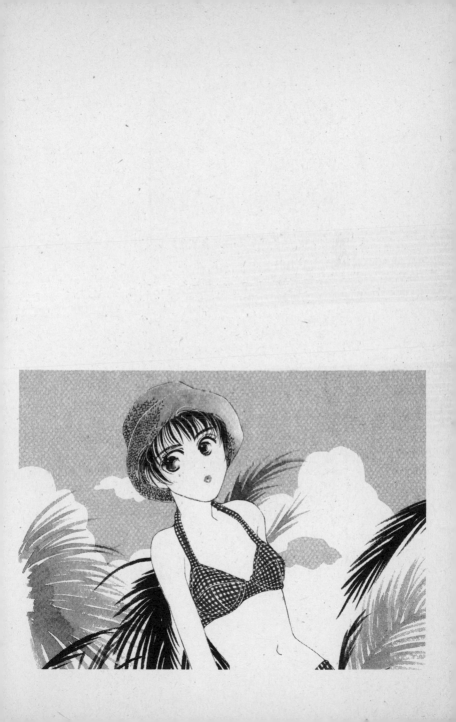

Miki Aihara was born in the Shizuoka prefecture of Japan and currently lives in Tokyo. She made her debut in 1991 with *Lip Conscious!*, published in *Bessatsu Shôjo* Comic. Her immensely popular manga *Hot Gimmick* is published in English by VIZ Media. Aihara moves houses frequently, and loves to go to movies and shop for clothes. One of her hobbies is keeping tropical fish.

Shojo Beat

TOKYO BOYS & GIRLS VOLUME 4
The Shojo Beat Manga Edition

STORY AND ART BY
MIKI AIHARA

English Adaptation/Shaenon Garrity
Translation/JN Productions
Touch-up Art & Lettering/Bill Schuch
Design/Courtney Utt
Editor/Urian Brown

Managing Editor/Megan Bates
Director of Production/Noboru Watanabe
Vice President of Publishing/Alvin Lu
Vice President & Editor in Chief/Yumi Hoashi
Sr. Director of Acquisitions/Rika Inouye
Vice President of Sales & Marketing/Liza Coppola
Publisher/Hyoe Narita

Printed in the U.S.A.

Published by VIZ Media, LLC
P.O. Box 77010
San Francisco, CA 94107

Shojo Beat Manga Edition
10 9 8 7 6 5 4 3 2 1
First printing, April 2006

VIZ media

RATED T+ FOR OLDER TEEN

PARENTAL ADVISORY
TOKYO BOYS & GIRLS is rated T+ for Older Teen and is recommeded for ages 16 & up. This volume contains strong language and sexual themes.

store.viz.com

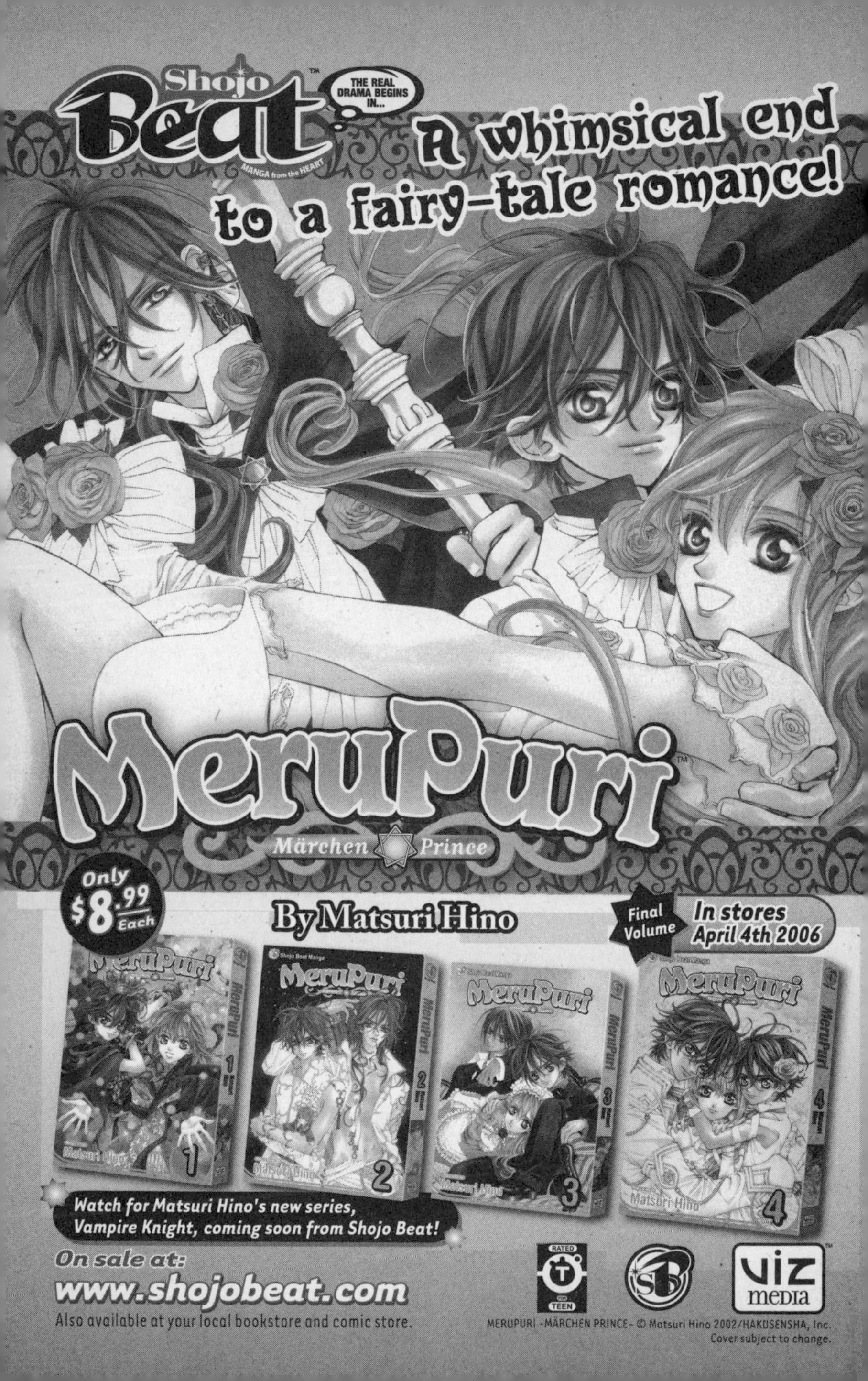
Shojo Beat™
MANGA from the HEART
THE REAL DRAMA BEGINS IN...
A whimsical end to a fairy-tale romance!
MeruPuri™
Märchen Prince
Only $8.99 Each
By Matsuri Hino
Final Volume
In stores April 4th 2006
Watch for Matsuri Hino's new series, Vampire Knight, coming soon from Shojo Beat!
On sale at:
www.shojobeat.com
Also available at your local bookstore and comic store.
RATED T FOR TEEN
viz media™
MERUPURI -MÄRCHEN PRINCE- © Matsuri Hino 2002/HAKUSENSHA, Inc.
Cover subject to change.

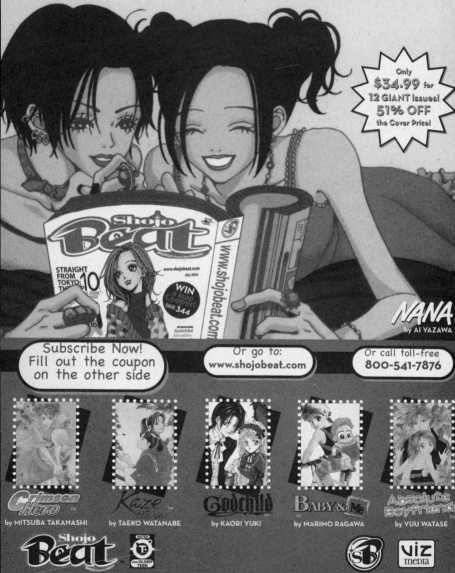